DANIEL

PETER A. STEVESON

BOB JONES
UNIVERSITY PRESS

Greenville, South Carolina

Library of Congress Cataloging-in-Publication Data

Steveson, Peter A. (Peter Allan), 1934-
Daniel / Peter A. Steveson.
p. cm.
Includes bibliographical references and index.
Summary: "This book is an exegetical commentary on the book of
Daniel"—Provided by publisher.
ISBN 978-1-59166-855-8 (perfect bound pbk. : alk. paper)
1. Bible. O.T. Daniel—Commentaries. I. Title.

BS1555.53.S755 2008
224'.507—dc22

2008025622

BWHEBB [Hebrew] and BWGRKL [Greek] Postscript® Type 1 and True-
TypeT fonts Copyright © 1994–2006 BibleWorks, LLC. All rights reserved.
These Biblical Greek and Hebrew fonts are used with permission and are
from BibleWorks, software for Biblical exegesis and research.

Cover Photo Credits: Do Hoai Nam (Lion) from iStockphoto

The fact that materials produced by other publishers may be referred to in
this volume does not constitute an endorsement of the content or theological position of materials produced by such publishers.

All Scripture is quoted from the Authorized King James Version unless
otherwise noted. See p. xi for a list of other versions cited.

Daniel
Peter A. Steveson

Design by Nick Ng
Page layout by Kelley Moore

© 2008 BJU Press
Greenville, South Carolina 29614
Bob Jones University Press is a division of BJU Press

Printed in the United States of America

ISBN 978-1-59166-855-8

15   14   13   12   11   10   9   8   7   6   5   4   3   2   1

Dedicated to
Dr. Robert D. Bell,
mentor, colleague, and friend.

TABLE OF CONTENTS

PREFACE

The book of Daniel is the indisputable foundation for the study of prophecy. Setting forth, as it does, a panoramic view of the future history of the world, the book gives Christians a framework in which to fit world-influencing events as they occur. Daniel's writings support the view that this world is living in the end times preceding our Lord's return. It is likely for this reason that the Lord commanded His followers to understand the book (Matt. 24:15). Such an understanding leads to the hope of our Lord's soon return, and this hope moves believers to pure living (1 John 3:3).

The writings of Daniel not only guide our understanding of God's plan for the future but also have a practical emphasis that Christians do well to understand. The opening chapter illustrates the need for believers to be faithful to God's Word. Daniel and his friends demonstrate tactful yet godly behavior among the heathen. We see here as well God's blessing on those who put Him first in their actions. The following chapters show many of the wicked habits followed by those who live apart from God. Among other sins, we see a reliance on false gods, anger, pride, and a lack of concern for righteous actions. They also reveal still other desirable traits of character and behavior in God's followers. Daniel and his friends demonstrate reliance on God to guide them, refusal to break His Word, prayer, boldness in the face of opposition, and other godly practices.

My own study of the book goes back about forty years when I first taught the book to an adult Sunday school class. Since that time, I have taught the book to classes and have preached from it in churches. Many of the commentaries on Daniel follow a liberal approach, redating the authorship to a later date and turning its prophecies into mere history. This view of the book dates back to the mid-third century AD when Porphyry, a Greek opponent of Christianity, wrote a fifteen-volume set of books titled *Against the Christians*. He devoted the twelfth book of this to arguing that an unknown second-century-BC author wrote the book of Daniel. This unknown author wrote to kindle hope in the hearts of his fellow Jews. Porphyry based his argument on the belief that the book was too accurate in its details to be prophetic. His work no longer exists, but the early Christian scholar Jerome, writing toward the beginning of the fifth century, quoted extensively from it. With variations, liberal authors set forth basically the same position as Porphyry. The prevalence of this false view has led me to write this commentary to explain and defend a conservative interpretation.

I appreciate the help of others who have assisted my work on the book. Mrs. Jackie Eaves, Mr. Phil Adams, and Dr. Robert Bell have answered my questions. Mr. Roger Eaves read much of the rough draft and made many helpful comments. The library staffs of Bob Jones University, Furman University, and Emory University have helped me find research materials. The editors at Bob Jones University Press—especially Mr. Todd Jones and Mrs. Mary Schleifer—have corrected my grammar and other human foibles. Once again, Bob Jones University has made it possible for me to complete my writing of the book.

CHIEF ABBREVIATIONS

AB   Anchor Bible

ANET   *Ancient Near Eastern Texts*, ed. James B. Pritchard (Princeton, N.J.: Princeton University Press, 1955)

Antiquities   *The Antiquities of the Jews*, Josephus

AUSS   Andrews University Seminary Studies

BAR   *Biblical Archaeology Review*

BDB   Francis Brown, S. R. Driver, and Charles A. Briggs, eds., *Hebrew and English Lexicon of the Old Testament* (1974 rpt.)

BibSac   *Bibliotheca Sacra*

BV   *Biblical Viewpoint*

CBQ   *Catholic Biblical Quarterly*

DOTT   *Documents from Old Testament Times*, D. Winton Thomas, ed. (New York: Harper & Row, 1958)

ET   *Expository Times*

ETL   *Ephemerides Theologicae Lovaniensium*

GKC   *Gesenius' Hebrew Grammar*, E. Kautzsch, ed., and A. E. Cowley, rev. (1970)

JATS   *Journal of the Adventist Theological Society*

JBL   *Journal of Biblical Literature*

JETS   *Journal of the Evangelical Theological Society*

JSOT   *Journal for the Study of the Old Testament*

ISBE   *International Standard Bible Encyclopaedia*, ed. James Orr (Grand Rapids, 1952)

KB   *The Hebrew and Aramaic Lexicon of the Old Testament*, rev. Walter Baumgartner and Johann Jakob Stamm, trans. and ed. M. E. J. Richardson (New York: E. J. Brill, 1995)

LXX   Septuagint

ms, mss   manuscript, manuscripts

NT   New Testament

OT	Old Testament
OTTP	A. R. Hulst, *Old Testament Translation Problems* (Leiden: E. J. Brill, 1960)
TB	*Tyndale Bulletin*
TWOT	*Theological Wordbook of the Old Testament*
VT	*Vetus Testamentum*
WBC	Wesleyan Bible Commentary

BIBLES

AB   Scripture quotations taken from the Amplified® Bible, Copyright © 1954, 1958, 1962, 1964, 1965, 1987 by The Lockman Foundation. Used by permission.

CB   *The Complete Bible: An American Translation.* Translated by J. M. Powis Smith and Edgar J. Goodspeed et al. Chicago: University of Chicago Press, 1939.

DV   Scripture taken from Douay Version. New York: P. J. Kennedy & Sons, n.d.

ESV   Scripture quotations marked ESV are from The Holy Bible, English Standard Version®, copyright © 2001 by Crossway Bibles, a publishing ministry of Good News Publishers. Used by permission. All rights reserved.

HCSB   Scripture quotations marked HCSB are taken from the Holman Christian Standard Bible®, Copyright © 1999, 2000, 2002, 2003 by Holman Bible Publishers. Used by permission. Holman Christian Standard Bible®, Holman CSB®, and HCSB® are federally registered trademarks of Holman Bible Publishers.

NAB   Scripture texts in this work marked NAB are taken from the *New American Bible with Revised New Testament* © 1986, 1970 Confraternity of Christian Doctrine, Washington, D.C. and are used by permission of the copyright owner. All Rights Reserved. No part of the *New American Bible* may be reproduced in any form without permission in writing from the copyright owner.

NASB   Scripture taken from the NEW AMERICAN STANDARD BIBLE®, Copyright © 1960, 1962, 1963, 1968, 1971, 1972, 1973, 1975, 1977, 1995 by The Lockman Foundation. Used by permission.

NCV   Scriptures quoted from The Holy Bible, New Century Version, copyright © by Word Publishing, Dallas, TX 75039. Used by permission.

NET   Scripture quoted by permission. Quotations designated (NET) are from the NET Bible® copyright ©1996–2006

INTRODUCTION

The book of Daniel describes events from the late seventh century BC into much of the sixth century BC. This was a dark period in Israel's history. The nation had been under Egyptian domination (2 Kings 23:29–35). Babylon now has displaced Egypt and, to worsen the situation, carried many of the nation's future leaders into bondage in a distant land (2 Kings 24:1–25:21). The Jews have every reason to question what the coming years hold in store for them. Daniel now comes forth, however, with a message designed to build confidence among the nation. God is in control. He not only knows the future but also controls it. He raises up kings to rule, and He puts kings down from their lofty positions. He lifts up nations of His choice, and He causes other nations to fall. Throughout it all, He still has a plan for Israel. Daniel's prophecies sketch enough of this message to rekindle the hope of his people. As believers today study the book, we also find our hope rekindled and our confidence in God strengthened.

The Authorship of Daniel

The author of the book is Daniel, a young man taken captive by the Babylonians (1:1–6). The Talmud, *Baba Bathra* 15*a*, says, "The men of the Great Synagogue wrote . . . Ezekiel, the twelve Minor Prophets, Daniel, and the scroll of Esther." The statement, however, is not correct. Since "the men of the Great Synagogue" were not present for the events recorded in Daniel, they could only have recorded an oral tradition or revised an earlier written work.

Evidence for Daniel's authorship comes from the author's knowledge of details, and from his use of the first-person pronoun in the narrative (e.g., 7:28; 8:1–7, 15, 27; 9:2; 10:2, 7; 12:5). In the first six chapters of the book, Daniel generally refers to himself in the third person (e.g., 1:8–11, 17; 2:46–49; 5:13, 17, 29). This is not unusual in historical writings. In his *History of the Peloponnesian War*, the Greek general Thucydides writes of himself in the third person, e.g., 1.1, 4.104. The Greek general Xenophon, in service to the Persian satrap Cyrus the Younger and later the author of several works, does the same, e.g., *Anabasis* 1.8.15, 2.4.15, 2.5.37, 2.5.41; *Memorabilia*

1.3.10, 1.3.12–13.[1] The final chapters of the book of Daniel relate events in which Daniel is the central character. As he relates these personal experiences, it is appropriate for him to write in the first person.

In *The Antiquities of the Jews* 11.8.5, the Jewish historian Josephus records an early belief in Daniel's authorship: "When the book of Daniel was showed [Alexander], wherein Daniel declared that one of the Greeks should destroy the empire of the Persians, he supposed that himself was the person intended."[2] First Maccabees 2:60, written about 80 BC, also reveals an early belief in the book. This states that "Daniel for his innocence was delivered from the mouths of the lions."[3] Further proof of his authorship comes from the Lord's comments in the NT referring to "Daniel the prophet" (Matt. 24:15; Mark 13:14). Hebrews 11:33 does not mention Daniel by name but clearly alludes to his escape from being eaten by the lions.

Liberal authors often reject the accuracy of the book. Di Lella concludes that the stories of Daniel and his companions should not be taken literally. He states that "in a Jewish composition . . . the absence of a genealogy, contrary to custom, gives probability to the suggestion that the characters of Daniel and his pious companions are legendary." He sees several authors writing in Aramaic over a broad span of time. To give the book canonical recognition, 1:1–2:4*a* and c. 8–12 were translated into Hebrew. A redactor compiled the individual stories and edited them in the second century BC. While the lack of a genealogy is unusual, it is not unique. There are no genealogies recorded for Amos, Obadiah, Nahum, Habakkuk, Haggai, or Malachi. Di Lella's argument for multiple authors and dating rests on subjective grounds. No manuscript evidence supports the view. Without proof, André Lacocque asserts that "Daniel is the name of a mythical personage mentioned along with Noah and Job in Ezek.

---

[1]Thucydides, *History of the Peloponnesian War*, trans. Charles Forster Smith (Cambridge, Mass.: Harvard University Press, 1962); Xenophon, *Anabasis*, trans. Carleton L. Brownson (Cambridge, Mass.: Harvard University Press, 1968), and *Memorabilia and Oeconomicus*, trans. E. C. Marchant (Cambridge, Mass.: Harvard University Press, 1988). Branson L. Woodard Jr., "Literary Strategies and Authorship in the Book of Daniel," *JETS* 37 (March 1994): 40–53, surveys the literary features of the first six chapters as support for Daniel's authorship.

[2]*The Works of Josephus*, trans. William Whiston (Peabody, Mass.: Hendrickson Publishers, 1987).

[3]Edgar J. Goodspeed, translator of the Apocrypha in the CB.

14.14 and 20." The statement rejects the inspiration of Scripture as well as ignoring the weight of Jewish tradition. These views are typical of the approach taken by liberal authors.[4]

The book of Daniel covers the seventy-year captivity of the Jews in Babylon. The Jews placed the book in the Writings, the third section of the Hebrew Bible. This was because of Daniel's office as a statesman rather than serving as a priest or acting as a prophet to the nation.[5] Although the book was placed in the Writings, at least some of the Jews considered it prophecy. In *Against Apion* 1.8, Josephus says that of the "twenty-two books" of the Jews, "five belong to Moses. . . . The prophets, who were after Moses, wrote down what was done in their times in thirteen books. The remaining four books contain hymns to God, and precepts for the conduct of human life." The books by Moses are the five books of the Pentateuch. The "four books" include Psalms, Proverbs, Ecclesiastes, and the Song of Solomon. The remaining thirteen books, the authors of which Josephus calls "prophets," include the other OT books, some bound as a single book, e.g., the twelve Minor Prophets. Daniel is one of the thirteen books. The *Manual of Discipline* at Qumran refers to the OT books as "Moses and the Prophets." Nonetheless, despite its position in the OT, the NT makes it clear that Daniel was a prophet (Matt. 24:15).

The Background of Daniel

We know little of Daniel's personal background, other than that he was descended from one of the kings of Judah and thus was a descendant of David. According to 1:3, Daniel and the other captives in training had a princely heritage. The prophet Isaiah had before predicted that the king's sons would be taken captive (2 Kings 20:18; Isa. 39:7). While we do not know that Daniel was in the direct kingly line, he was of "the king's seed, and of the princes," 1:3.

---

[4]Louis F. Hartman and Alexander A. Di Lella, *The Book of Daniel*, in *The Anchor Bible* (Garden City, N.Y.: Doubleday, 1978). Di Lella is the author of the Introduction, p. 8, from which the above statement is taken; André Lacocque, *The Book of Daniel*, trans. David Pellauer (Atlanta: The Society for Promoting Christian Knowledge, John Knox Press, 1979), pp. 2–3.

[5]E. H. Horne, *The Meaning of Daniel's Visions* (London: Marshall, Morgan & Scott, n.d.), p. 24, asserts that Daniel was excluded from a place in the prophets since he was a eunuch. This is not necessarily the case. See the discussion of "eunuch" at 1:3.

The rabbis disagreed over the tribal heritage of the four. The Talmud, *Sanhedrin* 93*b*, gives two views: either (1) the four young men were all of the tribe of Judah, or (2) only Daniel came from Judah, while the other three were from other tribes. As the word "Judah" occurs in Daniel, it refers to the Southern Kingdom, not the tribe; cf. 1:1, 2, 6; 2:25; 5:13; 6:13; 9:7. Either of these views may be correct. Since Daniel and his three friends receive similar treatment in Babylon, it is reasonable to see them as coming from a similar background in Judah.

Josephus *Antiquities* 10.10.1 states that Daniel, Hananiah, Mishael, and Azariah were all "of the family of Zedekiah." When the Lord brought the Babylonians to judge Judah for their sins in 605 BC, they included Daniel in the first deportation of captives by Nebuchadnezzar from Judah to Babylon. The OT does not mention this deportation but does refer to a conflict between Babylon and Egypt (2 Chron. 36:20; Jer. 46:2–26). It would have been natural for Nebuchadnezzar to take a spoil from Judah at this time.

The name Daniel means "God is my judge." Some authors, e.g., Gangel, Lederach, Young, variously give the meaning as "God is judge" or "God has judged."[6] The Hebrew consonants of *dnyʾl* are open to interpretation either way, depending on the vowel pointing of the word. The vowels of the MT support the above sense of the name.

This name likely reflects a godly heritage for the man. Because Daniel was a young man in chapter one, the godly qualities displayed throughout the book must have begun early in his life. This is a clear indication of early training in godliness by his parents. Daniel's faithfulness to God appears early in the book (1:8) as does God's blessing on him for his faithfulness (1:9, 17). The book often refers to Daniel's prayers (e.g., 2:18; 6:10–11). Over and over, the Babylonians describe Daniel as one filled with the "spirit of the holy gods" (4:8, 9, 18; 5:11, 14), a heathen way of referring to the Holy Spirit's guidance. He gives glory to God for his accomplishments (2:28; 6:22). He confesses the sin of his people (9:5, 8) and shows his concern that others turn to a righteous way of life (4:27).

---

[6]Kenneth O. Gangel, *Daniel* (Nashville: Broadman & Holman Publishers, 2002), p. 20; Paul M. Lederach, *Daniel* (Scottsdale, Pa.: Herald Press, 1994), p. 36; Edward J. Young, *The Prophecy of Daniel: A Commentary* (Grand Rapids: Wm. B. Eerdmans Publishing Co., 1949), p. 43.

The Character of Daniel

As an individual, Daniel's character shows his dedication to God. He is one of only a few people in the Bible about whom there is no moral weakness or inconsistency recorded. From his initial decision not to "defile himself" with the king's rations (1:8) to his willingness to rebuke the king (5:27) and his continuing in prayer to God against the king's command, which results in his being thrown among hungry lions (6:16), Daniel shows himself faithful to God. Daniel 10:11 refers to him as "a man greatly beloved" by God.

Ezekiel went into captivity in Babylon in 597 BC (2 Kings 24:11–16; cf. Ezek. 1:2), about five years after Daniel had completed his training. Since Ezekiel's ministry lasted at least twenty-two years (Ezek. 29:17; cf. 1:2), he would have known of Daniel, possibly personally and certainly by reputation. In Ezekiel 14:14, 20, he groups him with Noah and Job as righteous individuals. In Ezekiel 28:3, he refers to his wisdom, a statement echoed when the Babylonian queen mother described him as having wisdom "like the wisdom of the gods" (5:11).[7]

The Date of Daniel

According to 1:1–6 and 10:1, the author of the book wrote from 605 BC to 536 BC. Liberal theologians object to this date on the basis that the book speaks of events that happen as late as the Greek period. The first to suggest a later date was Porphyry, an anti-Christian philosopher from the early third century AD. While his writings on the subject no longer exist, we know of it from the commentary on Daniel written by Jerome a little more than a century later.[8]

It is a basic tenet of liberal philosophy to reject the possibility of supernatural revelation. Kepler explicitly states that Daniel is "not

---

[7]Raymond Hammer, *The Book of Daniel*, in *The Cambridge Bible Commentary*, ed. P. R. Ackroyd, A. R. C. Leaney, and J. W. Packer (London: Cambridge University Press, 1976), p. 3, suggests that these references in Ezekiel show that Daniel "belongs to the dim and distant past" of OT history. Ezekiel, however, wrote long after the start of the Captivity; cf. Ezek. 1:2; 29:17. He surely would have known of Daniel and his position in the Babylonian court.

[8]*Jerome's Commentary on Daniel*, trans. Gleason L. Archer Jr. (Grand Rapids: Baker Book House, 1958).

prophetic" but an apocalyptic writing "which re-interpret[s] the past so that people in the present will remain faithful and courageous." Driver notes linguistic reasons for assigning a late date to the book. Driver also notes that the Hebrew of Daniel is late. This conclusion is based on Driver's late date for other books, e.g., Isaiah and Chronicles. The vocabulary, syntax, and style of Daniel can be explained by its content. In addition, the LXX, completed about 250 BC, includes Daniel. Hammer dates the book in the mid-second century BC. André Lacocque places its writing ca. 166 BC. He sees a Greek influence in the book and places c. 10–11 during the rule of Antiochus Epiphanes. Hartman sees multiple authors of an Aramaic original that was later translated into Hebrew. He dates the book ca. 164 BC. Gowan also rejects the prophetic nature of the book. He asserts that "no human being knows anything about the future" and that Daniel's prophecies therefore reflect the hope of the authors that God would deliver them from persecution.[9] This is a liberal view commonly held by those who reject the inspiration of the Bible. Other liberal authors are similar in their dating of the book.[10]

Among others, Driver, Hammer, and Montgomery point to the presence of Persian and Greek words, especially in the Aramaic section of the book, as evidence for a late date.[11] Since Daniel held a political position, he may well have had contact with these nations. In any case, the language of every nation contains loanwords that for various reasons have been adopted from other nations, e.g., the use

---

[9]Thomas S. Kepler, *Dreams of the Future*, in *Bible Guides*, ed. William Barclay and F. F. Bruce (New York: Abingdon Press, 1963), p. 12; S. R. Driver, *The Book of Daniel*, in *The Cambridge Bible for Schools and Colleges* (London: Cambridge University Press, 1936), pp. lvi–lxii; Hammer, p. 1; André Lacocque, *Daniel and His Time*, trans. Lydia Cochrane (Columbia: University of South Carolina Press, 1983), p. 8; Hartman, p. 14; Gowan, pp. 38–39.

[10]F. A. Gosling, "Is it Wise to Believe Daniel?" *Scandinavian Journal of the Old Testament* 13:1 (1999): 142–53, discusses the book from a liberal viewpoint and concludes that it is wise to believe it because of the spiritual lessons it teaches or illustrates. Gosling's view is open to question. How can one base personal spiritual values on a flawed foundation? If the book is not what it claims to be, it is an unreliable basis upon which to rest spiritual values.

[11]Driver, pp. lvi–lxiii; Hammer, p. 5; James A. Montgomery, *A Critical and Exegetical Commentary on the Book of Daniel* (Edinburgh: T. & T. Clark, 1927, rpt. 1972), pp. 20–23.

of "kimchi" (Korean), "sayonara" (Japanese), "mañana" (Spanish), "amour" (French), and "lei" (Hawaiian) in the English language.

Another reason for a late date often given is the failure of Ecclesiasticus, dated ca. 180 BC, to mention Daniel. Charles, Driver, and Kepler are among the authors who bring up this fact.[12] The author of Ecclesiasticus, Jesus Ben Sirach, lists several OT prophets: Moses, Samuel, Nathan, Elijah, Isaiah, Jeremiah, the Twelve, and Ezekiel (although he does not call him a prophet). The book written by Ben Sirach, however, fails to list others whom the OT clearly identifies as prophets. In fact, Ben Sirach omits more prophets than he lists. In addition to Daniel, there is no mention of Deborah (Judg. 4:4); Gad (2 Sam. 24:11); Micaiah (1 Kings 22:8); Asaph, Jeduthun, and Heman (1 Chron. 25:1); Zaccur, Joseph, Nethaniah, and Asarelah (1 Chron. 25:2); or Ahijah (2 Chron. 9:29).

Also, since the Jews did not place the book of Daniel in the prophetic section of the OT, there is no reason why Ben Sirach would have included him as a prophet. These liberal authors date the book ca. 165 BC. In effect, they criticize the book for being too accurate! By redating it, the prophetic sections become historical material written in the form of prophecy.[13]

This view is wrong! If the book does not set forth the prophetic writings of Daniel, it should be omitted from the pages of Scripture. Edward M. Panosian has well said, "Daniel is clearly presented as an eyewitness of and participant in the events described in the Book; if he were not, the Book would be a deception and a fraud, and the Holy Spirit of God would have honored and preserved for these two and a half millennia a lie and have called it Holy Scripture. That is worse than absurd."[14]

---

[12]Charles, pp. lxx–lxxi; Driver, p. xlviii; Kepler, p. 32.

[13]Hammer, pp. 1–11, mentions nine proofs to support a late authorship of the book of Daniel: the Masoretic location of the book, the lack of mention in Ecclesiasticus, the failure of any contemporary of Daniel to mention him, historical inaccuracies in the record of Belshazzar and Nabonidus and in the relationship of Darius and Cyrus, the misuse of the term "Chaldeans," errors in prophecy (which Hammer sees as earlier history), the use of Greek loanwords, and the interpretation of Daniel's seventy weeks (9:24–27). Gleason L. Archer Jr., "Modern Rationalism and the Book of Daniel," *BibSac* 136 (April–June 1979): 131–47, effectively refutes each of these arguments.

[14]Edward M. Panosian, "No Half Measures," *BV* 8:2 (November 1974): 100.

The Holy Spirit is well able to inspire the biblical authors, including Daniel, to forecast the future accurately. The sixth-century-BC prophet Ezekiel mentions Daniel (Ezek. 14:14, 20; 28:3). Gowan notes that the consonantal text in Ezekiel refers to "Danel" rather than "Daniel," as in the book of Daniel. For this reason, he concludes that Ezekiel writes about a Danel, also mentioned in the apocryphal book of Jubilees. Ezekiel perhaps "knew of legends about him that are lost to us." KB and BDB both recognize *dani'el* as simply a variant spelling of *danîye'el*. Gowan dismisses the fraudulent authorship with the comment that this was "a common practice" in the second century BC. While this was true of extrabiblical literature in that period, it is not true of biblical material.[15]

The Dead Sea Scrolls include several copies of the book, with the oldest dated in the late second century BC. This is evidence that the Essene inhabitants of Qumran considered the book a part of the canon of Scripture.[16] In *Antiquities* 12.7.6, Josephus states that Daniel uttered his prophecies "four hundred and eight years before" the desolation of the temple by Antiochus Epiphanes ca. 168 BC. This is long before the liberal date. The reference already referred to in Josephus's writings, *Antiquities* 11.8.5, has the book completed before ca. 332 BC, when Alexander overthrew the Persian Empire.

It has been aptly noted that "the period of the captivity is the only one during the whole range of Jewish history in which one of the Jewish books could have been written [in Hebrew and Aramaic]. . . . This was the only period in the entire national history of the Jews in which they understood both these languages.—Again, this was the only period in which the Chaldee portion [the Aramaic section, 2:4b–7:28] could have been reasonably written, for the benefit of the Chaldee period."[17]

It is also important to note that Daniel mentions Babylon and Media and Persia. He clearly prophesies both Greece and Rome but

---

[15]Donald E. Gowan, *Daniel* (Nashville: Abingdon Press, 2001), p. 22.

[16]Roger Beckwith, "Early Traces of the Book of Daniel," *TB* 53:1 (2002): 75–82, discusses three works from the intertestamental period—Tobit, Enoch, and Ecclesiasticus—all of which show knowledge of Daniel but were written before the date commonly proposed by liberal authors for its writing. Manuscripts of Tobit and Enoch were also found at Qumran.

[17]Henry Cowles, *Ezekiel and Daniel: With Notes, Critical, Explanatory, and Practical* (New York: D. Appleton, 1868), p. 277.

does not mention either by name. If he wrote as late as the liberals assert, we would expect him to mention the empires by name that developed out of the Grecian rule—Greece and Macedonia, Asia (including Syria and Babylon), and Egypt—and the growing power of Rome. Instead, he prophesies without mentioning these names.

The empire under Greece replaced the one controlled by the Medes and Persians, then divided into several smaller empires. The empire under Rome overcame and replaced these empires. Although the leaders of these kingdoms exercised a significant influence on Israel, Daniel does not mention any of them by name. This is inexplicable if he wrote as late as liberal authors assert. In Matthew 24:15, the Lord sets the fulfillment of "the abomination of desolation" (11:31) in the future, not in history.

Finally, it is difficult to explain Daniel's use of the name Belshazzar if he wrote in the mid-second century BC. How would he have known the name? We have no certain record of this name from history, outside of the Babylonian cuneiform records. While Herodotus (fifth cent. BC) and Xenophon (fourth cent. BC) refer to the fall of Babylon,[18] they do not mention Belshazzar's name. There is no reason to set aside the testimony of the book. Disbelief in prophecy is not an adequate ground for rejecting an early date for the writing of the book.

After referring to the NT references to Daniel, Keil concludes that "this testimony of our Lord fixes on the external and internal evidences which prove the genuineness of the book of Daniel." Keil calls this testimony "the seal of divine confirmation."[19] Stephen Miller notes that "traditionally, it has been held that Daniel wrote the book substantially as it exists today, that the prophecy is historically reliable, and that its predictions are supernatural and accurate."[20] H. C. Leupold states, "The matter boils down to this: the critical objections have been answered time and again in such a manner as to satisfy those that still believe in the veracity of God's Word, who also are fully convinced

---

[18]Herodotus 1.191; Xenophon *Cyropaedia* 7.5.15.

[19]C. F. Keil, *Biblical Commentary on the Book of Daniel*, trans. M. G. Easton (Grand Rapids: Wm. B. Eerdmans Publishing Co., rpt. 1978), p. 57.

[20]Stephen R. Miller, *Daniel*, in *The New American Commentary*, ed. E. Ray Clendenen and Kenneth A. Matthews (Nashville: Broadman & Holman, 1994), p. 23.

that, on the basis of sound logic, not one valid objection against the historical truth of the Bible can be pointed out."[21]

The Outline of Daniel

The outline of the book generally follows the chapter divisions.

I. Personal History 1:1–6:28
   A. Proving God 1:1–21
   B. Nebuchadnezzar's Image Vision 2:1–49
   C. Fiery Furnace 3:1–30
   D. Nebuchadnezzar's Tree Vision 4:1–37
   E. Belshazzar's Feast 5:1–31
   F. A Lion's Den 6:1–28

II. Prophetic Ministry 7:1–12:13
   A. Four Beasts 7:1–28
   B. Ram and Goat 8:1–27
   C. Seventy Weeks 9:1–27
   D. God's Glory 10:1–11:1
   E. Ptolemies and Seleucids 11:2–45
   F. End Times 12:1–13

This outline takes into account Daniel's writing of the first six chapters as history, mentioning himself as only one of several characters. While these chapters are generally historical, they also include some significant prophecy. In the remaining chapters, other than God, the Lord, and the angels, Daniel mentions only himself. The last six chapters deal with the four revelations received by Daniel and introduced in 7:1; 8:1–2; 9:20–21; and 10:1. Since these come to Daniel, he writes these chapters in the first person. These chapters are primarily prophetic, although they include historical matter as well.

Lenglet proposes an inverse parallel structure for c. 2–7. He parallels c. 2 and 7, c. 3 and 6, and c. 4 and 5. While this analyzes the Aramaic part of the book, it suffers from the failure to comprehensively consider the entire book. Gooding sees a parallelism between c. 1–5 and c. 6–12. Chapters 1 and 6 deal with a refusal to obey the king; c. 2–3 discuss two images and c. 7–8 two visions.

---

[21]H. C. Leupold, *Exposition of Daniel* (Grand Rapids: Baker Book House, rpt. 1969), p. 26.

Chapters 4–5 describe the discipline of two kings, while c. 9–12 explicate two writings (9, 10–12). In my judgment, Gooding's comparisons are artificial. For instance, c. 2 and the dream image parallels c. 7 and the four beasts, but Gooding places these differently. In c. 4, Gooding parallels Nebuchadnezzar's discipline and restoration with c. 9, which he sees as developing Jeremiah's prophecy but is in reality far more than this. In addition, his structure groups c. 7–8 but gives no reason for the change from Aramaic to Hebrew in them.[22]

Tanner proposes an "overlapping structure" with c. 7 belonging to both major parts of the book. Chapter one introduces the book, c. 2–7 adopt Lenglet's structure showing "God's Sovereignty over Gentile Empires," and c. 7–12 present the "Visions Given to Daniel." This has advantages in noticing the linguistic divisions in the book and giving a structure to the Aramaic portion in c. 2–7 while also noting that c. 7 begins the final section describing Daniel's visions. It has the disadvantage of an unusual structure with one chapter located in two parts of the book. It also fails to consider the differences between c. 1–6 and 7–12. Leupold considers c. 7 as the close to the first part of the book. He notes that c. 2 and 7 deal with the same subject and that c. 7 ends the use of Aramaic in the book. The chapter includes the reign of Jesus Christ over the world, a fitting close to the first part of the book.[23] His arguments are valid. Ultimately, however, the outline of the book rests on subjective reasoning. I have given my reasons above.

The Content of Daniel

As a whole, the book of Daniel gives us significant historical information relating to the captivity of the Jews. We find historical information in it regarding those captives placed in a position for leadership training. The book gives us specific information regarding the lives and character of Daniel and his three friends. We gain from it some insight into the character and nature of the Babylonian

---

[22]A. Lenglet, "Las structure littéraire de Daniel 2–7," *Biblica* 53:2 (1972): 169–90; David W. Gooding, "The Literary Structure of the Book of Daniel and Its Implications," *TB* 32 (1981): 52.

[23]J. Paul Tanner, "The Literary Structure of the Book of Daniel," *BibSac* 60 (July–September 2003): 277–82; Leupold, p. 270.

kings. We see the transition from Babylonian kings to Medo-Persian rulers. These historical parts give us vivid illustrations of faithful service to the Lord. Despite these contributions to our knowledge of the history of these times, the book is not primarily historical.

The book is of the highest value in introducing biblical prophecy. Daniel's interpretations of the visions given in the book sketch for us the outline of world history—the kingdoms of Syria (including Babylon), Media and Persia, Greece, and Rome. These four kingdoms span the interval from Daniel's own time to the second coming of the Lord. The prophetic portions tell us of great eschatological themes—the Tribulation with an emphasis on Antichrist and the Great Tribulation of the Jews, the second coming of Jesus Christ, the times of the Gentiles, and the resurrections of the dead and the subsequent judgments. These parts of the book devote more space to the person and work of Antichrist than any other book of the Bible. The only great prophetic themes omitted by the book are the development of the church and its later apostasy.

The book is apocalyptic in nature, similar in style to the Apocalypse of the NT. As with the book of the Revelation of Jesus Christ, so in Daniel we find prophetic revelations presented in highly symbolic form. In many cases, Daniel and Revelation deal with the same events but use different imagery to describe them (compare 7:7–8 with Rev. 13:1–2; 7:18 with Rev. 2:26 and 3:21; 8:23–24 with Rev. 13:11–14).

The Additions to Daniel

The book of Daniel served to influence other books that added to it as they developed their plots. These appear in the Apocrypha, a section included in the LXX translation of the OT and in the Latin Vulgate, in the Roman Catholic version of the Bible, and in several modern translations (NAB, NEB, NJB, REB). Although the original translation of the King James Version of the Bible included them, more recent conservative versions generally omit them. Church leaders as early as Augustine rejected these writings as noncanonical. In general, these books contain historical and geographic errors and teach false doctrinal practices. Several of these books, however, are valuable sources of historical information.

The books that draw on Daniel are *The History of Susanna, The Song of the Three Children,* and *The Story of Bel and the Dragon. The History of Susanna* tells of a godly woman who is accused of adultery by two men. Daniel questions the men and proves their accusation false. The story occurs before the book of Daniel in the LXX and as c. 13 in the Vulgate.

The Song of the Three Children recounts Azariah's prayer while in the fire of the furnace. After the miraculous deliverance of the three men, the story records a song of praise to God from them. Both the LXX and Vulgate insert this after 3:23, although the Vulgate notes that the account does not occur in the Hebrew.

The Story of Bel and the Dragon is a fanciful tale. It tells how Daniel proves the deception of the priests at an idol of Bel, then kills a serpent worshiped by the Babylonians, and finally escapes unharmed from a den of lions. Both the LXX and Vulgate append this narrative as a final chapter to Daniel.

At the Council of Trent in 1546, the Roman Catholic Church decreed these three stories as canonical. For this reason, the Roman Catholic Church accepts them as part of the OT. Historically, Protestant churches have rejected them as not belonging to the canonical book of Daniel.

The Theology of Daniel

We find a great deal of theological teaching in the book. This generally occurs incidentally, in connection with some event related by the prophet. The book gives several illustrations of man's sinfulness: his inherent pride, 4:30; 5:20, 22–23; his reliance on false gods, 2:11; 3:4–7; and his contempt toward the true God, 5:2–4. Daniel refers to man's anger, 3:19, and deceitfulness, 6:4–13. He urges the practice of righteousness on others, 4:27. Daniel describes God as righteous, 9:7, 14, 16, and merciful, 9:18. He speaks about the power of God, e.g., 1:17; 6:22. He includes illustrations of God's judgment on sin, 4:28–33; 5:18–21, 22–30, and speaks specifically of God's judgment on His people, 9:24*a.*

The prophet describes his emotional reaction to divine truth as God reveals it to him, 7:15, 28; 8:27; 10:8, 15. He gives incidents that show the faithfulness of the saints, e.g., 1:8, 11–15; 3:16–18. Daniel's actions teach the value of prayer, e.g., 2:17–18, 19–23; 6:10–11; 9:3–19; and of confession of sin, 9:5–6, 11, 15–16, 20.

One of the more fully developed teachings in the book concerns angels. Daniel mentions these creatures and the variety of service they render to God, 4:23; 5:5; 6:22; 7:16; 8:13, 16; 9:21. He also touches briefly on the organization of the angels that serve God and the opposition of those angelic beings that serve Satan, 10:12–13, 20–21; 12:1.

The major theological emphasis in Daniel, however, lies in the realm of eschatology.[24] The book describes the four major kingdoms that have dominated and will continue to dominate the world's government until the Lord's return, 2:37–43; 7:2–8, 17, 23–24a. It gives special emphasis to the Medo-Persian Empire, 8:3–4, 20; 11:2; the Greek Empire, 8:5–12, 21–22; 11:3–4a, with the continued development of the Egyptian and Syrian leaders who followed Alexander, 11:4b–35. Daniel prophecies of the tribulation judgments that are yet to come, 7:25; 9:27; 12:1. He speaks briefly of the first coming of Jesus Christ and His sacrificial death, 9:24b–26a. He predicts the kingdom of God, 2:44–45; 7:13–14, 18, 27, and His final victory over Antichrist, 7:9–11, 20b–22, 24b–26; 8:23–25; 9:26b–27; 11:36–45. Daniel mentions briefly the resurrection of the godly and the ungodly, 12:2. He mentions the reward that God will give for faithful service, 12:3.

King sees the theological emphasis as "the Universal Sovereignty of God," and Bell sees its message as "a divinely inspired philosophy of history."[25] The eschatology of the book embraces both of these topics. God demonstrates His "Universal Sovereignty" as He guides the events of this world toward their inevitable end. Likewise, we see the "divinely inspired philosophy of history" revealed as Daniel summarizes the world kingdoms that will end with the divine kingdom ruled by the Son of God.

---

[24]E. W. Heaton, *The Book of Daniel* (London: SCM Press, 1956), p. 107, sees the major emphasis as wisdom. This "is more explicitly and maturely expounded than anywhere outside those Old Testament books which are by general consent ascribed to the tradition of the sages." While the book does demonstrate wisdom, the word occurs only in c. 1, 2, and 5. The eschatological emphasis is dominant.

[25]Geoffrey R. King, *Daniel: A Detailed Explanation of the Book* (Grand Rapids: Wm. B. Eerdmans Publishing Co., 1966), p. 20; Robert D. Bell, "The Theology of Daniel," *BV* 8:2 (November 1974): 143.

The Value of Daniel

The emphasis of Daniel on eschatology gives the book a practical nature for believers today. 1 John 3:3 states that the Christian who looks for the appearing of Jesus Christ "purifieth himself, even as he is pure." The prophetic teaching of Daniel suggests that the Lord's return is near. There is therefore a need for Christians to purify themselves. In addition, we see the emphasis placed on the book in the Lord's command in Matthew 24:15, repeated in Mark 13:14: "When ye therefore shall see the abomination of desolation, spoken of by Daniel the prophet, stand in the holy place, (whoso readeth, let him understand) . . ." Since the Lord Himself commanded understanding, it is well that we take the time to study carefully this book and its prophetic truths.

After summarizing Daniel's prophecies, Josephus wrote that those who "read his prophecies, and see how they have been fulfilled" should "wonder at the honor wherewith God honored Daniel" (*Antiquities* 10.11.7). Merrill F. Unger wrote that the book is "one of the most important prophetical books of the O. T., indispensable as an introduction to N. T. prophecy." William Stuart Auchincloss stated that the book "is a most important part of the Word of God, and is set like a gem among jewels." John R. Walvoord describes the book as "the most comprehensive revelation of the Old Testament, giving the only total view of world history from Babylon to the second advent of Christ. . . . Daniel provides the key to the overall interpretation of prophecy, is a major element in premillennialism, and is essential to the interpretation of the book of Revelation."[26]

---

[26]Merrill F. Unger, *Unger's Bible Dictionary* (Chicago: Moody Press, 1957), p. 237; W. S. Auchincloss, *The Book of Daniel Unlocked* (New York: D. Van Nostrand Company, 1905), p. 10; John R. Walvoord, *Daniel: The Key to Prophetic Revelation* (Chicago: Moody Press, 1971), p. 27.

PROVING GOD 1:1–21

The first chapter serves as a preface to the whole book. It not only tells the readers of the early part of the Babylonian captivity but also introduces them to the character of Daniel and his companions. We see in the chapter the example of faithfulness to God's Word. This is the reason behind Daniel's commendation as one of the great examples of righteousness (Ezek. 14:14, 20) and wisdom (Ezek. 28:3) and the statement that Daniel was "greatly beloved" by God (9:23; 10:11, 19). In addition, we see some of the reasons that allow God to use Daniel in such a significant way. His refusal to break God's law and his willingness to prove God, coupled with his tactful interaction with the Babylonians, open the way to a life of fruitful service for God and for his nation.

Captivity of Jerusalem 1:1–2 The chapter begins with the conquest of Judah by Nebuchadnezzar, one of the great heathen kings of biblical times. As his name appears in Daniel, the spelling is $n^e b\hat{u}kadne^{\jmath}ssar$ or a close variant spelling. It is found more frequently elsewhere in the OT as $n^e b\hat{u}kadre^{\jmath}ssar$. From the Akkadian parallel $nab\hat{u}\text{-}kudurri\text{-}usur$, the latter is the proper spelling. This spelling occurs (with some variation) thirty-three times elsewhere, all in Jeremiah and Ezekiel. Some have described the name in Daniel as a wrong form.[1] Since variant spellings of the king's name also occur in 2 Kings, 1 and 2 Chronicles, Ezra, Nehemiah, Esther, and Jeremiah and the Greek form of the name in the LXX, it is not appropriate to find Daniel in error. The interchange between n and r is due to the transition from Akkadian to Hebrew.

The name Nebuchadnezzar means "Nebo, protect the boundary." Nebuchadnezzar served as the general of the army for his father Nabopolassar and, later, during his own rule over the Babylonian empire. Verse 1 gives him the title of "king." Gowan and Hartman understand 1:1–2 as giving wrong historical information. Nebuchadnezzar was not king of Babylon at the time he besieged Jerusalem in 606 BC. These authors assert that the first deportation of Jews

---

[1]E.g., Heaton, p. 122, and Norman W. Porteous, *Daniel: A Commentary* (Philadelphia: The Westminster Press, 1965), p. 26, both call the spelling "inaccurate." R. H. Charles, *A Critical Commentary on the Book of Daniel* (Oxford: Clarendon Press, 1929), p. 5, refers to it as "incorrect."

took place in 597 BC, not in 605 BC.[2] Daniel, however, uses the title of "king" in a proleptic sense. He writes from Babylon, after Nebuchadnezzar has ascended to the throne. It is natural that he would refer to him as the king who had earlier besieged Jerusalem and taken captives.

Daniel 1:1 establishes the date of the first deportation at 605 BC. Josephus *Antiquities* 10.11.1 refers to "captive Jews" at the time of Nebuchadnezzar's conquest of Jerusalem before his father's death.[3] After defeating Judah in 605 BC, Nebuchadnezzar carried away captives, including Daniel and his friends, to Babylon. The OT does not discuss this event clearly, but it gives enough information that we can accept this date with confidence. Pharaoh Necho, an Egyptian ruler, placed Jehoiakim on the throne of Judah (2 Chron. 36:4–5) in 608 BC. In Jehoiakim's fourth year, Nebuchadnezzar led Babylon's troops against Egypt (Jer. 46:2). This was Egypt's final battle in Palestine against the Babylonians and their allies. Earlier in his book, Jeremiah had stated that Nebuchadnezzar would defeat Judah in Nebuchadnezzar's first year, which was also Jehoiakim's fourth year (25:1–9). This is the beginning of the seventy years of captivity prophesied in Jeremiah 25:11–12 (cf. 29:10).

According to Daniel, the Babylonian king besieges Jerusalem "in the third year" of Jehoiakim, best dated at 605 BC.[4] The date introduces a minor problem. Among others, Hammer and Driver deny that Nebuchadnezzar besieged Jerusalem in "the third year" of Jehoiakim. They cite Jeremiah 25:1, which places Jehoiakim's

---

[2]Gowan, pp. 43–44; Hartman, p. 34.

[3]Miller, p. 56, and Frederick A. Tatford, *The Climax of the Ages: Studies in the Prophecy of Daniel* (London: Marshall, Morgan & Scott, 1953), p. 19, consider Nebuchadnezzar as reigning jointly with his father. There is, however, no evidence in the records from this time to support this conclusion.

[4]Hersh Goldwurm, *Daniel* (Brooklyn, N.Y.: Mesorah Publications, 1980), p. 58, places this at the end of Jehoiakim's eleven-year rule (cf. 2 Kings 23:36). He asserts that the phrase "third year" refers to the third year of Jehoiakim's "independent rule." Prior to this, he had been under the domination of either Egypt or Babylon. There is, however, no need to so interpret the phrase. Jehoiakim replaced his brother Jehoahaz in 608 BC with the nation subject to Egypt. Three years later, Nebuchadnezzar routed Egypt at Carchemish. As the Egyptians fled southward through Palestine, the Babylonians followed. It was at this time that Nebuchadnezzar took a spoil from the temple at Jerusalem. Jehoiakim continued as king over the Jews for another eight years.

"fourth year" as the first year of Nebuchadnezzar. This is the typical view of authors with a liberal view of Scripture.[5] There is a ready explanation for the supposed discrepancy between the third and fourth years. The Jews and Babylonians calculated the accession year of a king differently. The Babylonians counted a king's rule from his first *full* year, while the Jews began with the earliest part, including a *partial* year. Daniel, writing from the standpoint of his years in Babylon, gives the Babylonian dating of Jehoiakim's rule. Jeremiah, however, gives the Jewish dating. Taylor adopts this view. Walvoord notes, "Having spent most of his life in Babylon, it is only natural that Daniel should use a Babylonian form of chronology." Yamauchi is similar.[6]

Other explanations have also been given. Leupold suggests that Nebuchadnezzar's raid in Jehoiakim's "third year" is not mentioned elsewhere due to its nature as being a minor conflict. Keil argues that "came," v. 1, refers to the start of the campaign, which ended later, in the fourth year. These views also give reasonable explanations of the different biblical dates.[7]

Upon the death of his father Nabopolassar, Nebuchadnezzar returned from warring in Palestine to Babylon to be inaugurated as king. Accordingly, Judah's defeat took place in his first year as the Babylonian ruler. When Judah allied itself to Egypt in 597 BC, Nebuchadnezzar defeated them again and carried away a second group of captives (2 Kings 24:11–16). He took a third set of captives to Babylon in 586 BC (2 Kings 25:8–11).

Nebuchadnezzar devoted much of his rule to building. He rebuilt the Temple of Marduk in Babylon and the Temple of Ezida in Borsippa. He built streets in Babylon and strengthened the city's walls. He built canals in and near the city. He built the Hanging Gardens of Babylon, one of the seven wonders of the ancient world. He carried out a variety of building projects in the cities of Ur, Larsa, Sippar, Erech, and Cutha. He ruled Babylon forty-three years (605–562 BC), v. 1.

---

[5]Hammer, p. 18; Driver, p. 2.

[6]Richard A. Taylor, "The Life God Blesses," *BV* 8:2 (November 1974): 105; Walvoord, p. 31; Edwin Yamauchi, "The Archaeological Background of Daniel," *BibSac* 137 (Jan–Mar 1980): 3.

[7]Leupold, p. 52; Keil, p. 63.

Jehoiakim had been a wicked king (2 Chron. 36:5, 8). In punishment, the "Lord" (*ᵃdonay*) gave his capital city into the hands of the Babylonian king (2 Kings 24:1–3; 2 Chron. 36:5–7). The word *ᵃdonay* occurs twelve times in Daniel, eleven of them in c. 9. The word stresses the position of God as man's "master" or "lord." As such, He exercises His right to punish His people for their sins by sending them into captivity.

The judgment is appropriate. The Jews had polluted the temple with images of heathen gods (2 Kings 21:4, 5, 7; 23:11). God now allows "part" of its vessels to occupy the "house" of a heathen god (cf. 2 Chron. 36:7). John Calvin identifies the "house" as "the temple of Belus."[8] This temple, also known as the temple of Esagila, was in the southern part of Babylon, at the end of the processional street. It served as a worship center for the god Marduk, called Bel in Isaiah 46:1 and Jeremiah 50:2; 51:44. Since Nebuchadnezzar restored Esagila, this may well be the "house" in which the temple vessels were stored.

The mention of this action prepares for the description of Belshazzar's wicked actions in 5:1. The vessels come from "the house of God [*ᵉlohîm*]," more literally from "the house of the God." In Daniel, when *ᵉlohîm* appears without a qualifying pronoun to refer to the true God, the definite article is always attached. This distinguishes the true God from the false gods of the Babylonians.

The article is attached to the name *ᵉlohîm* when it refers to the true God in 1:2*a*, 9, 17, and 9:3, 11. When the name refers to false gods in 1:2*b* (twice) and 11:8, 37, the article is lacking due to attached pronouns. In 1:2 and 9:3, Daniel uses apposition rather than prepositions or a construct state but still maintains the use of the pronoun with the true God. In 9:4, 9, 10, 13, 14, 15, 17, 18, 19, 20 (twice); 10:12, and 11:32, the attached pronoun makes it clear that this is the true God.

The Babylonians carry the vessels to "the land of Shinar," an ancient name for the southern part of Babylon (cf. Gen. 10:10; 11:2; 14:1, 9). The action fulfilled the prophecy made by Isaiah after Hezekiah's sin of pride (2 Kings 20:17). Later, the Babylonians carried away additional temple vessels (2 Kings 24:13; 25:14–15), v. 2.

---

[8]John Calvin, *Commentaries on the Book of the Prophet Daniel*, trans. Thomas Myers (Grand Rapids: Wm. B. Eerdmans Publishing Co., 1948), I, 83.

Introduction of Daniel 1:3–7 Almost 200 years earlier, the prophet Isaiah had foretold that the descendants of Hezekiah would be captives at Babylon (2 Kings 20:18; Isa. 39:7). The group of captives introduced in Daniel 1:3–6 fulfills this prophecy.

Nebuchadnezzar now assigns Ashpenaz, chief of the Babylonian "eunuchs" (or "officers," *sarîs*), to choose some of the "children [lit. 'sons'] of Israel" for training. The word *sarîs* occurs seven times in Daniel, all in this chapter (vv. 3, 7, 8, 9, 10, 11, 18). It may be translated here either as "eunuch" or "officer." The word likely comes from the Akkadian *ša reši*, "he who is the head." The sense of "eunuch" comes from the use of emasculated men in certain court positions. In some places in the OT, the word clearly refers to a eunuch (e.g., Esther 2:3; Isa. 56:3–4). In Genesis 39:1, where it refers to Potiphar, a married man, it clearly refers to a highly placed official. The word often occurs simply as a general term for "officer" (e.g., Gen. 40:2; 1 Sam. 8:15). A related title, Rabsaris ("chief of the heads"), occurs in 2 Kings 18:17; Jeremiah 39:3, 13.

Josephus *Antiquities* 10.10.1 asserts that the four Israelites were made eunuchs. Although Greene accepts the view that the trainees became eunuchs, most authors reject this position. Even liberal authors reject the possibility of emasculation. Montgomery says that "it is not necessary to draw the conclusion that the youths were made eunuchs." Driver comments, "It is not said that Daniel and his companions were made eunuchs, and it is too much to infer this." Charles notes that "the perfection here asserted is physical, as in Lev. 21[17]. Such perfection could not be asserted of eunuchs."[9]

It is not necessary to conclude that Daniel and his friends became eunuchs. There is no mention of wives or children, but there is no reason why they should be mentioned. They play no part in the ministry and testimony of these men. Leviticus 21:17–21 shows that God held a high physical standard for those who served Him as priests. While Daniel and his friends were not priests, they played very important spiritual roles in the nation. Their example had to be blameless. In addition, the phrase "children in whom was no blemish" (or "youths in whom were no physical defects," v. 4) argues against the possibility of later emasculation.

---

[9]Oliver B. Greene, *Daniel* (Greenville, S.C.: The Gospel Hour, Inc., 1964), p. 29; Montgomery, p. 119; Driver, p. 4; Charles, p. 13.

The Babylonians choose the captives on the basis of their heritage, their appearance, and their abilities. They are "of the king's seed, and of the princes," having a royal background. Although we cannot prove it, it may be that these members of the royal family were taken as hostages for Jehoiakim's continuing subjection to Babylon. This custom was widely practiced in this period of the world's history. Antiochus Epiphanes, a character whose life and reign is summarized in Daniel 8:9–12 and expanded on in 11:21–35, received his education while a hostage at Rome for his father, v. 3.

The hostages are "children" (*yeled*), i.e., youths. The noun *yeled* occurs five times in Daniel, again all in this chapter (vv. 4, 10, 13, 15, 17). Elsewhere in the OT, it describes a range of ages. These include a fetus (Exod. 21:22), a babe (Exod. 2:7), a child (2 Kings 4:18), an adolescent (Gen. 37:30), and young adults (1 Kings 12:8). From the fact that the "children" in Daniel enter into training, it is reasonable to see them as late teens or young adults.

We may only speculate on Daniel's age at the time of his capture. We have information about the Persians from pre-Christian writings. Plato states that "the most excellent of the Persians" were chosen at the age of fourteen for further training.[10] Xenophon places the training at the age of "sixteen or seventeen years of age."[11] Herodotus 1.136 makes the age "from five to twenty years old," while Strabo gives the age as from "five years of age to twenty-four."[12]

Modern authors give various ages and backgrounds to the captives. On the basis of 9:24 ("thy holy city"), Josephus *Antiquities* 10.10.1 describes the four as being of "the family of Zedekiah." Barnes tentatively suggests that Daniel was born in Jerusalem. Larkin states that the four "were of royal blood [and] were descendants of . . . Hezekiah." Luck sees all of them as "from the tribe of Judah and of noble lineage."[13]

---

[10]Plato, *Alcibiades*, trans. W. R. M. Lamb (Cambridge, Mass.: Harvard University Press, 1964), 1.121.

[11]*Cyropaedia* 1.2.8.

[12]Strabo, *The Geography of Strabo*, trans. Horace Leonard Jones (Cambridge, Mass.: Harvard University Press, 1966), 15.4.18.

[13]Albert Barnes, *Daniel*, in *Notes on the Old Testament: Explanatory and Practical*, ed. Robert Frew (Grand Rapids, 1950), I, 1–2; Larkin, *The Book of Daniel* (Philadelphia: Rev. Clarence Larkin Estate, 1929), p. 22; G. Coleman Luck, *Daniel* (Chicago: Moody Press, 1958), p. 25.

Barnes relies on Daniel 1:4 ("children") to make Daniel and his friends "somewhere about twelve to fifteen years." William LaSor agrees with the view that he was "twelve or fifteen at the time." William Taylor conjectures an age of fourteen." Thurman Wisdom states that he "was probably not more than fifteen years old." Gene Getz suggests an age of fifteen at the time of Daniel's captivity. Morton Wharton makes him "about sixteen years of age" when he was taken from Jerusalem. Thomas Kirk assigns a birth date in 623 BC with the fall of Jerusalem occurring in 606 BC.[14] This gives Daniel an age of seventeen or eighteen when he entered into his training.

It is clearly impossible to be dogmatic about the age of the four Israelites mentioned in c. 1. The book describes Daniel's activities over a range of a little more than seventy years, from 605 BC (the captivity) to ca. 536 BC ("the third year of Cyrus," 10:1). This sets an upper limit in the early twenties for Daniel's age. The description of Daniel's interaction with "the prince of the eunuchs" (1:8–16) together with the performance of the four Jewish youths at Nebuchadnezzar's examination (1:18–20) suggests a level of maturity greater than that of a mere child. I would suggest an age of between eighteen and twenty years at the time of the captivity.

From Daniel's longevity in service, approximately seventy years, he could have been no more than in his late teens or early twenties when chosen. The young men chosen for training have no "blemish," or physical defects, and are "well favoured," with a pleasing appearance. They are "skilful in all wisdom," "cunning in knowledge," and "understanding science [or 'knowledge']." There is no great distinction in these phrases. The heaping of commendation on commendation simply conveys the readiness of these men to learn new things, in particular the ways of the Babylonians. Nebuchadnezzar probably

---

[14]Barnes, pp. 1–2; William Sanford LaSor, *Great Personalities of the Old Testament: Their Lives and Times* (Westwood, N.J.: Fleming H. Revell Company, 1959), p. 164; William M. Taylor, *Daniel the Beloved* (New York: Harper & Brothers, 1878), p. 11; Thurman Wisdom, *A Royal Destiny: The Reign of Man in God's Kingdom* (Greenville, S.C.: Bob Jones University Press, 2006), p. 265; Gene A. Getz, *Daniel: Standing Firm for God* (Nashville: Broadman & Holman, Publishers, 1998), p. 2; Morton Bryan Wharton, *Famous Men of the Old Testament* (Chicago: W. P. Blessing, 1903), p. 260; Thomas Kirk, *Daniel the Prophet* (Edinburgh: David MacDonald, 1906), pp. 2, 13.

felt that the youths were too young to have developed a loyalty to their nation.

Captives from other nations may well have been included among those receiving training. Josephus *Against Apion* 1.19 records that Nebuchadnezzar took captives from "the Jews, and Phoenicians, and Syrians, and of the nations belonging to Egypt." He relocated these captives to Babylon.

After completing the early training, Persian youths received further training in hunting and military matters. The Persians also had a "college of the magi" in which hymns and worship of the deities was practiced. Some boys received instruction in the medicinal effects of plants.[15] From other references to medicine, trades, and law, it is clear that education encompassed many fields.[16] Archaeology also shows that there were schools at Babylon. Babylon was a center of learning. Excavations of the city revealed hundreds of tablets in which students practiced language skills and copied earlier writings. There was also instruction in astrology (which required the knowledge of astronomy), mathematics, and business.[17] The captives in their training likely embraced such topics as the Akkadian language, literary material, mathematics, astronomy, business matters, and the interpretation of dreams.

After training and becoming accustomed to Babylonian ways, these young men would be of service to Babylon. They had the "ability [*koah*] . . . to stand in the king's palace." The noun *koah* normally refers to physical strength. This produces an ability to act in some area. Elsewhere in Daniel, *koah* is translated "power" (8:6, 7, 22, 24 [twice]; 11:6, 25) or "strength" (10:8 [twice], 16, 17; 11:15). Elsewhere in the OT, however, *koah* may refer to "ability" without any reference to strength (e.g., Gen. 31:6; 1 Chron. 29:14; Ezra 2:69). This is the sense in which it occurs here.

The context describes these captives as "well favoured, and skilful in all wisdom, and cunning in knowledge [*da‘at*], and understanding science [*madda‘*, or 'knowledge']." There is no clear distinction between *da‘at* and *madda‘*. Both come from the root *yd‘*.

---

[15]Xenophon, *Cyropaedia* 1.2.8–13; 8.1.23; 8.8.14.

[16]Herodotus 7.181; Xenophon, *Cyropaedia* 8.2.5–6.

[17]D. J. Wiseman, *Nebuchadrezzar and Babylon* (New York: Oxford University Press, 1985), pp. 86–93.

The word *daᶜat* occurs widely in the OT, about ninety times, while *maddaᶜ* is limited in use, occurring only six times. Both words occur twice in Daniel (*daᶜat* also at 12:4, and *maddaᶜ* also at 1:17). This context of *koaḥ* here suggests that both words refer to the captives' mental ability to serve wisely.

Following their transport to Babylon, the Jewish youths are placed in some form of school. Here, they receive training in the "learning" (*seper*, lit. "writing," i.e., knowledge preserved in writing, or "books")[18] and speech of the "Chaldeans" (*kaśdîm*), a term that here refers to the inhabitants of Babylon. The word *kaśdîm* occurs widely in the OT, referring to either a region (Jer. 51:24, 35), a group of wise men (Dan. 2:2, 4), or the inhabitants of Babylon (2 Chron. 36:17; Dan. 9:1). In each case, the context must guide as to the meaning given to the word.

Lederach, Hartman, and Montgomery refer "the tongue of the Chaldeans" to the study of omens, incantations, prayers, kabbalism, and other specialized areas used by the Babylonian priests.[19] The view is speculative. The normal use of the language supports the view adopted above. While it is possible to limit the word to a class of professional wise men, we do not know of any special writing or language unique to the "priest-seers" of Babylon. It is more logical that the young men received training to let them communicate freely with the Babylonians.

Daniel 2:4 (cf. 2 Kings 18:26) indicates that "Syriack" (better "Aramaic") was spoken at the court. The historic language of the Babylonians was Akkadian, and many official documents must have used this. Written Akkadian used cuneiform with its combinations of wedge-shaped markings. There are many transliterated Akkadian words that are cognate to Hebrew. We cannot be dogmatic about which language is in view here. The "tongue of the Chaldeans" may refer to a late Babylonian form of Akkadian, to Aramaic, or to both languages, v. 4.

---

[18]Lacocque, *The Book of Daniel*, p. 27, restricts Daniel's study to "the cuneiform writing practised up to the Seleucid period in literate circles addicted to the occult." The word also occurs in 9:2; 12:1, 4, where it cannot be so restricted. The word likely has a broader sense here and refers generally to the learning of the Babylonians.

[19]Lederach, p. 36; Hartman, p. 129; and Montgomery, pp. 120–21.

The Israelite youths receive a diet of "the king's meat [i.e., 'food,' *pat·bag*] and . . . wine." The noun *pat·bag* occurs in the OT only in Daniel (1:5, 8, 13, 15, 16; 11:26). It is a Persian loanword that refers to fine food, delicacies, and here indicates the choice food served at the king's table each day. Tatford derives *pat·bag* from the Persian word *patibaga* (1:5), "offering or tribute." He suggests that the word implicitly refers to "food which, before being placed upon the king's table, had first been presented before the gods." This supports the idea that Daniel and his friends requested a different diet for religious reasons. Keil and Young also adopt this view.[20] While it is possible that this food had been dedicated to the Babylonian gods, the context in 11:26 does not require it.

The intention of the diet is for "nourishing them" (lit., "making them great," i.e., developing them) for three years. This would give time to let the Jewish young men develop both physically and mentally before putting them into their service for the king. The verse introduces the dilemma faced by the Israelites and developed more fully in vv. 8–16. Some of the food undoubtedly had been dedicated to the Babylonian gods. Some of it likely violated the dietary laws of Israel (e.g., Lev. 11). The youths must choose, v. 5.

Four of the captives taken from the southern kingdom of Judah stand out. Their Israelite names hint that they have a spiritual heritage, with their parents giving them names to reflect their relationship to God. The name Daniel means "God is my judge." Hananiah means "the Lord is gracious." Mishael asks the question, "Who is like God?" The name Azariah affirms that "the Lord is my help," v. 6.

As one way of helping them forget their spiritual heritage, the "prince of the eunuchs [or 'officers']" gives them new names. It is not possible to identify this "prince." The word may simply vary the title "master of [the] eunuchs," given to Ashpenaz in v. 3. It may as well indicate an unnamed official in overall charge of the training program. Daniel receives the name Belteshazzar ("protect his life"). The name is a prayer addressed to an unnamed Babylonian god, probably Bel (cf. "according to the name of my god," 4:8). Daniel 5:12 says that the king himself gave the name of Belteshazzar to Daniel. This probably, however, indicates that the king commanded

---

[20]Tatford, p. 23; Keil, I, 80; Young, p. 44.

that Babylonian names should be given to the captives. Hananiah receives the name of Shadrach ("command of Aku," the Sumerian moon god). Mishael is renamed Meshach ("of the goddess Shach," the Babylonian name for Venus; or "who is what Aku is"; the name cannot be related clearly to Akkadian). Azariah is given the name Abed-nego ("servant of Nebo").[21]

The giving of new names follows a pattern seen elsewhere in the OT. The Egyptians renamed Joseph to Zaphnath-paaneah (Gen. 41:45). Hadassah received the new Persian name Esther (Esther 2:7). Names in the Bible are often theologically significant. This can be seen in the changes of Hebrew names in the OT. Abram ("high father") became Abraham ("father of a multitude"), Genesis 17:5. Jacob ("one who overreaches," i.e., seeks to supplant his brother) became Israel ("he who strives with God"), Genesis 32:28. There are many examples of significant names, e.g., Noah ("rest"), Moses ("drawn out" of the water), Samuel ("asked of God"), and Ichabod ("inglorious"). Undoubtedly, the Babylonians hope to relate these men to their Babylonian gods by means of their new names, v. 7.

Test of the Israelites 1:8–16 Daniel, the leader among the four Israelites, refuses to "defile" himself with the "portion" (*pat-bag*) of meat from the king. The verb "defile" shows that there was some violation of the Law involved with eating the Babylonian diet. The OT dietary laws guided Israel to practice holiness (Exod. 22:31; Lev. 11:44–45; Deut. 14:21).

Goldwurm asserts that Daniel's abstention from Babylonian food was to avoid the temptation of intermarriage with a non-Jewish woman: "An eating and drinking relationship strengthens social bonds, and may ultimately lead to intermarriage." Goldwurm also suggests "since Daniel alone had been named for a Babylonian idol, he suspected that he was being consecrated to this idol and that his

---

[21]Various authors also give other meanings for these names. Uriah Smith, *The Prophecies of Daniel and the Revelation* (Mountain View, Calif.: Pacific Press Publishing Association, 1944), p. 23, equates Belteshazzar with "prince of Bel." Tatford, p. 24, understands Shadrach as "the inspiration of Rach [the Babylonian word for sun]." Lenormant, quoted by Thomson, p. 18, renders Meshach as "who is as Merodach." Matthew Henry, *Commentary on the Whole Bible*, (reprint, New York: Fleming H. Revell Company, 1935), IV, 1019, gives Belteshazzar as "keeper of the hidden treasures of Bel" and Abed-nego as "servant of the shining fire." The meanings given above generally follow the lexicon definitions.

food consisted of animals sacrificed to the idol, including wine used for libations." While either of these views may be so, the record does not give any reason other than that implied by the word "defile." Watkinson asserts "that indulgence in animal food retards spirituality, and an abstinent and vegetable diet is conducive to the opening of the spiritual faculties, prophetic powers, and mediatorial states."[22] The widespread practice of God's servants argues against the view.

There are several distinct reasons for the OT dietary laws that governed the diet and sacrificial system of Israel. (1) The law excluded some food for health reasons, e.g., pork (Lev. 11:7). With the limited refrigeration available and the lack of food processing capability, it was best to keep Israel from eating certain foods. For this same reason, the Jews avoided meat from animals that had died naturally (Deut. 14:21) or been killed by another animal (Exod. 22:31). (2) The people could not eat certain food because of the degrading symbolism attached to it. Some animals were carrion-eaters or had personal habits that made them unfit to be used for food (Lev. 11:13–19). Jewish laws forbid the eating of meat from unclean animals (e.g., Lev. 11:4–8). Meat that had been dedicated to an idol could not be eaten (Exod. 34:15). (3) The Jews could not eat raw meat with blood still in the flesh (Deut. 12:16, 23). Blood in the OT symbolically looked forward to the sacrificial blood of the Lord. (4) Certain foods were given to the Lord, thus picturing Israel giving Him their best. Fatty parts of sacrificial animals were not eaten but burned on the altar (Lev. 3:15–17; 7:23–25). (5) The Lord excluded some food simply to set Israel apart from the heathen nations around them (e.g., crab, lobster, oysters, clams, cf. Lev. 11:9–12). There was nothing wrong with this food. Refraining from it marked Israel as being in submission to God.

There were other dietary rules as well. Since Daniel and his friends cannot control the nature of the food served him by the Babylonians, they ask "the prince of the eunuchs [or 'officers']" to limit their diet. Since the Babylonians would not have eaten food that was unhealthy, the primary reason behind the request was spiritual. Daniel and his friends did not want to displease God.

---

[22]Goldwurm, p. 67; Redford A. Watkinson, *The End, as Foretold in Daniel* (New York: C. S. Westcott & Co., 1865), p. 81.

Daniel, speaking for the group, asks the "prince of the eunuchs [or 'officers']" to excuse them from eating the diet prescribed by the Babylonians, v. 8. God (*ᵉlohîm*, see v. 2) has given this official a special liking for Daniel. This friendship gives Daniel the opportunity to make his petition, v. 9. The Babylonian leader of the "eunuchs" (or "officers"), however, expresses his concern over the request. He anticipates that the Israelites will appear "worse liking," in poor health, compared to others "of your sort" (i.e., "of your age"), the other men also receiving training. If that happens, the king will blame him for it. This will "endanger my head," place him in a position subject to severe punishment, possibly even death, from the king, v. 10.

Daniel speaks with the "Melzar" (or "the overseer," *hammelṣar*), set over the four Israelites by the "prince of the eunuchs [or 'officers']." The word *melṣar* occurs only here and in v. 16. It clearly is an Akkadian loanword, but we cannot be dogmatic about the meaning. Since the word occurs in both places with the definite article, it is clear that it is a title rather than a personal name. BDB suggests "keeper, guardian." KB gives "overseer." Since the context here deals with providing food and drink, the meaning of "steward" is often suggested, v. 11.[23]

Daniel presents his plan to prove God by a ten-day trial period. Young suggests that it would have been presumptuous for Daniel to make this offer on his own initiative. In view of the guidance elsewhere in the book, Young thinks it likely that God has given special guidance to Daniel here. In proposing the test, Daniel demonstrates his faith in God.[24] While this may be true, it is also possible that Daniel proposes a test in order to follow the Lord's dietary regulations, already made known to him through His Word.

The test involves all four of the Jewish friends. They will eat "pulse" (better "seeds," *hazzeroᶜîm*). The word comes from the verbal root *zrᶜ*, "to sow, scatter seed," and indicates the results of sowing or scattering seeds. There is no reason to limit these results to any particular kind of vegetable. It could include peas, beans, parched grain, lentils, and possibly fruits, nuts, and bread made from grain. In addition, the four will drink water rather than the king's

---

[23]So Gangel, p. 23, and Leupold, p. 70.

[24]Young, p. 46.

wine, v. 12. At the end of the time, the Babylonians can examine them and compare them with others who have eaten the prescribed diet for the captives. They can decide at that point how to handle the matter, v. 13. The overseer approves, giving the four men a ten-day trial period. Young suggests that the number "ten" is a round number here, as in 1:20.[25] It is likely, however, that the test had to have a definite end so that the overseer could make an evaluation. Verse 14 supports the view that a definite time passed before drawing a conclusion regarding the diet. Note that the four Israelites took their stand under a king who did not hesitate to torture others (cf. Jer. 29:22; 39:6–7; Dan. 3:15). The key is that Daniel agrees to test God in the matter. The Babylonian official will make the decision.

With the approval of the overseer, Daniel and his friends test the Lord's ability to sustain them during the ten-day period, v. 14. At the end of that time, they visibly appear healthier than any of the other Jews. It is possible to speculate about this, since a ten-day test would not normally show such a distinct difference. It may well be that the Lord sent some sickness to the others who had accepted the Babylonian food, v. 15. The "Melzar" (or "overseer") now agrees to let Daniel and his friends continue eating "pulse," vegetables, v. 16.

Success of the Test 1:17–21 "God" (*ᵉlohîm*, see v. 2) blesses the four Israelites who have trusted Him. He gives them unusual knowledge and skill in all "learning" (or "writing," *seper*, see v. 4) and wisdom. In addition, Daniel receives the ability to interpret "visions and dreams." The phrase prepares the way for Daniel's later experiences in which God communicates prophetic truth to him through visions, v. 17. At the end of the three-year training period (cf. 1:5), the "prince of the eunuchs [or 'officers']" brings the captives who have completed their training to Nebuchadnezzar, v. 18. The king himself examines them and finds that the four faithful Israelites rank above the others. "Therefore stood they before the king," i.e., Nebuchadnezzar appoints them to positions in which they will have regular contact with him, v. 19.

Nebuchadnezzar finds that in matters requiring "wisdom and understanding" (lit. "wisdom of understanding"), they are "ten times better," i.e., much better, than his own wise men. This is the only

---

[25]Ibid.

time in the OT that the phrase "wisdom of understanding" occurs, although the words "wisdom" (*ḥokmâ*) and "understanding" (*bînâ*) often occur together. In many cases, these two words have a similar sense, simply referring to the mental processes that underlie grasping a situation rightly (e.g., Job 28:12, 20; 38:36). Here, where *ḥokmâ* is in construct to *bînâ*, the thought is of the wisdom that develops out of a right discernment. Daniel and his friends correctly interpreted the information given them and made right judgments concerning the required actions.

Nebuchadnezzar's wise men include "magicians" (or "diviners," *ḥarṭom*)[26] and "astrologers" (or "conjurors," those capable of casting a spell, *ʾaššap*). The book gives other groups of wise men later (e.g., 2:2; 4:7). The word *ḥarṭom* is related to *ḥereṭ*, "stylus." It probably indicates a learned person, someone able to write. As a loanword, *ḥarṭom* refers to the magicians of Egypt in Genesis and Exodus. We cannot be precise as to the nature of their work. The noun *ʾaššap* appears only here and 2:2. The related word *ʾašpâ* appears elsewhere referring to the quiver, a holder for arrows, e.g., Job 39:23; Isaiah 22:6. It may be that these wise men used arrows or sticks in divining or conjuring some mystical pronouncement. The Aramaic *ʾaššap*, "enchanter," and the Assyrian *ʾašipu*, "exorcist," are both cognate to the Hebrew *ʾaššap*.

The number "ten" often occurs as a round number, an approximation (see Num. 14:22; Neh. 4:12). This is the best way of understanding it here. The character of the four Israelites is without reproach in this test. They refuse to defile themselves as they tactfully take their stand. God honors their faithfulness by giving them success in the test as He allows their wisdom to be superior to that of other advisors to the king. *Yoma 77a*, in the Talmud, records the apt comment of a Jewish rabbi that "if all the wise men of other nations were in one scale of the balance, and Daniel, the man of pleasant parts, in the other, would he not be found to outweigh them all?" The example of these four faithful Israelites should serve to challenge Christians today to follow the standards of God's Word as they take their stand for the Lord before others, v. 20.

---

[26]Goldwurm, p. 72, identifies the *ḥarṭummîm* as "necromancers," those who examined the bones of the dead. This is speculative.

Another summary statement notes that Daniel continues his service until the "first year" of Cyrus the Great.[27] This covers about seventy years. We meet Daniel in Jehoiakim's third year, corresponding to Nebuchadnezzar's first year (1:1). He continues until at least the third year of Cyrus (10:1). This period covers the reigns of Nebuchadnezzar (605–562 BC), Amel-Marduk (the biblical Evil-Merodach, 2 Kings 25:27; Jer. 52:31, who reigned 562–560 BC), Nergal-shar-usur (the biblical Nergal-sharezer, also known as Neriglissar, Jer. 39:3, 13, who usurped the throne from his brother-in-law, Amel-Marduk, and reigned 560–556 BC), Labashi-Marduk (several months, 556 BC), Nabonidus (556–539 BC), and Cyrus the Great (whose rule over Babylon covered 539–530 BC), v. 21.[28]

---

[27]Thomson, p. 29, suggests that Cyrus did not call himself the "King of Babylon" until his third year. In his first two years, he was the "King of Nations." His first year as king over Babylon would then coincide with his third year as King of Nations. The explanation is contrived. Lacocque, *The Book of Daniel*, p. 33, sees the chronology here as contradicting 10:1, where Daniel speaks of the "third year" of Cyrus. There is no conflict between these dates. Here, Daniel refers to his continuing service to the nation of Babylon, a service that ended with the fall of the nation to Cyrus, who then began his first year of rule. There, Daniel refers to an event that takes place in the Medo-Persian era.

[28]Watkinson, pp. 84–90, inserts the apocryphal *History of Susannah*, included in the Douay Version after c. 12, at this point. He considers this "a crude allegory of a prophetic character" that parallels the book of Daniel, a book beginning "in a crude and imperfect state" that becomes "more and more finished and explicit as it progresses to the last chapter." Protestants have long since rejected the *History of Susannah* as noncanonical. Watkinson's view has little to support it. Since the book of Daniel gives the history of his life, it is natural that it begins as unfinished and progresses to a conclusion.

NEBUCHADNEZZAR'S IMAGE VISION 2:1–49

Chapter 2 develops the first prophecy of the book. Nebuchadnezzar's vision here serves as the basis for other later prophecies. These include the writing on the wall that tells of the end of the Babylonian rule in c. 5; the parallel vision to c. 2 in c. 7; the ram and goat, developing the second and third kingdoms, in c. 8; Daniel's seventy weeks, giving details of Israel's future and climaxing with Antichrist's fall prior to the Lord's kingdom, in c. 9; and the detailed prophecy of c. 11 that expands on the third kingdom, then adds details of Antichrist's rule and eventual fall, again occurring before the reign of Christ.

Dream of the King 2:1–3 Daniel 1:1–2 states that the captivity took place in Jehoiakim's third year. The first year of Nebuchadnezzar as king was Jehoiakim's fourth year (Jer. 25:1). The closing of Daniel's three years of training and Nebuchadnezzar's dream take place at about the same time, ca. 603 BC. There is a minor chronological problem here. The verse locates the dream and its interpretation in Nebuchadnezzar's "second year." In 1:5, Daniel's period of training is said to take three years.

The approach to the chronological problem generally follows the conservative or liberal approach to the book taken by an author. Gowan and Heaton illustrate the liberal view, setting the account as in conflict with the three-year period of training set forth in c. 1.[1] Other views are more conservative, attempting to explain the difficulty. Mercer thinks that "Dan 2 records an incident that took place after the story in Dan 1:8–17, but before the end of the three-year period." It is difficult to reconcile vv. 48–49 with the view. Goldwurm understands the second year as "the second year of [Nebuchadnezzar's] direct reign over Judah and Jerusalem" after he had ruled Judah through regents, including Jehoiakim. This contradicts history. 2 Kings 24:17–18 states that Nebuchadnezzar appointed Zedekiah king over Judah and that he ruled for eleven years. At the end of that time, Nebuchadnezzar sacked Jerusalem and carried many of the Jews into Babylonian captivity. There is no indication that he ruled Judah independently. Bultema explains the chronology by having Nebuchadnezzar rule as co-regent

---

[1]Gowan, p. 52; Heaton, p. 124.

with his father. The date here "counts from the time Nebuchadnezzar was ruling alone." This is also difficult to defend since we know that Nebuchadnezzar returned to Babylon to assume the throne shortly after conquering Jerusalem and taking Daniel captive. Knoch advances the view that "Daniel was not even out of school." Leon Wood adopts the same view.[2] This conflicts with 1:18–20, where Daniel and his friends are examined "at the end of days" with the other captives. It also conflicts with 2:48, where Nebuchadnezzar appoints Daniel to a position over the other Babylonian wise men.

A better approach notes that the Babylonians dated regnal years from the first *full* year of rule while the Jews dated it from the first *fraction* of a year. From archaeology, we know that Nebuchadnezzar became king in the fall of the year. The last two tablets of Nabopolassar Nebuchadnezzar's father, are dated May and August 605 BC. The first two tablets of Nebuchadnezzar have dates placing them in August and September of 605 BC.[3] The Babylonians would have counted his regnal years from 604 BC, the first full year of his rule. The Jews would have considered his reign as starting in 605 BC. If c. 2 follows the Babylonian practice by referring to the second *full* year of Nebuchadnezzar's reign, this event takes place toward the end of Daniel's training or, possibly, shortly after its completion. The reference to "three years" (1:5) may be a rounded number. The actual training may have been between two and three years.

Nebuchadnezzar "dreamed dreams." The reliance on dreams to convey spiritual guidance was common in biblical times. God spoke to the Philistine king of Gerar, Abimelech, through a dream (Gen. 20:3, 6). God spoke to Jacob in dreams (Gen. 28:12; 31:10–11). Later, He warned "Laban the Syrian" in a dream (Gen. 31:24). God revealed His will to Joseph through dreams (Gen. 37:5–10). Later, in prison, Joseph interpreted the dreams of the butler and baker (Gen. 40:5, 8–9, 16). The heathen Midianite soldier received a dream that forecast the defeat

---

[2]Mark K. Mercer, "Daniel 1:1 and Jehoiakim's Three Years of Servitude," *AUSS* 27 (Autumn 1989): 187–88; Goldwurm, p. 74; Harry Bultema, *Commentary on Daniel* (Grand Rapids: Kregel Publications, 1988), p. 59; A. E. Knoch, *Concordant Studies in the Book of Daniel* (Saugus, Calif.: Concordant Publishing Concern, 1968), p. 41; Leon Wood, *A Commentary on Daniel* (Grand Rapids: Zondervan Publishing House, 1973), pp. 49–50.

[3]Merrill F. Unger, *Archaeology and the Old Testament* (Grand Rapids: 1956), p. 290.

of their army (Judg. 7:13). The Lord spoke to Joseph in dreams (Matt. 1:20; 2:13, 19–22). Nebuchadnezzar's dream here is only the first time in the book in which God will reveal the future through a dream (also 4:5–9, 18–19; 7:1).

There is also secular history regarding the meaning of dreams. For example, in Egypt, if a man saw a large cat in a dream, it meant that a large harvest would come to him. Dreaming of a deep well meant that prison lay ahead, and dreaming of a shining moon suggested forgiveness of some wrong. Plunging into the river in a dream was good, while seeing the face in a mirror was bad.[4] In Mesopotamia, a date appearing on a man's head in a dream indicated coming distress. A fish on the head, however, indicated that the man would be powerful. Salt on the man's head meant that his house would be well protected.[5]

The Chronicle of Nabonidus speaks of the gods showing him "a vision in a dream" in which Marduk and Sin charged him to build a temple.[6] Thutmose IV recorded a dream in which the sphinx told him that he would one day become Pharaoh over Egypt and that he should clear the sand from the feet of the sphinx to show his gratitude.[7]

The plural word "dreams" occurs here (also in v. 2) but elsewhere the singular "dream" occurs (vv. 3, 4, 5, 6, 7, 9, 26, 28, 36, 45). Since all of the characters in the chapter—Nebuchadnezzar (vv. 3, 5, 6, 9, 26), the wise men (vv. 4, 7), and Daniel (vv. 28, 36, 45)—refer to the dream in the singular, it is clear that the "dreams" involved a single dream. From Daniel's explanation given later, this was a complicated dream that involved significant details. By causing the king to dream the dream several times, God impressed these details on his mind.

Young understands the plural as referring to "a state." He paraphrases the statement: "Nebuchadnezzar was in a state in which a dream came to him." The occurrence of the plural in v. 2 argues

[4]*The Interpretation of Dreams*, trans. John A. Wilson, taken from *Hieratic Papers in the British Museum. Third Series. Chester Beaty Gift*, ed. A. H. Gardiner (London, 1935), 2 vols., *Ancient Near Eastern Texts*, ed. James B. Pritchard (Princeton, N.J.: Princeton University Press, 1955), p. 495.

[5]Morris Jastrow, *The Religion of Babylonia and Assyria* (Boston: Ginn & Company, 1898), p. 403.

[6]Joan Oates, *Babylon* (London: Thames & Hudson, Ltd., 1979), p. 89.

[7]Willis Goth Regier, *Book of the Sphinx* (Lincoln: University of Nebraska Press, 2004), pp. 21–22.

against this. Keil calls the plural one of "intensive fulness," indicating that the "dream in its parts contained a plurality of subjects." This leaves unexplained, however, the use of the singular by the king elsewhere.[8]

Because of the nature of his dream, the king is "troubled," causing him to awaken, v. 1. Nebuchadnezzar sees this incident as a way of testing his advisors. If they can tell him the dream, he will know that their interpretation is true. If they can't describe his dream, he will know that any interpretation they give him is false.

Some authors think that the king has forgotten his dream. Among others, Cowles, Gaebelein, Henry, and Knoch understand that Nebuchadnezzar has forgotten the dream but that, with his advisors recalling it for him, he will recognize it again.[9] Although possible, the view is unlikely because it goes contrary to God's use of dreams elsewhere. The Lord uses dreams and visions elsewhere in the book to communicate with both kings (4:5, 9, 10, 13) and Daniel (7:1–15; 8:1–27; 10:1–6). This is true also of the dreams given to Jacob (Gen. 31:11–12), Laban (31:24), Pharaoh (41:1), Solomon (1 Kings 3:5–15), and many other individuals in the OT to whom God communicated truth. Since God caused these dreams and visions to be remembered at other times, it would be unusual for Him to let the king forget the dream at this time.

The king calls several classes of wise men to recall the dream and interpret it for him. The "magicians" (ḥarṭom, see 1:20) likely cast spells or divined. The "astrologers" (or "conjurors," ʾaššap, see 1:20) were "conjurors." The "sorcerers" (kašap) practiced witchcraft or sorcery. This is the only time that kašap appears in Daniel. The Akkadian kišpû, referring to witchcraft, supports this meaning for kašap. The "Chaldeans" (kaśdîm, see 1:4) are thought to have been master astrologers.

Whitcomb tentatively suggests that the conjurors were "snake charmers." Watkinson makes the "astrologers and soothsayers" those "who were acquainted with magnetism, and used its power and who pretended to consult stars, entrails, &c."[10] We do not know enough

---

[8]Young, p. 56; Keil, p. 86.

[9]Cowles, p. 297; Gaebelein, p. 21; Henry, IV, 1023; and Knoch, p. 42.

[10]John C. Whitcomb, *Daniel* (Chicago: Moody Press, 1985), p. 36; Watkinson, p. 81.

about these groups to state the nature of their work. Those who claim such powers may practice any of several methods of divining the future including incantations, invoking the gods, divination from omens, etc. The OT does not clarify the nature of these practices.

In calling these classes of wise men, the king tests the broad range of his advisors. From vv. 4, 5, and 10, we see that the Chaldeans speak for everyone. From this, it is reasonable to assume that they are the most important group, v. 2. The king asks these men to tell him the dream and interpret its meaning.[11]

From the rest of the chapter, it is clear that Nebuchadnezzar does not call all of the wise men to come. Verses 12–13 indicate that the wise men had to be gathered. Daniel and his three friends had been trained under the wise men. The gathering of condemned wise men therefore includes them. A wide variety of suggestions have been made to explain the absence of Daniel and his friends from the wise men called by the king. Wood suggests that Daniel and his friends "were not full members [of the class of wise men], but only trainees." Lacocque proposes that Nebuchadnezzar had simply forgotten Daniel. King indicates "they would not bring captives of another race for so important a conference." Keil thinks that they were not called to the king "because . . . only the presidents or the older members of the several classes were sent for."[12]

We cannot be dogmatic as to the reason for omitting them from the group. From the record, it is reasonable to conclude that God ordained their omission to bring about the advancement in position of Daniel and his friends and to testify to His own greatness in giving the interpretation of the dream. It is likely that Nebuchadnezzar simply followed his habitual practice, not even thinking of the newly appointed advisors. It is also probable that God guided the king in this so that he forgot Daniel and the others. This allowed their interpretation of his dream to have a greater impact on the king, v. 3.

---

[11]The word "dream" is singular here. Gangel, pp. 39–40, concludes that "Nebuchadnezzar targets one particular dream among the various dreams mentioned in verse 1." While this is possible, it is likely that the plural in v. 1 refers to a repeated dream and that the singular here simply collects these dreams into the single dream.

[12]Wood, p. 55; Lacocque, *The Book of Daniel*, p. 40; King, p. 55; Keil, p. 96.

Failure of the Wise Men 2:4–13 The initial phrase, "Then spake the Chaldeans (*kaśdîm*) to the king" is in Hebrew. Beginning with the phrase "in Syriack [lit. 'Aramaic']," the text changes to Aramaic. The Hebrew noun *kaśdîm* is cognate with the Aramaic *kaśday.* Both may also refer to a group of wise men (2:5, 10; 3:8; 4:7; 5:7, 11) or to the inhabitants of Babylon (5:30).

From 2:4*b* to 7:28, the book of Daniel employs Aramaic rather than Hebrew. Several authors hold that the book was originally written wholly in Aramaic and that the Hebrew parts are a translation. Charles cites the occurrence of "frequent Aramaisms" as evidence for this. He suggests that the translation was made so "it could be adopted into the Canon." Hartman similarly notes the presence of Aramaisms as evidence for an Aramaic original. He also attributes the translation to the desire for "canonical recognition."[13] Since Daniel likely spoke the Aramaic trade language fluently, it is not surprising that his writings would include Aramaic cognates to Hebrew words. There is, of course, no textual evidence to support the view that the book was written originally in Aramaic.

Since the subject of this part of the book is the development of the heathen world powers, it is appropriate to use the heathen trade language of that day.[14] The other parts of the book, 1:1–2:4*a* and 8:1–12:13, use Hebrew. This section is one of several Aramaic passages in the OT. The biblical authors wrote in Aramaic in Genesis 31:47 (two words); Ezra 4:8–6:18; 7:12–26; and Jeremiah 10:11. There are also Aramaic loanwords used sporadically throughout the OT (e.g., *bar*, "son," Ps. 2:12; Prov. 31:2; *millîn*, "speaking," Job 4:2; *haga²*, "terror," Isa. 19:17). The use of Aramaic loanwords reflects the closeness of the two cultures, with the Jews adopting Aramaic words from time to time.

The Chaldeans greet the king in Aramaic with a normal greeting: "O king, live for ever." Similar greetings occur elsewhere (1 Kings

---

[13]Charles, p. xxxvii; Hartman, pp. 13–15.

[14]Bultema, p. 237, explains this by noting that "the first half of Daniel deals more with the realm of common grace, while the second half deals more with particular grace." Bultema considers this the equivalent of the traditional explanation that what concerned the Chaldeans was written in their language, and what concerned the Hebrews are written in theirs. The view and its explanation are not persuasive.

1:31; Neh. 2:3; Dan. 3:9; 5:10; 6:6, 21).[15] This greeting attempts to foster goodwill on the part of the king. The magicians urge him to tell them the dream so that they may interpret it, v. 4. Nebuchadnezzar, however, maintains his determination to test his advisors. The "Chaldeans" (*kaśday*) here represent the various groups of wise men.

The phrase "the thing is gone [*ʾazdaʾ*] from me" is better "the matter is certain from me." He has made up his mind. If they cannot describe the dream, he will execute and publicly degrade them. Barnes adopts the meaning "gone" and concludes that Nebuchadnezzar had forgotten the dream.[16] The LXX translates Ὁ λόγος ἀπ' ἐμοῦ ἀπέστη, "the word is apart from me." The Vulgate is similar, *sermo recessit a me*, "the word is hidden from me." These interpret *ʾazdaʾ* as *ʾazal*, "to go away." KB gives "promulgated" or "irrevocable," both meanings supporting the above view. BDB gives "sure, assured." This earlier meaning, followed by the KJV, likely came from misunderstanding the sense of the word. The word *ʾazdaʾ* is a Persian loanword, "assured, certain." The use of loanwords is common in every language since it is relatively easy to use words from nearby countries. Several other loanwords occur in the book. This is not surprising since Daniel would have heard many representatives from other nations at the Babylonian court.

Nebuchadnezzar's threat, "ye shall be cut in pieces [*haddamîn*]," is lit. "you shall be made into limbs [or 'members']," a threat describing their dismemberment. The noun *haddamîn* occurs only here and at 3:29. It is a Persian loanword that refers to members of the body. While this seems unduly harsh, we have evidence from Babylonian archaeology that such punishment was indeed inflicted at that time.

In addition, the homes of the wise men will be torn down and "made a dunghill" (*nᵉwalî*). The word *nᵉwalî* occurs again in 3:29 and Ezra 6:11. It refers to the houses being left as heaps of refuse. Public degradation of a person's possessions after his death was a

---

[15]Goldwurm, p. 79, notes that Daniel never greets Nebuchadnezzar this way. He suggests that Daniel "did not want to greet the idolatrous king with the same formula which was used . . . as a benediction for his ancestor King David." Daniel, however, greets Darius (another idolatrous king) with this phrase. Since the phrase occurs only four times in the book, it is likely that we simply do not have a large enough sample to see how Daniel used the phrase with Nebuchadnezzar.

[16]Barnes, I, 131.

way of showing his disgrace. 2 Kings 10:27 and Ezra 6:11 illustrate
this practice, v. 5. If, however, the wise men can tell him the dream
and interpret it, he will lavishly reward them with "gifts and rewards
[$n^e biz b\hat{a}$][17] and great [$\acute{s}agg\hat{i}$] honour." The word $n^e biz b\hat{a}$ is also a
loanword from Persia. The word is singular but likely has a collec-
tive sense. The word $\acute{s}agg\hat{i}$ refers to some form of greatness. This
may be numerical greatness, "much, many" (e.g., 2:48); a greater
degree, "very" (e.g., 2:12); or greatness in extent, "great" (e.g., 4:10).
The word occurs twelve times in Daniel and also in Ezra 5:11, v. 6.

Once more, the wise men urge the king to tell them the dream.
The interpretation of dreams was not new to them. Undoubtedly,
they could have given the king an interpretation that would have
seemed reasonable. But they needed the dream before they could
supply an interpretation, v. 7. Nebuchadnezzar realizes that they are
stalling for additional "time" ($^c iddan$) because "the thing is gone [or
'certain,' $^{?}azda^{?}$] from me," i.e., his firm statement of judgment. The
word $^c iddan$ occurs thirteen times in Daniel. In 3:5, 15, it refers to a
point in time. In 2:8 and 7:12, it refers to an indefinite period of time.
In 2:9, the changing of the time is equivalent to a new set of circumstances. In 7:25, it is generally interpreted as a year. In 4:16, 23, 25,
32, the interpretation is debated (see discussion at 4:25). This variation makes it impossible to be dogmatic here as to the exact sense.
It is likely, however, that the king refers to an indefinite extension of
time. When $^c iddan$ and $z^e man$ (see v. 16) occur together (2:21; 7:12,
25), the repetition gives its stress to all manner of time, including
appointed times as well as longer periods of time, v. 8.

If the wise men cannot tell his the dream, the king has one "decree" (*dat*) that he will apply to them as a group. The noun *dat* refers
broadly to law, either civil law (Ezra 7:26; Dan. 2:9, 13, 15; 6:8, 12,
15) or religious law (Ezra 7:12, 14, 21, 25, 26; Dan. 6:5; 7:25). In
each case, the context must guide as to the sense given to the word.
Here, of course, the king thinks of his own decree of judgment as
the law they will face. They have spoken "lying and corrupt words"

---

[17]Miller, p. 82, suggests that the king refers "to a particular gift and reward,
maybe a promotion or marriage to one of the king's daughters." Since the king
speaks to the group, he probably thinks of a group of rewards rather than a single
award.

until such "time" (*ʿiddan*) as the circumstances change.[18] The phrase suggests that they had implied to the king that something serious would happen if he continued to withhold the knowledge of the dream from them. Nebuchadnezzar's logic is impeccable. If they can tell the dream, he will know that they can tell its interpretation, v. 9.

In desperation, the wise men tactfully suggest that Nebuchadnezzar is unreasonable. In the first place, what he is asking is impossible. In the second place, no other "king, lord [*rab*], nor ruler" (better "great king or ruler") has made such a demand of a "magician" (*ḥarṭom*), "astrologer" (or "conjuror," *ʾaššap*), or "Chaldean" (*kaśday*, see v. 5). The word *rab* often has a sense of glory associated with its basic meaning of "great." For this reason, it often becomes a title, e.g., "captain," 2:14; "master," 4:9. It may also serve as an adjective, "great," e.g., 2:31, 35, 45. The word occurs twelve times in Daniel, four of these as titles and the remainder as adjectives.

The noun *ḥarṭom* is cognate to the Hebrew word used for the "magicians" in Egypt (e.g., Gen. 41:8; Exod. 7:11, 22). Both relate to the unused root *ḥrṭ*, "to cut, engrave," which underlies the noun *ḥereṭ*, "stylus." The connection is unclear. The Aramaic word is similar in meaning to its Hebrew cognate. The Aramaic word *ʾaššap* is also similar in meaning to its Hebrew cognate. It occurs six times in Daniel, always translated "astrologer" or "astrologers" (see the discussion of the Hebrew cognates *ḥarṭom* and *ʾaššap* at 1:20). The wise men mentioned in vv. 2, 10 include "magicians," "astrologers," "sorcerers," and "Chaldeans." The list is representative of the wise men and not intended as a complete listing, v. 10.

The king has asked "a rare [better 'difficult'] thing." Only the "gods" themselves could answer such a request, and they do not dwell with men. Various mss of the LXX understand "gods" as either an angel (singular) or angels (plural). Hartman includes "all superhuman beings." Price categorizes the gods into the "high gods," the supreme beings with whom the wise men had no dealings, and the "lower gods" with whom they could consult.[19] In all likelihood,

---

[18]Goldwurm, p. 84, understands the verse as a threat: "Wait until the time changes," i.e., "when morning changes to afternoon." This requires supplying the verb "wait," a change that has no support elsewhere.

[19]Hartman, p. 139; George McCready Price, *The Greatest of the Prophets: A New Commentary on the Book of Daniel* (Mountain View, Calif.: Pacific Press

the word refers to the whole range of gods worshiped by the Babylonians. Unless these deigned to reveal hidden truth to the wise men, they had no way of recalling and interpreting the dream.

The response of the wise men reveals the fraudulent nature of their counsel to the king. Babylonian records regularly proclaim the guidance of the gods in various matters. Yet the king's counselors now acknowledge that they lack contact with the gods. This answer is important since it providentially prepares for Daniel's interpretation by the power of God. The NT reveals the real reason for the inability of the wise men to give the dream and its interpretation. Unsaved men do not have the Holy Spirit within them to guide them in understanding spiritual truth (1 Cor. 2:14). This dream, as now revealed by Daniel, conveys significant spiritual truths to Nebuchadnezzar, v. 11.

Nebuchadnezzar now gives in to his emotions. He becomes furious at the failure of his wise men to know and interpret his dream. He concludes that his "wise men" (*hakkîm*) are either traitors or that they have no contact with the gods and are therefore useless.[20] The phrase "wise men" (*hakkîm*) did not occur earlier as one of the groups called before the king, 2:2. The term here is general, embracing all who based their advice on various signs in nature. The word occurs frequently in Daniel 2, 4, and 5. Nebuchadnezzar commands the execution of his wise men, v. 12.

The "decree" (*dat*) for the arrest of the "wise men" (*hakkîm*) goes forth. The Aramaic suggests that the execution of the wise men began immediately. A *waw* introduces the phrase, and the participle is passive here, i.e., "were slain." This suggests the translation "and the wise men were slain." The LXX and Vulgate support the view, and v. 14 implies that the execution had begun. Because of their recently completed training as wise men, Daniel and his friends are also sought.[21] They are not among the king's usual counselors at this time and therefore would not have been present at the first, v. 13.

Publishing Association, 1955), p. 65.

[20]With no firm evidence, Porteous, p. 39, suggests that events from King Nabonidus "have been transferred to the earlier and better-known evidence." The suggestion lacks merit. It requires a late date for the book, and the parallels suggested by Porteous are tenuous at best. Even Porteous admits that "the parallels . . . are not on the whole very close."

[21]Philip R. Newell, *Daniel: The Man Greatly Beloved and His Prophecies* (Chicago: Moody Press, 1951), pp. 20–30, considers Nebuchadnezzar's decree the

Revelation to Daniel 2:14–30 Arioch is the "captain" (*rab*) of the king's "guard" (or "executioners," *ṭabbaḥ*). This is the only time that *ṭabbaḥ* occurs in the OT. The Hebrew and Akkadian cognates suggest that the root meaning is "slaughterer" or "executioner." Charles relates "Arioch" to the Akkadian Eri-aku, "servant of the moon-god," a possible derivation. Goldwurm accepts the statement from the Midrash, the Hebrew exposition of the OT, which identifies Arioch with Nebuzaradan, e.g., 2 Kings 25:8, 11, 20. He suggests that the name Arioch comes from *ʾaryeh* ("lion") "because he growled like a lion at the exiles of Jerusalem till he drove them over the Euphrates."[22] Since Arioch was a soldier, it would rather seem that the name, meaning "lion-like," would refer to a quality of fierceness in combat. This meaning for the name is often suggested. Because of the lack of a clear derivation for the name, we should not be dogmatic.

Arioch comes to arrest Daniel and his friends as part of the "wise men" (*ḥakkîm*). Daniel speaks with "counsel and wisdom" as he tactfully asks why the "decree" (*dat*, see v. 9), the king's word as an authoritative statement, is so "hasty" (better "harsh"), vv. 14–15. Upon hearing the reason, Daniel makes his request of the king. He asks for additional "time" (*zeman*) to determine the dream and give its interpretation. In addition to its occurrence at Ezra 5:3, the word *zeman* occurs ten times in Daniel (2:16, 21; 3:7, 8; 4:36; 6:10, 13; 7:12, 22, 25). It is another Persian loanword variously translated as "time" or "season." It generally refers to a specific or an appointed time. It is possible that Daniel made his request for time through channels and that he did not actually stand before the king. He "went in" to an official that could present his request to Nebuchadnezzar. This would explain the boastful statement of Arioch later (v. 25) when he claims to have found Daniel. If Nebuchadnezzar had seen Daniel, he would have known that Arioch's statement was false. If, however, he had only received the request for time, he may not have known that Daniel was involved.

Note Daniel's faith in this matter as he states his confidence in God's ability to give him the interpretation. This faith likely draws

---

result of a satanic plan to remove Daniel. Since the dream revealed God's plan for the ages, and its interpretation placed Daniel in a position where he could serve the Lord with significant influence, it is unlikely that Satan was involved.

[22]Charles, p. 34; Goldwurm, pp. 87–88.

on his ability to interpret other dreams that have been described to him (1:17). God had given him the gift earlier in preparation for this time when he would desperately need it, v. 16.

After receiving an extension of time, Daniel goes home to tell Hananiah, Mishael, and Azariah of the situation.[23] The use of the Hebrew names for Daniel's friends is natural in view of the Jewish context to the situation. Elsewhere, where the Babylonian names of his friends occur (2:49; 3:12–30), there is a Babylonian context, v. 17. Daniel asks them to join him in praying that God will grant "mercies" (*raḥᵃmîn*) to them. This is the only time that the Aramaic verb *rᵉḥam* occurs in the OT. It is, however, cognate to widely used Hebrew words that refer to "tender love, mercy, or compassion." The plural form here likely embraces the whole range of needs faced by Daniel and his friends—knowledge of the dream, its interpretation, and the reversal of the king's decree so that they will not perish with the other "wise men" (*ḥakkîm*). The LXX adds that they fasted, an addition without support from the text.

A matter as important as this requires the united prayers of the group (Matt. 18:19–20). They address their prayers to the "God of heaven," the Creator of all things and therefore the Omnipotent One Who is able to reveal dreams. Phillips and Vines suggest that Daniel uses the name "God of heaven" because God has withdrawn from His people and now acts from heaven rather than from between the cherubim in the temple. While the thought lends itself to preaching, the explanation overlooks a similar occurrence (using *ʾel* rather than *ʾᵉlah*) in Psalm 136, a psalm written before the destruction of the temple. Abraham uses the same name in Genesis 24:7, before the construction of the temple but during the time when God was working among His people on earth. Lederach aptly suggests that the name counteracted "the astral worship of peoples like the Babylonians" and emphasized "that God is the Creator also of planets and stars."[24]

---

[23]Goldwurm, p. 90, suggests that Daniel went home to pray because Nebuchadnezzar's palace was filled with idols. It is more likely that he returned home to get his friends to join with him in prayer.

[24]John Phillips and Jerry Vines, *Exploring the Book of Daniel* (Neptune, N.J.: Loizeaux Brothers, 1991), pp. 39, 259–60; Paul M. Lederach, *Daniel* (Scottsdale, Pa.: Herald Press, 1994), p. 62.

Daniel's approach differs from that of the Babylonian wise men. They rely on the movements and positions of the planets and stars and on other omens drawn from nature. Daniel and his friends rely on the "God of heaven," a name that stresses His creation and control of the movements and positions of the heavenly bodies. They go beyond the mere motions of the heavenly bodies to the One Who established and continues to control these motions, v. 18. After praying, the four go to sleep, an act that shows the peace that comes from their confidence that God will answer their prayers. In the night, God reveals the dream to Daniel in a vision.[25] This lets Daniel see the image and, at the same time, understand its significance, v. 19a.

Daniel immediately responds with a psalm of praise. This spontaneous note of praise reveals that Daniel has saturated himself with the Word of God. These thoughts come naturally to him as he expresses his gratitude to the God Who has answered his prayers. The thought of virtually every phrase in his psalm occurs elsewhere: 20a (Ps. 113:2), 20b (Job 12:13, 16), 21b (Ps. 75:6–7), 21c (Prov. 2:6), 22a (Job 12:22), and 22b (Ps. 139:12). Daniel's attitude of praise to God is also a revelation of his humility. Rather than taking the credit for uncovering the interpretation of the dream, he spontaneously praises the God Who has given him the interpretation.

Daniel begins by blessing, i.e., worshiping, the God Who dwells in and rules over heaven, v. 19b. He blesses "the name [i.e., the nature] of God" forever because He possesses "wisdom and might." The phrase recognizes God's knowledge of how to control the actions of mankind and His "might" to exercise control, v. 20. While God's wisdom and power include much more than the actions of men, Daniel focuses here on God's relationship to men. God controls "the times [*ᶜiddan*, see v. 8] and the seasons [*zᵉman*, see v. 16]" in which men live. He removes kings (e.g., Saul, 1 Sam. 28:15–19; Ahab, 2 Kings 21:17–19; 22:34–38) and raises up new ones (e.g., David, 1 Sam. 16:12–13; Jehu, 2 Kings 9:1–6). He gives wisdom to "wise men" (*ḥakkîm*) and knowledge to those who have

---

[25]Miller, pp. 85–86, thinks that the four men "continued in prayer until God revealed the dream." He argues that the seriousness of the "imminent death penalty" would have kept the four from sleeping. The addition of the word "night," however, argues that Daniel was asleep. Job 4:13; 33:15 along with Dan. 7:2, 7, 13; cf. v. 1, "upon his bed," support the thought of sleep.

understanding, v. 21. He reveals even "deep and secret things," unknowable to men except by divine revelation. He knows what is in the dark since He possesses the light of spiritual insight, v. 22. Daniel closes his psalm by giving thanks and praise to the "God of [his] fathers," Israel's God. God has imparted to Daniel wisdom and "might," the power to understand, at this critical time. He has answered the prayers of Daniel and his friends by revealing the king's dream, v. 23.

Since Arioch has been sent to destroy the "wise men" (ḥakkîm), Daniel's first step is to approach him. Daniel asks him to stop the slaughter of the Chaldean "wise men" (ḥakkîm) and assures him that he will tell Nebuchadnezzar the interpretation, v. 24. Arioch brings Daniel to the king in "haste" (beḥal). The verb beḥal is normally translated "trouble" (4:5, 19 [2X]; 5:6, 9; 7:15, 28), but here, at 3:24, and at 6:19, the KJV renders it as "haste." In each case, there is a sense of mental turmoil or alarm.

Arioch claims that he has found an Israelite captive who can interpret the king's dream. Because of the statement in v. 16, Goldwurm explains Arioch's statement in v. 25 by concluding that Arioch "had not been informed by Daniel about the talk he had had with the king." This is possible, but the question Nebuchadnezzar asks in v. 26 seems to favor the view that he had not previously seen Daniel. Since 1:19 and 2:16 suggest previous contact between Nebuchadnezzar and Daniel, Hammer sees Arioch's claim as a mistake due to the author's lack of concern "to mould his sources into a consistent whole."[26] Daniel's request in v. 16, however, may have been made through someone with access to the king.

Arioch's boastful statement is understandable from one who hopes to gain royal favor for the accomplishment. He has brought to pass what the king's advisors had failed to do, v. 25. Nebuchadnezzar speaks to Daniel, using his Babylonian name of Belteshazzar. He asks if he can indeed tell him the dream and its interpretation, v. 26.

In sharp contrast to Arioch's boastful claim, Daniel gives all the glory to God. Daniel's humility is refreshing. Rather than claiming any glory for himself, he acknowledges that God has revealed the dream and its interpretation to him. As with his psalm of praise

---

[26]Goldwurm, p. 98; Hammer, p. 28.

earlier, vv. 20–23, so now he gives the credit to God for his newly acquired knowledge of the dream and the ability to interpret it. The example is a wholesome one that Christians should still follow in their accomplishments!

None of the king's "wise men" (ḥakkîm), "astrologers" (ʾaššap, see v. 10), "magicians" (ḥarṭom, see v. 10), or "soothsayers" (gᵉzar) can give the dream. The list of advisors given here differs from those in v. 2. As in v. 12, the phrase "wise men" is general, embracing all of his advisors. Daniel omits the "sorcerers" and "Chaldeans" mentioned in v. 2 but includes the "astrologers" (or "conjurors"), "magicians," and a new group, the "soothsayers" (gᵉzar). The basic idea of gᵉzar is "to cut off, divide." This leads to making them "astrologers," those who divided the heavens into spheres of influence. Daniel does not attempt to identify those advisers earlier consulted by the king. The groups in vv. 2, 10, and here simply give a general list of wise men called in to interpret the king's dream, v. 27.

In sharp contrast to these failed advisors, the God of heaven is well able to give an interpretation. The king's "dream" (ḥelem) and the "visions" (ḥᵉzû) relate to "the latter days," the future of the world up to and including the kingdom governed by Messiah. These words are similar to their Hebrew cognates. When they occur together in Aramaic, as they do in 2:28; 4:5, 9; and 7:1, the word ḥᵉzû is always plural. In Hebrew, however, the cognate words may occur in the singular together, Job 20:8; 33:15, or in the plural, Job 7:14; Joel 2:28. In addition to referring to normal dreams or visions, both ḥelem and ḥᵉzû may refer to modes of divine revelation. TWOT makes the "[ḥᵉzû] individual segments within the [ḥelem]." In most of the places where the two words occur together, they are parallel with no significant difference in meaning. Occasionally, however, as here, the suggestion of TWOT is likely. In addition to the occurrence here of the phrase "latter days," the corresponding Hebrew phrase often occurs (e.g., Num. 24:14; Deut. 4:30; Isa. 2:2; Jer. 30:24; Ezek. 38:16; Dan. 10:14; and Mic. 4:1). The phrase regularly occurs in a messianic context. For that reason, it is appropriate to understand it so here, v. 28.

God has revealed to Nebuchadnezzar in his sleep things that will come to pass in the future. He now makes known to him the significance of these "secrets" (or "mysteries"), v. 29. God has not revealed this to Daniel because of any greater wisdom that he possesses compared with other men. Rather, it has been revealed so that Nebuchadnezzar might understand his dream. The phrase "but for their sakes that shall make known the interpretation to the king" reads better "but for the purpose that the interpretation may be known to the king," v. 30.

Details of the Dream 2:31–45 Daniel first describes Nebuchadnezzar's dream. Nebuchadnezzar had seen an "image" (or "statue") with the form of a man. This image was both "great" (*śaggî*, see v. 6) in size and "great" (*rab*, see v. 10) in glory. It had an excellent "brightness" (*zîw*) and a "terrible" (or "awesome") form. The word *zîw* occurs here and at 4:36; 5:6, 9, 10; and 7:28. In each of these places, it refers to appearance. BDB translates as "brightness, splendour." KB translates as "radiance, brightness." In the three plural appearances in c. 5, the word refers to the king's face. In c. 4 and c. 7, it likely refers to the face. Here it may refer to the overall appearance.[27]

As becomes clear in v. 34, the statue stands in a plain with a nearby mountain, v. 31. The head is "of fine gold," gold that has been refined and is therefore pure. In view of the interpretation given to this head later, it is likely that it has the face of Nebuchadnezzar. This would let the king readily accept Daniel's words that "thou art this head of gold" (v. 38). The breast and arms were of silver, and the belly and thighs of "brass" (better "bronze"), v. 32. Below the knees, the legs were made of iron, and the feet from iron mixed with "clay" (*ḥᵃsap*).

This is the first of nine times that the noun *ḥᵃsap* appears in the chapter (vv. 33, 34, 35, 41 [2X], 42, 43 [2X], 45). The word does not occur elsewhere. There is no cognate word in Hebrew, but cognates in other Semitic languages refer to formed clay, small pots, or potsherds. The major question here is whether *ḥᵃsap* refers to workable clay or to hardened clay. The word *ṭîn* occurs only twice (vv. 41, 43), both in the determinate form *ṭîna*, and gives emphasis to the phrase. Verse 35 describes the clay as part of that which is "broken to pieces" and becomes like "chaff." The NASB suggests "common clay," while the NIV offers "baked clay." Whatever translation we give to the phrase *ḥᵃsap ṭîna* must be interpretive. I accept "baked clay" because of its agreement with v. 35, v. 33.

---

[27]Leupold, p. 204, refers *zîw* to "renown" and Barnes, I, 271, to "intellect." These views are contrary, however, to the regular sense.

A stone was "cut out without hands," i.e., began rolling down a mountain (v. 45) with no human force directing it. It hit the statue on the feet and "brake them to pieces" (*deqaq*), causing them to crumble. The verb *deqaq* indicates a strong action of crushing or tearing into pieces some object. This is vividly seen with its Hebrew cognate when Moses grinds the golden calf to power (Exod. 32:20). This same picture occurs each time the word occurs in Daniel. Matthew Henry is devotional but incorrect with his comment that "God can bring about great effects by weak and unlikely causes."[28] The stone here is not a weak and unlikely cause. It represents the Lord Himself as He casts down the kingdoms of this world and establishes His own rule over the earth, v. 34.

The remainder of the statue also was "broken to pieces" (*deqaq*), becoming small particles like "chaff" that the wind blows away from "the summer threshingfloors." These places for threshing were located in areas where the wind would blow the chaff to the side and allow the heavier grain to fall. The stone in turn became a "great" (*rab*, see v. 10) mountain, glorious in its appearance, and filling the earth. It becomes clear later (vv. 44–45) that the mountain is another kingdom that embraces the whole earth, v. 35.

The "we" refers to Daniel and his friends, although Daniel is the spokesman. They had joined him in prayer that God would reveal the dream and its interpretation, vv. 17–19. He now associates them with him as he interprets the dream to the king, v. 36. For this reason, he later requests additional authority for them (v. 49).

Daniel addresses Nebuchadnezzar as "king of kings," an appropriate title in view of his position as the ruler of many countries conquered by Babylon. Goldwurm translates, "You, O king—whom the King of kings, Who is the God of heaven, has given a strong kingdom . . ."[29] This agrees with the rabbinical view given in the Talmud (*Shebuʾoth* 35*b*) but also interprets the verse with the presupposition that "Daniel would not have called Nebuchadnezzar *King of Kings*." The word *melek* ("king"), however, occurs over 180 times in Ezra and Daniel, however, always referring to a human king and never to God. The phrase *melek malkayyaʾ*, "king of kings," also occurs in Ezra 7:12, where it refers to a human king over other kings. When

---

[28]Henry, IV, 1030.
[29]Goldwurm, p. 103.

Nebuchadnezzar refers to God as ruling over earthly kings, he calls Him "a Lord of kings" (*mare³ malkîn*, 2:47), not a "King of kings."

Yet despite all of this exaltation, Nebuchadnezzar needs to realize that the "God of heaven" (cf. v. 18), the God Who has all power, has given him this eminence, v. 37. Daniel mentions the animals and birds as under Nebuchadnezzar's rule. This statement uses poetic superlatives to describe the authority given to Nebuchadnezzar. While the description seemingly includes the whole earth, the biblical focus is on the Mediterranean world. Nebuchadnezzar, the representative of the kingdom controlling this area, is the head of fine gold. The dream employs gold appropriately since the Babylonians used it lavishly in their temples and images of their gods, v. 38.

Following the Babylonian kingdom, another kingdom, represented by the "breast and . . . arms of silver," will rise. This kingdom will be inferior to Babylon. Its inferiority will not be in the extent of its rule since the Medo-Persian Empire actually covered more territory than the Babylonian Empire. Rather, it will be inferior in that the Medo-Persian ruler will have less power than Nebuchadnezzar. Young follows Keil in identifying the inferiority as the lack of "inner unity," with the Medes and Persians contending with one another. There is, however, no historical evidence for this. Henry sees the Medo-Persian Empire as "not so rich, powerful, or victorious." Since that empire actually covered more territory than the Babylonian Empire, the view is difficult to accept. Miller and Strauss argue that this is a moral inferiority, but all secular kingdoms are morally bankrupt. Barnes understands the deterioration to lie in the ability and character of the Medo-Persian kings, in the defeats suffered by its armies, in growing degeneracy, and a gradual weakening of its power. Only this last idea can be defended. Leupold notes that Babylon's empire continued the Assyrian rule and thus lasted about 2,000 years. This empire is superior to the Medo-Persian Empire in that "the two thousand years of Babylonian culture and its dominance in western Asia certainly outweighed the two hundred years of Persian dominion in its effect upon contemporary and later developments."[30] The view suffers when we consider the impact of the later Grecian and Roman

---

[30]Young, p. 74; Keil, p. 106; Henry, IV, 1031; Miller, p. 94; Lehman Strauss, *The Prophecies of Daniel* (Neptune, N.J.: Loizeaux Brothers, 1969), p. 70; Barnes, I, 159–60; Leupold, p. 116.

Empires on civilization. Both exercised a greater influence than the Medes and the Persians. Although unstated, the deterioration in the value of the metals suggests a continuing deterioration in the empires. I have related this to the nature of the ruling powers in each.

In the Babylonian Empire, the king was supreme. In the Medo-Persian Empire, however, numerous peers and satraps exercised independent powers. Although the kings descended from Cyrus until the fall of the Medo-Persian Empire, there is an implied division into two regions. Daniel 7:5 repeats this emphasis with its mention of the two sides of the bear, one raised higher than the other to suggest the Persian dominance. Here, the two arms of silver suggest the inclusion of Media and Persia in the kingdom. The dream uses silver appropriately, as the Medo-Persian rulers placed an emphasis on acquiring wealth, v. 39*a*.

The third kingdom is of "brass" (or "bronze") and represents Greece. A common view makes the four kingdoms Babylon, Media, Persia, and Greece. This is an older view that finds support today from liberal commentators (e.g., Lacocque, Lederach, and Porteous).[31] This position follows from the rejection of prophecy and the re-dating of the book to ca. 165 BC. The interpretation faces problems in that the Medes never had a significant world-dominating kingdom. They co-existed with Babylon until ca. 559 BC, when the Median kingdom came under the control of Cyrus, king of Persia. In addition, 6:8, 12, 15 refer to the "law of the Medes and Persians," i.e., the law of a single empire. Daniel 5:28 makes "the Medes and Persians" follow Babylon, with the Babylonians falling to "the Medes and Persians" joined into a single army. Daniel 8:20 identifies the ram with two horns as "the kings of Media and Persia," with the Persian kings controlling the empire "last," 8:3. Finally, the Lord sets up His kingdom to replace the fourth kingdom, 2:44–45, something that did not take place after the fall of the Grecian Empire. It is difficult to harmonize the liberal view with the details given both here and in c. 7, where the four kingdoms are again in view, and in c. 8 (especially v. 20), which focuses on the second and third kingdoms. In addition,

---

[31]Lacocque, p. 51; Lederach, p. 69; Porteous, p. 47.

history does not support the view. No worldwide Median kingdom existed at the time of Babylon's fall.

Alexander, born in mid-356 BC, was the son of Philip of Macedon.[32] As the king of Macedonia (359–336 BC) and commander of her army, Philip extended his control over most of the Greek mainland. From this base he conquered the surrounding nations and even planned the further conquest of the Persian Empire, but he fell prey to an assassin before he could execute this plan.

In addition to educating Alexander under the noted philosopher Aristotle, Philip involved him as a youth in both government and the army. When Alexander was but sixteen, Philip appointed his son regent while he led the army in a siege of Byzantium. During this time, Alexander commanded the army in a campaign against Thrace, northwest of Greece bordering on the Black Sea. Two years later, he commanded the Macedonian cavalry in a battle against Chaeroneia, a city in Greece located southeast of Mt. Parnassus. After the assassination of his father in 336 BC, Alexander gained the support of the generals in the army and took his father's place.

Alexander first put down rebellions by the Greek states and by barbarians in the north. By almost annihilating the city of Thebes, he warned other Greek cities against rejecting his leadership. He next led the troops across the Hellespont into battle against the Persian army. Although the Persians outnumbered the Greeks 150,000 soldiers to 75,000 soldiers, Alexander led his army to defeat them at the Granicus River in May 334 BC. In November 333 BC, the Persians, with a still larger army, were routed again at Issus, in southeast Asia Minor. Alexander then marched through Syria, Palestine, and Egypt. Because he offered cities and nations terms that were favorable compared to those demanded by the Persians, most opponents readily accepted his control. Those who attempted to resist received cruel treatment after their conquest. It was during this time that Alexander conducted his successful seven-month siege of Tyre, followed by the crucifixion of two thousand of its inhabitants. After

---

[32]Much of the information about Alexander the Great and the breaking up of his empire into four smaller kingdoms is from Paul Cartledge, *Alexander the Great* (New York: The Overlook Press, 2004), and from volume I of Edwyn Robert Bevan, *The House of Seleucus* (London: Edward Arnold, 1902).

his successful campaign in Egypt, Alexander founded the city of Alexandria in April 331 BC.

During this time, Darius gathered a third army in Persia. Alexander led his army back and fought a third battle against the Persians at Gaugamela, two hundred fifty miles north of Babylon, in October 331 BC. Despite choosing the battlefield and having a numerical advantage, the Persians again suffered defeat due to Alexander's superior strategy. Alexander now took the crown of Babylon to show his rule over the empire. He next conquered Bactria and Sogdiana, both to the northeast of Persia. In 326 BC, he campaigned in India. At this point his troops refused to go farther, and Alexander was forced to return home. He died in 323 BC of an unknown cause.

While the Greeks, under Alexander, conquered more territory than did either of the preceding kingdoms, the empire was relatively weak. The use of bronze to represent the kingdom suggests the continuing deterioration in the power of its leadership. In the Grecian Empire, numerous city-states and independent kings continued to govern themselves, with their only connection to the empire being their yearly tribute.[33] Bronze is also an appropriate metal to represent Greece in view of its armament. Bronze was the metal used in the armor and weaponry of the Grecian army.

As further evidence of the kingdom's weakness, four of Alexander's generals divided the empire between them following his death. There was conflict between the various rulers. Two of the generals, the rulers of Syria and Egypt, became dominant. The division of the third empire into two "thighs" suggests this later importance of the Syrian and Egyptian Empires. The reference to bearing rule "over all the earth" has its focus on the biblical world, v. 39*b*.

The final kingdom is of iron, of still lesser value.[34] The Roman Empire sprawled throughout the known biblical world, but the

---

[33]Henry, IV, 1031, sees the inferiority "in wealth and extent of dominion to the Persian monarchy." The Grecian Empire, however, actually covered more territory than did the Medo-Persian Empire. It is impossible to say which of the empires was the wealthier.

[34]Phillips, p. 265, notes that "the only empire which will, in fact, rule the whole world will be the last one, the empire of antichrist." This empire, however, and other Gentile empires, e.g., Britain, France, are "not part of this prophecy." While Antichrist will have a dominant role in world politics, nothing in the Bible indicates that he will rule the world. The focus of biblical prophecy is on the biblical

Roman emperor was relatively weak as a ruler. Technically, he was the representative of a republic. Others thus heavily influenced him in political power. Despite the weakness of its government, Rome became the strongest of the empires in the biblical world. Cowles adopts an older view that finds the fourth kingdom fulfilled in the fragments of the third kingdom, especially Syria and Egypt. The view neglects the many details that better apply to Rome. Knoch relates the iron to force and the clay to wealth. He understands apostate Israel as developing into a wealthy power that will control the world through its wealth. History since the publication of Knoch's commentary argues against the view.[35]

Iron appropriately represents the Roman Empire in its strength. Although it has the least value of the metals, it is by far the strongest metal involved in the dream. The statement "break in pieces [$d^e qaq$, see v. 34] and bruise [better 'crush']" aptly describes Rome's conquest of the biblical world. Rome "breaketh all these," the previous three empires mentioned. Rome used iron in its weapons, giving it an advantage over other armies. This again supports the use of iron to represent Rome in the dream, v. 40.[36]

The two legs suggest that the Roman Empire will include two distinct parts. Goldwurm mentions the view that the division represents the development of two religions, Christianity and Islam, in "the area occupied by the Roman empire." Since the toes represent kingdoms (cf. 7:7, 20), it is more likely that the initial division is political rather than religious. Montgomery sees no symbolism to the two legs since "the human body naturally has two legs." West likewise understands "the two legs and two feet" as simply normal part of a man

---

world. The Bible does not mention such areas of the world as North and South America, Australia, and Antarctica.

[35]Cowles, p. 308; Knoch, p. 65.

[36]J. Charleton Steen, *God's Prophetic Programme* (London: Pickering & Inglis, n.d.), pp. 67–68, understands the proportions of the image to represent the length of the kingdoms. The head, a shorter part, is Babylon, dominant for 66 years. The arms and breasts, the Medo-Persian Empire, stands for 207 years. The belly and thighs, Greece, lasts 210 years. To overcome the difficulty of the more than 2,000 years since the fall of Greece, he notes the gap in time before Daniel's seventieth week (9:24–27) and has the Roman Empire stopping at the fall of Jerusalem in AD 70. Steen understands this to follow the image down to the ankles, with the remainder from the ankles still awaiting fulfillment. The view is speculative and requires some arbitrary application of dates.

and claims that "the duality of the parts means nothing in itself."
He does let the ten toes represent ten kingdoms. The symbolism of
the legs, however, seems natural in light of the later division of the
Roman Empire into eastern and western parts. It is true that the body
naturally involves two legs, but v. 33 makes the point of mentioning the legs. Since the statue is virtually all symbolic, it is natural to
associate symbolism with the legs as well. Some authors, e.g., Archer
and Bloomfield, refer the division to the toes but do not mention the
legs.[37] While it is true that the toes represent further division, the
division begins with the legs.

In the mid-fourth century, the empire divided into the Western
Empire, dominated by the Papal church, and the Eastern Empire,
under the influence of the Greek church and pagan religions. Despite
sporadic persecution, Christianity flourished during the first three
centuries of the Roman Empire. With the conversion of the Emperor
Constantine (306–37), the Roman government looked upon Christianity with favor. Under Theodosius (379–95), Christianity was
declared the state religion and became dominant in the western part
of the empire. In the east, however, Zoroastrianism still held dominance. When Byzantium, later known as Constantinople, became
the capital of the eastern part of the empire, it also became the center
of the Eastern church. The onslaught of barbarian tribes from the
north toppled the western part of the empire in 476. The eastern part
continued until its fall in 1453. From the seventh century on, Islam
spread throughout the empire. The two legs of the statue suggest this
division into the eastern and western parts.

Goldwurm cites the older Jewish view that makes the third kingdom Rome and the fourth kingdom that of the Arabs. It is difficult,
however, to identify an Arab kingdom. No unified Arab kingdom
has approached Rome in extent or duration. Lang argues that the
fourth kingdom is that of Antichrist, centered in Babylon.[38] While

---

[37]Goldwurm, p. 107; Montgomery, p. 187; George W. West, *Daniel: The Greatly
Beloved* (London: Marshall, Morgan & Scott, Ltd., n.d.), p. 18; Gleason L. Archer
Jr., *Daniel*, in *The Expositor's Bible Commentary*, ed. Frank E. Gaebelein (Grand
Rapids: Zondervan Publishing House, 1985), pp. 72–73; Bloomfield, p. 92.

[38]Goldwurm, pp. 104, 109; G. H. Lang, *The Histories and Prophecies of Daniel*
(London: The Paternoster Press, 1950), p. 29.

Antichrist will come out of the Roman Empire (7:8), the empire exists before his rise to power.

In addition, there will be further division into the "feet and toes."[39] While the text does not mention the number of toes, the usual number of "ten" toes has caused great debate. This number sometimes refers to an exact number (e.g., Gen. 18:32; Exod. 34:28) but also sometimes indicates a round number (e.g. Gen. 31:7, 41; Lev. 26:8). This has led to taking the number either to an exact number of kingdoms developing from the two legs or to a large number of kingdoms developing. Price states, "It is quite probable that the number *ten* is used as an indefinite but comparatively large number, rather than as an exact number." Thomson says of the number, "It may be more than ten or fewer than ten." Leupold concludes that "there might in reality be nine or eleven or nineteen or twenty." Barrett understands the number as representing "the totality of its power."[40] Despite these views, when we compare the number with 7:7, 20, and 24 (also Rev. 13:1; 17:3, 7, 12, 16) we see that it represents an exact number of kingdoms.

Watkinson has God setting up His kingdom "in the reign of Tiberius Caesar." He identifies ten kingdoms making up Rome at that time: "Italia, Gaul, Pannonia, Rhoetia, Illyricum, Romelia, Maesia, Iberia, Syria, and Egypt." Smith understands the reference as ten kingdoms that arose between 351 and 476 AD out of Rome's fall. He names these as the Huns, Ostrogoths, Visigoths, Franks, Vandals, Suevi, Burgundians, Heruli, Anglo-Saxon, and Lombards.[41] These views give a historical application. More naturally, the passage is prophetic of the end times. The fact that the "stone" destroys these nations supports a prophetic view.

---

[39]King, pp. 75–77, interprets the feet as "Mohammedan power," the ongoing domination of Israel by Islamic nations. This leads him to conclude that Antichrist will be a Muslim who assumes the Jewish faith. The problem that he fails to address is the lack of an Islamic world-dominating kingdom. While Islamic nations will undoubtedly be involved in the end-time conflicts with Israel, there has never been a single Islamic nation to which we can point as fulfilling the symbolism of the feet. The emphasis of the chapter is on the toes of the feet, not the feet themselves.

[40]Price, p. 80; Thomson, *Daniel*, in *The Pulpit Commentary*, p. 72; Leupold, p. 122; Michael P. V. Barrett, *God's Unfailing Purpose: The Message of Daniel* (Greenville, S.C.: Ambassador Emerald International, 2003), p. 71.

[41]Watkinson, p. 106; Smith, p. 58.

As the kingdoms develop, they combine "the strength of iron" with "miry clay [or "baked clay," *ḥᵃsap ṭînaʾ*, see v. 33]," v. 41. This mixing of iron and baked clay results in the kingdoms being "partly strong" in leadership and "partly broken [or 'brittle']," subject to change and therefore weaker in leadership, v. 42. The mixing of iron and clay pictures mingling "with the seed of men." This refers to the amalgamation of different nations into the empire. The empire brings together different nationalities, different economies, different governments, different cultures, etc. This mixing results in further weakening as the nations contribute various pressures. Just as iron and clay do not mix, so these parts of the empire will not harmoniously mix.

Other views also explain the symbolism of iron mixed with clay. Leupold suggests the iron of "old Roman stock" mixed with the clay of "the more plastic Germanic and other peoples who were at that time not such good material for empire building." Gaebelein understands the iron of monarchial rule and the clay as democratic forms of government. Thomson sees "the infusion of barbarous races into the midst of a civilized [race]." Henry interprets the iron and clay as warring parties within Rome, e.g., "Marius and Sylla, Caesar and Pompey." Keil offers "inner disharmony or discord" yet an overall "firmness of iron." Archer proposes the iron of "the old Roman culture and tradition" and the clay of "a socialist society based on relativism in morality and philosophy." Ford accepts the joining of the church and state. Lederach proposes "marriages between royal families as attempts to unite kingdoms."[42] There are other possible views. We can only be sure of some form of weakness mixed with strength, v. 43.

"In the days of those kings," the final leaders of the Roman Empire, the powerful "God of heaven" (cf. vv. 18, 37) will "break in pieces" (*dᵉqaq*) the remaining power of these four empires. The reference to the "days of those kings" does not refer to a revival of the Roman Empire. This empire has continued to exist in various forms since it began. Daniel here speaks of this empire in its final form. This will be a union of ten strong and weak governments, pictured

---

[42]Leupold, p. 120; Gaebelein, p. 31; Thomson, p. 71; Henry, IV, 1031–32; Keil, p. 108; Archer, p. 48; Desmond Ford, דניאל, (Nashville: Southern Publishing Association, 1978), p. 99.

by the mingling of the iron and clay in the feet and ten toes, all under the control of the Antichrist.

While the narrative does not place any emphasis on a gap in time between vv. 43 and 44, we must nevertheless place one there. Verse 44 refers to the final kingdom established by the Lord, an act that is still future.[43] Verses 35 and 45 both refer to the breaking of the iron, clay, brass, silver, and gold. Remnants of all these kingdoms exist when God establishes the final kingdom. This new kingdom will not be left to the vagaries of "other people." For this reason, it will "stand for ever," a promise repeated in 7:14, 18, and 27, v. 44.

The stone (ʾeben) is Christ, the ruler of the final kingdom. The OT elsewhere pictures Christ as an ʾeben. He is the cornerstone (Ps. 118:22; Isa. 28:16). To those who reject Him, He is the "stone of stumbling" (Isa. 8:14). The NT carries on this picture of the Lord as a "stone." The NT Greek equivalent of ʾeben is λίθος. The λίθος is Christ in Matthew 21:42, 44 (Mark 12:10; Luke 20:17, 18; Rom. 9:32, 33; 1 Pet. 2:7, 8); Acts 4:11; and 1 Peter 2:4, 6.

This stone "is cut out of the mountain without hands." When used as a symbol in the OT, a mountain most often refers to Mt. Zion, the location of the temple and an appropriate symbol of the kingdom of Judah (e.g., Exod. 15:17; Pss. 30:7; 48:1; Isa. 2:2). Everywhere else in Daniel, the word refers to Mt. Zion, the location of the temple in Judah (9:16, 20; 11:45). It is reasonable to make that same association here. The kingdom of the Lord arises from Judah "without hands," i.e., without human assistance. As stated in v. 35, this final kingdom "filled the whole earth." Although men have tried to establish world-dominant kingdoms in the past, they have failed. Only when the Lord establishes His kingdom on earth will all people be brought under His control. The NT repeats the promise of v. 44 that the kingdom will last forever (Matt. 6:13; Luke 1:33; 2 Pet. 1:11).

An early view related the phrase "cut out of the mountain without hands" to the virgin birth of Christ. Justin Martyr and Jerome suggest this view. The view, however, requires that the verse refer to both the first and second comings of Christ. Leupold understands the

---

[43]Gerhard Pfandl, "Interpretations of the Kingdom of God in Daniel 2:44," *AUSS* 34:2 (Autumn 1996): 249–69, has an excellent summary of the historical interpretations of the kingdom in this passage. I have drawn on this article for much of the historical information relating to the interpretation of the kingdom.

mountain as having no meaning at all. It is "merely a part of the necessary framework of the dream." If this were true, there is no reason why a mountain should be mentioned at all. Walvoord understands the mountain as a "picture of political sovereignty." The final kingdom originates in God, not in mankind.[44] While the view is possible, it suffers from the lack of this symbolism elsewhere in the OT. It is more consistent to see here only the Lord's second coming.

His conquest is violent and abrupt, not peaceful and gradual. He will "[break] in pieces" (d^eqaq, see v. 34) the remnants of the other kingdoms. This will take place when the Lord returns visibly to the earth with His church and sets up His kingdom. Notice that the breaking of the ten toes is not gradual but sudden. This argues against the postmillennial view of the kingdom, a view that sees the world as growing better until it finally is ready for the Lord to begin His rule. It also opposes the amillennial view, in which the kingdom of the Lord exists alongside of the kingdoms of men. The interpretation declared by Daniel to Nebuchadnezzar is certain because it comes from the "great" (rab, see v. 10) God.

Leupold understands the final kingdom as that established by Christ "during the first centuries of *the Christian Era*." The context here, however, indicates a violent establishment. Leupold makes this "still future, for the final victory of the church coincides with the day of judgment." Since the violence in Daniel's vision coincides with the destruction of earthly kingdoms, it is better to set the establishment entirely in the future, at the second coming of the Lord to the earth. Henry describes the final kingdom: "The kingdom of Christ shall wear out all other kingdoms, shall outlive them, and flourish when they are sunk with their own weight, and so wasted that their place knows them no more."[45] This, however, suggests a gradual overcoming rather than a sudden coming of the final kingdom. The Scripture teaches that the Lord's kingdom will begin suddenly, following the defeat of Antichrist's army at the end of the Tribulation, v. 45.

It is appropriate to note that the times of these kingdoms make up what the NT calls "the times of the Gentiles" (Luke 21:24). This

---

[44]Justin Martyr, *Dialogue with Trypho*, in *The Fathers of the Church: Writings of Saint Justin Martyr*, trans. Thomas B. Falls (New York: Christian Heritage, Inc., 1948), p. 268; Jerome, p. 32; Leupold, p. 126; Walvoord, p. 76.

[45]Leupold, pp. 123–24; Henry, IV, 1032.

is the period in which Jerusalem is under the control of the Gentile nations. This began with Babylonian control, continued under the Medes and the Persians, remained during the Grecian era, and culminated during the period of Roman rule. Even those times when the Jews have been permitted to live in Jerusalem have been precarious times when the Gentile nations exerted significant influence on them. Only when the Lord establishes His worldwide rule will the city finally be free.

Reward of Daniel 2:46–49 Nebuchadnezzar is so overwhelmed by Daniel's knowledge of the dream and its interpretation that he falls upon his face to worship him. Verse 47 makes it clear that in worshiping Daniel, Nebuchadnezzar worships Daniel's God.[46] He offers "an oblation," a meal offering, and "sweet odours," incense, to Daniel, again the representative of God. To Nebuchadnezzar, Daniel's God has revealed Himself through Daniel, and so he thinks it appropriate to honor Daniel with these sacrifices, v. 46.

Nebuchadnezzar praises "your God" as the greatest of all gods and therefore as ruler over all earthly kings. The pronoun "your" translates the plural pronominal suffix *kôn*. In all likelihood, the plural refers to the nation of Israel. It is possible that Nebuchadnezzar limited his thought to the God of Daniel and his friends.[47] They, however, have not been mentioned in this context, leaving it more likely that the king thinks of the nation's God.

On the basis that God has given Daniel the knowledge of his dream and its interpretation, Nebuchadnezzar recognizes God's ability to reveal secrets, v. 47. He makes Daniel a "great man" by elevating him to the position of chief "ruler" and "chief [*rab*] of the governors [*s^egan*]." The noun *s^egan* occurs five times in Daniel, here and 3:2, 3, 27; 6:7. The Hebrew cognate, *sagan*, also refers to a governmental official.

Although he is young in years and experience, Daniel's abilities are evident and Nebuchadnezzar places him in a position as

---

[46]Heaton, pp. 135–36, suggests that Daniel is "the embodiment of true Israel." In prostrating himself, Nebuchadnezzar fulfills the prophecies that the Gentiles would lick the dust of the Gentiles, Isa. 49:23; cf. 45:14; 60:14. Those prophecies, however, relate to the millennial kingdom more than to Daniel. Nebuchadnezzar in no way exalts Israel at this point in his life.

[47]Moses Stuart, *Commentary on the Book of Daniel* (Boston: Crocker & Brewster, 1850), p. 70, adopts this position.

head over the other "wise men" (*ḥakkîm*). He gives Daniel "many" (*śaggî*, see v. 6) gifts, v. 48. At Daniel's request, his three friends are appointed over the routine affairs of the kingdom. Daniel, however, "sat in the gate of the king," serving as Nebuchadnezzar's chief advisor. The "gate" of a city was normally the place at which the city leaders made political decisions (e.g., Deut. 25:7; 1 Kings 22:10; Amos 5:15). With this background, the term has the sense here of the place where Daniel made decisions that affected Babylon, v. 49.

FIERY FURNACE 3:1–30

Worship of Nebuchadnezzar's Image 3:1–7 Nebuchadnezzar erects an "image" (or "statue"). The ratio of sixty cubits high compared to only six cubits wide, approximately ninety feet high and nine feet wide, has caused a variety of views. Gowan thinks that the image "existed only in the mind of this author" and considers the dimensions "very strange." Lacocque suggests that the "image" was "a stele covered with bas-reliefs." While this is possible, the word $ṣ^elem$ elsewhere refers to a statue-like image, e.g., 2:31 (2X), 32, 34, 35, the only occurrences outside of c. 3. The Assyrian cognate $ṣalmu$ refers to a statue. The Hebrew $ṣelem$ refers to an "image." Other than referring to the likeness of God in the historical and prophetic books, the word $ṣelem$ also refers to various idols. It was common to erect images with massive proportions to impress their viewers. Tatford thinks that Nebuchadnezzar got the idea of a statue from seeing "the colossal statue of Rameses the Great" during his successful campaign in Egypt.[1] Because of the length of his reign, there are more statues of Rameses II than of any other pharaoh. It is possible that Nebuchadnezzar saw one or more of these. We do not know, however, enough about his Egyptian campaign to be certain. Nothing in Daniel's description excludes a pedestal base with a human figure on top.

The erection of large statues was not unusual in ancient times. A statue of Zeus, located at Olympia, in Greece, stood almost forty feet high. The Colossus, a statue of the sun god overlooking the city of Rhodes on the island of Rhodes in the Aegean Sea, was almost one hundred feet tall. The statues erected by the early Egyptian pharaohs range up to sixty feet in height.

In the day in which we live, we still find large statues. In 2001, the terrorist group known as the Taliban destroyed a 175-foot statue of Buddha that was located in the Bamiyan Valley in Afghanistan. The statue was estimated to be almost 1,600 years old. The well-known statue of Lord Nelson, at Trafalgar Square in London, is 18 feet high and located on a 185-foot pedestal. The Statue of Liberty is one inch over 151 feet and rests on a pedestal about 154 feet high.

---

[1]Gowan, p. 63; Lacocque, *The Book of Daniel*, p. 56; Tatford, p. 55.

China is home to the tallest statue in the world today, a 71-meter (approximately 233 feet) statue of Buddha that is 1,200 years old.

The book does not give a date for this event. The LXX sets these events in the "eighteenth year." If this is so—and there is no way to support the date—this would place the chapter ca. 586 BC. This is the year in which Nebuchadnezzar defeated Judah and carried away much of its population into captivity (2 Kings 25:8–12).[2] This would have been a natural time for the king to celebrate the power of his god that had so blessed him.[3] We cannot, however, certainly date the events of the chapter.

Miller dates the event close to the dream of c. 2. He relies on "the position of the chapter in the book, the probability that the king received the idea for the image from the dream in chap. 2, and the likelihood that the image was constructed to test the loyalty of the king's officials to his new administration."[4] Of these arguments, however, only the position of the chapter has any viability. Nebuchadnezzar's dream in c. 2 dealt with a completely different subject, and the empire was at least two years old if this took place after c. 2.

Wood sets the event "four or five years" after the king's reign begins. Without giving a reason, Henry suggests Nebuchadnezzar's seventh year. Shea dates the convocation in 594 BC, in the eleventh year of the king's reign. Strauss concludes that the event was "between eighteen and twenty-three years" after the dream of c. 2. Wiersbe notes that some believe the event took place "twenty years after the promotion of Daniel and his friends, about the time Jerusalem was finally destroyed (586 B.C.)." Leupold places the chapter "at some time when [Nebuchadnezzar] had completed his major conquests and had felt the magnitude and the strength of his

---

[2] 2 Kings 25:8 and Jer. 52:12 place the captivity in the "nineteenth year." This reflects the differing ways of counting the length of a king's reign. See the discussion of dating at 1:1.

[3] William H. Shea, "Daniel 3: Extra-Biblical Texts and the Convocation on the Plain of Dura," *AUSS* 20:1 (Spring 1982): 30, presents an impressive argument supporting his view that the ceremony took place after Nebuchadnezzar had put down a rebellion against him. This event brought leaders of the king's empire together to pledge their loyalty. While this may have been the purpose, there is no direct statement in either the OT record or from archaeology to support the view. Shea has brought evidence together that he has interpreted this way.

[4] Miller, p. 107.

empire."[5] These dates are possible but not provable. The chapter is later than c. 2 since v. 12 refers to 2:49. It is earlier than c. 4 since that chapter closes with Nebuchadnezzar extolling God. This likely places the event during the first half of Nebuchadnezzar's forty-three-year reign.

Nothing describes the nature of the figure other than the verses (vv. 5–7, 10–12, 14–15, 18) that show it to be a god requiring worship. As with the date of the event, there are considerable differences in describing the statue. Keil states that "the statue is not designated as the image of a god." He concludes that it "was a symbol of the world-power established by Nebuchadnezzar." Falling down before it gave reverence to this power and also paid homage to its gods.[6] The view is possible. Falling down before the statue implied worship of heathen gods, an action forbidden to the Jews.

Wallace presents the view that the king "knew that most would think of it as there to stimulate common devotion to the gods of Babylon . . . yet he desired to leave minority communities with his . . . empire free to adapt the meaning of the outward ritual to their conscience about images and idolatry." He thinks that "the statue could represent whatever anyone wanted it to symbolize . . . the spirit of Babylon, or for the emperor himself, or for one of the traditional national gods."[7] It is doubtful that the king would have erected an image with an uncertain meaning.

Gangel tentatively suggests that the statue was "a reproduction of the likeness of Nebuchadnezzar himself" and that it "was designed for the direct worship of Nebuchadnezzar." West also suggests that the image was of the king, so that "the King indirectly received idol worship."[8] From archaeology, we know that Nebuchadnezzar built temples to both Bel and Nebo. It is unlikely that he would have invented a new god to worship or commanded worship of himself.

---

[5]Wood, p. 79; Henry, IV, 1034; Shea, pp. 30–31; Strauss, p. 89; Warren W. Wiersbe, *Be Resolute* (Colorado Springs, Colo.: Victory, 2000), pp. 37–38; Leupold, p. 135.

[6]Keil, p. 120.

[7]Ronald S. Wallace, *The Lord Is King: The Message of Daniel* (Downers Grove, Ill.: InterVarsity Press, 1979), p. 64.

[8]Gangel, pp. 75, 77; West, p. 23.

Jastrow refers to "colossal statues of themselves" placed by
Gudea and other rulers in temples. They placed inscriptions expressing devotion to their gods on these statues. Henry concludes that
the statue represents a new god, one more among the many already
worshiped by the Babylonians. King suggests the unlikely view that
the image "was a replica of the one he had seen in his dream in ch.
ii."[9] This image required worship, vv. 5–7; that image represented
kingdoms, all of which ultimately perished.

From the reaction of the three Israelites later (vv. 16–18), it may
have been a representation of Bel or Nebo, Babylon's chief gods.
The name "Bel" comes from the Akkadian word $b\bar{e}lu$, "lord." With
the passing of time, the name Bel was given to Marduk, the chief
god of Babylon. He was the sun god. The Temple of Esagila ("lofty
house") was given over to the worship of Bel. As the city grew in
importance, Bel received a greater prominence. Eventually, the
Babylonians recognized him as head of the pantheon of gods. The
extent of his influence at Babylon can be seen by the names of the
Babylonian kings: Evil Merodach ("Marduk"), Labashi-Marduk,
and Belshazzar.

Nebo, also called Nabu, was the Babylonian god of wisdom
and literature. He was specially worshiped in the Temple of Ezida
("enduring house") at Borsippa, about ten miles south of Babylon. In
early times, he was considered more important than Marduk. Several
Babylonian kings had names compounded in some way with Nebo
(Nabopolassar, Nebuchadnezzar, and Nabonidus).

Whatever the identification of the statue, the construction likely
involved a wooden frame with gold leaf applied over it (cf. Isa.
40:19; 41:7; Jer. 10:3–4). Archer and Young suggest that Nebuchadnezzar used gold for the statue because the golden head of the
statue in the dream represented him. While this is possible, the use
of gold to make an ornate figure is in keeping with what we know
of ancient rulers. Herodotus 1.183 refers to "a great golden image
of Zeus sitting at a great golden table" and to "a statue of solid gold
twelve cubits [eighteen feet] high." Oates relates that during the time
of Babylon's submission to Assyria, Merodach-Baladan gave large
amounts of gold in tribute. Nebuchadnezzar covered the walls of the

---

[9]Jastrow, p. 57; Henry, IV, 1034; King, p. 79.

shrine to Marduk "with sparkling gold [and] caused it to shine like the sun." King aptly notes that the image was "outwardly imperishable, inwardly inferior."[10]

There are also differing views as to the location of the "plain of Dura." Goldwurm refers to tradition that locates Dura "near the famous ruins of Babylon . . . as the place where Chananyah, Mishael, and Azaryah were thrown to the flames. Tradition places the lions' pit into which Daniel was thrown (ch. 6) near this area." Miller suggests a location sixteen miles south of Babylon where archaeological investigation has discovered a large brick structure that may have served as the base for a statue. The distance from Babylon and inconvenience of traveling this far (and back again) argues against this. Walvoord suggests a site located in a plain six miles southeast of Babylon. Montgomery suggests the river Dûra that flows into the Euphrates six miles south of Babylon. A large square of brick has been found there that could have served as the base for the image. Again, the distance argues against these views.[11]

That Nebuchadnezzar located the statue in a "plain" possibly suggests that Dura was outside the city. Beside this, we cannot locate the "plain of Dura" other than to place it close enough for the people of Babylon to come to it readily at the time set for giving homage to the image. The word *dûraʾ* occurs only here. A related verb means "to dwell." The Akkadian noun *duru* refers to a wall. Dura may have been some enclosed place in the city or, more probably, an area outside the city but near the city's wall, v. 1.

Nebuchadnezzar plans the ceremony to include the leaders of the empire. He calls the nation's leaders to come. The "princes" (*ʾaḥašdarpᵉnayyaʾ*, or "satraps") are governors of various provinces; cf. 6:1. The title *ʾaḥašdarpᵉnayyaʾ* is a Persian loanword. According to KB, it refers to a "protector of the empire." The word occurs in 3:2, 3, 27 and in 6:1, 2, 3, 4, 6, 7. Although translated differently, a related word occurs in Ezra 8:36 and Esther 3:12; 8:9; 9:3.

The "governors" (or "prefects," *sᵉgan*, see 2:48) held lesser roles of administration over parts of the Babylonian empire. The "captains" (or "governors," *paḥᵃwataʾ*) were likewise administrators although we cannot clearly distinguish their role. The plural form

---

[10]Archer, p. 50; Young, p. 84; Oates, pp. 115, 157; King, p. 81.

[11]Goldwurm, p. 114; Miller, p. 111; Walvoord, p. 81; Montgomery, p. 197.

pahᵃwataʾ occurs four times in Daniel (3:2, 3, 27, 6:7). The singular *pehâ* occurs six times in Ezra. It is apparently an Akkadian loanword referring to a political leader of some sort. We cannot be specific as to the exact responsibilities carried by the holders of this office.[12]

The "judges" (or "counselors," *ʾᵃdargazrayyaʾ*)[13] may have served to advise governmental leaders in various areas or acted as higher-level judges. The noun *ʾᵃdargazrayyaʾ* occurs only in vv. 2 and 3. It seems to be a Persian loanword. From the context, it refers to some type of governmental position although we cannot be certain as to its nature. The word is compounded from the roots *ʾdr*, "great," and *gzr*, "to cut, divide" and thus "to determine." In this context, the word would indicate a "great judge."

The "treasurers" (*gᵉdabrayyaʾ*) held responsibilities in government, possibly financial in nature. The title *gᵉdabrayyaʾ* occurs only in vv. 2 and 3. A similar Hebrew word occurs in Ezra 1:8, where it indicates a "treasurer." That is likely the function here as well.

The "counsellors" (or "judges," *dᵉtabrayyaʾ*) are thought to administer the law. This title also appears only in vv. 2 and 3. The title *dᵉtabrayyaʾ* is a Persian loanword that designates a counselor. The "sheriffs" (or "magistrates," *tiptayeʾ*) may have served as judges in the legal system. As with the previous three titles, the noun *tiptayeʾ* occurs only in vv. 2 and 3. BDB considers it a personal name, but this does not fit into the context of Babylonian officials. Once more, we can only speculate as to its meaning.

The "rulers of the provinces" included various district officials. We cannot precisely distinguish the individual responsibilities of the officers mentioned since we do not know enough about the Babylonian rule. It is clear, however, that these are highly placed leaders of the empire under Nebuchadnezzar. Since a gathering of all of the nation's leaders would have been unwieldy, these leaders probably

---

[12]Hartman, p. 156, notes that the *waw* prefix occurs before only the third title in this group of seven classes of officials. He suggests "that the first three kinds of officials form a group distinct from the last four," with the first three groups of higher rank than the last four. This is possible although we do not know enough about these officers and their responsibilities to be certain.

[13]Goldwurm, p. 115, considers the last four names as names of officials. He also mentions the view of Rashi that these names refer to nations. The view follows *Sanhedrin 92a* in the Talmud. The view goes against the context, however, which groups these with words that clearly refer to officials of various types.

represented the different areas of the empire. Young understands that "no [official] in the whole kingdom was to be exempt from obeying the command." He suggests, "Soldiers would have remained at their posts throughout the province to quell any uprisings." Knoch is similar, seeing "a gathering of the entire executive staff of the empire."[14] This seems extreme for a one-time ceremony. It is more likely that the various areas of the kingdom were represented by officials rather than having the entire group of officials journey to Babylon. The Babylonian leaders, of course, would have all attended, v. 2. These leaders gather at the site of the image for its dedication, v. 3.[15]

The herald announces Nebuchadnezzar's decree. This command is for all of the people, including representatives from various nations and languages, v. 4. At the "time" (ʿiddan, see 2:8) when the music starts, they should fall in worship before the image. In bowing before the image that in some way represented Babylon's god, this worship recognized the power of Babylon's god over the different gods of the various nations.

The narrative lists the musical instruments in three groups. The first group contains two wind instruments. The horn of a ram or a goat served as the source for the "cornet" (qarnaʾ). The noun qarnaʾ refers to a horn of some kind. In vv. 5, 7, 10, and 15, it is a musical horn. In 7:7, 8, 11, 20, 21, 24, it is an animal's horn, used to symbolize various human leaders. The "flute" (mašrôqîtaʾ) was a whistle-like instrument carved from wood or ivory. The noun mašrôqîtaʾ occurs only in this chapter, vv. 5, 7, 10, and 15. It comes from the root šrq, "hiss, whistle," and indicates a "pipe" or "flute," possibly one of a double-reed type.[16]

---

[14]Young, pp. 86–87; Knoch, p. 88.

[15]Hector Avalos, "The Comedic Function of the Enumeration of Officials and Instruments in Daniel 3," *CBQ* 53 (Oct 1991): 584–86, considers the repetition of officials (vv. 2, 3) and musical instruments (vv. 5, 7, 10, 15) satirical, showing the mechanical and mindless actions of the Babylonians in contrast with the pious behavior of the Jews. It is more likely that this repetition merely reflects Daniel's style of writing. Repetition also occurs elsewhere in the book, e.g., names (1:6, 11, 19); titles of the king's wise men (2:2, 27); Daniel's name (4:8, 19; 5:12; 10:1); Belshazzar's offer (5:7, 16, cf. v. 29); the unchangeable law of the Medes and Persians (6:8, 12, 15, 17); king of the south (11:5, 9, 11, 14, 25 [2X], 40); king of the north (11:6, 7, 8, 11, 13, 15, 40).

[16]Charles H. Dyer, "The Musical Instruments in Daniel 3," *BibSac* 147 (Oct–Dec 1990): 429, identifies the mašrôqîtaʾ as a double-reed pipe, more prominent in

The second group of instruments includes three instruments that involve the plucking of strings. The "harp" (or "lyre," *qayt^erôs*, a loanword from Greek)[17] was a stringed instrument plucked with a plectrum and mounted over a sounding board. The strings were cut from the intestines of a sheep. Verses 5, 7, 10, and 15 also mention the *qayt^erôs*. The Vulgate translates as *citharae*, "harp" or "zither." The word is related to the NT word κιθάρα, "harp, lyre" (e.g., 1 Cor. 14:7). The "sackbut" (*sabb^eka^ʾ*) was a triangular-shaped instrument with four strings. The word *sabb^eka^ʾ* occurs only in v. 5. It is a variant spelling of *śabb^eka^ʾ*, which occurs in vv. 7, 10, and 15. The Vulgate translates as *sambucae*, "sackbut," and the LXX σαμβύκης, also an instrument with a triangular shape and having four strings. The "psaltery" (*p^esanterîn*, a Greek loanword) was a small, triangular, harp-like instrument, possibly a lyre but having a different shape from the *qayt^erôs*. The word *p^esanterîn* occurs only in vv. 5, 10, and 15. A variant spelling, *p^esanṭerîn*, occurs in v. 7. The instrument is akin to the Greek word ψαλτήριον, some type of harp.

The final instrument stands by itself in the third group of instruments. The "dulcimer" (*sûmpon^eyâ*) is commonly suggested to be a bagpipe or some form of pipes. The translations display this variation. The AB, ESV, NAB, NASB, and NJB all translate "bagpipe." The NCV, NET, NIV, and NLT translate "pipes." Others understand the word generally, not as a specific instrument. By combining *sûmpon^eyâ* with the phrase "all kinds of musick," they obtain something like "full consort of music" (REB), "every other kind of music" (CB), or "in symphony with all kinds of music" (NKJV). The grammatical construction—a sequence of six names followed by the copulative introducing the phrase "all kinds of musick"— argues against this.

The failure to group *sûmpon^eyâ* with the first two instruments suggests that it differs from them in some way. The word *sûmpon^eyâ* occurs here and in v. 15. In v. 10, it is spelled *sîpon^eyâ*. As written, it

---

Babylon than the flute. Archaeological evidence supports the view.

[17]Authors often cite the presence of Greek loanwords as evidence of a late date, e.g., Driver, p. lviii; Montgomery, p. 22. Edwin M. Yamauchi, "Daniel and Contacts Between the Aegean and the Near East Before Alexander," *The Evangelical Quarterly* 53 (Jan–Mar 1981): 37–47, cites archaeological evidence to show that this contact occurred as early as the seventh century BC. The presence of this word does not therefore support a late date for the book.

is related to the Greek συμφωνία, "music" (Luke 15:25). It is evident, however, that it is some kind of instrument here.[18] In recent years, the word has been related to τύμπανον, "drum." The exchange of the τ and σ often occurs with Eastern Greek dialects. This would place a percussion instrument in the third group. The use of percussion instruments occurs in archaeological portrayals of music. Dyer, Mitchell, and Joyce adopt this position. Both the HCSB and the NRSV translate *sûmpon^{e}yâ* as "drum." Whitcomb suggests "drum" or "tympanum."[19] The list ends with the phrase "all kinds of musick," probably a general reference to other musical instruments playing a lesser role in the ceremony, v. 5.

The herald warns that any who do not worship will be thrown "the same hour [or 'immediately,' *ša^{c}â*]" into a furnace heated with burning fire. The word *ša^{c}â* occurs five times (3:6, 15; 4:19, 33; and 5:5). It is clear from these that it does not mean precisely an "hour." It rather indicates a brief period of time, the length of which is left undefined. Jeremiah 29:21–22 shows that this is not an idle threat. The prophet refers there to two false prophets that were roasted in a fire by Nebuchadnezzar, v. 6. At the "time" (*z^{e}man*, see 2:16) when the music begins, the people prostrate themselves in worship before the image. Since these represent a variety of nations (vv. 2–3), the act symbolizes the submission of nations to Babylon's chief god and therefore to Babylon itself, v. 7.

Accusation of the Faithful Israelites 3:8–18 At that "time" (*z^{e}man*), probably out of jealousy, some of the "Chaldeans" (*kaśday*, see 2:5) approached the king and "accused" (*^{a}kalû qarṣêhôn*) the Jews[20]

---

[18]BDB gives "double-pipe [NIV, 'pipes'] or Pan's pipe." William L. Holladay, *A Concise Hebrew and Aramaic Lexicon of the Old Testament* (Grand Rapids: Wm. B. Eerdmans Publishing Co., 1971), p. 414, gives "bagpipe" (so NASB) but also mentions the view that the word refers to "concord" or "harmony."

[19]Dyer, pp. 433–36; Terence C. Mitchell and Ray Joyce, "The Musical Instruments in Nebuchadnezzar's Orchestra," in *Notes on Some Problems in the Book of Daniel* (London: The Tyndale Press, 1965), pp. 25–27; and Terence C. Mitchell, "And the Band Played On . . . But What Did They Play On?" *Bible Review* 15:6 (Dec. 1999): 39; Whitcomb, *Daniel*, p. 55.

[20]Thomson, p. 100, speculates that the failure to name "the three friends" shows that the purpose of the Chaldeans was to involve "the whole Jewish people." There is nothing in the narrative to hint at any purpose other than an attack on the three Jews mentioned in the narrative. Verse 12 gives the names of the three "Jews."

of not worshiping according to the king's command.[21] Leupold identifies the "Chaldeans" as "the prominent leading class of court astrologers." Henry calls them "some of those magicians or astrologers that were particularly called Chaldeans (ch. ii. 2, 4)."[22] While this is possible, the word also occurs with a general use, 5:30. From its use here, it is likely that the word simply refers generally to the Babylonian leaders without distinguishing any particular group among them.

The phrase *ᵃkalû qarṣêhôn* has as its underlying meaning "to eat the morsels of." Figuratively, it refers to chewing someone up, as by slander or malicious accusations. A similar phrase occurs at 6:24 ("men which had accused Daniel"). Along with Daniel, his three friends, Shadrach, Meshach, and Abed-nego, had refused to compromise their beliefs earlier, during their training period (1:11–16). Now, several years later, they remain steadfast in their determination to honor the Lord. As a result, they become the target of an accusation made for the sole purpose of harming them, v. 8.

After an ingratiating greeting, v. 9 (cf. 2:4), the Chaldeans remind Nebuchadnezzar of his decree to put to death any who fail to worship the image. This failure to bow before the image was a refusal to worship the god represented by the image, vv. 10–11. The Chaldeans then accuse the three Israelites of this failure in worshiping the image. The Chaldeans use the Babylonian names given to the three Israelites, cf. 1:7, the names by which they have come to be known. The gravity of their actions is worsened by their position of leadership "over the affairs of the province," where they would set an example for others. They "have not regarded" Nebuchadnezzar because, by failing to bow down before the image, they have ignored the king's command. Their actions showed that they worshiped a God other than Nebuchadnezzar's god, v. 12.

There is no clear answer to the question about Daniel's absence. The call to attend (v. 2) goes out to governmental officials. Since

---

[21]Henry, IV, 1036, suggests that the three Jews deliberately attended the ceremony. Rather than remaining away, they "being in office thought themselves obliged to stand" in defiance of the king's command. While this is possible, it is probable that they had no choice but to attend the ceremony. Verse 2 indicates that the nation's leaders were brought to give homage to the idol.

[22]Leupold, p. 147; Henry, IV, 1036.

Daniel was "ruler over the whole province of Babylon" (2:48), he clearly held a position of authority over the other wise men. Daniel's three friends were "over the affairs of the province of Babylon," also positions holding governmental responsibilities. A wide range of suggestions have been made to account for Daniel's absence.

Henry offers three reasons. Either (1) Daniel was away on business; or (2) he had permission from the king to withdraw; or (3) he stood so high with Nebuchadnezzar that no one dared complain about him. Thomson adds some other possibilities. (1) His presence may not have been required, or (2) he may have been sick. Lacocque relies on 2:49 to conclude that Daniel was no longer involved in government. He served as a counselor to the king and "may have been somewhere far from the province of Babylon" while these events took place.[23]

The Talmud, in *Sanhedrin* 93*a*, gives three somewhat confusing views. In the first, God kept Daniel away so that people will not say "that they were delivered through his merit." The second view holds that Daniel avoided the scene to keep from fulfilling the prophecy that "the graven images of their gods shall ye burn with fire" (Deut. 7:25). In the final view, Nebuchadnezzar "let Daniel depart, lest people say he has burnt his god in fire."

Bultema tentatively mentions the possibility that Daniel was present and that he briefly bowed before the image. Because of his later faithfulness, the Lord does not let his name occur here.[24] In view of Daniel's faithfulness in other situations, even at the risk of incurring royal punishment (1:8–10; 4:27; 5:17–23), we may reject this suggestion.

Whatever the reason for his absence, Daniel does not record it. It is clear from his character, seen elsewhere in the book, that he either did not worship or was not present at the ceremony. Further speculation can have no value since no proof can be given for any reason that is advanced.

In "rage and fury," the inclusion of multiple terms indicating the extreme nature of the king's anger at the three men who have spurned his command, Nebuchadnezzar commands his servants to bring the Israelites before him, v. 13. The phrase "is it true" ($ṣ^eda^{\circ}$)

---

[23]Henry, IV, 1036; Thomson, p. 101; Lacocque, *The Book of Daniel*, p. 55.

[24]Bultema, p. 126.

has the sense of "is this true?" This is the only occurrence of *ṣᵉdaʾ*.
Nebuchadnezzar's question is not meant to gain an answer. He
knows already what they have done. The question introduces his
offer in the next verse, v. 14, where he gives them a second chance to
worship the statue.[25] If they will worship at the "time" (*ʿiddan*, see
2:8) when the music starts, there will be an implied deliverance from
punishment. If they do not, however, they will be thrown "the same
hour" (or "immediately," *šaʿâ*, see v. 6) into the burning furnace, a
place from which their God will not be able to deliver them, v. 15.

The three men answer the king. The phrase "we are not careful
to answer" is lit. "we do not need to answer." Because they have
already determined not to worship the idolatrous statue, there is no
need to discuss the matter further, v. 16. The phrase "if it be [*ʾîtay*]
so, our God whom we serve is able to deliver us" can be rendered "if
our God exists, whom we serve, He is able to deliver us." The particle *ʾîtay* occurs often in both Ezra and Daniel. When the particle is
without a personal pronoun, the noun following *ʾîtay* is normally the
subject of the particle, e.g., "a man does not exist," 2:10; "men of the
Jews exist," 3:12; "a man exists in your kingdom," 5:11. Here, then,
it refers to God's existence. The men do not doubt His existence.
They rather draw the king's attention to Him. He is a God Who is
well able to deliver them from Nebuchadnezzar's burning furnace.
The statement counters Nebuchadnezzar's assertion that no God can
deliver them from his wrath, v. 17. If, however, He chooses not to deliver them—a possibility since they do not know His intention—they
still will not worship the heathen god represented by the "golden
image."

Note that Shadrach, Meshach, and Abed-nego demonstrate
spiritual obedience and true faith in God. Their actions follow God's
command: "Thou shalt have none other gods before me. Thou shalt
not make thee any graven image, or any likeness of any thing that
is in heaven above, or that is in the earth beneath, or that is in the
waters beneath the earth: thou shalt not bow down thyself unto them,

---

[25]Thomson, p. 102, suggests that the festival dedicating the idol lasted several
days. Nebuchadnezzar will overlook the first failure to worship "if, probably at
the sunrise of the following day, they were willing . . . to fall down and worship
this golden image." Since it is unlikely that the king would have gathered everyone together with the musicians simply to give the three a second chance, this may
indeed explain Nebuchadnezzar's offer.

nor serve them: for I the Lord thy God am a jealous God, visiting the iniquity of the fathers upon the children unto the third and fourth generation of them that hate me" (Deut. 5:7–9). They do not serve the Lord because He will deliver them. They serve Him because He is God and is therefore worthy of service! Regardless of the consequences, they will do right; cf. Job 13:15*a*. There is no hint of compromise here that will let them do good later, v. 18.

Deliverance of the Faithful Israelites 3:19–30 Filled with rage to such a degree that it shows on his face, Nebuchadnezzar orders that the furnace be heated "seven times" hotter than normal. The idiom "seven times" implies the fullness of heat (cf. Lev. 26:18, 24, 28), v. 19. The king orders his "most mighty men," the strongest of the soldiers present, to bind the three Israelites. Smith understands the phrase "most mighty men" as the "most famous of Nebuchadnezzar's warriors." Powell refers the phrase to "the very pick of [Nebuchadnezzar's] body-guard."[26] While these views may be true, the situation here calls for strength. This would prevent the Israelites from resisting at the time when the soldiers throw them into the fire, v. 20.

The binding takes place while the three are still dressed in their court attire. This includes "coats" (*sarbal*). The word *sarbal* occurs only here and in v. 27. Various cognates suggest "shoes" or "trousers." The Vulgate *braccis* supports "trousers." The LXX reads σαραβάροις, "sandals." From the act of binding, I would relate it to some garment enclosed in the rope, likely the "trousers" or, more appropriate to the times, "tunics" or "mantles."

The men wear "hosen" (*paṭṭᵉyšêhôn*, or "garments"). Henry renders this as "breeches," Leupold as "leggings," Bultema as "hose," and Walvoord as "hosen."[27] Both the LXX and Theodotion translate as a form of τιάραις, some form of headdress. The Vulgate renders the word *tiaris*, "caps" or "turbans." This is the only appearance of the word in the OT. The meaning is dubious although, again, the act of binding suggests some garments worn by the men and enclosed in their bonds. BDB suggests "leggings" or "tunic." The three keep

---

[26]R. Payne Smith, *Daniel* (Cincinnati, Ohio: Cranston & Curtis, n.d.), p. 129; F. Ellsworth Powell, *Uncle Frank and Daniel or Pen Pictures from Babylon* (Largo, Fla.: privately published, 1970), p. 47.

[27]Henry, IV, 1040; Leupold, p. 155; Bultema, p. 116; Walvoord, p. 89.

their "hats" (*karbᵉlâ*, or "turbans"). This is the only time that *karbᵉlâ* occurs in the OT. Keil gives "mantles," taking the word from the root *kbl*, "to bind," with an intercalated *rêš*. This root appears in Hebrew but not in Aramaic. Barnes suggests some "outer garment," possibly a cloak.[28] As is so often true with rare words, we cannot be certain of the meaning.

The phrase *"other* garments" (*lᵉbûšêhôn*, or simply "garments") sums up the remaining articles of clothing not mentioned. The word *lᵉbûšêhôn* is similar to the Akkadian word *lubašu* and the Hebrew *lᵉbûš*, both of which also refer to garments. The listing of these garments shows that the young men are fully clothed when the soldiers throw them into the heated furnace. The description of the clothing prepares for the observation made in v. 27. We see there that the Lord fully protects them, even to the extent that there is no smell of burning clothes, v. 21.

The furnace must have been similar to the large brick kilns used in some modern industries. If it were built against a hillside, the top could be reached by an elevated path. It is not surprising that Nebuchadnezzar would have had such a furnace. An estimated fifteen million kiln-fired glazed bricks were used in the king's various building projects. The bricks were fired at a temperature of 850–950 degrees centigrade (≈ 1560–1740 degrees Fahrenheit).[29] The large number of glazed bricks used in the various building projects probably required several large furnaces.

In response to the "urgent" (better "harsh") nature of Nebuchadnezzar's command (v. 19), the furnace has been brought to its highest level of heat. The heat is so great that the soldiers who take the Israelites up the ramp to throw them into the furnace are themselves overcome, v. 22. The description of the furnace's heat makes it clear that the future deliverance of the three men is miraculous. The soldiers manage to push Shadrach, Meshach, and Abed-nego into the furnace. The fact that they are bound, v. 20, is repeated to give still another detail that prepares for the divine deliverance.

Following v. 23, the LXX inserts a lengthy passage commonly titled the *Song of the Three Children*. This supposedly contains the prayer of Azariah in which he praises God, confesses the sins of

---

[28]Keil, p. 129; Barnes, I, 220.

[29]So Wiseman, p. 112.

the nation, and beseeches God's continuing favor. The Vulgate also includes the *Song of the Three Children* but adds a note that the passage is not found in the Hebrew text. This apocryphal song gives the height of the flames as forty-nine cubits, about seventy-three feet, an unlikely height. A brief passage describes the deliverance of the three Israelites. A lengthy section follows in which the three praise God for His deliverance. We have no knowledge of the origin of this passage although, since it appears in these ancient versions, it must have been written early. Since there is no evidence that it belongs with Daniel, it is rightly left out of the Bible and included among the Apocrypha.[30]

The Talmud, *Sanhedrin* 92*b*, describes the "burning fiery furnace" as a pit, dug into the ground. It further describes six miracles that took place. These include (1) the furnace floating upward so that everyone may see the miracle; (2) the partial collapse of the walls; (3) the crumbling of the foundation of the furnace; (4) the image set up by the king being overturned on its face; (5) four kings, and their aides who had helped throw the Israelites into the fire, being consumed; and (6) the prophet Ezekiel raising the dead in the plain of Dura (cf. Ezek. 37). The view is clearly fabricated from someone's imagination, v. 23.

Nebuchadnezzar sits down to watch the death of those who had refused to obey him. In astonishment at what he sees, he rises to his feet in "haste" (*beḥal*, see 2:25). The king rhetorically asks his "counsellors" (*haddabar*), his advisors, if they had not cast three men into the fire. The noun *haddabar* occurs here, v. 27, 4:36, and 6:8. From the association of *haddabar* with other governmental

---

[30]Watkinson, pp. 113–132, follows the Roman Catholic position in accepting the *Song of the Three Children* as well as *Bel and the Dragon* as canonical. He interprets both of the stories as allegories, developing such spiritual applications as come to his mind. Watkinson also interprets the biblical text as an allegory, asserting that inconsistencies exist if it is taken literally. He understands the dimensions of the statue, sixty cubits by six, to equal 360 cubits of surface area. The number 360 represents a complete circle, a symbol of Deity, with the number nine [six cubits], the number of man, contained in it. This represents "a natural projection of the material man" with "the outward signs of the Divine humanity." The three Hebrews represent "the unspotted truths preserved in Babylon," and the fiery furnace is "a false and perverted world." This is enough to show that Watkinson is the authority, and not the Bible. The Introduction discusses the apocryphal writings that relate to Daniel.

leaders, it is clear that it has a similar sense. We cannot tell precisely the nature of their function. The counselors agree that three men had been cast into the furnace, v. 24.

Nebuchadnezzar describes what he now sees. Instead of men that are bound and not able to move, he sees men calmly walking around. Instead of men screaming from the burning flames, he sees men who "have no hurt." Instead of three men, he sees four. Instead of only men, he sees another who is like "the Son of God." *Pesaḥîm* 118*a*, in the Talmud, identifies the fourth person as the angel Gabriel. *Sanhedrin* 95*b* states that Nebuchadnezzar recognized Gabriel because he had survived the destruction of the Assyrian army at Jerusalem (Isa. 37:36) and had seen the angel there. The view is fanciful.[31] Nothing in the account of the destruction of the Assyrian army identifies Gabriel as the destroying angel. Daniel does not identify the fourth person. While this person may have been an angel, the appearance may also have been a theophany, a pre-incarnate appearance of Jesus Christ. The fourth man is like "the Son of God" (lit. "a son of the gods"). In v. 28, Nebuchadnezzar refers to him as an "angel," a messenger of God. We would not expect Nebuchadnezzar to describe the fourth man in Christian terms.

There is no agreement as to the identity of the fourth person. Among others, Driver, Hammer, and Lederach identify him as an angel. Support for this comes from 6:22, in which an angel delivers Daniel from the lions. Psalm 34:7 and 91:11 speak of angels delivering men from their trials. Also among others, Barrett, Gangel, and Wiersbe identify the fourth person as the Son of God.[32] Although I believe that the fourth person was the Lord, it is not possible to be dogmatic with the view. It would have been an encouragement to the three Hebrews to see the Lord they had honored by their refusal to

---

[31] Jack Van Impe, *Final Mysteries Unsealed: Opening the Door to Your Destiny* (Nashville: Word Publishing, 1998), pp. 56–58, understands the king as seeing "a son of one of the Babylonian deities" in the fire. In view of Nebuchadnezzar's reaction in vv. 28–30, this is unlikely. He describes the fourth man as an "angel," and praises "the God of Shadrach, Meshach, and Abed-nego." Van Impe would translate *malʾak* (translated in the KJV as "angel") as "deity," but this is contrary to its normal sense. In Aramaic, the word occurs only here and 6:22. The Hebrew counterpart occurs 214 times, never referring to deity.

[32] Driver, p. 44; Hammer, p. 42; Lederach, p. 86; Barrett, p. 140; Gangel, p. 81; Wiersbe, p. 44.

bow to the idol. On the other hand, angels appear to Daniel in other parts of the book, e.g., 6:22; 9:21, v. 25.

Nebuchadnezzar comes as close to the "mouth" (or "door," t^era^c) of the furnace as he dares. The noun t^era^c occurs only here and at 2:49, where it is translated "gate." The Hebrew counterpart $ša^car$, "gate," employs the normal shift between the $šîn$ and the taw and transposes the $rêš$ and the ^cayin. Since Nebuchadnezzar seated himself in front of the furnace to watch, there must have been an opening of some kind. He calls to the three men to come out. Notice that he addresses them as "servants of the most high God" ($^{>e}laha^{>}$ $^cillaya^{>}$). The name $^{>e}laha^{>}$ $^cillaya^{>}$ is the Aramaic equivalent of the Hebrew $^{>}el$ $^celyôn$. As a name for God, it emphasizes His position with respect to the Creation. He is higher than all else, higher than man or any other god that man can conceive of. The use of the name early in the OT (Gen. 14:18–20, 22) supports the belief that man held a high view of God from the earliest times.

Nebuchadnezzar's reference to "the most high God" shows that he recognizes the God of the three Israelites as higher than his own gods. He had earlier stated that no god could deliver from the fire. He now recognizes a god higher than any he had known before. While not recognizing the uniqueness of Israel's God, this title does place Him as the chief of the gods. In response to the king's call, the three men leave the furnace, v. 26.

The many officials who had gathered to view the execution serve as witnesses to the fact that no harm has come to the three men. As before, v. 2, the "princes" (or "satraps") are governors of various provinces. The "governors" (or "prefects," s^egan, see 2:48) occupy lesser roles of administration over parts of the Babylonian empire. The "captains" (or "governors," $paḥ^awata^{>}$, see v. 2) have an unknown role in administration. The "counsellors" ($haddabar$) serve as advisors to the king. These highly placed Babylonian leaders attest that the fire has not hurt the men. It has not singed their hair. It has not "changed" their "coats" for the worse, i.e., damaged them, significant since they had been walking in the flames. There is not even an odor to show that their clothing has burned, v. 27.

The deliverance of the three men illustrates Isaiah 43:2: "When thou walkest through the fire, thou shalt not be burned; neither shall the flame kindle upon thee." The apocryphal books refer to the deliverance twice: "Bless the Lord, Hananiah, Azariah, and Mishael,

Sing praise to him and greatly exalt him forever. For he has rescued us from Hades and saved us from the hand of death, and delivered us from the burning fiery furnace" (*Song of the Three Children* 1:66); and "Hananiah, Azariah, and Mishael had faith in God and were saved from the fire" (1 Macc. 2:59). The NT also recognizes the faith of the three Jews when it speaks of those who "quenched the violence of fire" (Heb. 11:34). While the passage does not name these men, no other OT incident satisfies the reference.

Before, v. 15, Nebuchadnezzar had thought that no god could deliver the Israelites from the fire. Now he blesses the God of the Israelites. He recognizes that God has sent His "angel" to deliver the three men. They had (1) trusted their God; (2) "changed the king's word," making it ineffective; and (3) risked their lives, all because they had refused to worship any god but their God, v. 28. Nebuchadnezzar therefore issues a decree that no one shall speak "amiss" (or "careless *words*," *šalû*) against Israel's God. The KJV and most modern versions adopt the q^{e}rê, *šalû*, and translate something akin to "amiss." Shalom M. Paul relates the k^{e}tîb to the Akkadian *šillatu*, "blasphemy," i.e., "a verbal offence against humans," and thus "improper speech" against Daniel. In all likelihood, we should relate the k^{e}tîb to the Hebrew *šalâ*, "to be at ease" and thus "careless."[33]

From the phrase "every people, nation, and language," it is evident that this decree is proclaimed throughout Nebuchadnezzar's realm. Anyone defying the decree will be "cut in pieces" (better "made into limbs," *haddamîn*, see 2:5) and his house torn down and left as refuse (*n^{e}walî*, see 2:5). The decree is still that of a heathen king. He recognizes the power of God, but nothing indicates that he has accepted Him as the only true God, v. 29.

Nebuchadnezzar now rewards the three Israelites. The word "promoted" (*ṣ^{e}laḥ*) is better translated as "prospered." The word also occurs in 6:28 and Ezra 5:8; 6:14. In each of these places, it is translated as a form of "prosper." The three men had already been appointed to guide the affairs of the province. Nebuchadnezzar now supports and furthers them in their work over against the opposition of others.

---

[33]Shalom M. Paul, "Daniel 3:29—A Case Study of 'Neglected' Blasphemy," *JNES* 42 (Oct 1983): 291–94.

There is no mention of Hananiah (Shadrach), Mishael (Meshach), or Azariah (Abed-nego) in the remainder of the book. In the Talmud, *Sanhedrin* 93*a* offers several speculative explanations. (1) They died through an "evil eye," the normal cause of death. (2) The nations showed their scorn of the apostate Jews who had bowed before Nebuchadnezzar's idol by spitting on them. "So much spittle collected that the three heroes were drowned in it." This has been explained as a metaphor: The three, by their actions having "caused Israel to be spat on, died to save them from further disgrace." (3) They returned to Palestine, where they married and had children. While the views are interesting, they are clearly fanciful or speculative, v. 30.

NEBUCHADNEZZAR'S TREE VISION 4:1–37

The approach to the events in this chapter differs from that found in the other historical parts of the book. Rather than Daniel giving his description of the events, this chapter gives Nebuchadnezzar's own words. He issues a decree for his empire in which he speaks of the events that have led him to acknowledge Israel's God as "the King of heaven" (v. 37). Led by the Holy Spirit, Daniel includes the decree in his book.

Verses 1–3 in the English Bible are 3:31–33 in the Hebrew Bible. These verses connect better to c. 4, however, than to c. 3. Daniel 3:28–30 gives the outcome of Nebuchadnezzar's experience in c. 3. Rather than continuing the king's proclamation, 3:28–29, vv. 1–3 begin a new thought in this chapter. Nebuchadnezzar's mention of "signs and wonders . . . wrought toward me" (v. 2) connects logically with the events related in the following verses.

Nebuchadnezzar's Dream 4:1–18 The opening words, "all people, nations, and languages, that dwell in all the earth," are a typical exaggeration from an ancient king; cf. 6:25. On the Cyrus cylinder, Cyrus refers to himself as "king of the world, great king, mighty king of the four quarters."[1] Hammurabi, king of the Amorites in ancient Babylon, pictured himself as "the powerful king, the sun of Babylon, who causes light to go forth over the lands of Sumer and Akkad; the king who has made the four quarters of the world subservient."[2] Thutmose III of Egypt described his kingdom: "His southern frontier is to the horns of the earth, to the southern limit *of this land*; [his] northern to the marshes of Asia, to the supporting pillars of heaven."[3] Still, the fact that Nebuchadnezzar addresses his salutation to his whole realm shows the importance of the decree.[4]

---

[1]Trans. T. Fish, in *DOTT*, p. 93.

[2]Prologue to *The Code of Hammurabi*, trans. Theophile J. Meek, in *ANET*, p. 165.

[3]*The Asiatic Campaigns of Thutmose III*, trans. John A. Wilson, taken from *The Temples of Armant. A Preliminary Survey* (London, 1940), in *ANET*, p. 240.

[4]Barnes, I, 244, understands this as a decree to "all the people of the world," including nations not under the control of Babylon. It is difficult to see how Nebuchadnezzar would feel free to interfere with the worship of other nations.

The phrase "Peace be multiplied unto you" is a ritualistic addition to the decree of an ancient king; cf. 6:25. It is equivalent to the Hebrew greeting "Shalom" or the Arabic "Salaam," both expressing the wish for "peace," v. 1. Nebuchadnezzar speaks of the "signs [ʾat] and wonders [tᵉmah]" done by the "high God" (better "most high God," ᵉlahaʾ ᶜillayaʾ, see 3:26) for his benefit. The word ʾat is cognate to the Hebrew ʾôt, a word that normally indicates a religious sign of some kind. From its correspondence to its Hebrew cognate tamah, tᵉmah refers to something that causes astonishment or wonder. In Daniel, ʾat and tᵉmah are always paired together. Both words occur here, in v. 3, and at 6:27. In these places, tᵉmah refers to a display of God's power that brings "wonder" to man, v. 2. Nebuchadnezzar has been so impressed with God's work in his life that he praises God openly in his decree. This is an extraordinary step for the king, v. 3.

The king describes the vision that had come to him while he was resting. This happened at a time when he was "flourishing" (raᶜᵃnan) in the palace, i.e., a time when the kingdom was prospering. The adjective raᶜᵃnan occurs only here in the OT. The Hebrew cognate raᶜᵃnan occurs twenty times and is translated "fresh, flourishing" and, most often, "green." A green plant is one that is flourishing.

It is not possible to date the chapter's events precisely. The LXX notes that the dream took place in the eighteenth year of Nebuchadnezzar's reign. Since he ruled forty-three years (604–562 BC), this would place the dream at not quite the halfway point of his reign. No evidence supports the conclusion of the LXX that the dream occurred in this year. Neither the MT nor Theodotion's translation includes this date.

Wood locates the event "between the thirtieth and thirty-fifth year of Nebuchadnezzar's reign." Whitcomb suggests a date of 570/569 BC for Daniel's warning, about the thirty-fifth year of the king's reign. Clarence Larkin states that Nebuchadnezzar "lived only about a year after his restoration to his throne." He dates his death at 562 BC and places the dream eight years earlier, about 570 BC.[5] While these dates are possible, the lack of evidence to prove the date leaves the actual setting uncertain. Verse 4 describes Nebuchadnezzar as "at rest . . . and flourishing." Verse 30 suggests that his building

---

[5]Wood, p. 99; Whitcomb, *Daniel*, p. 62; Clarence Larkin, *The Book of Daniel*, p. 77.

projects were complete. In my judgment, these verses place the events in the latter half of Nebuchadnezzar's reign. Unfortunately, we cannot date the king's decree more closely than that, v. 4.

Because Nebuchadnezzar has concluded that Babylon's success is due to his leadership (see v. 30), God chooses to teach him the lesson that "pride goeth before destruction, and an haughty spirit before a fall" (Prov. 16:18). The king has a "dream" (*ḥelem*, see 2:28) that makes him "afraid" (*dᵉḥal*). The root *dᵉḥal* refers to something awesome or, more generally, to a frightening experience that causes severe fear, e.g., 5:19 and 7:7, 19 (both "dreadful"). The word "nightmare" probably best describes Nebuchadnezzar's dream. These "thoughts" (*harhor*) and "visions" (*ḥᵉzû*, see 2:28) "troubled" (*bᵉhal*, see 2:25) him. This is the only time the word *harhor* occurs. From the context, it must refer to nightmarish thoughts. The plural "visions" occurs again in v. 9 in such a way as to indicate that these are the various parts included in the king's dream, v. 5.

In ancient times, people took visions seriously, looking at them as means by which the gods communicated with men. Herodotus 1.107, 108, 128 relates two visions of Astyages concerning his daughter. Based on the interpretation of the Magi, he married his daughter to Cambyses, feeling that he would not rebel against him. The second vision caused him to order the death of his daughter's child, a son, lest he rise against him. Later, when Cyrus revolted against him, Astyages had the Magi put to death. Herodotus 7.12–19 tells of several visions received by Xerxes that guided him in the direction of his army.

Some liberal authors relate this dream to an incident in the life of Nabonidus, the final ruler over Babylon. Hartman notes the similarities and differences between Daniel 4 and The Prayer of Nabonidus. He suggests that both stories "go back to an early folk tale first transmitted in oral form." He also states that the Qumran text of the prayer "appears to have preserved the early tale more faithfully than the one in Daniel 4." There is, however, no warrant for making the chapter an adaptation of a nonexistent original. Hammer also comments on The Prayer of Nabonidus. He concludes that "the parallels are too close to be accidental, and it is likely, therefore, that the story in ch. 4 was originally about Nabonidus." Montgomery calls this chapter "historically absurd" and implies a relation to similar secular stories. Porteous refers Nebuchadnezzar's madness to Nabonidus at "his strange retirement to the oasis of Teima at a critical time in his empire's fortunes."[6] There are other explanations for Nabonidus's stay at Tema and no warrant for rejecting Nebuchadnezzar as the central figure here. These suggestions deny inspiration.

In the Dead Sea Scrolls, one fragmentary document found in cave 4 bears the title "The Prayer of Nabonidus." While the document comes from the first century BC, it records a tradition describing events in the time of Daniel. In the prayer, the king tells of being smitten for several years. During this time, he is put away from men. After he confesses his sins, God sends one of the Jewish exiles to tell him he needs to honor God rather than the gods of silver, gold, iron, wood, stone, and clay.

While there are similarities between the biblical narrative and The Prayer of Nabonidus, there are also differences.[7]

(1) the difference in the names of the kings

(2) the difference in the nature of the affliction, Nebuchadnezzar suffering a mental illness and Nabonidus from some skin disease[8]

(3) the difference in the location, Nebuchadnezzar being in Babylon and Nabonidus in Tema

(4) the possible difference in duration, Nebuchadnezzar suffering for "seven times" and Nabonidus for "seven years"

(5) the difference in the time required to reach animal-like behavior, Nebuchadnezzar becoming such in "the same hour" (v. 33), while Nabonidus "came to be *like the animals*"[9]

---

[6]Hartman, pp. 178–79; Hammer, pp. 48–49; Montgomery, p. 222; Porteous, p. 70.

[7]I have made the comparison using the translation of the prayer in *Aramaic Texts from Qumran*, in *Semitic Study Series*, trans. and annotated B. Jongeling, C. J. Labuschagne, and A. S. Van Der Woude, ed. J. H. Hospers, T. Jansma, and G. F. Pijper (Leiden: E. J. Brill, 1976), pp. 121–31.

[8]Jongeling et al., ibid., translate "malignant boils." Others have translated "malignant inflammation" or "severe inflammation." The Hebrew cognate $š^e\hat{h}în$ refers to "boils" or some skin eruption, e.g., Exod. 9:9–11; Isa. 38:21.

[9]The translators have supplied the phrase "like the animals." There is a lacuna at this point. Others have supplied differently, referring to banishment from among men or the changing of his facial appearance. It is possible that the desire to make The Prayer of Nabonidus the basis for Daniel's account has influenced the translators to supply similar words.

(6) the difference in the work of God, Nebuchadnezzar regaining his health by the sovereign work of God and Nabonidus saying of God that "He pardoned my sins" without mentioning any physical healing

(7) the difference in the reference to God, Nebuchadnezzar referring to "the most High" (v. 34) and "the King of heaven" (v. 37) and Nabonidus to "the gods of silver and gold, bronze, iron, wood, stone and clay"[10]

(8) the difference in the timing by the approaching Jew, Nebuchadnezzar being approached before his madness and Nabonidus while still suffering

(9) the difference in the Jew who approaches the king, Nebuchadnezzar being approached by Daniel and Nabonidus by an unnamed "diviner, who was a Jewish man [from the exiles]"[11]

(10) the difference in the timing of the proclamation, Nebuchadnezzar proclaiming the work of God after his healing and Nabonidus doing so in order to gain healing

(11) the difference in the spiritual results, Nebuchadnezzar giving evidence of his conversion and Nabonidus continuing to refer to a variety of "gods"

Because the visions in his dream have brought such a strong emotional response, Nebuchadnezzar calls "all the wise men [ḥakkîm, see 2:12]" in the city to come to him to interpret the dream, v. 6. He summons the "magicians" (ḥarṭom, see 2:10), the "astrologers" (ʾaššap, see 2:10), the "Chaldeans" (kaśday, see 2:5), and the "soothsayers" (gᵉzar, see 2:27). None of these can interpret his vision, v. 7.

Daniel comes "at the last." There are a wide variety of suggestions to explain his delay in coming. Keil concludes that the king had forgotten Daniel's success in interpreting his dream some twenty-five to thirty years earlier. He therefore calls the wise men "without

---

[10]While the translation in *Aramaic Texts from Qumran* refers four times to "God Most High," in every case these words come from a conjecture to fill in a lacuna in the tablet. In the only place clearly referring to deity, the word is ʿly², "gods" rather than "God."

[11]The phrase "from the exiles" is conjectured. Since the lacuna at this point is of a length to allow several words to be supplied, the translation becomes subjective here.

expressly mentioning their president." It is difficult to see how the king could have forgotten the chief officer over his wise men. Henry suggests either that (1) Daniel "declined associating with the rest because of their badness, or they declined his company because of his goodness," or that (2) "the king would rather that his own magicians should have the honour of doing it if they could," or that (3) "Daniel, being governor of the wise men . . . was, as is usual, last consulted." None of these views have much to commend them.[12]

Bultema offers the additional views that (1) it was Nebuchadnezzar's custom to call the lower class of wise men first, or (2) Daniel may have been away or ill. There is no reason to accept the first view. Since Daniel came a relatively short time later, we may discard the last suggestion. Leupold tentatively gives the view that the king "may have been . . . apprehensive about soliciting Daniel's assistance, being mindful of the general purport of the early dream." Cowles makes it the king's usual practice to call the Babylonian interpreters of dreams "to make known to him the significance of this dream." Knoch considers Nebuchadnezzar as being "more or less beside himself." Acting impulsively, he calls the Babylonian wise men first. By calling his Babylonian wise men, he gives priority to the Babylonian gods from whom he hopes to gain understanding of his dream.[13] With this variety of views to choose from, it is clear that the narrative does not give the reason. We can only speculate.

Daniel may have been occupied with administrative responsibilities. His delay may have been deliberate, giving the Babylonian wise men the time to fail. Whatever the reason, the lateness is providential. As in 2:10–11, the "wisdom of this world" fails. The Lord sets the timing of Daniel's entrance so as to emphasize his ability, and thus the ability of his God, over the others and their gods. Where they have failed, Daniel and his God will succeed.

At Daniel's arrival, the king addresses him by his Babylonian name of Belteshazzar, cf. 1:7. This identifies him to those throughout the empire who read the king's narrative. Many of these officials would not have known Daniel by his Jewish name. Nebuchadnezzar describes Daniel as one named after "my god," Bel. Daniel is also a person "in whom is the spirit of the holy gods." The description

---

[12]Keil, p. 146; Henry, IV, 1046.

[13]Bultema, p. 131; Leupold, p. 175; Cowles, p. 318; Knoch, p. 108.

reflects Nebuchadnezzar's pagan beliefs at this time. Although the king had earlier ordered that the people of his kingdom should worship Israel's God (3:29), he still thinks of Him as one among many gods, v. 8.[14]

Nebuchadnezzar also greets Daniel by his title. Daniel is the "master [*rab*, see 2:10] of the magicians [*ḥarṭom*]," i.e., the highest of Nebuchadnezzar's advisors. The king comments once more that Daniel is one "in whom is the spirit of the gods." As in v. 8, the statement reflects the king's polytheism at this time. He asks Daniel to interpret the "visions" (*ḥᵉzû*) of his "dream" (*ḥelem*), v. 9.

Nebuchadnezzar describes the "visions," the different parts of his dream that have come to him while he was sleeping. As the king carefully looked in his dream, a tree dominated the earth "in the midst" (or "center") and had a "great" (*śaggî*, see 2:6) height, v. 10. The tree grew until its top was high in the sky and visible "to the end of all the earth," embracing the full extent of Babylon's rule. Phillips suggests that this is a cedar tree.[15] This is possible. The cedar typically grows to a height of eighty to one hundred feet, with some varieties growing even higher. The cedar elsewhere represents Israel (Ezek. 17:22–23) and Assyria (Ezek. 31:3). Since the narrative does not specify a tree, we should not be dogmatic in identifying it. The meaning of the vision does not depend on the kind of tree seen by Nebuchadnezzar, v. 11.

The foliage of the tree is beautiful. It bears "much" (*śaggî*) fruit. This lets it serve as "meat for all," the source of food for both animals and mankind. Animals rest in its shade and birds nest among its branches, v. 12. As the vision continues, "a watcher and an holy one" come down from heaven. The name "watcher" suggests "a vigilant one," an angel that carefully carries out his commission

---

[14]A. R. Hulst, *OTTP*, p. 224, understands the phrase as a singular, "spirit of a holy God." He concludes that "the writer of the book has interpreted such an apparent, polytheistic expression in a monotheistic way." The view requires Hulst to explain the plural form of the adjective as "an assimilation to agree with the nominal form." Normally, the adjective has the same number as the noun it modifies. With the word "God," the adjective may indeed assimilate to the plural form; cf. Josh. 24:19. It is difficult to believe, however, that Daniel would so have interpreted the words of a heathen king, not only here but also in vv. 9, 18; and 5:11.

[15]Phillips, p. 224.

from God, v. 13.[16] He commands unknown agents to cut down the tree, trimming its branches, stripping off its leaves, and scattering its fruit. The beasts and birds no longer find shelter or food in it, v. 14.

The command of the angel keeps the tree from complete destruction. He orders that "the stump of [the tree's] roots" should be compassed about with "a band," i.e., a "chain," of iron and bronze. The pronouns change now so that the dream is personalized. Nebuchadnezzar "shall be wet" with dew and "his portion [shall] be with the beasts in the grass" of the fields, v. 15. He will receive the "heart," i.e., the understanding, of a beast so that he no longer acts as a normal person. "Seven times" will pass over him (cf. v. 25), v. 16.

Perhaps to humble the king further, God carries out this work through the angels rather than by Himself.[17] The angelic "watchers," also called "holy ones," decree the matter. The purpose is that mankind may know that the "most High" (*illay*) is the power behind human authorities. The word *illay*, "most High," occurs ten times, four times in the phrase "most high God" (or "high God"), 3:26; 4:2; 5:18, 21, and elsewhere at 4:17, 24, 25, 32, 34; 7:25. The word is a shortened form of *elaha* *illay*a, "most high God" (see 3:26), and is comparable to the Aramaic *elyônîn*, "most high," which occurs four times in c. 7 (vv. 18, 22, 25, 27). He alone raises up kings, even establishing "the basest of men," the lower classes of mankind, as rulers, v. 17. Nebuchadnezzar attests to the accuracy of what he has described. His "wise men" (*hakkîm*, see 2:12) have failed him. Still clinging to his pagan view that Daniel possesses "the spirit of the holy gods,"[18] he asks him to interpret the dream, v. 18.

---

[16]Watkinson, p. 135, identifies the "holy one" as Jesus Christ and the "watcher as either "Elias, or John in the spirit of Elias." The view overlooks the fact that both "watchers" and "holy ones" are plural in v. 17. From the grammatical construction, the "holy one" is parallel to the "watcher," i.e., both name the same being.

[17]Lang, pp. 62–63, asserts that "there is a court of superior angels who judge men on earth, and are themselves supervised and judged by Jehovah." The decree of the angels here, however, does not come from a permanent court of angels. The action here is unique. Through the work of the angels, God humbles the proud king. Angels minister on behalf of mankind, Heb. 1:14, while the Lord Himself presides over man's judgment, John 5:22–23.

[18]Calvin, I, 267, considers the phrase "holy gods" as a reference to angels. With the pagan background of Nebuchadnezzar, it refers to the multitude of Babylonian deities.

Daniel's Interpretation 4:19–27 The king's description of his dream troubles Daniel. He is stunned for "one hour" (better "a while," *ša͑â*, see 3:6) and has "troubled" (*bᵉhal*, see 2:25) thoughts. He does not know how to relate the unpleasant interpretation to Nebuchadnezzar.[19] The king encourages him to proceed and Daniel finally speaks. He wishes that the dream would refer to the king's enemies ("the dream be to them that hate thee"), v. 19. He summarizes the dream for the king, vv. 20–21. Nebuchadnezzar himself is the strong tree that dominates the earth and supplies the needs of those who rely on him.

In his interpretation, Daniel refers to the details given in the dream to describe the tree. It is "strong," speaking of Nebuchadnezzar's power in ruling over nations. Its "height" (v. 11) alludes to his greatness as the world's dominant monarch. Its "sight" (v. 11) by all the earth suggests Babylon's dominion over other nations. Its beauty and fruitfulness, with "fair" leaves and "much" fruit (v. 12), calls to mind the prosperity of the empire. The dwelling of "beasts" under its branches and the nesting of "the fowls of the heaven" in them (v. 12) naturally relates to the reliance of the nations on Babylon's protection. All this is true, yet Daniel does not stress this. The message of the dream does not focus on what Nebuchadnezzar has done in the past; it develops what Nebuchadnezzar will experience in the future, v. 22.

The decree of the angelic "watcher," again called a "holy one," is that the tree should be cut down with its stump protected by a chain. It shall be left unprotected in the field until "seven times" (see v. 25) pass, v. 23. Daniel now gives the interpretation decreed by the "most High" (*͑illay*, see v. 17), v. 24. Nebuchadnezzar will be deposed due to mental illness. We can only speculate on the exact nature of the illness. Among others, Pusey and Tatford say that it is *lycanthropy*, the delusion letting a person see himself as a wolf or some other animal. Bultema and Wood represent a second view which holds that

---

[19]Watkinson, p. 137, thinks that a literal view "is too trivial to record." He makes the hour equal one-twelfth of a day. According to Watkinson, the day in Daniel represents 360 years. The hour then is thirty years. "Daniel did not have his prophetic powers fully developed until . . . Belshazzar's reign, some thirty years after" beginning his service at the Babylonian court. This hour thus refers to that period of time. The view shows the fallacy of trying to interpret every period of time by the "day = year" theory.

the king fell into *boanthropy*, a more specific term referring to a person acting like an ox. Thomson calls the illness *acute mania*. With this, a person will show degraded habits, stripping off his clothes, eating garbage, making wild gestures and howling noises, and disregarding personal decency. Nutz and Hammer are among those who hold that Nebuchadnezzar suffered from *zoanthropy*, thinking he is an animal while still retaining his reasoning power and understanding that the "most High" (*ʿillay*) was punishing him.[20] Whatever the nature of the illness, it is clear that the king will be incapacitated for a while, v. 25*a*.

Nebuchadnezzar will be "wet . . . with the dew of heaven" and "eat grass [*ʿiśbaʾ*] as oxen" as he practices animal-like behavior. The word *ʿiśbaʾ* is better "herbiage," i.e., grains, vegetables, etc., that his body could digest. All of this will last for "seven times [*ʿiddanîn*, see 2:8]." This phrase is variously interpreted as seven months, three and one-half years (seven seasons, a possible meaning of "times," embracing summers and winters), seven years, or an indefinite period of time. Auchincloss argues that "seven times" refers to seven months. He bases this on the fact that Nebuchadnezzar's probationary period was twelve months, v. 29, and that "the events in the years of his reign are too well known to admit of a much longer season of affliction." Thomson also supports the meaning of months. Walvoord and Porteous agree that *ʿiddanîn* can refer to seven years or simply to an unspecified period of time. Nutz and Van Impe make it seven years. Leupold considers it an indefinite period, "enough time for God to finish his specific work upon the man . . . more time than a few months. . . . Yet seven years seems too long a time."[21]

Other views have also been suggested. Gowan concludes from the lack of evidence that Nebuchadnezzar was not disabled for any prolonged period and that "the meaning of the bizarre behavior attributed to him should thus be interpreted theologically rather than psychologically . . . the result of seeking to become more than

---

[20]Edward Bouverie Pusey, *Daniel The Prophet* (New York: Funk & Wagnalls, Publishers, 1885), p. 360; Tatford, p. 79; Bultema, p. 142; Wood, p. 121; Thomson, p. 147; Nutz, "Nebuchadnezzar: The Tree Cut Down," *BV* 8:2 (1974): 123; Hammer, p. 52.

[21]Auchincloss, pp. 38–39; Thomson, p. 148; Walvoord, p. 103; Porteous, p. 69; Nutz, p. 123; Van Impe, p. 66; Leupold, p. 185.

human is the loss of humanity." The view ignores the normal meanings of the root ᶜdn. Goldwurm mentions the view held by Malbim (an acronym for his name, Meir Leibush, ben Yechiel Michael), a nineteenth-century Polish rabbi, that the "seven times" were seven different stages of punishment. The view also requires an unusual meaning for "times." Young gives the view of Hippolytus that the phrase may refer to "seven seasons," i.e., seasonal changes of a year, a total of two and a quarter years. The root ᶜdn does not have this meaning. Watkinson presents a fanciful view in which "seven times" is 7 × 360 years, or 2,520 years, "which passes over the church on earth that had lost the spirit of the word."[22]

We cannot be certain of the length of time involved. It may have been seven months, seven seasons, seven years, or an indefinite period. The Babylonian records do not mention any period in which Nebuchadnezzar was unable to rule. It is, however, expected that they would not be negative toward their greatest king. Further, we have a scarcity of documents from the latter years of his rule, so the Babylonian records cannot be relied on here.

Since Daniel uses the word "time" with an indefinite sense elsewhere (2:8; 7:12), it may well have that sense here. The phrase "seven times" would simply indicate a fullness of time. In my judgment, it is doubtful that the Babylonians would have held the throne open for Nebuchadnezzar after a long period of seven years. It is also worth noting that the description uses ᶜiddanîn, "times," not the word šᵉnâ, "year," although šᵉnâ occurs fifteen times elsewhere in the book. In addition, Daniel refers to the time generally in 5:21 ("till he knew . . .") as he speaks with Belshazzar. Finally, Nebuchadnezzar later refers to "the end of the days" (v. 34), a phrase that seems to refer to a shorter period of time than seven years. The time must have been significant, more than a few weeks, since v. 33 describes the king as having hair like "eagles' feathers" and nails like "birds' claws." At the end of this time, Nebuchadnezzar will know that it is God Who is the real power in human government.

The major alternative view equates "seasons" with years, making Nebuchadnezzar go through seven years of madness. Those who give reasons for the view generally cite 7:25 and 12:7, where the

---

[22]Gowan, p. 81; Goldwurm, p. 142; Young, p. 105; Watkinson, p. 136.

word "times" refers to years. This oversimplifies the interpretation of ʿiddanîn. The word refers to "times," which at these references is correctly interpreted as "years." As the discussion at 2:8 points out, the noun ʿiddan may refer to a point in time, an indefinite period of time, or new times (i.e., a change in circumstances) or may be interpreted as a definite amount of time. The context must guide in the sense given to the word. In my view, the context here argues for an indefinite period of time, v. 25b.

The "stump of the tree roots" represents the fact that Nebuchadnezzar will not be completely cut off. Verse 23 notes that there will be a "band" (or "chain") about the stump. The chain likely is some form of restraint that keeps the mad king from wandering away. A variety of other interpretations have been suggested to explain the band. Wiersbe gives the band a symbolic sense, indicating "that [Nebuchadnezzar] was marked by God and protected by Him until His purposes for him were fulfilled." Jerome argues that the chain bound the king to keep him from destroying himself or attacking others. Wood sees it as a fence that symbolizes "the care given by assigned guards as they would watch over Nebuchadnezzar, while allowing him to live in the open with animals." Bevan understands iron and brass as "familiar types of firmness and unflinching severity." This leads him to see the band as picturing "the stern and crushing sentence under which the king is to lie." Keil concludes that it is "the withdrawal of free self-determination through the fetter of madness."[23] These are also possible views. Since the text does not explain the band, we cannot be certain of its purpose. Once Nebuchadnezzar admits that "the heavens," standing by metonymy for God,[24] serve as the power behind his government, the kingdom will be restored to him, v. 26.

---

[23]Wiersbe, p. 52; Jerome, p. 51; Wood, p. 110; Anthony Ashley Bevan, *A Short Commentary on the Book of Daniel* (Cambridge: University Press, 1892), p. 92; Keil, p. 152.

[24]Heaton, p. 151, is inaccurate in his comment that "this is the only time that 'heaven' is used for God in the OT." This is normally true, but there are exceptions. While not using Aramaic, there are places where "heaven" can refer either to the heavenly abode of God and His angels, or to God Himself, e.g., Deut. 32:40; 2 Chron. 18:18. In 2 Chron. 32:20, the word "heaven" clearly refers to God. In the Aramaic of Dan. 4:34, 35, God is also in view.

Daniel now goes beyond mere interpretation to advise Nebuchadnezzar. He urges him to turn away from his sins and to display
righteous actions. Perhaps this will bring "lengthening of thy tran-
quility" (or "prolonging of your prosperity"), turning God's wrath
from him. The advice does not mean that Daniel teaches salvation by
works. The Vulgate translation reads *Peccata tua elemosynis redime,
et iniquitates tuas misericordiis pauperum*, "Redeem your sins by
alms, and your iniquities by kindnesses to the poor." Salvation,
however, has never been conferred as a reward for good works (cf.
Rom. 11:6; Eph. 2:8–9; Titus 3:5). The Bible does not support the
view that man must work to earn salvation. The deliverance from sin
that God offers to man requires a right relationship with Him. This
comes only by faith in Jesus Christ's death as satisfying the penalty
for your sins. Such righteousness will appear, however, in subsequent
good works.

Salvation involves (1) recognizing that you have sinned (cf. Rom.
3:10, 23); (2) knowing that God punishes sinners (cf. Rom. 5:12; 6:23);
(3) realizing that you cannot save yourself (cf. Rom. 4:5); (4) understanding that Jesus Christ can save you (cf. Rom. 10:9–10); and
(5) confessing your sins and asking the Lord to save you (cf. Rom.
10:13). When you repent of your sins and ask Jesus Christ to become
your Savior, God forgives your sins and adopts you into His family.

The faith in Jesus Christ that saves is a complete trust. It is a total
reliance on Him and His atoning death at Calvary as the only means
of salvation. God requires nothing else. Jesus Christ bore your sin
and took the penalty that you deserved. When you confess your sins
to God and tell Him that you believe Jesus Christ died for you, you
take the step that makes you a child of God. Just as Daniel urged
Nebuchadnezzar to act righteously, so you should now live in a manner fit for a member of God's family, v. 27.

Nebuchadnezzar's Experience 4:28–37 All that Daniel has
prophesied comes to pass on the anniversary of the vision.[25] While
Nebuchadnezzar walks, apparently on the flat roof of the palace where

---

[25]Goldwurm, p. 150, asserts that Nebuchadnezzar followed Daniel's advice in
v. 27 and thus his "philanthropy deferred his punishment twelve months." Had he
"kept up his philanthropy, he would have escaped his doom indefinitely." It is more
likely that God graciously gave the king one year to repent rather than that he punished him after his repentance.

he can see the city, he exults in what he has accomplished with his work on the buildings of Babylon and other cities. This is in keeping with what we know of this king. Almost every document from his reign speaks of his building and restoration of the walls, temples, and palaces of the city. He rebuilt the Temple of Esagila at Babylon for the worship of Marduk. He likewise rebuilt the Temple of Ezida at Borsippa for the worship of Nebo. In addition, he carried out various building projects in the cities of Cutha, Erech, Larsa, Sippar, and Ur. At Babylon, he built a new palace for himself and rebuilt one of his father's palaces. He built the Hanging Gardens of Babylon, one of the Seven Wonders of the Ancient World. He built the Ishtar Gate (see the description at 5:5) and many streets in the city. He strengthened the defenses of Babylon and built large loading areas in the port area of the city. It is no wonder that Nebuchadnezzar could look out over the city and call it "great [*rab*, see 2:10] Babylon that I have built . . . by the might of my power, and for the honour of my majesty," vv. 28–30.

At this moment, a voice from heaven announces judgment on him. He will rule no longer, v. 31. Men will drive him from dwelling with them. His madness will cause him to dwell with the wild beasts in the field. He will eat "grass" ("herbiage," ʿiśbaʾ, see v. 25) like grazing oxen. "Seven times" will pass before he knows that the "most High" (ʿillay, see v. 17) rules the kingdom of mankind, sovereignly placing over it whom He will, v. 32. In "the same hour" (i.e., immediately, šaʿâ, see 3:6), Nebuchadnezzar begins to act in an animal-like manner. He is deposed from his rule over the nation and spends his days in the field with wild donkeys (cf. 5:21) where he eats "grass" (ʿiśbaʾ), the grains that sustain his life. His hair and nails grow.

Eusebius (ca. AD 260–340) was born in Caesarea and later rose to become its bishop. Only about one-third of his writings have survived, but his *Ecclesiastical History* is our primary source for information about the early church. In his historical writing about Nebuchadnezzar, he cites a now-lost fragment from the Greek historian Abydenus (second or third century BC) to say that the king "being possessed by some god or other" uttered a prophecy concerning a Persian conqueror and then "immediately disappeared."[26]

---

[26]Eusebius, *Praeparatio Evangelica*, trans. Edwin Hamilton Gifford (Oxford: Clarendon Press, 1903), rpt. *Preparation for the Gospel* (Grand Rapids: Baker Book House, 1981), 9.41.1.

While the quote cannot be related directly to Daniel's account, the reference to Nebuchadnezzar's speech is intriguing. It is possible that the reference to Nebuchadnezzar's disappearance refers to the period of his madness when he was hidden from public view.

At the end of the "days," the period corresponding to the "seven times" mentioned earlier (vv. 16, 23, 25, 32), "understanding" (or "reason," *manda^c*) returns to Nebuchadnezzar. The same word occurs in v. 36, where it is translated "reason." In 2:21 and 5:12, it is translated "knowledge." Since Aramaic has another word for "understanding" and "knowledge" doesn't quite seem to express the sense in c. 4, I have opted for "reason" in these two verses.

Nebuchadnezzar lifts his eyes to God in heaven and praises the "most High" (*^{c}illay*) as the everlasting God Who eternally rules (cf. v. 3) over earth, v. 34. In comparison with this God, the inhabitants of the earth are as nothing. God works out His own will in "the army of heaven," the host of angels that serve Him, as well as in earth. No one can "stay his hand," restraining it from carrying out His will. No one can successfully question His working. Clearly, God has worked sovereignly in Nebuchadnezzar's life. A God Who is so great that He can humble the leader of the world's dominant nation deserves man's worship, v. 35.

At that "time" (*z^eman*, see 2:16), Nebuchadnezzar's "reason" (*manda^c*), the mental processes including knowledge, rational thinking, and understanding, returned. In order that he might take the "glory" of his position as emperor, his "honour and brightness [i.e., appearance, *zîw*, see 2:31]" also returned. His "counsellors" and "lords" once more sought his approval on their decisions. He was established again as the nation's leader with all of the earthly glory that came with the position. The phrase "excellent majesty was added unto me" indicates that the final years of Nebuchadnezzar's reign brought increased glory to him, v. 36. Nevertheless, he gives glory to the God Who works in "truth" and "judgment." He recognizes that God is able to put down those who exalt themselves.

It is possible that Nebuchadnezzar's statement reflects his conversion to faith in God as the God of gods. There is a progression of Nebuchadnezzar's view of God. In c. 2, he praises Him as "a God of gods," the highest among many gods (2:47). In c. 3, he is so impressed with God's power to deliver His servants that he decrees that no one shall speak evil against Him (3:29). In c. 4, Nebuchadnezzar adopts Daniel's description of God as the "most High" (vv. 17, 24, 25, 32, cf. v. 34) and praises Him as the everlasting God Whose reign is forever, v. 34. He speaks of Him as sovereign with no one able to withstand His will, vv. 3, 35. He recognizes the truth and justice of God's work, v. 37. Taken together, these statements likely indicate Nebuchadnezzar's faith in God.

As with many other matters in the book, there are differences of opinion regarding the possibility of Nebuchadnezzar's conversion. Cowles concludes "that the temptations of royalty were too strong for his moral nature to overcome" and that Nebuchadnezzar "would not bow his whole heart to truth and to God." Calvin argues against Nebuchadnezzar's conversion since he "does not embrace the grace of God." Leupold follows Calvin, noting that Nebuchadnezzar admits "God's justice" but says nothing of "His mercy." On the other hand, Henry sees Nebuchadnezzar's conversion as evidence of God's "free grace, by which [the king] lost his wits for a while, that he might save his soul for ever." Wallace refers to Nebuchadnezzar's words as "the personal testimony of a converted soul—his peace." Vines comments that "the last we hear of this pagan king is a thoroughly converted man praising God with all his heart and soul."[27] Good men thus differ on Nebuchadnezzar's conversion. It is not possible to state dogmatically that Nebuchadnezzar possessed saving faith. It is in my judgment, however, a reasonable conclusion, v. 37.

---

[27]Cowles, p. 325; Calvin, I, 304; Leupold, p. 204; Henry, IV, 1053; Wallace, p. 83; Vines, p. 74.

BELSHAZZAR'S FEAST 5:1–31

Message From the Lord 5:1–9 A gap of more than twenty-three years separates this chapter from the events of c. 4. Nebuchadnezzar died in 562 BC, and Babylon fell to Cyrus in 539 BC. The separation of the chapters in years depends on the date assigned to Nebuchadnezzar's madness.

Liberal authors often accuse the book of historical inaccuracy when it refers to "Belshazzar the king." Hartman accuses Dan. 5:1–2 of error in calling Belshazzar the "king" and making Nebuchadnezzar his "father." Later, however, he admits, "Belshazzar was, for all practical purposes, ruler of the Neo-Babylonian empire." After admitting the historical accuracy of the chapter with regard to Belshazzar, he inconsistently calls the account in c. 5 "mostly legend and fiction." Gowan makes the reference to Belshazzar as king a "historical [error]" because the Babylonian records call him the "son of the king [Nabonidus]." He dates the book at 165 BC and assumes that Belshazzar's true position as regent under his father had been forgotten by then. After discussing the cuneiform evidence linking Belshazzar with his father, Montgomery concludes that Daniel's account is "unhistorical." As regent, however, Belshazzar for all practical purposes served as king since his father was absent for most of his reign away from Babylon. The chapter gives the title of "king" to Belshazzar seventeen times. It is inconceivable that this emphasis is in error.[1]

Others, however, have identified him with historical figures from that period of time. Keil equates him with Evil-Merodach. Goldwurm mentions a rabbinical view that he was a son of Nebuchadnezzar. He himself, however, adopts the view that he is a son of Evil-Merodach. Moses Stuart considers the name "a mere appellation or title of honor." Later, however, he identifies Belshazzar with Labynetus, i.e., Labashi-Marduk. Jerome considers him the son of Labashi-Marduk. Clarence Larkin thinks that he was a grandson of Nebuchadnezzar that was adopted by Nabonidus.[2] Josephus *Antiquities* 10.11.2 states that Belshazzar is another name for Nabonidus.

---

[1]Hartman, p. 50; Gowan, p. 86; Montgomery, p. 249.

[2]Keil, pp. 175–76; Goldwurm, p. 156; Stuart, pp. 146, 149; Jerome, p. 55; Clarence Larkin, *The Book of Daniel*, p. 82.

From the Babylonian cuneiform writings, we now know that Daniel 5 is accurate in describing Belshazzar as the king. While his father Nabonidus was the actual king, he was absent from Babylon for many years. During this time, Belshazzar directed the affairs of the nation, serving as its ruler.

According to the cuneiform texts, the Babylonian kings after Nebuchadnezzar include

Amêl-Marduk (Evil-Merodach), Nebuchadnezzar's son, 562–560 BC

Nergal-šar-ʾuṣur (Neriglissar), Nebuchadnezzar's son-in-law, 560–556 BC

Lâbâši-Marduk (Labashi-Marduk), Nebuchadnezzar's grandson, several months in 556 BC

Nabû-nâʾid (Nabonidus), not clearly but probably related to Nebuchadnezzar, 556–539 BC

Evil-Merodach, also known in secular history as Amel-Marduk, was the son of Nebuchadnezzar. Calvin, not having the benefit of modern archaeological information, considered him as reigning twenty-three years.[3] Josephus *Antiquities* 10.11.2 has him reigning eighteen years (although, in *Against Apion* 1.20, he makes it two years). We know now that Evil-Merodach succeeded his father as king and reigned two years, 562–560 BC. The OT mentions him in 2 Kings 25:27 and Jeremiah 52:31, both times in connection with his release of the captured king of Judah, Jehoiachin. We know little of his reign. After ruling for only two years, his brother-in-law, Neriglissar, assassinated him and assumed the throne. Neriglissar ruled until his death four years later.

Labashi-Marduk was the ill-fated son of Neriglissar. After his father's death, Labashi-Marduk, also called Laborosoarchod, ascended the throne of Babylon. His reign may have lasted as few as three months. Josephus *Antiquities* 10.11.2 and *Against Apion* 1.20 quotes the historian Berossus in stating that he ruled nine months. He also quotes Berossus to the effect that those who later placed Nabonidus on the throne assassinated Labashi-Marduk. The cuneiform reference to him calls him a "young" man "who had no ability in governing." Not surprisingly, it also sees him as placed "on the throne of

---

[3]Calvin, I, 305.

the kingdom contrary to divine wish."[4] After his death, Nabonidus came to the throne.

The father of Nabonidus, *Nabû-balâṭsu-iqbi*, was a prince, although we do not know how close his connection was to Nebuchadnezzar. The wife of Nabonidus likely was a daughter of Nebuchadnezzar.[5] The mother of Nabonidus, *Šumûa-damqa*, was the high priestess of the moon god Sin at Haran.[6] Nabonidus also worshiped this god as the chief god rather than Bel or Nabu. Later, his daughter, *Bêl-šalṭi-Nannar*, was high priestess of the moon god Sin at Ur.

Nabonidus served as the leader of a city while under Nebuchadnezzar. This political appointment may suggest some connection to the king. Herodotus 1.74, 77, 188 refers to Labynetus. The reference in 1.74 is disputed. Some think that the name refers to Nebuchadnezzar but others refer it to Nabonidus. In 1.77, 188, Herodotus clearly refers to Nabonidus, who represented Babylon in negotiations with Lydia and the Medes. The background of Nabonidus through his father, and his subsequent activity in government, likely accounts for his replacing Labashi-Marduk as king.

For reasons that are not clear, Nabonidus spent several years, most of his reign, living at the Oasis of Têmâ, located about two hundred sixty miles southeast of Petra and almost five hundred miles southwest of Babylon in the Arabian Desert. His failure to return to Babylon for the annual New Year's feast honoring Bel was typical of actions that alienated the people. Although he ruled seventeen years, 556–539 BC, we know little of his accomplishments. He rebuilt the ziggurat dedicated to the moon god Sin at Ur. Before the fall of Babylon, Nabonidus returned to the city and led the Babylonian army against Cyrus. After he lost the battle, Cyrus received him kindly. He was exiled to Carmania, about 250 miles west of Persepolis, where he died of natural causes a year later.

Bêl-šar-ʾuṣur ("Bel, protect the king"), known to us by the name of Belshazzar, was the son of Nabonidus, king of Babylon.

---

[4]Quoted by Raymond Philip Dougherty, *Nabonidus and Belshazzar: A Study of the Closing Events of the Neo-Babylonian Empire* (New Haven, Conn.: Yale University Press, 1929), 71.

[5]So Dougherty, pp. 40–43; Auchincloss, p. 43; Barnes, I, 281; Gangel, p. 136.

[6]Dougherty, pp. 16–28, discusses the cuneiform records mentioning the heritage of Nabonidus.

Nabonidus spent most of his reign at the Oasis of Têmâ. During this time, Nabonidus left his son to rule in his place in Babylon, ca. 553–539 BC. The Chronicle of Nabonidus says, "He entrusted a camp to his eldest, firstborn son; the troops of the land he sent with him. He freed his hand, he entrusted the kingship to him; then he himself undertook a distant campaign; the power of the land of Akkad advanced with him; toward Têmâ in the midst of the West-land he set his face. . . . He slew the prince of Têmâ with the [sword]; the dwellers in his city (and) country, all of them they slaughtered. Then he himself established his dwelling [in Têmâ]. . . . That city he made glorious. . . . They made it like a palace of Babylon."[7]

Another cuneiform text records "the oath of Nabonidus, king of Babylon, and Belshazzar, the king's son." Theophilus Pinches concludes that this "places Belshazzar practically on the same plane as Nebuchadnezzar [*sic*] his father, five years before the latter's deposition. . . . It seems clear that he was in some way associated with him on the throne, otherwise his name would hardly have been introduced into the oath with which the inscription begins."[8]

Josephus *Antiquities* 10.11.4 refers to Belshazzar as "king." The evidence available from both the cuneiform records and from history supports Belshazzar as serving as regent and having the authority of a king while his father Nabonidus remained at Têmâ. The biblical record is accurate.

At the time of this chapter, Belshazzar is about fifty years old. He had earlier served as "the chief officer of the king [Neriglissar], gaining administrative experience through the responsibilities."[9] Undoubtedly, he had held other administrative positions before this. We assume that he was in his early thirties at the time of his service to Neriglissar, mature and experienced enough to carry the responsibilities. The events of this chapter are about twenty years later.[10]

---

[7]Dougherty, pp. 106–7.

[8]Theophilus G. Pinches, "Fresh Light on the Book of Daniel," *ET* 26 (April 1915): 297.

[9]Dougherty, pp. 67–69.

[10]Price, p. 115, makes the king "not much more than thirty years of age" at this time. Boutflower, p. 114, gives his birth at 575 BC. This makes him about thirty-six at his death. These views go counter to the historical evidence about Belshazzar.

It was customary for ancient kings to hold great feasts, cf. Esther 1:3. Ctesias, born about 416 BC, was a Greek doctor and early historian of Persia and India. He records that the Persian king provided food for 15,000 persons daily in his royal court.[11] The Roman poet Statius, in a poem offering thanksgiving to the emperor Domitian, refers to Caesar hosting the Roman chieftains and knights "reclin[ing] together at a thousand tables."[12] Pliny the Elder, also a Roman, writing in his *Natural History*, mentions that the Roman general Pompey gave "a lavish feast to a thousand guests" and that the Bithynian king Pythes "gave a banquet to the forces of Xerxes" which amounted to 788,000 men.[13]

Belshazzar follows this practice by hosting a "great" (*rab*, see 2:10) banquet with "a thousand of his lords," the number likely being an approximate total of the guests. Herodotus 1.191 and Xenophon *Cyropaedia* 7.5.15, 21, 25 record that the Babylonian leaders were at a banquet on the night the city fell to the armies of Cyrus.

At the banquet, the king drinks wine "before" (*q°bel*) the others, probably on a raised platform that allows the guests to view him. The preposition *q°bel* occurs widely, with a variety of meanings. When taking a spatial sense in 2:31; 3:3; and 5:5, as here, the KJV translates as "before" or "over against." The context does not demand that the king occupy a raised position, but, in view of his position, this is likely. This would place him in view of the guests, "before" them at the banquet, v. 1.

While "he tasted the wine," not merely a sip but rather under its influence, Belshazzar orders the vessels taken by "his father [*°ab*] Nebuchadnezzar" from the Israelite temple to be brought out. Among others, Driver, Hartman, Heaton, and Porteous adopt the view that the record is mistaken in describing Nebuchadnezzar as the "father" of Belshazzar.[14] The relationship may be understood, however, in different ways. The word "father" (*°ab*) corresponds to

---

[11]Referred to in Athenaeus, *The Deiphnosophists*, trans. Charles Burton Gulick (Cambridge, Mass.: Harvard University Press, 1967), vol. II, 4.146.

[12]"Silvae," in *Statius*, trans. J. H. Mozley (Cambridge, Mass.: Harvard University Press, 1961), vol. I, 4.4.31–33.

[13]Pliny, *Natural History*, trans. H. Rackham (Cambridge, Mass.: Harvard University Press, 1968), vol. IX, 33.47.

[14]Driver, p. 62; Hartman, p. 186; Heaton, p. 158; Porteous, p. 72.

the similar Hebrew word, which has a wide variety of meanings. It may refer to a literal father (Gen. 2:24) or grandfather (Gen. 28:13), to ancestors (Gen. 15:15), a man in a position of authority (1 Sam. 24:11), the founder (Gen. 4:20) or protector (Ps. 68:5) of a group, or an advisor to a king (Gen. 45:8). It often refers to God, the One Who had begotten Israel (Isa. 63:16) or held a spiritual relationship to the individual (Ps. 89:26). From 2:23, it is clear that the Aramaic ʾab may have the sense of "ancestor." The term here may thus refer to Nebuchadnezzar as the "father" (5:2, 11 [3X], 13, 18) of Belshazzar in his heritage as Nebuchadnezzar's grandson. The word may also refer to Nebuchadnezzar as a king that had gone before Belshazzar.

The Talmud, *Megillah* 11*b*, records the Jewish tradition that Belshazzar calculated that the Jews had been in captivity for more than seventy years: forty-five years under Nebuchadnezzar, twenty-three under Evil-Merodach, and three under himself. Since Jeremiah's prophecy told of their deliverance after seventy years, Belshazzar concluded that "of a surety they will not be redeemed." He therefore ignored Israel's God and used the vessels from their temple. While an interesting story, it assigns wrong lengths to the reigns of the Babylonian kings.[15]

Long before, the prophet Jeremiah had predicted that the temple vessels would be taken to Babylon (Jer. 27:21–22). The presence of the "wives [*šegᵉlateh*][16] and concubines" at the feast agrees with what we know of banquets in ancient times.[17] Herodotus 5.18 mentions the presence of Persian women at banquets. The presence of women at the feast suggests that the occasion was social, and not an official meeting to consider the siege of the Medes and Persians or other political problems, v. 2. After the temple vessels arrive at

---

[15]Goldwurm, pp. 157–58, also adopts the view that the Babylonian kings knew of Jeremiah's prophecy that the Jews would return from captivity after seventy years (Jer. 29:10). When this time passed without the return of Israel, the Babylonians assumed that they had triumphed over Israel's god. "They proceeded to desecrate the vessels of the temple without fear of retribution." Belshazzar miscalculated the starting date and therefore offended God by his actions. It is more likely, however, that the judgment came more for Belshazzar's overall wickedness than for this one action.

[16]The Talmud, *Rosh Hashanah* 4*a*, translates *šegᵉlateh* as "Queen." The word, however, is plural here and in vv. 3 and 23.

[17]Leupold, p. 216, understands the presence of the king's wives and concubines as evidence of degeneracy at the feast.

Belshazzar's feast, the Babylonians use them as common drinking vessels. The use of these vessels may have served as an example to show the power of the Babylonian gods as being above the gods of other nations, v. 3.

The Babylonians praise their heathen gods. The description "gods of gold, and of silver, of brass, of iron, of wood, and of stone" hints at the numerous deities worshiped by the Babylonians. Several cuneiform texts refer to gifts by Belshazzar to various temples devoted to Babylonian gods.[18] Whether the praise of these gods at this time is deliberate or not is of no importance. The end result of the action is that the Babylonians use vessels sanctified to the Lord's service and turn them into means for worshiping their false gods, v. 4.

"In the same hour" (or "at that time," *šaᶜâ*, see 3:6), Belshazzar sees the "fingers" (*ʾeṣbaᶜ*) of what appears to be a man's hand writing on the plastered wall. The last half of the verse describes this as "part [*pas*] of the hand." There are a wide variety of views as to the meaning of *pas*. Hartman refers it to the "palm," which he defines as "the hand from the wrist to the tips of the fingers." Heaton makes it the "back" of the hand. Young calls it the "extremity," which he defines as "the hand from the wrist to the tips of the fingers." Stuart also translates as "extremity," which he considers just the "fingers." Keil interprets it as the "end of the hand," i.e., the fingers. Knoch understands it as "fingertip." Jerome presents the novel view that it refers to the "joints of the hand." Theodotion translated ἀστραγάλους, "wrist," referring to the whole of the hand. Porteous translates "palm" but makes the hand one that writes on the wall behind him so that Belshazzar sees the palm as he looks up. It is, however, unlikely that the writing occurred behind the king.[19]

The word *ʾeṣbaᶜ* elsewhere refers to either "toes" (2:41, 42) or, as here, "fingers." The Hebrew cognate to *ʾeṣbaᶜ* also refers to fingers or toes (e.g., Exod. 8:19; 29:12; 2 Sam. 21:20). Verse 5*b* notes that the king saw the "part" (*pas*) of the hand that wrote. The word *pas* occurs elsewhere only in v. 24, where it parallels the sense here. A corresponding Hebrew noun (*passîm*, occurring only in describing a robe) is always translated "colours" in the KJV, but this translation is

---

[18]Dougherty, pp. 87–91.

[19]Hartman, p. 184; Heaton, p. 159; Young, p. 120; Stuart, p. 130; Keil, p. 181; Knoch, p. 133; Jerome, p. 57; Porteous, p. 78.

conjectured. BDB suggests "flat of hand or foot" as though the robe reached to the palms and soles. KB offers "palm of the hand, sole of the foot." The corresponding Hebrew root *pss* occurs only in Psalm 12:1, where it is rendered "fail," i.e., vanishing. This lends support to referring *pas* to the end of the hand, the fingers. Since the king observed the hand from across the room, it probably does not refer to the palm, unseen from Belshazzar's perspective.

We can only speculate on whose hand was seen. Bultema and Van Ryn refer to the "hand" as that belonging to Jesus Christ.[20] While this is possible, it is conjectured. The account does not make this clear. Most commonly, the writing is thought to be that of God Himself. Calvin, Tatford, Strauss, and Vines all suggest that the hand of God Himself writes to give Belshazzar the message. To justify this, they often refer to Exodus 8:19, "this is the finger of God," and Exodus 31:18, where the tablets of the law were written "with the finger of God."[21] Against this is the human appearance of the hand (5:5), and the fact that God elsewhere in the book communicates with man by means of visions (e.g., 4:10–17; 7:1–14; 8:2–14) or by angels (e.g., 7:16–27; 8:15–26; 9:21–27). Whatever view we take, we cannot be certain in identifying the writer.

Archaeologists excavated Babylon between 1899 and 1918. The inner part of the city covered about 500 acres and had a population of about 100,000 people. The Euphrates River flowed through the middle of the city. The Babylonians laid out the streets at right angles to one another. A wall surrounded the inner city. Outside the wall was the suburban part of the population. Mud houses and reed huts housed the people. Around this area was another wall about ten miles long. This outer wall was thirty-six feet wide, enough to let troops move along the perimeter of the city. Nebuchadnezzar built the Ishtar Gate, decorated with 575 brick-relief dragons and bulls, in 575 BC. The gate, one of eight gates to the inner city, opened on the north side of the city into the processional street. A smaller reconstruction of this gate, containing much of the original material, is located now in the Pergamon Museum in Berlin. The reconstruction is forty-seven feet high and one hundred feet wide. The processional

---

[20]Bultema, p. 160; August Van Ryn, *Daniel: The Man and the Message* (Kansas City, Kans.: Walterick Publishers, 1969), p. 52.

[21]Calvin, I, 315; Tatford, p. 83; Strauss, pp. 154–55; Vines, p. 78.

street was over one-half mile long and sixty-three feet wide and was paved with red and white stone slabs. Enameled tiles showing 120 lions decorated the walls along the street. A reconstructed portion of this street is also in the Pergamon Museum.

The city included several temples. The worship of Bel (Marduk), the chief god of the city, took place at the Temple of Esagila, located near the center of the city. The Hanging Gardens of Babylon, built by Nebuchadnezzar for his wife, were on the north side of the city. Enameled lions elaborately decorated Nebuchadnezzar's palace.

From archaeology, we know there was a large court in the center of the palace. Next to this was a large chamber, about 56' × 170', which served as the king's throne room[22] and would have been appropriate for large banquets. The hand writes directly across from the king, "over against" (or "before," i.e., opposite, $q^o bel$, see v. 1) a "candlestick" ($nebrašta^{\,\flat}$, or "lampstand") that lighted it. In the context here, "over against" the king is on the "opposite" wall, where he could see the fingers writing. Although $nebrašta^{\,\flat}$ occurs only here, early translations of the OT support the translation "lampstand." Theodotion translated it λαμπάδος, "torch, lamp," and the Vulgate *candelabrum*, "candlestick, lampstand." This was not just a simple candleholder, but rather an ornate fixture with enough candles or torches to illumine the writing from a distance, v. 5.[23]

Belshazzar is so shaken by the writing that his "countenance [$zîw$, see 2:31] was changed," i.e., becoming pale rather than its normal swarthy color, and his thoughts "troubled" ($b^e hal$, see 2:25) him. In addition, "the joints [$q^e tar$] of his loins were loosed," i.e., he was not able to stand. Goldwurm understands the translation of the phrase "joints of his loins were loosed" as "the belt around his waist opened." The plural word "joints" (or "knots") either indicates that he wore several belts or that he had several fasteners in one belt. Due to fright, his loins constricted, letting the belt open. While the translation is conceivable, it is unlikely that the king's waist would

---

[22]Authorities give different dimensions for the throne room, all within a foot or two of the above. I have taken these numbers from James G. MacQueen, *Babylon* (New York: Frederick A. Praeger, 1965), p. 170.

[23]Thomson, p. 164, suggests that this was the golden candlestick from the Jews' temple. While this is possible, since the vessels from the temple had been brought in, it is speculative. The text does not identify the candlestick.

constrict to the point of letting his belt open. Wolters understands
$q^e\underline{t}ar$ as "knots." He refers this to the sphincter muscle, the loosing
of which leads to incontinence. The repetition of the word in vv. 12
and 16 becomes "a mocking and ironic allusion to this ignominious
incontinence on the king's part." To explain vv. 12 and 16, he makes
the speakers—the queen mother and Belshazzar himself—fail to
understand the meaning, while it "is obvious to the readers of the
story."[24] The view is unlikely. BDB and KB both give the meaning of
"joints" in v. 6. While the sense of "knots" lies in the background of
the word's development, by Daniel's time this sense no longer dominates. It is unthinkable that either the queen or Belshazzar would
use the word without awareness of what they were saying. Note the
contrast between the insolent actions of Belshazzar before and his
fearfulness now, v. 6.

Belshazzar "cried aloud" (lit. "called with strength"), i.e., loudly.
He is frightened and desperate for understanding. He calls for the
"astrologers" (ʾaššap, see 2:10), the "Chaldeans" (kaśday, see 2:5),
and the "soothsayers" (gᵉzar, see 2:27) of the kingdom. He speaks to
them all as "wise men" (ḥakkîm, see 2:12) and asks them to interpret the writing. He does not call Daniel, who, because of his age, is
probably no longer over the wise men at this time.

As an incentive, the king offers great honor to the one that
interprets it. "Scarlet" (ʾargᵉwanaʾ) is lit. "purple," a royal color.
The Aramaic ʾargᵉwanaʾ occurs only here and in vv. 16 and 29.
The Hebrew cognate ʾargaman refers to the similar color. People in
places of authority wore purple (cf. Exod. 28:15, 33; Esther 8:15).
The tabernacle of Israel widely used fabric with this color (Exod.
36:8, 35). The golden chain may also have marked royalty (cf. Gen.
41:42). Several references in the Apocrypha (1 Esd. 3:5–7; Jth.
10:21; Ecclus. 40:4; 1 Macc. 8:14; 10:17–20; 11:57–58; 14:41–45)
suggest that purple cloth and gold jewelry marked royalty and other
highly placed officials. Xenophon, writing in *Anabasis* (1.5.8; 1.8.29;
2.2.27) and *Cyropaedia* (1.3.2; 2.4.6), also associates gold and purple
with nobility.

In addition to the visible symbols of royalty, Belshazzar offers to
reward the one who interprets the writing with a high position: he

---

[24]Goldwurm p. 161; Al Wolters, "Untying the King's Knots: Physiology and
Wordplay in Daniel 5," *JBL* 110 (Spring 1991): 117–22.

shall "be the third [taltî] ruler" (better "have authority as third") in
the kingdom. There is disagreement about the meaning of taltî (and
the related form, talîtî, which occurs in 2:39). Leupold refers taltî
to a position of leadership, i.e., "shall occupy the position of 'talti'
in the kingdom." Heaton is similar, making it simply a "high officer
under the king." KB suggests that taltî originally referred to an Assyrian title of an official, either third in rank or ruling over a third
part of the empire. Charles objects that neither taltî (here) nor talta᾽
(vv. 16, 29) occurs elsewhere as an ordinal. He understands Daniel
as one of three rulers, i.e., as ruling over one-third of the kingdom.[25]
It is highly unlikely, however, that Belshazzar would offer Daniel a
position equal in rank to himself.

Shea argues that the Babylonians did not practice co-regency.
He suggests that Belshazzar had heard of the defeat of Nabonidus
by Cyrus. He thus proclaims himself king to give authority to his
leadership. The banquet in this chapter likely celebrated this new
position. Against the view is the historical statement in the *Nabonidus Chronicle* that Nabonidus "entrusted the kingship" (Dougherty, p. 106) to Belshazzar.[26]

Keil expresses an older view, developed before archaeology
revealed more information about Nabonidus and Belshazzar. He
suggests that the government was a triumvirate "regulated by the
Median king Darius." The view violates the historical record given
in Daniel. Ford understands the phrase "third ruler" as "an idiom for
a superior officer." When a literal meaning makes sense, there is no
reason to adopt an idiomatic one.[27]

The word is generally considered as an ordinal. With the normal interchange between the *tau* and the *šîn*, taltî corresponds to
the ordinal šᵉlîšî in Hebrew. Since this form occurs only here in the
Aramaic portions of the OT, we cannot be dogmatic. The identification of taltî as an ordinal, however, agrees with what we know of
Babylonian history at this time, a nation ruled by both Nabonidus
and Belshazzar. The frightened Belshazzar may well have offered an
exalted position of leadership to whoever interprets the writing.

---

[25]Leupold, p. 222; Heaton, p. 159; Charles, pp. 126–27.

[26]William H. Shea, "Nabonidus, Belshazzar, and the Book of Daniel: An Update," *AUSS* 20:2 (Summer 1982): 141–43.

[27]Keil, p. 184; Ford, p. 129.

Becoming the "third [*taltî*] ruler" would be to take a leadership position behind Nabonidus and Belshazzar. In addition to increased power in the land, the *taltî* would lead the nation in the absence or sickness of Nabonidus and Belshazzar. Since Nabonidus was already absent, the position held great promise for influence in the nation, v. 7. The "wise men" (*ḥakkîm*), however, are not able to read or interpret the message.

The Talmud, *Sanhedrin* 22*a*, gives several views: (1) None except Daniel could read it. (2) The message was a cryptograph giving either a numerical value for each word or a cipher produced by the permutation of the letters. (3) The message followed the ʾ*at baš* principle with the letters interchanged, the first with the last, the second with the next to last, etc. (4) The letters were written left-to-right rather than right-to-left. (5) Daniel moved the second letter of each word to its beginning.

Goldwurm gives several rabbinical views to explain the difficulty of interpretation, some of which duplicate the views given in the Talmud: (1) The words were written in the squared script used today rather than the older form of Hebrew. (2) The words developed a code, with each letter of the alphabet substituted for its counterpart from the other end of the alphabet. (3) The words were out of sequence with the message reading *aalrn mmtws nnqpy*. (4) The letters were written as three five-letter words with the message being written vertically rather than horizontally. (5) There were five groups of three letters each, with the groups arranged vertically; the message required reading every fifth letter with the first word composed of letters 1, 6, and 11, the second of letters 2, 7, and 12, etc. (6) The words were written backwards.[28]

Rembrandt, in his painting of the scene, adopted a rabbinical view that the words were written vertically. Archer suggests the possibility that the "writing was in symbols unlike any known to the wise men." Albrecht Alt argues that the consonants were "ohne Trennung der Wörter von einander," without separation of the words from one another. Millard states that the Babylonian wise men had "catalogued thousands of ominous signs." This writing, however, was new to them and therefore could not be interpreted. Calvin offers the

---

[28]Goldwurm, p. 163.

thought that either the writing was visible to the king but concealed
from the wise men or God sent a stupor that prevented the wise men
from understanding the message. Brewer proposes "that the inscription was a number written in cuneiform, which was translated into
Aramaic and then interpreted."[29]

Donald C. Polaski thinks that these words referred to monetary
values: *mene* to the minah, *tekel* to the shekel, and *parsin* to the half-
minah. The wise men saw no meaning in this, but Daniel's "clever
(mis)reading of the list [made] it 'significant' for Belshazzar." Kraeling also agrees with the idea that the words refer to coins. He sees
the repeated *mene* as representing Neriglissar and Amel-Marduk, the
tekel standing for Labashi-Marduk, and the plural *parsin* indicating
Nabonidus and Belshazzar.[30]

All of these suggestions are speculative. We do not know why
the wise men could not read the message. It may well be that the
phrase "could not read the writing" indicates that they could not read
it with understanding. The message *m^{e}ne$^{\jmath}$ m^{e}ne$^{\jmath}$ t^{e}qel parsîn*, i.e.,
"Number, Number, Weigh, Divide" is nonsensical without spiritual
enlightenment.

Although they may have proved themselves by solving man's
problems, they are once more powerless to solve God's message,
cf. 2:10–11; 4:7, v. 8. As before (2:11; 4:7), the natural man cannot
understand spiritual truth (cf. 1 Cor. 2:14). When they fail to give an
interpretation to Belshazzar, he becomes "greatly [*śaggî$^{\jmath}$*, see 2:6]
troubled [*b^{e}hal*, see 2:25]." His "countenance" (*zîw*) changes, giving
evidence of his emotions. His inability to know what is clearly a
divine message gives rise to fear, v. 9.

Interpretation of the Message 5:10–29 The "queen" is likely
the queen mother, Nito-cris, the wife of Nabonidus and possibly
the daughter of an earlier king.[31] She exercised a great amount of

---

[29]Archer, p. 71; Albrecht Alt, "Zur Menetekel-Inschrift," *VT* 4 (1954): 303–5;
Alan Millard, "Daniel and Belshazzar in History," *BAR* 11 (May–Jun 1985): 77;
Calvin, I, 322; David Instone Brewer, "*Mene Mene Teqel Uparsin*: Daniel 5:25 in
Cuneiform," *TB* 42 (Nov 1991): 310–16.

[30]Donald C. Polaski, "*Mene, Mene, Tekel, Parsin*: Writing and Resistance in
Daniel 5 and 6," *JBL* 123 (Winter 2004): 657; Emil G. Kraeling, "The Handwriting
on the Wall," *JBL* 63 (1944): 17–18.

[31]Josephus *Antiquities* 10.11.2 identifies her as the grandmother of Belshazzar,
i.e., Nebuchadnezzar's widow. William H. Shea, "Nabonidus, Belshazzar, and the

influence in Babylon since her husband, Nabonidus, was gone for at least fourteen of his seventeen years of rule. Herodotus 1.185–86 tells us that under her directions, the channel of the Euphrates River was re-routed north of Babylon to make a potential approach by the Median army more difficult. She earlier had caused a bridge to be built across the Euphrates River in Babylon to connect the two halves of the city. She apparently died following the fall of Babylon to Cyrus and the death of her son Belshazzar.

She has not been at the banquet but has heard of the event, probably through her servants. After greeting the king,[32] she advises him not to be "troubled" (b^ehal) or to show fear on his "countenance" ($z\hat{\imath}w$), v. 10. The most likely explanation as to why Daniel had not been called with the other wise men is that he no longer held an official position.[33] Daniel went into captivity in 605 BC. Babylon fell October 13, 539 BC. If we assume that Daniel was 18 years at the time of his captivity, he would have been 85–86 years old at this time. Belshazzar may well have replaced Daniel with a younger man. In the intervening years, he had forgotten him and, in fact, no longer recognized him due to the changes brought about by age.

Daniel is old at this time, at least in his upper eighties, and likely no longer carries a full load of responsibilities in the court. The queen, however, remembers that Nebuchadnezzar had made him "master" (rab, see 2:10) over "the magicians [$hartom$, see 2:10], astrologers [$^{\jmath}a\check{s}\check{s}ap$, see 2:10], Chaldeans [$ka\acute{s}day$, see 2:5], and soothsayers [g^ezar, see 2:27]." She suggests that Belshazzar call him.

Book of Daniel," p. 138, tentatively adopts this view. Dougherty, pp. 60–63, and Cowles, p. 327, suggest that Nito-cris was a daughter of Nebuchadnezzar. This is possible, perhaps probable, but can only be inferred from the cuneiform references to Nabonidus and Nito-cris.

[32]See the discussion of the phrase "O king, live for ever" at 2:4. Leupold, p. 211, suggests that the queen was a young widowed queen of Nebuchadnezzar that Nabonidus married to gain standing among the Babylonians. He also mentions the possibility that Nabonidus had adopted Belshazzar, a son of Nebuchadnezzar. This view, however, violates a Persian inscription that refers to Belshazzar as the "eldest, firstborn son" of Nabonidus (Dougherty, p. 106).

[33]Hammer, p. 64, sees a conflict with 8:27, where it speaks of Daniel carrying out the business of Belshazzar. Chapter 8, however, takes place in Belshazzar's third year, while the events here occur about eleven years later, hours before Babylon's fall in 539 BC. Daniel may well have left an active service to the king in these additional years.

Knowing of Daniel's past service to the nation, the queen commends him to Belshazzar as one who is led by "the spirit of the holy gods." This is the Holy Spirit, although we would not expect her to phrase it in a monotheistic way. See also 4:9; 5:14; 6:3; Romans 8:5; Galatians 5:16, 25; Ephesians 5:18. The description testifies to the fact that Daniel had consistently given God the credit for the decisions that he made, v. 11.

Nebuchadnezzar had recognized Daniel's "excellent spirit," his "knowledge" and "understanding," his "interpreting of dreams," his "shewing of hard sentences," and his "dissolving of doubts." The phrase "dissolving [$š^era^{\circ}$] of doubts [q^etar]" is more literally "loosing knots," a metaphor for solving knotty problems. The word q^etar occurs three times, all in this chapter (vv. 6 ["joints"], 12, 16). It is thought to refer to a knot in which the rope forms a joint (cf. v. 6) as it passes across another part of the rope. This follows the verb $š^era^{\circ}$, "to loosen," i.e., to untie the knot. This description of Daniel heaps up superlatives as the queen mother seeks to persuade Belshazzar to call for Daniel. The reference to Daniel being named by Nebuchadnezzar (cf. 1:7) likely refers to a general command from the king that the Jewish men were to receive Babylonian names, v. 12.

After Daniel arrives, the king rhetorically identifies him as the same Daniel that had come in the captivity of the Jews. The question may or may not show that Belshazzar was acquainted with Daniel's past history. The earlier conversation with the queen mother recorded here is likely a summary. Belshazzar may actually have received more information about Daniel, v. 13. He repeats the comments of the queen mother. He has heard that Daniel is led by "the spirit of the gods," again the Holy Spirit. The words "light," "understanding," and "excellent wisdom" are parallel, all referring to Daniel's skill in giving interpretations, v. 14. Other "wise men" ($hakkîm$, see 2:12), including the "astrologers" ($^{\circ}aššap$, see 2:10), have not been able to interpret the writing, v. 15. He has heard of Daniel's ability to "dissolve doubts," again solving knotty problems. He makes Daniel the same offer of honor and material reward as he has earlier made to the other wise men: "scarlet" ("purple," $^{\circ}arg^ewana^{\circ}$, see v. 7), a gold chain, and the position of being the third ($talta^{\circ}$) ruler.

The Aramaic word $talta^{\circ}$ differs slightly in vv. 16 and 29 from that given in v. 7 ($taltî$). BDB suggests the words are different, although both related to the thought of a "third" in some way. KB makes them variant spellings of the same word. It is possible that the form *talta²* is emphatic, denoting determination, "the third" (cf. *²alpa²*, "the thousand," 5:1; *qadmay²ta²*, "the first," 7:4; *r²bî²ay²ta²*, "the fourth," 7:19, 23), v. 16. Daniel responds, making it clear that the interpretation is not for the purpose of personal "rewards" (*n²bizbâ*, see 2:6); cf. Genesis 14:23; 2 Kings 5:15–16.[34] Later, in v. 29, the situation is different. At that point, there was no hint that Daniel had interpreted the writing for personal gain. To refuse the king's honor then would have insulted Belshazzar, v. 17.

Daniel reminds the king that it was the "most high God" (*²laha² ²illay²a*, see 3:26) who had established Nebuchadnezzar his "father" as king and given him glorious success, v. 18.[35] As a result, other nations "feared" (*d²ḥal*, see 4:5) him. He held absolute power, sovereignly judging and promoting others, v. 19. But when Nebuchadnezzar let pride dominate him, he became mad and temporarily lost the throne, v. 20. He was as a wild beast, living in the fields with wild donkeys, eating "grass" (*²iśba²*, see 4:25) and becoming wet from the dew, until he recognized the sovereign rule of the "most high God" (*²laha² ²illay²a*), v. 21.

In his rebuke of the king, Daniel refers to him as the "son" of Nebuchadnezzar. Just as Nebuchadnezzar is addressed as Belshazzar's "father," vv. 2, 11, 13, 18, so Belshazzar is Nebuchadnezzar's "son." Corresponding to the Hebrew *ben*, the Aramaic *bar* has a variety of meanings. It may refer to a literal son (Ezra 5:1), a legal son (Zerubbabel, Ezra 5:2), a divine being (Dan. 3:25), or even to age (Dan. 5:31). Daniel uses the word here to refer to Belshazzar's position in following Nebuchadnezzar as king of the nation.

---

[34]Bultema, p. 167, suggests that the customary greeting, "O king, live for ever" (2:4; 3:9; 5:10; 6:6, 21) was "a sign of communion." Daniel's failure to use this indicated his rejection of "even the least communion with this base mocker of Israel's holy things." But cf. 2:27; 4:19, where Daniel addresses Nebuchadnezzar without this formal greeting. He is about to refuse the king's offer of reward. A formal greeting was not appropriate at this point.

[35]Leupold, p. 230, refers "majesty" to the king's "ability to manage the kingdom," "honour" to that which "results from successful administration of office," and "glory" to "the well-deserved reputation that grows up among men." This same combination of words occurs again at 4:30. Leupold's view goes beyond the normal use of these words and of their cognates in Hebrew. It is more likely a piling of superlatives meant to stress the glorious position held by Nebuchadnezzar.

Belshazzar has known these things. Although several kings had ruled between Nebuchadnezzar and Belshazzar, only a few years had intervened. Evil-Merodach ruled two years, Neriglissar for four years, and Labashi-Marduk for a few months. In these years, Belshazzar had been involved with governmental affairs and would likely have known of Nebuchadnezzar's plight. Even if Nebuchadnezzar's madness occurred as much as twenty years before his death, Belshazzar would have been alive at the time. Such an unusual humbling of the great king Nebuchadnezzar would have stood out. Belshazzar would not easily have forgotten such an event, v. 22.

Despite this knowledge of God's power, Belshazzar has arrogantly lifted up himself against the God of heaven. He has taken vessels sanctified to the service of God and used them in a profane way. He has praised the heathen gods instead of giving praise to the true God, v. 23. God, therefore, has sent the message to Belshazzar. The "part of the hand" refers here to the fingers that held the writing implement. Note Daniel's courage in speaking boldly to the king, v. 24.

Daniel first reads the message, something the other wise men had not been able to do sensibly (v. 8), v. 25. He then gives the interpretation of the writing to Belshazzar. The word "mene," doubled in v. 25 to give emphasis, means "numbered."[36] God has numbered the days of the kingdom and brought it to its end. This use of numbering is seen elsewhere (Job 14:5; 15:20; Ezek. 4:5), v. 26. The word "tekel" means "weighed." The OT regularly refers to God weighing a man to see if he measures up to the divine standard (e.g., 1 Sam. 2:3; Job 31:6; Ps. 62:9; Isa. 26:7). Belshazzar has been weighed in God's balances and found lacking according to God's standards, v. 27. The word "upharsin" includes the conjunction u, "and," and the verb parsîn, "divide." Taken together, the message says that Belshazzar's kingdom has been numbered, with its days fixed. God has weighed Belshazzar in His balance and found him wanting. His kingdom, therefore, will be divided, taken away from Babylon, and given to the Medes and the Persians, v. 28.[37]

---

[36]Gowan, p. 89, calls the text "puzzling," since v. 26 makes no reference to the doubling of mene in v. 25. There is, however, no need to repeat or refer to the doubling since this would have been readily seen to emphasize the statement.

[37]Lacocque, The Book of Daniel, p. 103, sees the words as referring to Babylon, Media, and the Persians, the sequence implying that Babylon is about to be

Belshazzar now shows his lack of spiritual discernment. He promptly forgets Daniel's warning and proceeds as though everything is normal. Despite the presence of an enemy besieging the city, he shows no concern that Daniel's interpretation might soon come to pass. He heaps material rewards on Daniel and proclaims his new position as the "third ruler" of the kingdom, v. 29.

Judgment of the King 5:30–31 In "that night," during the revelry of the banquet, the Medo-Persian army takes the city. Babylon's fall fulfills the prophecy in which Isaiah describes the Babylonians as setting their table with food, enjoying themselves at a banquet (Isa. 21:5). Jeremiah 51:39, 57 also alludes to this. Darius the Mede (Dan. 5:31; 6:1, 6, 9, 25, 28), called Gubaru in ancient records, becomes the ruler. He was the son of Ahasuerus (Dan. 9:1) and governed in Babylon under the authority of Cyrus the Great, who "made" him king in Babylon (Dan. 9:1). His rule covered roughly the area in the "fertile crescent," Palestine, Syria, Phoenicia, the Mesopotamian Valley, and some area to the east of that. His decree "unto all peoples, nations, and languages, that dwell in all the earth" (Dan. 6:25) reflects the custom of that time of exalting the king by exaggerating the extent of his rule. The invaders put Belshazzar, king of the "Chaldeans" (*kaśday*, see 2:5), to death.[38]

Hilton mentions the legend which states that Belshazzar's death came when "Cyrus and Darius crushed his skull with a branch from the *menorah* [the candlestick of v. 5] while he was on his way back from the privy in the night."[39] While perhaps of interest, the story has no basis in either the Bible or history.

The Cyrus who ruled the victorious Medo-Persian alliance rose to this position from a lesser role as a minor king. Cyrus led his troops to overthrow his grandfather Astyages, the Median king, ca.

---

replaced by the Medes and they, in turn, by the Persians. Lacocque sees the whole account as fictional, developed by a second-century-BC author as a posthistorical explanation of the succession of the kingdoms. The view rests on a wrong dating of the book and the rejection of an inspired text.

[38]Thomson, pp. 172–73, follows the LXX to translate, "And the interpretation came upon Belshazzar the king." He concludes that the fall of Babylon may have been "six, eight, or ten years" later. The LXX translation of Daniel is, however, often inaccurate. Theodotion follows the MT. Thomson's view ignores the biblical statement of Belshazzar's death.

[39]Michael Hilton, "Babel Reverses—Daniel Chapter 5," *JSOT* 66 (1995): 102.

559 BC. Allying the Median army to himself, he marched north to attack Lydia, ruled by the fabulously wealthy king Croesus. His first encounter was inconclusive. But Cyrus followed the Lydians and surprised them. After stampeding their horses, he drove their army back into Sardia. After scaling that city's wall, his troops overcame the Lydian resistance, 546 BC. The Ionian and coastal Greek cities surrendered to him. He then marched to Babylon and overcame that city without significant resistance, 539 BC.

Shortly after the conquest of Babylon, Cyrus issued the decree that let the Jews in the Captivity return to Palestine. Zerubbabel led the first return in 536 BC. The remainder of Cyrus's rule was marked by building projects, especially his palace in Pasargadae, the capital of ancient Persia located a little more than fifty miles northeast of Persepolis in the area occupied by present-day Iran. At the end of his reign, nomadic tribes in the east rebelled against him. Cyrus was killed in battle, 530 BC. His tomb is located at Pasargadae.

Cyropaedia is an imaginative history of Cyrus the Great written by Xenophon. This early historian lived ca. 430–355 BC. After studying under Socrates, he served as a Greek soldier in the Persian army. After the death of their generals, he was chosen as one of the leaders of the army. He later wrote essays and several histories.

According to *Cyropaedia* 7.5.1–36, Cyrus the Great, emperor of the Medo-Persian alliance, ordered the Euphrates River diverted into ditches that his army had dug. The army then marched along the bed of the river under the walls of Babylon into the city while the Babylonian leaders caroused. After entering the city, they attacked the palace and killed the king and many of the nobles.[40] Daniel 11:1 indicates that Darius received angelic help in the conquest. The nature of the help is not made clear. The account given in Herodotus 1.190–91 also supports the biblical record that Cyrus captured Babylon by a surprise attack while the Babylonian leaders caroused at a banquet.

---

[40]Lester L. Grabbe, "The Belshazzar of Daniel and the Belshazzar of History," *AUSS* 26:1 (Spring 1988): 60–61, asserts that Belshazzar did not die on the night of Babylon's fall. He argues that neither the *Nabonidus Chronicle* nor Berossus say anything of Belshazzar's death at the conquest of the city. Berossus wrote more than two centuries after the event and may not have had access to the full record of Belshazzar's death. Nabonidus, being his father, may not have wished to dwell on his son's death. In any case, Grabbe argues from silence, not from actual evidence. This does not justify setting aside the biblical account.

The *Nabonidus Chronicle* 3.16 dates the fall of Babylon on the 15th day of Tishri. This places the conquest of the city by the army under Darius at the end of September, 539 BC, v. 30.

In the MT, v. 31 is 6:1. The thought of the verse connects it better with c. 5. The MT recognizes this connection by leaving a space between 6:1 and 6:2. After the conquest, Darius the Median "took" (better "received") the kingdom, serving as a vassal king under Cyrus, v. 31. The "kingdom" was the Babylonian kingdom previously ruled by Nabonidus and Belshazzar, not the Persian Empire that remained under Cyrus. There is archaeological confirmation of this event. The *Nabonidus Chronicle* says, "Cyrus entered Babylon and they waved branches before him. Peace settled on the city (and) Cyrus proclaimed peace to Babylon. Gobaru [i.e., Darius], his district-governor, appointed local governors in Babylon."[41]

Liberal authors often deny the position of Darius as king over Babylon. Grabbe closes his study by saying that "there is no room for a king named Darius the Mede . . . early in Cyrus' reign." Driver states that "contemporary monuments allow no room for a king, 'Darius the Mede.'" Rowley describes Darius as "a fictitious creation." Porteous asserts that the "supposed existence" of Darius is the result of "a historical blunder." Later, he concludes that "Darius is almost certainly a figment of the writer's imagination," created to fulfill the biblical prophecies of a Median king between the fall of Babylon and the rise of Persia. Charles is similar. He refers to Darius as a "mythical king" invented to fulfill the prophecies of Isaiah 13:17; 21:2; Jeremiah 51:11, 28.[42] These views, of course, set aside the truth of the biblical record.

Some liberal authors, however, along with others holding a more conservative position, identify Darius with historical figures. Colless identifies Darius as Cyrus the Great. Wiseman, followed by

---

[41]D. J. Wiseman, "Historical Records of Assyria and Babylonia," in *DOTT*, p. 82. Nabonidus, the final ruler of the Neo-Babylonian Empire (556–539 BC), is also called Nabunaid in the Babylonian records. He is not named in the OT. The *Nabonidus Chronicle* records the major events taking place in Babylon during the almost seventeen years of his reign.

[42]Lester L. Grabbe, "Another Look at the Gestalt of 'Darius the Mede,'" *CBQ* 50 (1988): 211; Driver, p. 70; H. H. Rowley, *Darius the Mede and the Four World Empires in the Book of Daniel* (Cardiff, Wales: University of Wales Press Board, 1964), p. 5; Porteous, pp. 47, 83; Charles, p. 141.

Walvoord, adopts this same position.[43] Shea identifies Darius with Gubaru, the general who captured Babylon. He advances the position that Daniel served as governor of Babylon until his death. He places this shortly after the beginning of Cyrus's third year of rule; cf. 10:1. At this point, a second Gubaru takes the position.[44] Later, in a second article, he abandons this identification and adopts the position advocated by Wiseman, that Darius is another name for Cyrus.[45] The view that identifies Darius with Cyrus faces the difficulty of making Cyrus the son of Ahasuerus; cf. 9:1.

Boutflower identifies Darius with Cambyses. Both the age and relationship of Darius to Ahasuerus argue against this. The Persian inscriptions tell of the elevation of Cambyses to co-regency with Cyrus several years later. Tatford suggests that Darius is Astyages, the son of Cyaxares, a Median king. He, however, would have been older than the sixty-two years given in 5:31. Hasel tentatively makes Darius a title used by Cyaxares II, the uncle of Cyrus and father-in-law of Cyrus. Taylor also equates Darius with Cyaxares II. Once again, the age of Darius argues against the view. Horner argues for Gobryas, the commander of the army that took Babylon. The inscriptions, however, tell us that Gobryas died about three weeks after entering the city, while Darius ruled several years. Lacocque misidentifies Darius as Darius Hystaspes, the king preceding Xerxes and not his son (con. 9:1). Hammer sees the mention of Darius as "a possible confusion with the capture of Babylon by Darius I . . . in 520 BC after an uprising." Daniel's account is not confusion. In declaring his burden against Babylon, Isaiah (21:1) forecasts its fall to Elam and Media. Jeremiah 51:11, 28 prophesies that Babylon

---

[43]Brian E. Colless, "Cyrus the Persian as Darius the Mede in the Book of Daniel," *JSOT* 56 (1992): 113–26; Wiseman, pp. 9–16; Walvoord, p. 134.

[44]William H. Shea, "A Further Note on Daniel 6: Daniel as 'Governor,'" *AUSS* 21:2 (Summer 1983): 169–70.

[45]William H. Shea, "Darius the Mede in His Persian-Babylonian Setting," *AUSS* 29:3 (Fall 1991): 238–39, 243, 252. To explain the mention of Ahasuerus as the father of Cyrus (9:1), Shea relates the Hebrew ʾaḥašwerôš to the Old Persian name of Cyaxares, *uvaxštra*. He admits that "the correspondence is not perfect" but concludes that "there are enough resemblances so that the words can be recognized as related to one another." In my judgment, Shea stretches the association to support his view.

will fall to the Medes. The record in Daniel is consistent with these prophecies.[46]

Whitcomb has considered the arguments for and against the various positions.[47] He concludes that Darius is best taken as Gubaru, an otherwise unknown individual mentioned many times in Babylonian inscriptions. The name "Darius" is apparently an honorific title given to him in his position as ruler over Babylon and the surrounding regions. I have followed Whitcomb's view in this.

From the account of c. 6 as well as incidental references in 9:1 and 11:1, it is clear that Darius is the Median of 5:31, the son of Ahasuerus (9:1). It is further clear that he ruled at a time when the Medes and Persians were allied (5:28; 6:8, 12, 15). Cuneiform records frequently mention a Gubaru (with several variant spellings) who serves as governor over Babylon during the reign of Cyrus the Great. Gubaru is also often identified as the general of the army that captured Babylon. That view, however, poses a chronological problem since Ugbaru, the name of the general in the cuneiform records, died a few days after the conquest. Gobaru, the governor of Babylon, ruled at least until the reign of Cambyses over the empire. It is better to understand Darius as Gubaru without associating him with the army. The phrase in 5:31 is "Darius the Median took [or 'received,' qabbel] the kingdom." The pa^{c}el verb qabbel may be translated with "take" or "receive." In the book of Daniel, however, the sense of "receive" fits in all three occurrences, here, 2:6; and 7:18. It is cognate to the Hebrew verb qabal, also "to take, receive." The use of the verb suggests that he ruled under Cyrus, the only one with power to designate those sub-rulers who served him in administering the empire.

---

[46]Boutflower, p. 145; Tatford, p. 93; Gerhard F. Hasel, "The Book of Daniel: Evidences Relating to Persons and Chronology," *AUSS* 19:1 (Spring 1981): 47; William M. Taylor, *Daniel the Beloved* (New York: Harper & Brothers, Publishers, 1878), p. 105; Joseph Horner, *Daniel, Darius the Median, and Cyrus* (Pittsburgh, Pa.: Joseph Horner, 1901), p. 98; Lacocque, *The Book of Daniel*, pp. 109, 179; Hammer, pp. 65–66.

[47]John C. Whitcomb, *Darius the Mede: A Study in Historical Identification* (Grand Rapids: Wm. B. Eerdmans Publishing Co., 1959).

A LION'S DEN 6:1–28

Plot Against Daniel 6:1–9 Cyrus the Great appoints Darius (discussed at 5:31) as the leader of Babylon and of the region in which most of the biblical history takes place. In this position, it is appropriate to refer to him as king. As part of his governmental organization, he appoints 120 "princes" (*ʾaḥašdarpᵉnayyaʾ*, better "satraps," see 3:2) as governors over the various portions of his dominion, v. 1. Three "presidents" (i.e., "administrators") lead the group.

Josephus *Antiquities* 10.11.4 refers to 360 provinces. This (apparently) confuses the biblical record by assigning 120 provinces to each of the three presidents. The *Nabonidus Chronicle* states that Darius "appointed local governors in Babylon."[1] While this does not give any number, it supports the biblical account of leaders set by Darius over the area ruled by him. Esther 1:1; 8:9; 9:30; and 1 Esdras 3:2 refer to 127 provinces. In the Talmud, *Megillah* 11*b* explains the difference by saying that Darius did not rule over seven of the provinces. It is more likely that Darius organized his kingdom differently by combining some of the smaller regions and thus having fewer satraps ruling under him.

The main responsibility of these "three presidents" seems to have been financial, with the lesser administrators giving "accounts unto them." This let the king avoid "damage," shortages in collecting taxes, v. 2. Daniel's natural abilities, augmented by the leading of the Holy Spirit, allow him to become the most influential of these administrators.[2] Darius may have been influenced by Belshazzar's

---

[1]*Nabonidus Chronicle*, "Historical Records of Assyria and Babylonia," in *DOTT*, trans. D. J. Wiseman, p. 82.

[2]Watkinson, pp. 163–68, continues his scheme of numerology in the chapter. Considering the account "taken literally [as] a very improbable story," he develops an interpretation from the numbers. The three represents the three Babylonian kings: Nebuchadnezzar, Belshazzar, and Darius (*sic*). The three presidents suggest the Trinity. Daniel represents the Holy Spirit, "not yet in power but subordinate" to Darius. The thirty-day length of Darius's decree is "three cycles of 360 years which is 1080 years." This time from Darius brings us to 424 AD, about the time when Theodosius decreed that the Roman Empire should follow Christianity. This suggests that the three Babylonian rulers represent three eras: Nebuchadnezzar, the phase of idolatry given to image worship; Belshazzar, perversion and desecration of the Word; and Darius, intolerance in the practice of religion. There is more, but this is enough to show the foolishness of an overemphasis on numerology.

proclamation of Daniel as the third ruler in the kingdom. Undoubtedly, his reputation for wisdom would have been widely known in Babylon, v. 3.

While the text does not give any reason for the opposition of the other administrators, it is clear that they are jealous of Daniel's position. They cannot, however, find any point on which they may attack him. Daniel is not only faithful in his worship of God but also faithful in his administrative responsibilities. His enemies find no occasion to accuse him and no "fault" (or "corruption," $š^eḥat$). While the word $š^eḥat$ occurs only three times, twice here and in 2:9 ("corrupt"), it is closely related to the Hebrew cognate $šaḥat$, "to become corrupt." It is appropriate to give it the sense of "corruption," some weakness in Daniel's work that would let his foes accuse him.

Authors have advanced a wide variety of possible reasons for the princes' animosity. Lang and Henry suggest that the other leaders may have sought devious means to gain wealth and seen Daniel as an obstacle to their plans. Knoch and Wiersbe mention the possibility that the accusation may be a way to rid themselves of an older man who kept the younger princes from gaining authority. Bultema and Thomson see the Medo-Persian leaders as resentful that a Jew held authority over them. Keil and Jerome understand the other administrators as being jealous of Daniel's authority. Leupold and Vines mention the possibility that the incident may reveal a wicked reaction against Daniel's godliness, v. 4.[3]

The leaders decide to strike at Daniel through his faithfulness to "the law [*dat*, see 2:9] of his God." Notice the clarity of Daniel's testimony that lets others seize on it as something through which they can attack him. He does not have a secret witness. He does not hold one standard while he is with the heathen and another standard when he is with Jewish friends. He is faithful, and the Medo-Persian leaders see this as a point at which they can attack him, v. 5.

The events of the chapter take place ca. 537 BC. Babylon's fall occurred late 539 BC. It is reasonable to assume that the organization of the government and appointment of governmental officials took several months. After an additional time, perhaps one or two years,

---

[3]Lang, p. 71; Henry, IV, 1062; Knoch, p. 150; Wiersbe, p. 74; Bultema, p. 179; Thomson, p. 186; Keil, p. 207; Jerome, p. 64; Leupold, p. 251; Vines, p. 85.

the jealousy of the other leaders causes them to scheme against Daniel.

The other "presidents" (or "administrators") and some of the "princes" (or "satraps") of the kingdom "assembled together" (*r^egaš*, or "thronged together") to Darius. The word *r^egaš* only occurs in vv. 6, 11, and 15 of this chapter. It is cognate to the Hebrew *ragaš*, "to be in tumult, commotion." While the cognate verb *ragaš* occurs only at Psalm 2:1 ("rage"), a related noun occurs with a sense of noise or disturbance at Psalm 64:2 ("insurrection"). The excitement here reflects their enthusiasm for the plot against Daniel.

It is doubtful that all of the administrators join in this plot.[4] A group of over one hundred men would have been unwieldy. Later, v. 24, it is unlikely that Darius commands that a group of several hundred, including the wives and children, be cast into the lion's "den" (*gob*, or "pit"). Several of the most outspoken satraps join the two presidents in coming to Darius and greeting him, v. 6.[5] They mislead him by saying that they represent "all" of the nation's leaders. These include the "presidents" (or "administrators"), "governors" (or "prefects," *s^egan*, see 2:48), "princes" (or "satraps," *^{ɔa}hašdarp^enayya^ɔ*, see 3:2), "counsellors" (*haddabar*, see 3:24), and "captains" (or "governors," *pah^awata^ɔ*, see 3:2).

They ask Darius to issue a "royal statute" and "firm decree" that no one shall pray to anyone other than himself for thirty days. Heaton thinks it unlikely that Darius would have proscribed the practice of private prayer. He concludes that "the writer has borrowed a traditional tale and given it a new setting in the reign of Darius and a new hero in Daniel." Montgomery considers the account one of a series of "apocryphal" stories in the book. These liberal views reject the inspiration of Scripture and are not worthy of serious consideration. Thomson suggests that Darius was "a timid ruler," fearing nothing "more than a religious riot." Darius accepts the suggestion of the administrators since it effectively forbad all religious observances that might cause strife among the people. The suggestion is ludicrous. There is no hint in Babylonian history that

---

[4]King, pp. 191, 199, includes all of the 120 princes except Daniel in the proposal that Darius issue the decree forbidding prayer to anyone other than himself. I have answered this view above.

[5]See discussion of the greeting at 2:4.

Darius was weak. His quickness later in punishing the leaders of this plot argues that he was forceful.[6]

Such a decree would have appealed to the king's ego. It would also solidify his authority over the people and would test their willingness to submit to him. The thirty-day period is long enough to accomplish these goals, yet short enough so as not to offend the normal religious tendencies of the people.[7] From the religious writings that have survived from this time, we know that prayer was an important part of Babylonian religion. Various texts that relate to Nabonidus, the Cyrus Cylinder, the Babylonian Theodicy, and the Counsels of Wisdom, all mention prayer.[8] The king was regarded as divine, the earthly representative of the gods.

Anyone violating this decree will be cast into "the den of lions," v. 7. According to "the law [dat, see 2:9] of the Medes and the Persians," this decree could not be changed. Diodorus Siculus, a first-century Greek historian, tells of a decree in which Darius III condemned one of his military leaders, a man named Charidemos. Later, Darius changed his mind but was not able to reverse his own decree.[9]

The book of Esther also illustrates this characteristic of Medo-Persian law. Ahasuerus issues a decree condemning the Jews and allowing their property to be taken as spoil (Esther 3:2–12). Later, after the death of Haman and following Esther's plea, he issues a second decree giving the Jews the right to defend themselves from attacks (Esther 8:11–13). In this way, he makes his will known even though the first decree is still in effect (cf. Dan. 6:12, 15; Esther 8:8), v. 8. Darius agrees to the decree and signs it into law, v. 9.

---

[6]Heaton, p. 165; Montgomery, p. 268; Thomson, p. 186.

[7]In the Apocrypha, the book of Judith records a similar incident. Holofernes, the Assyrian general under Nebuchadnezzar, defeated the Syrians. Other groups in Palestine, fearing his power, sent leaders to negotiate a peaceful settlement. He brought his army into the region and "broke down all their frontier landmarks and cut down their groves, and he succeeded in destroying all the gods of the country, in order that all the nations should worship Nebuchadnezzar alone, and that their tongues and tribes should call upon him as god," Jth. 3:8 (Goodspeed's translation).

[8]T. Fish and W. G. Lambert, in *DOTT*, pp. 89–90, 93–94, 99, 106.

[9]*Diodorus of Sicily*, trans. C. Bradford Welles (Cambridge, Mass.: Harvard University Press, 1963), VIII, 203.

Faithfulness of Daniel 6:10–24 Knowing of the decree, Daniel continues to pray to God as he has done before.[10] He kneels before the windows that face toward Jerusalem.[11] The practice of facing toward Jerusalem naturally follows Solomon's prayer (1 Kings 8:28–48). In this prayer, he mentions praying toward the temple eight times (vv. 29, 30, 33, 35, 38, 42, 44, 48). The psalmist mentions the practice (Pss. 5:7; 28:2; 138:2). From the inside of the "great fish," Jonah made this same pledge (Jon. 2:4). In earlier times, the Lord dwelled in the Holy of Holies at the temple. It became natural to face in that direction and, even though the temple no longer existed at this time, Daniel continues the practice, praying three "times" ($z^e man$, see 2:16) each day (cf. Ps. 55:17). These prayers took place at the times of the morning and evening sacrifices (cf. 1 Chron. 23:30) and at midday. The Talmud, *Berakoth* 31*a*, enjoins this same practice of praying three times each day while facing toward Jerusalem. Even today, orthodox Jews follow this practice.[12]

Daniel's outward posture of kneeling reflected his inward attitude. While kneeling in prayer is an appropriate posture that reflects one's submission to God, the Bible does not command any one position for prayer. The OT gives us examples of different postures during prayer. Abraham's servant prayed while standing by a well (Gen. 24:12–14). Jacob prayed while wrestling with the Lord (Gen. 32:26). Hezekiah prayed while lying down (2 Kings 20:2). Nehemiah prayed while sitting down (Neh. 1:4) and standing before his king (Neh. 2:4). It is not the position of the body that is important in prayer but rather the attitude of the heart. The NT command to "pray without ceasing" rules out the need for any one position during prayer. Since

---

[10]Goldwurm, p. 180, expresses the view that Daniel changed his habit of praying publicly in the synagogue "where he no doubt prayed up to now." He prays at home instead so as "not to anger the king." He justifies this with the rabbinical teaching that the rule that "one must let oneself be killed rather than transgress" applies only to the cardinal sins of "idolatry, immorality, and murder." The view is speculative and goes against the description of Daniel's prayer life seen throughout the book.

[11]In the Talmud, *Berakoth* 34*b* records the trivial view of Rabbi Ḥiyya ben Abba. Based on this verse, he taught that "a man should not pray save in a room which has windows." This is contrary to both the example set elsewhere, e.g., Abraham, Jonah, and the teaching of 1 Thess. 5:17.

[12]*The New Encyclopedia of Judaism*, ed. Geoffrey Wigoder (Washington Square, N.Y.: New York University Press, 2002), p. 614.

the open windows in his house faced toward Jerusalem, Daniel kneeled before them as he prayed.

Prayer was so important that Daniel chooses to obey God's command (e.g., Luke 18:1; 1 Thess. 5:17) rather than the king's decree. By praying, he follows the example of Samuel (1 Sam. 12:23), David (Pss. 17:1; 55:1), Solomon (1 Kings 8:54), Jeremiah (Jer. 42:4), and many others. The other tests of the faith of Daniel and his friends involved sins of commission (1:8; 3:18). The failure to pray would have been a sin of omission.

Although the windows were likely covered with some latticework, Daniel is visible through them. He goes into his "chamber" (or "roof chamber," ʿillî), where his enemies can see him through his window. This is the only occurrence of ʿillî in the OT. It is, however, related to the Hebrew ʿalâ, "to go up," and the derived adjective ʿillî, "upper," and noun ʿalîyâ, "roof-chamber," v. 10. His adversaries "assembled" (or "thronged," rᵉgaš, see v. 6) outside his house to spy on him. Their excitement comes from their anticipation of trapping Daniel.

Keil understands that Daniel's enemies "rushed into the house while he was offering his supplications." Leupold describes the group as "coming thronging in." The word rᵉgaš occurs three times in Aramaic, 6:6, 11, 15. In neither v. 6 or v. 15 is the sense of "thronging in" appropriate. While a throng may have gathered, such a group would not come bursting in to the king. The cognates in Hebrew may have the sense of a noisy group (Ps. 2:1) but may also refer to a more orderly group ("company," Ps. 55:14).[13] Nothing here requires that his adversaries do anything more than excitedly gather to watch Daniel through the windows of his house. Not surprisingly, they find him carrying out his customary prayers. The fact that Daniel's enemies went to his home to watch him praying suggests that this was Daniel's regular habit, not something adopted out of expediency, v. 11.

Having observed Daniel praying, his enemies accuse him to the king. This was the whole purpose of their actions in vv. 6–9. They lead the king to comment on his decree that forbids prayer. He agrees that he has made the decree, even noting that it is an unchangeable decree, "according to the law [dat, see 2:9] of the Medes

---

[13]Keil, p. 213; Leupold, p. 262.

and the Persians, which altereth not," v. 12. This lets Daniel's foes accuse him of violating the decree by praying three "times" (z*eman*) each day to his God. In the accusation, they call him one "of the captivity of Judah." This is likely meant to demean him as being one of a lower group within the nation. They hopefully seek to prejudice the king against him.

The accusation that Daniel prays "three times a day" shows that his enemies had waited for at least a couple of days before making their charge against him. The original decree from Darius would have been issued some time during the day. It would have then been proclaimed throughout the city so that all would know of it. The Medo-Persian leaders probably began their watch on Daniel the next day and continued it to be certain that he had not changed his habit of praying in the morning, midday, and evening. Later (v. 14), the king spends several hours until "the going down of the sun" trying to find a way to avoid carrying out the punishment. This suggests that the accusation comes in the middle of the day, probably the third or fourth day after the decree.[14] This would explain why they begin by reminding Darius of his decree, something he may well have forgotten if it occurred several days before, v. 13.

When Darius hears the accusation, he realizes that his decree has been a mistake. He is "sore [or 'greatly,' *saggî*, see 2:6] displeased." It is likely that he has come already to recognize Daniel's abilities in his leadership role and does not want to lose this. He sets his "heart" (or "mind") on a way to change his decree, keeping up his efforts until sundown. The indication of time shows how speedily Medo-Persian justice was executed, v. 14. His nobles "assembled" (r*egaš*) before the king, once more excitedly anticipating the end of their plot against Daniel. Although Darius tries to change his "law" (*dat*),

---

[14]A. S. van der Woude, "Zu Daniel 6,11," *ZAW* 106 (1994): 123–24, argues that the spying, observing, and accusation came on the first day following the decree. He sees the pronoun *hûʾ* as a demonstrative pronoun. He concludes, "Dan Pronomen *huʾ* soll nicht mit *barek* ["he kneeled"], sondern mit *bᵉyômaʾ* ["in that day"] verbunden werden!" Even granting that *huʾ* serves as a demonstrative pronoun—a view that is debatable—the narrative still suggests a longer period of time. The reference to praying "three times" alone requires a full day. Gathering the group at Daniel's residence, spying, accusing Daniel to the king, the need to remind the king of his decree, and the king's effort to evade the consequences of his decree combine to support a longer period of time.

the nobles will not permit this. They point out that his decree is not subject to change, v. 15.

Reluctantly, the king commands that Daniel be cast into the lion's "den" (or "pit," *gob*).[15] The noun *gob* occurs ten times, all of them in this chapter. This gives us only a single context for the word. It is cognate to the Hebrew *geb*, which refers to a pit or ditch dug in the ground (e.g., 2 Kings 3:16; Jer. 14:3). From this, we can visualize here a pit with an opening at the top that allows viewing and an underground entrance for feeding and attending to the needs of the lions. The opening above ground was probably walled to keep people out while at the same time letting them look down on the lions.[16] While we can only speculate on the purpose of the lion's den, we do know that lions were part of everyday life at that time. The excavation of Babylon revealed several thousand enameled lions used as decorations. There was one large statue of a lion standing over a man. In the same general area, thousands of colored tiles had pictures of lions. Some of these had white bodies and yellow manes. Others had yellow bodies and red manes. A cylinder-seal shows Darius hunting with a lion as his target. One hundred twenty enameled tiles with pictures of lions line the walls along the processional street that led into the city from the Ishtar Gate.

It is worth noting that Daniel was persecuted because of his faithfulness, not because he had denied his God. Persecution is part of spiritual warfare as Satan and his hosts try to turn God's people away from Him. At the same time, persecution helps believers grow stronger. The experience of God's sustaining grace enables believers to trust Him more. It is in the blackness of trials that Christians find the light of God's presence.

---

[15]The Talmud, *Baba Bathra* 4a, states that Daniel's being cast into the lion's den was a punishment for giving advice to Nebuchadnezzar; cf. 4:27. The conclusion comes from Esther 4:5, where Esther calls to "Hatach." Some rabbis identified Daniel with Hatach (*ḥatak*, "to cut down," referring to Daniel's punishment). Others relate his name to the *nipᶜal* of *ḥatak*, "to determine," referring to his power to decide matters of state. The view rests upon a random word that has no clear identification with Daniel. In addition, the book of Esther describes events that take place about three-quarters of a century after Daniel.

[16]Van Impe, p. 111, estimates that the den held "as many as two hundred hungry lions." He gives no reasons for the conclusion. While possible, the view is speculative.

Darius encourages Daniel with the thought that his God is able to "deliver" (*šêzib*) him.[17] The conversation must have taken place before the actual casting of Daniel into the den of lions, v. 16. A stone is placed over the den to prevent anyone from helping Daniel climb out. Seals placed by the king and the nobles guarantee the security of the den. The seals indicate the lack of trust between Darius and the nobles. The king's seal prevents them from approaching Daniel to kill him; their seals prevent the king from later rescuing Daniel or protecting him while in the den of lions, v. 17.

Darius spends the night fasting, a sign that he has repented of his hasty decree and regrets the outcome. He goes without "instruments of musick" (or "entertainment," *dah^awan*). This is the only place that *dah^awan* occurs. From the context, it was some form of entertainment. Different suggestions have been made, but we cannot be specific as to its nature. Lacocque tentatively translates as "concubines." King suggests "dancing girls." Hulst gives "diversion" and supports it as being "a fairly general word" with "the form of the diversion . . . not known." Matthew Henry understands it as "music." Jerome refers to skipping food. These are possible views, but the text does not let us be dogmatic as to the nature of the entertainment.[18] Whatever the king gives up, it is of no help. He is not able to sleep, v. 18.

The king rises "early" the next day, lit. "at the dawn." He goes in "haste" (*b^ehal*, see 2:25) to the lion's den, v. 19, and calls to Daniel with a "lamentable [or 'troubled'] voice" to see if his God has indeed been able to deliver him from the lions, v. 20. Daniel responds to the question with a typical wish for the king's long life (cf. v. 6), v. 21. He adds that he has been kept safely. God has delivered him because of his "innocency" (*zakû*), including his lack of harm to the king. The noun *zakû* occurs only here. It is cognate, however, to the Hebrew *zakâ*, "to be clean, pure," and to an Akkadian cognate, *zakû*,

---

[17]Bultema, p. 189, and Wood, p. 168, consider that the statement "he will deliver thee" is not appropriate for a heathen king to make. They translate as a wish, "may your God deliver you!" The verb *šêzib* is a *šap^cel* imperfect. The imperfect occurs again in 3:15, 17, neither one of which expresses a wish. Although *šap^cel* verbs occur relatively infrequently, they normally have a causative sense. While Darius may not have had strong faith, he may still have stated his hope positively as an encouragement to Daniel.

[18]Lacocque, *The Book of Daniel*, p. 117; King, p. 196; Hulst, p. 225; Henry, IV, 1067; Jerome, p. 68.

"to be clean." It thus refers here to Daniel's moral purity. He had not committed any sin to justify the actions of the Medo-Persian leaders against him. God had sent "his angel" therefore to shut the mouths of the hungry lions.

Daniel does not identify the angel and so leaves any attempt to do so as speculative. Bultema identifies the angel as Michael, the one whose responsibility seems to have been the guarding of Israel. The view is possible but speculative. Among others, West and Miller suggest that this is the Lord Himself coming to deliver His servant. Nothing in the chapter, however, indicates that this is more than the appearance of an angel. The fact that God "sent" the angel suggests that this is an unidentified angel rather than the Angel of the Lord, the Son of God, v. 22.[19]

Charles Spurgeon commented on the failure of the lions to eat Daniel. Different versions of his comment may be found. He is supposed to have said that lions didn't eat Daniel "because the most of him was backbone and the rest was grit." Someone else has described Daniel as "two-thirds grit and one-third gristle."

The king is "exceedingly [śaggî'] glad" and hurriedly commands that Daniel be "taken up" (sᵉleq) from his prison. The word sᵉleq occurs here and at 2:29; 3:22; 7:3, 8, and 20. It refers to being "taken up." Rather than being drawn up by a rope or climbing a ladder, from 3:22, we can visualize Daniel going through an opening in the side of the lion's den and then ascending a ramp to the surface. Such an opening would have let caretakers feed and care for the animals and clean the pit. Walvoord and Wood suggest that Daniel was taken up through the opening by means of ropes.[20] This is also a possible view. Because of Daniel's trust in the Lord, no harm has come to him. The incident is the basis for the NT comment that "through faith" the OT prophets "stopped the mouths of lions" (Heb. 11:33), v. 23.

With typical oriental justice, those men who had "accused" (ᵃkalû qarṣôhî, see 3:8) Daniel are themselves judged. They receive the same punishment that they had thought to bring upon Daniel. In *Antiquities* 10.11.6, Josephus gives an interesting account of this judgment:

---

[19]Bultema, p. 193; West, p. 39; Miller, p. 187.
[20]Walvoord, p. 142; Wood, p. 173.

[Daniel's enemies] would not own that he was preserved by
God, and by his providence; but they said, that the lions had
been filled full with food, and on that account it was, as they
supposed, that the lions would not touch Daniel, nor come to
him; and this they alleged to the king; but the king out of an
abhorrence of their wickedness, gave order that they should
throw in a great deal of flesh to the lions; and when they had
filled themselves, he gave farther order that Daniel's enemies
should be cast into the den that they might learn whether the
lions, now they were full, would touch them or not; and it
appeared plain to Darius, after the princes had been cast to
the wild beasts, that it was God who preserved Daniel, for
the lions spared none of them but tore them all to pieces, as
if they had been very hungry and wanted food.

While we do not know the source of Josephus's information, it
does point to an early view that Daniel was not spared because the
lions were full. His deliverance was a miracle from God. 1 Maccabees 2:60, written about 80 BC, states that "Daniel for his innocence
was delivered from the mouths of the lions."

As indicated in the discussion of v. 6, the judgment involved only
part of the Babylonian leaders. The lions "break [them] . . . in pieces"
(*deqaq*, see 2:34), tearing them apart as they kill and eat the bodies.
The inclusion of their families in the judgment is an oriental practice
that was undertaken to prevent retaliation later by family members
(cf. Herodotus 3.119; Marcellinus 23.6.81).[21] The LXX states that only
two men (likely the other two administrators that served with Daniel)
and their families were slain. This is interpretive, doing away with
the difficulty of including all of the other leaders and their families in
the judgment. The number involved, however, must have been fairly
small. We can only guess at the total, v. 24.

Decree from Darius 6:25–28 After the punishment of the conspirators is complete, Darius addresses a decree to the empire. The
statement "peace be multiplied" is a standard formula found also in
Nebuchadnezzar's decree; cf. 4:1, v. 25. He decrees that the region
under his control should "fear" (*dehal*, see 4:5) Daniel's God. He is

---

[21]*Ammianus Marcellinus*, trans. John C. Rolfe (Cambridge, Mass.: Harvard
University Press, 1972).

both living and steadfast, and His kingdom will continue forever, v. 26. He works signs and wonders in heaven and earth. Coming to the cause of the decree, Darius mentions that this God has delivered Daniel from the lions.

Coming so soon after the first decree, the king's statement may indicate his conversion, accepting Daniel's God as his own. The LXX translation of the Hebrew adds the words "I Darius will worship and serve him all my days, for none of the idols that are made with hands are able to deliver as the God of Daniel did Daniel." This is an addition to the text. It does reflect, however, an early belief in the conversion of Darius. Leupold and Keil reject the conversion of Darius. Storz and McGee accept it.[22] Since the OT record is scant concerning Darius, it is not possible to be dogmatic concerning his conversion. It is a possibility, v. 27. After these events, Daniel continues to exercise a significant influence in both the reigns of Darius and Cyrus, v. 28.[23]

[22]Leupold, p. 274; Keil, p. 218; Elizabeth B. Storz, *Daniel: The Triumph of God's Kingdom* (Wheaton, Ill.: Crossway Books, 2004), p. 99; J. Vernon McGee, *Daniel* (Nashville: Thomas Nelson Publishers, 1991), pp. 106–7.

[23]A. C. Gaebelein, *The Prophet Daniel* (Grand Rapids: Kregel Publications, 1955), pp. 67–68, refers to Isa. 45:1, the prophecy of Cyrus that speaks of him as the Lord's "anointed." Gaebelein then concludes, "In this, [Cyrus] is a type of the Lord Jesus Christ." Scripture, however, is consistent in its types. It is unlikely that a Gentile king whose salvation is debated serves as a type of Christ.

FOUR BEASTS 7:1–28

Although the chapter is written in Aramaic, the outline of the book given in the Introduction groups it with c. 8–12.[1] The last six chapters of the book describe four visions given to Daniel. These primarily emphasize prophetic truth, just as the first six chapters of the book primarily deal with historical matters. There is, however, some marvelous prophecy in the first six chapters. There is also a great deal of historical information in the final six chapters of the book. Daniel basically writes the first six chapters as history, keeping himself in the narratives as only one of many characters. In the final six chapters, other than God, the Lord, and the angels, Daniel is the only character named. These chapters deal with the four revelations received by Daniel and introduced in 7:1; 8:1–2; 9:20–21; and 10:1. Since these come to Daniel, he generally writes these chapters in the first person.

The events in c. 7 occur during the reign of Belshazzar, before the events in c. 5–6. Chapter 8 is also out of chronological order. The order of the book according to time would be chapters 1, 2, 3, 4, 7, 8, 5, 6, 9, 10–12. Daniel has placed this chapter in the second half of the book because of its content, not because of when it occurred.

Vision of the Four Beasts 7:1–14 Chapter 7 describes four earthly kingdoms. In this, it parallels chapter two. Chapter 2 presents the external, the human side of the four great world kingdoms. This is Nebuchadnezzar's vision, given to a heathen king, and naturally emphasizes what man would see. Chapter seven presents the internal, the beast-like nature of the kingdoms. This is Daniel's vision, given to a godly prophet, and more naturally stresses what God sees, the character of the kingdoms. The vision climaxes with end-time events as it introduces the rise to power of Antichrist in the Tribulation, his defeat and judgment, and the establishment of the kingdom reign of the saints with the Lord.

Nabonidus appointed Belshazzar regent in the third year of his reign, ca. 553 BC. The date is disputed: Archer places it at 556 or 555 BC. Wood and Walvoord make it 553 BC. Hasel dates Belshazzar's

---

[1]Gaebelein's comment, p. 92, that "beginning with the seventh chapter to the end of the Book of Daniel the language employed is Hebrew" is apparently a mental slip. On p. 9, he correctly notes that the book uses Aramaic from 2:4 to 7:28.

first year as 550/549 BC. Powell sets the date at 541 BC. Our knowledge of the history of Babylon at this time is based on historical records that are often vague. It is often difficult to be certain in setting an exact date. Shea recognizes this difficulty and dates Belshazzar's first year some time between 553 and 539 BC.[2]

At some time during that year, Daniel had a "dream" (*helem*, see 2:28) and "visions" (*ḥᵉzû*, see 2:28). The "visions" are the different scenes within the "dream." Daniel now recalls the substance and writes the "sum" (or "summary," *reʾš*) of his dream, the essential details of it. Hulst draws on the reference to "the end" in v. 28 to conclude that the sense of *reʾš* here is "beginning," not "sum."[3] The word *reʾš* occurs fourteen times in the Aramaic portions of the OT and regularly refers to the "head." Only here and at Ezra 5:10 does the translation differ. The sense in Ezra, "chief," gives the clue to the translation here. Daniel wrote down the "chief" parts of the dream, i.e., he summarized it rather than giving a detailed record. While the translation "beginning" contrasts nicely with v. 28, it does not agree with the record related by Daniel in the chapter. He not only gives the beginning of his dream but also gives the middle, the end, and the interpretation. The translation "summary" agrees better with this.

Since this verse introduces the narrative, it is written in the third person, v. 1. Daniel "saw" activity after activity in his vision. The phrase "I saw" or its equivalents ("I beheld," "I considered") occurs ten times in the chapter (vv. 2, 4, 6, 7, 8, 9, 11 [2X], 13, 21). This repeatedly calls attention to Daniel's personal involvement. He speaks of that which he himself has seen.

In the dream, four winds "strove upon" (or "stirred up") the "great [*rab*, see 2:10] sea," the Mediterranean, here symbolically representing the nations of the biblical prophecy. Tatford understands the sea only as a symbol of mankind, "not necessarily the Mediterranean." Young relates the sea to "the world of nations in a tumultuous state." Keil and Leupold identify the "great sea" as

---

[2]Archer, p. 84; Wood, p. 179; Walvoord, p. 149; Hasel, p. 43; F. Ellsworth Powell, *Uncle Frank and Daniel or Pen Pictures from Babylon* (Largo, Fla.: privately published, 1970), p. 117; William H. Shea, "Nabonidus, Belshazzar, and the Book of Daniel," p. 135.
[3]Hulst, p. 225.

the ocean rather than the Mediterranean.[4] The phrase "great sea"
in Aramaic, *yamma' rabba'*, is equivalent to the Hebrew *hayyam
haggadôl*. Everywhere else, this phrase refers to the Mediterranean
(e.g., Josh. 1:4; Ezek. 48:28). All of the four kingdoms pictured in
c. 2 and c. 7 (Babylonian, Medo-Persian, Greek, Roman) lay about
the Mediterranean.

Waters often represent mankind in the Bible (e.g., Isa. 8:7; 48:1;
Jer. 46:7–8; 47:2; Rev. 17:1, 15). Gardner asserts that Babylon,
Media, and Persia "were [not] Mediterranean powers, thus to posit
that they emerged from the Mediterranean Sea is nonsensical." She
attempts to show that the "great sea" here is "the sea of mythologi-
cal chaos."[5] She bases her conclusion on the misinterpretation of
three passages (Isa. 51:9–10; Pss. 74:13–14; 104:24–25). While the
empires of Babylon and Medo-Persia encompassed territory several
hundred miles from the Mediterranean, all stretched to the shores
of the Mediterranean. It is not an error to say that these kingdoms
"came up from the sea."

The phrase "four winds" represents the four primary directions.
Strauss argues that the "four winds" are evil forces warring against
God's people throughout history. Whitcomb refers them to "angelic
forces through which God controls and moves the nations." Jerome
also refers the winds to the angels who oversee the nations. Gangel
and Walvoord understand the "four winds" as suggesting "God's
sovereign power." Gangel is extreme in saying that this is "the only
way Daniel uses the word."[6] The phrase occurs six times in the OT,
half of these in Daniel. In Jeremiah 49:36; Daniel 8:8; 11:4, the sense
of four directions is clear. In Ezekiel 37:9 and Zechariah 2:6, it is
reasonable to interpret as directions. Since the idea of four directions
agrees with its use elsewhere in the book, I have adopted that sense
here. The winds stir up the sea, with the turbulence suggesting that
the conflicts about to be described come from all directions, v. 2.

"Four great beasts" rise from the sea of mankind. In the OT,
"beasts" often represent nations. The "leviathan," probably a
crocodile, in Isaiah 27:1 represents first Assyria, then Babylon; the

---

[4]Tatford, p. 111; Young, p. 142; Keil, p. 222; Leupold, p. 284.

[5]Anne Gardner, "The Great Sea of Dan. VII 2," *VT* 49 (July 1999): 412–15.

[6]Strauss, p. 205; Whitcomb, *Daniel*, p. 93; Jerome, pp. 72–73; Gangel,
pp. 184–85; Walvoord, p. 152.

"dragon" in 51:9 represents Egypt. The "lion" in Jeremiah 4:7 represents an unnamed northern foe, probably Babylon. The "eagle" in Ezekiel 17:3, the "dragon" in 29:3, and the "young lion" and "whale" (or "monster") in 32:2 all represent Egypt.[7] Comparing v. 17 with v. 23 makes it clear that the four beasts here are four kings, the heads of four kingdoms.[8] They come from the "sea" of mankind. As the dream later makes clear ("the first," v. 4; "another," v. 5; "after this," vv. 6, 7), they come not all at once but successively, v. 3.

The first beast begins the series that parallels c. 2. Auchincloss understands the four beasts differently. He makes the lion with eagle's wings the Medo-Persian Empire, the bear Greece, the leopard Macedonia, and the fierce beast the Roman Empire. There is no warrant for making Greece and Macedonia separate empires. Philip, the first king of the Grecian Empire, was king of Macedonia when he conquered the Greek states. This became the basis for further expansion throughout the Mediterranean area. Knoch makes the four beasts represent the four great religions of the world. The lion stands for the Buddhism of eastern Asia, the bear for the Hinduism prominent in India and nearby nations, the leopard for the Islam of the Arab world, and the monstrous beast for the Christendom (perverted Christianity) of the west.[9] The view flies in the face of almost all conservative interpretation by its radically different interpretation of the visions of c. 2, 8, and 11.

---

[7]Several authors relate the biblical imagery of animals representing nations to earlier Babylonian or Ugaritic writings. Martin Noth, *The Laws in the Pentateuch and Other Studies* (Philadelphia: Fortress Press, 1967), trans. D. R. Ap-Thomas, p. 211, states that "the seer is working with traditional ancient Oriental illustrative materials." Heaton, p. 171, sees the origin in *Enuma Elish*, the Babylonian story of the Creation. Porteous, p. 98, suggests that these "myths and rituals" of Babylon "may have been mediated to Israel by way of Ugarit." Ernest Lucas, "The Source of Daniel's Animal Imagery," *TB* 41 (Nov 1990): 161–86, refutes this view by noting that animal imagery, including the same animals found in Daniel, is common in the OT.

[8]Watkinson, p. 187, understands the four kings as representing four types of religions. Babylon suggests the worship of images. The Medes and Persians worshiped fire and sun, thus indicating that "God under them [appears] as symbols." The Macedonian rule relates to paganism. Paul's comment that "whom ye ignorantly worship, him declare I unto you" suggests "a certain amount of spirituality in their worship." Rome is "unadulterated paganism, the worship of men." The view suffers from assigning spiritual meanings without any textual indication of such need.

[9]Auchincloss, pp. 53–55; Knoch, p. 175.

Hanhart concludes that the kingdoms of c. 2 succeed one another but that those of c. 7 "are related geographically, the one alongside the other." He identifies them as Egypt, Persia, Rome, and Syria, with the unidentified beast of v. 7 probably being an elephant. Wittstruck sees the winds as representing four quadrants: to the south, Babylon; to the north, Media; to the east, Persia; and to the west, Greece. Since "the four winds appear simultaneously . . . the kingdoms should be understood as contemporary with one another." Newell also understands the four winds as blowing at the same time, "suggesting a world-wide commotion arising in all directions." Since this did not happen during the rise of Babylon, Medo-Persia, Greece, or Rome, he sets the fulfillment of the chapter in the end times.[10] Nothing here requires that the four winds blow simultaneously. The emphasis on sequence ("first," v. 4; "another," vv. 5, 6; "after this," vv. 6, 7) argues against simultaneous winds. In addition, the parallelism between c. 2 and c. 7 indicates that the earlier kingdoms are Babylon, Medo-Persia, and Greece. The words that indicate sequence in vv. 4–7, together with the obvious chronological development of v. 8 and the standard interpretations of the descriptive phrases connected with each beast, argue against the view that these kingdoms exist side by side.

Each beast in this chapter corresponds to a section of the statue in c. 2. The lion with eagle's wings symbolizes Babylon under the leadership of Nebuchadnezzar. The combination of a lion with the wings of an "eagle" ($n^e\check{s}ar$)[11] suggests the coupled fierceness and speed of the Babylonian conquests. Jeremiah 49:19, 22 uses this same symbolism. The ruins of Babylon contained a large number of winged lions.[12]

---

[10]Karel Hanhart, "The Four Beasts of Daniel's Vision in the Night in the Light of Rev. 13. 2," *New Testament Studies* 27 (1981): 578–81; Thorne Wittstruck, "The Influence of Treaty Curse Imagery on the Beast Imagery of Daniel 7," *JBL* 97 (Mar 1978): 101–2; Newell, pp. 78–79.

[11]Tatford, p. 112 identifies the $n^e\check{s}ar$ as the "griffon-vulture," a bird also found in that part of the world. The view is possible since the OT connects several birds with the words $n^e\check{s}ar$ (Aramaic) and $ne\check{s}er$ (Hebrew). The eagle is generally considered the more majestic of the birds. The vulture is a carrion-eater with weaker claws than the eagle. For this reason, the eagle better pictures a king.

[12]Hartman, pp. 202–13, transposes from v. 5 the phrase "it had three tusks in its mouth [between its teeth], and it was given the command: 'Up, devour much flesh!'" He inserts it after the reference to "eagle wings." He further moves v. 4b

The plucking of the wings followed by its standing as a man probably indicates the madness and restoration of Nebuchadnezzar. The "man's heart" being given reflects 4:16, 34, where Nebuchadnezzar first becomes beastlike and then has his understanding restored, v. 4. Smith understands the plucking of the wings as a time when Babylon "no longer rushed upon its prey like an eagle. The boldness and spirit of the lion were gone. A man's heart—weak, timorous, and faint— took the place of a lion's strength." Calvin likened this to Babylon's being restrained "within due limits" when the Lord "checked their continual victories." Barnes understands the "man's heart" as a reference to the change as Babylon passed from Nebuchadnezzar's rule to "a succession of comparatively weak and inefficient princes." The nation no longer ravaged other nations but, instead, became weak and unable to defend itself. Barrett suggests that it is "the weakening of the kingdom as a whole."[13] Because the description is symbolic, it is not possible to be dogmatic in the interpretation. It is worth noting, however, that Babylon was not necessarily weak. The nation ceased to expand—thus wings were no longer needed to indicate rapidity— but Babylon still ruled a vast territory until its final defeat.

The second beast is similar to a bear. There is general agreement among conservative authors that this represents the Medo-Persian Empire (cf. 8:20). Liberal interpreters, e.g., Driver, Hartman, and Lacocque, adopt the same view here as in chapter two. They make the second kingdom Media, the third Persia, and the fourth Greece.[14] A note at 2:39b briefly discusses this view.

One side of the bear was raised higher than the other, a symbol of Persia's dominance in the alliance. This is similar to the symbolism in 8:3, where one horn is higher than the other horn, and relates to

---

to the end of v. 5. These changes have no significant support. Moving the phrases between vv. 4 and 5 gives them unnatural and incorrect interpretations. The three ribs become tusks that represent "the three Babylonian kings known to the author." The standing of the bear refers to Darius, "the only Median king known to the author." The four heads of the leopard in v. 6 are "the four kings of the Persian empire known to [the] author from the Bible." The ten horns of v. 7 become ten Greek kings. Since there were more than ten Greek kings, Hartman, p. 213, states that "our author believed that the tenth Greek king would be the last ruler of the Greek kingdom—a prediction not born out [sic] by events."

[13]Uriah Smith, p. 107; Calvin, II, 14; Barnes, II, 48–49; Barrett, p. 59.

[14]Driver, pp. 82–83; Hartman, pp. 212–13; Lacocque, p. 140.

the two arms of the statue in 2:32. Hartman sees this as the "animal standing only on its hind legs." This departs from the MT and has no significant sense in the interpretation. Barnes understands this as the bear "raising itself up from a recumbent posture" with the body partially raised. He interprets this as "a kingdom that had been quiet and at rest" but now rouses itself for conquest. The parallelism with 8:3 supports rather the dominance of Persia in the Medo-Persian alliance. Calvin translates "he stood on one side" and refers this to the obscure background of the Persian kingdom before Cyrus. We know, however, quite a bit about the Persians before Cyrus. Tregelles translates the phrase "it raised up itself on one side [śeṭar]" as "it made for itself 'one dominion.'"[15] The meaning "dominion" for śeṭar goes contrary to BDB and KB and does not agree with the common view of 8:3. The LXX translated πλευροῦ, "side." Theodotion is similar, πλευρά. These support the traditional sense given to śeṭar.

There are "three ribs [ʿilʿîn]" in the bear's mouth, symbolizing the substantial conquests of territory to the north, to the west, and to the south (cf. 8:4 for this interpretation). Ginsberg emends the text without manuscript support and concludes that the beast had three "fangs" rather than three ribs. Frank rejects Ginsberg's derivation but accepts the same translation. He argues from logic and Arabic although he acknowledges, "We have no corroborative evidence for this metaphorical use of the root in Aramaic."[16] The word ʿilʿîn occurs only here. It is, however, cognate to the Hebrew noun ṣelaʿ, "side" or "rib" (so Gen. 2:21, 22). The sense of "ribs" fits nicely with the thought of conquests, areas that have been devoured by the Medo-Persian "bear."

The Talmud, *Kiddushin* 72*a*, considers the ribs to represent three provinces (or towns), which were continually in revolt against their Medo-Persian overlords. We have no knowledge of such a state of continuous revolt. Walvoord makes the ribs represent Media, Persia, and Babylon, "the three major components of the Medo-Babylonian

---

[15]Hartman, p. 205; Calvin, II, 16; Barnes, II, 49; S. P. Tregelles, *Remarks on the Prophetic Visions in the Book of Daniel* (London: The Sovereign Grace Advent Testimony, 1863, rpt. 1965), p. 33.

[16]H. Louis Ginsberg, *Studies in Daniel* (New York: The Jewish Theological Seminary of America, 1948), pp. 13, 69; Richard M. Frank, "The Description of the 'Bear' in Dn 7,5," *CBQ* 21 (1959): 505–7.

Empire." Phillips and Wiersbe see the three ribs as representing Lydia, Babylon, and Egypt, three kingdoms conquered by the Medo-Persians under Cyrus and Cambyses. Van Ryn suggests Susiana, Lydia, and Asia Minor, not all of which was conquered by the Medes and Persians.[17] These views selectively choose three conquests of other nations but neglect the many other victories by the empire, e.g., Parthia, Bactria, Arachosia, Carmania.

Porteous sees the three ribs as "a cryptic allusion to Median greed for booty." Thomson considers the number "three" as "not important, but a general term for a few."[18] These views are better but overlook the obvious parallel with the three directions in c. 8. Un-identified voices, possibly the angels introduced in v. 16, command the bear to devour "much [*saggîʾ*, see 2:6] flesh" by undertaking further conquests, v. 5.

The leopard-like third beast has four wings on its "back" (better "sides"). It also has four heads. The beast with its four heads repre-sents Greece under Alexander the Great (discussed at 2:39*b*), who was followed by four generals (cf. 8:8, 21–22).[19] The figure of a leop-ard coupled with the four wings implies exceptional speed in con-quests.[20] In eleven years, Alexander the Great conquered more cities and territory than Cyrus the Great did in thirty years. He conquered Persia and much of Asia, Syria, Egypt, and India.

The "four heads" serve as symbols of the four generals who divided the empire between them after Alexander's death and, eventually, formed four lesser empires. Keil follows an older view not generally held today. He understands the four heads as "the four successive Persian kings whom alone Daniel knows (ch. xi. 2)." Bultema interprets the heads as representing "the fourfold mind and

---

[17]Walvoord, p. 156; Phillips, p. 98; Wiersbe, p. 87; Van Ryn, p. 76.

[18]Porteous, p. 105; Thomson, p. 210.

[19]After having let the second beast refer to Media and Persia, Lederach, p. 154, lets the third beast also represent "the Persian empire under four kings": Cyrus, Ahasuerus, Artaxerxes, and Darius the Persian. He does not explain the omission of Cambyses, Pseudo-Smerdis (Gaumata), Darius the Mede, Xerxes II, and several minor kings. The view also leads Lederach, p. 155, to equate the fourth beast with "the Greeks and especially the Seleucids."

[20]Miller, pp. 199–200, suggests that the four wings "allude to the four quarters of the earth, thus signifying world domination." While this is possible, the emphasis in 8:5 is on speed rather than dominion.

the unique talent of Alexander as a general." Cowles sees the four heads as stressing Greece as being distinguished "more by the power of thought than the power of brute force." The discussion in c. 11, particularly 11:4, argues against these views. Young holds that the four heads represent "the four corners of the earth [and thus] symbolize the ecumenicity of the kingdom." The view ignores the historical record of Greece after Alexander's death. Since the "four heads" compare to the "four notable" horns of 8:8, 22, they must relate to leaders of nations rather than directions.[21] Our knowledge of history today argues for the view given above. While Alexander had more than four generals, these were the four that gained dominance. A period of infighting lasting about thirty years followed Alexander's death. At the end of this time, the four kingdoms led by the former generals or their sons had replaced Alexander's rule. Seleucus Nicanor took Asia, including Syria, which at that time included the area between the Tigris and Euphrates Rivers. Lysimachus took Thrace and Bithynia. Cassander took Macedonia and Greece. Ptolemy took Egypt, v. 6.

Goldwurm identifies the generals as Ptolemy, Seleucas, Antigonus, and Phillip (Alexander's brother). History does not support this view. Henry sees them as Seleucus Nicanor, Cassander, Ptolemeus, "Perdiccas, and after him Antigonus." While Perdiccas and Antigonus were involved in the attempt to control a portion of Alexander's kingdom, the final success came to Lysimachus when he and Seleucus combined forces to defeat and kill Antigonus.[22]

The fourth beast differs from the other three.[23] The symbolism is so "dreadful [$d^{e}hal$, see 4:5] and terrible [$^{\flat}êm^{e}tan$]" that no beast suitably portrays it (cf. Rev. 13:1–2). Both $d^{e}hal$ and $^{\flat}êm^{e}tan$ convey the idea of strong fear. The noun $^{\flat}êm^{e}tan$ occurs only here. It is, however, cognate to the Hebrew noun $^{\flat}êmâ$, also "dread." The fourth

---

[21]Keil, p. 227; Bultema, p. 209; Cowles, p. 341; Young, p. 146.

[22]Goldwurm, p. 198; Henry, IV, 1071.

[23]H. A. Ironside, *Notes on the Minor Prophets* (Neptune, N.J.: Loizeaux Brothers, 1909), p. 7, and Tatford, pp. 114–15, note the similarity to Hos. 13:7–8. They suggest that Hosea's passage is a prophecy of the same four beasts: the lion, leopard, bear, and the "wild beast" a general reference to Daniel's fourth beast. It is more likely that Hosea simply prophesies generally of judgment upon Israel because of their sin. Hos. 13:8 refers to a fifth animal, the "lion" (lit., "lioness"), that does not fit into the future outlined in Daniel.

beast is distinct. It is fierce, having "great iron teeth" with which it devoured others and "brake [them] in pieces" (d^eqaq, see 2:34), then stamped on them with its feet.[24] Verse 19 describes its feet as having "nails" (or "claws") of bronze.

This beast differs from the earlier beasts in that it has ten horns, indicating that it comprises ten kingdoms.[25] Keil sees the ten horns as indicating "terrible strength, because a horn is in Scripture always the universal symbol of armed strength."[26] While it is true that a horn often represents strength, this strength may have different sources. It may be the strength of God (Ps. 18:2), of the wicked (Ps. 75:4, 5), of the righteous (Ps. 75:10), of an individual (Ps. 89:24), or of something else. Here, it refers to the strength of the kingdoms. In this way we can explain v. 8 where three of the horns are plucked up, i.e., the strength of three kingdoms is overcome, v. 7.

Goldwurm understands the "ten horns" as the ten emperors who ruled Rome prior to the destruction of the temple in AD 70. These include Julius Caesar (49–44 BC), Augustus Caesar (31–14 BC), Tiberius Caesar (14 BC–AD 37), Claudius Caesar (AD 41–54), Nero (AD 54–68), Galba (AD 68–69), Otho (AD 69), Vitellius (AD 69), and Vespasian (AD 69–79). This leads to his inability to interpret the overcoming of the three horns. He comments on v. 8: "The commentators offer many interpretations of this, none of which satisfy the text fully." Without choosing, Goldwurm gives a sampling of interpretations from Jewish commentators, none of which have much to commend them.[27]

Calvin refers the ten kings to Roman provinces, with their proconsuls acting as "kings" over them. The "little horn" relates to "Julius Caesar and the other Caesars who succeeded him." The cutting

---

[24]Joseph Coppens, "Dan. VII, 1–18—Note Additionnelle," *ETL* 55:4 (1979): 384, describes the fourth beast as "purement imaginarie," pure imagination. He suggests that the author was afraid of making too clean an allusion to the Seleucids at a time when Syrian power dominated the country. Further, if he was too clear, it became difficult to present the distinction of the ten horns in his description. The view fails by referring the fourth beast to Syria.

[25]Archer, p. 87, tentatively suggests that the horns come on "two five-pronged antlers." While possible, the emergence of an eleventh horn that overcomes three of the original horns better supports the idea of ten separate horns.

[26]Keil, p. 228.

[27]Goldwurm, p. 201.

off of the three horns denotes loss of power by the Roman Senate leading to greater power by the emperor.[28] The view suffers from its historical inaccuracy. There is no evidence that limits Rome to ten proconsuls. The "little horn" is a single king, not several caesars.

Caragounis sees the horns as representing the Seleucids, beginning with Alexander, continuing through his sons Philip Arrhidaeus and Alexander Aegus (both of whom were children and under the control of others), and including seven Seleucid kings. The eleventh king is Antiochus Epiphanes. The three horns that are overcome are Alexander and his two sons who, in contrast with the vision, were overthrown long before the birth of Epiphanes.[29]

Isaac Newton understands the ten horns as historical kingdoms, remnants after the breaking up of Rome. He lists the Vandals and Alars, Suevians, Visigoths, Alans, Burgundians, Franks, Britains, Hunns, Lombards, and Ravenna. The view ignores the prophetic sense suggested by the phrase "time and times and the dividing of time" (v. 25). It also leads Newton to interpret the eleventh horn as the church of Rome.[30]

Young considers the number "ten" as symbolic and indicating several kings. "From the time of the destruction of the Roman Empire to the appearance of the little horn there will be a number of kingdoms, which may truly be said to originate from the ancient Roman Empire." The view is inconsistent in that it considers the kingdoms to be sequential except for the final three, which must exist at the same time.[31]

Van Impe finds the ten horns as the nations in the European Union, later increased to thirteen nations with the addition of three nations that Antichrist will overcome.[32] The European Union, however, already includes more than two dozen nations. This modern-day organization also includes nations not connected with the biblical world. In addition, v. 8 has Antichrist overcoming three of "the first horns," not an additional three.

---

[28]Calvin, II, 25–29.

[29]C. C. Caragounis, "The Ten Horns of Daniel 7," *ETL* 63:1 (1987): 106–13.

[30]Isaac Newton, *Sir Isaac Newton's Daniel and the Apocalypse*, ed. William Whitla and trans. W. H. Semple (London: John Murray, 1922), pp. 170, 188.

[31]Young, pp. 147–49.

[32]Van Impe, p. 125.

These ten kingdoms exist at the same time in the final form of the Roman Empire. Another "little horn" arises after them and over-comes three of the original horns. Wood understands the conquest as "a gradual process, where new growth pushes out old. The new king will not take control of all three areas at once, then, but over a period of time."[33] The verb translated "plucked up by the roots," $\partial et^{c a}qar\hat{u}$ ($q^{e}r\hat{e}$, $\partial et^{c a}qar\hat{a}$) is an $itpe^{c}el$ perfect-tense verb. This has a reflexive sense but not particularly one of gradual action. While Antichrist may take some time to subdue three other kingdoms, it cannot be much time. He only has a short time to dominate the earth, and his role as king must be in place before he can establish his covenant with Israel.

There is another "little horn" in c. 8, but it refers to a different ruler. The "little horn" of c. 8 rises out of the Greek Empire and refers to Antiochus Epiphanes. The "little horn" of this chapter comes out of the Roman Empire and refers to Antichrist. Among others, Barnes and Horne understand the "little horn" as the papacy. This rises to dominant world influence and lasts "a time and times and the dividing of time" (v. 25), which they both interpret as 1260 years.[34] The view is subject to many criticisms. When did the papacy begin? Not in the eighth century as would be required since it still exists. Horne has the power of the papacy ending in 1870, but vv. 21–22 indicate continu-ing conflict until the coming of the Lord. What three kingdoms did it overcome? There is no general agreement on this. Why should we understand the duration as 1260 years when 42 months agrees better with Daniel 12:6–12 and Revelation 11:2–3; 13:5?

The phrase "little horn" occurs here and at 8:9. The adjective "little" here is $z^{e c}\hat{e}r$, "small, little." In 8:9, the Hebrew adjective is $mi\d{s}^{c}ar$, "insignificant." The distinction makes the point that Anti-christ, here, has a small beginning from which he rises to great power. In 8:9, Antiochus Epiphanes, for all of his earthly influence, is but an insignificant power in God's eyes.

The "little horn" stands for a man who speaks "great things" against God; cf. v. 25. Revelation 17:3, 12–18 sets the time of this beast in the Tribulation. The reference to his "eyes" suggests his per-sonal magnetism. With the mention of his speech (vv. 8, 11, 20, 25),

---

[33]Wood, p. 188.

[34]Barnes, II, 82–93; Horne, pp. 56–62.

we gather that he will exploit his personality as he exercises leadership on the earth, v. 8.

A new scene appears to Daniel. He watches until "the thrones were cast down [better 'were set up']." The Talmud, *Sanhedrin* 38*b*, gives several rabbinical views to explain the plural "thrones." One throne may be for God and one for David, the name here referring to the Messiah. One throne may be for mercy and the other for justice. One throne was for a seat, and the other for a footstool. Others refer the plural to the twenty-four "seats" (lit., "thrones") of Revelation 4:4. There is no mention here, however, of anyone other than the "Ancient of days."

Gangel tentatively suggests that the plural thrones "may indicate the seating of the Son and the Holy Spirit." While the Son has a role in the judgment (John 5:22, 27), the Bible nowhere depicts the Holy Spirit as participating. Leupold states that many judgment seats appear "because courts are usually represented thus." Only courts of appeal have more than one judge. There is no appeal from this court.[35] Since the description does not refer to others assisting in the judgment, the plural "thrones" is best understood as a plural of majesty. This is appropriate when referring to the seat taken by God in the judgment.

The placing of the throne takes place in anticipation of the judgment that follows. The "Ancient of days," the Eternal God, enters to conduct the judgment. Gaebelein interprets the "Ancient of days" as Christ, the Son of God. The phrase "Son of man" also refers to Christ but in His human nature. The view is impossible. Thomson translates "one ancient in days," calling the phrase "not appellative, but descriptive."[36] There is, however, no preposition "in" connected to *yômîn*. Further, it is normal in Aramaic for a name to be determinative. The appearance of the Lord as "the Ancient of days" is appropriate for the Eternal One. The name occurs again in vv. 13, 22.

Older expositors wavered between two identifications. Hippolytus, Eusebius, Cyril of Jerusalem, and Chrysostom identified the "Ancient of days" as God the Father. Jerome, Cyril of Alexandria, John of Damascus, and Germanus of Constantinople identified Him

---

[35]Gangel, p. 192; Leupold, p. 303.
[36]Gaebelein, pp. 77–78; Thomson, p. 213.

with Christ.[37] Modern authors generally identify Him with God the Father. Others have been suggested as assisting the Judge—angels, glorified men, David—but these views do not agree with Scripture. The Bible does not teach that others join the Lord in judging the wicked.

There are several distinct judgments mentioned in the Bible, e.g., the judgment of Israel (Ezek. 20:34–38), the judgment of the nations (Matt. 25:31–46), and the judgment of angels (Jude 6). In some cases, the Son of God is the Judge (e.g., John 5:22, 27; Acts 10:42). In this judgment, however, the focus is on God the Father as the Judge. It must therefore refer to the Great White Throne judgment of Revelation 20:11–15.

The "Ancient of days" wears white clothing, a suggestion of His personal purity and fitness to carry out the judgment (cf. Ps. 51:7; Isa. 1:18). His white hair, appropriate to His eternality as the "Ancient of days," suggests His maturity and ability to judge wisely (cf. Rev. 1:14).[38]

The "fiery flame" of the throne and the "burning fire" associated with the wheels adds to the awesome atmosphere of the judgment, v. 9. The presence of the Lord is often associated with fire (e.g., Exod. 3:2; 19:18; 2 Chron. 7:1–3). Here, a "fiery stream" flows from Him, a picture of the consuming of the wicked by God. *Berakoth* 59*a*, in the Talmud, gives a trivial view of the "fiery stream," referring it to the Milky Way. Fire is often connected to judgment elsewhere (e.g., Deut. 4:24; Ps. 97:3; Heb. 12:29), which is sometimes connected with God's throne (e.g., Ps. 9:4, 7; Isa. 16:5; Matt. 25:31).

The fiery throne of the Judge is on wheels. There are several possible views that attempt to explain the "wheels" of the throne. The movable throne is often compared to the wheels in Ezekiel 1:15–21 and 10:2–19, e.g., Hartman, Montgomery, and Porteous. Wood sees them as evidence of the "universality of authority." Boutflower suggests that thrones in the East had wheels that let them be moved.

---

[37]Wilfred Sophrony Royer, "The Ancient of Days: Patristic and Modern Views of Daniel 7:9–14," in *St. Vladimir's Theological Quarterly* 45:2 (2001): 137–62, has surveyed many of the church fathers in this matter.

[38]Cowles, pp. 343–47, argues that this is not the final judgment but only "the destruction of the fourth beast and his horns." It is difficult to apply the description of v. 10, with its mention of numberless multitudes being judged from "the books," to anything other than the final judgment.

Young describes the throne as appearing as a chariot. Keil and Leupold suggest that the wheels, allowing mobility of the throne, symbolize the omnipresence of God.[39] Since the text does not state the use of the wheels, we can only speculate as to their purpose. Since God chooses to reveal Himself in this scene, it is appropriate to let the "wheels" indicate His mobility, i.e., His omnipresence, as He confronts each person in judgment.

The judgment is awe-inspiring. A "thousand thousands" of angelic beings serve God. "Ten thousand times ten thousand" more stand before Him, awaiting His directions for service (cf. Ps. 68:17; Matt. 26:53). Both of these numerical expressions involve hyperbole, conscious exaggeration for the sake of making a point. They convey the fact that an uncountable body of angels serves God.

The phrase "the judgment was set" is better translated "the court was set," i.e., everything is now ready for the judicial proceedings. The "books" are the books in which God keeps the record of man's works (cf. Rev. 20:12). Among these is the Lamb's Book of Life (cf. 12:1), which contains the names of all who belong to God through faith in His Son as their Savior, v. 10.

The speech of the "little horn" captures Daniel's attention. Daniel continues to watch him "because of" (lit. "from") the beginning of his arrogant speech until God sends judgment upon him. Verse 25 sums up the nature of these words as directed against God, the saints, and divine directions for life. There is no description of the agent bringing the judgment or of its nature. Divine judgment of some sort takes place as "the beast was slain." The parallelism with c. 2 tells us that this last beast represents the Roman Empire. The destruction of its "body" pictures the complete overthrow of the empire. The little horn, Antichrist, its final leader, is given to "the burning flame."

Barnes asserts that the fire is symbolic, not literal: "It is to be remembered that all this is symbol, and no one part of the symbol should be taken literally more than another."[40] In this case, however, Scripture elsewhere supports the literal nature of the judgment (cf. Rev. 20:11–15). The "little horn" represents Antichrist. At the end of

---

[39]Hartman, p. 218; Montgomery, p. 299; Porteous, p. 108; Wood, p. 189; Boutflower, p. 219; Young, p. 151; Keil, p. 230; Leupold, p. 302.

[40]Barnes, II, 62.

the Tribulation, when the Lord visibly returns to the earth with His saints to defeat the armies of Antichrist, he and the False Prophet will be cast into the "lake of fire" (cf. Rev. 19:20; 20:10). The "burning flame" here refers to that eternal judgment, v. 11.

The end of this fourth beast, the final form of the Roman Empire, differs from the end of the three previous beasts (Babylon, Medo-Persia, Greece). The end here is complete as God brings the empire under the absolute authority of Jesus Christ in His reign over the earth. The previous empires had been absorbed within the rule of new leadership while still retaining a measure of some authority. All authority now passes to the Lord. This continues for "a season [see the discussion of time, 2:8] and time," v. 12.

As the climax of Daniel's vision, he sees one "like the Son of man." Literally, this is one "like a son of man." He is like man yet different because He is the divine Son of God. This is the only time in the OT the phrase refers to the Lord. Similar phrases occur more than one hundred times in Hebrew, but they consistently refer to mankind (e.g., Job 25:6; Isa. 51:12).

Driver argues that "there is nothing [in the book] which lends support to the Messianic interpretation." He bases this on the fact that in vv. 18, 22, 27, it is the saints who receive the kingdom. Here, then, the phrase simply refers to "the ideal people of God." Further, the chapter uses figures—beasts to represent kingdoms, horns to represent kings.[41] By analogy, the figure here must be symbolic. Driver's arguments are faulty. While the chapter does use figures, the figures are explained. There are also real images and persons in the chapter—the "Ancient of days," vv. 9, 13, 22, described in some detail; the angelic hosts, v. 10; the burning fire, v. 11; the "saints," vv. 18, 22, 25, 27. While the saints receive the kingdom, it is clear from vv. 9, 13, and 22 that the "Ancient of days" rules over it. The phrase is the basis for the Lord's use of the phrase "Son of man" when referring to Himself (e.g., Matt. 9:6; 12:8). The phrase also occurs in referring to the glorified Lord (Acts 7:56; Rev. 1:13; 14:14).

In a similar way, the OT often associates clouds with the presence of God (e.g., Exod. 13:21; Ps. 97:2; Isa. 19:1). In the NT, the Lord referred to His return to the earth as being in the clouds of heaven

---

[41]Driver, pp. 103–4.

(cf. Matt. 24:30; 26:64; Mark 13:26; 14:62; Luke 21:27; Acts 1:9; 1 Thess. 4:17; Rev. 1:7). After "a cloud" received the Lord so that the apostles no longer saw Him, an angel announced to them that the Lord's return would be in a "like manner." (Acts 1:10–11).

The "Son of man" comes before the "Ancient of days" (vv. 9, 22), the eternal God. The name appropriately conveys the thought that He has ruled from days long since gone by, v. 13. The Son of man receives what no king before Him has ever achieved, eternal dominion over the whole earth. Barnes continues his insistence on a symbolic interpretation. He rejects the literal rule of Christ over the earth in favor of a spiritual rule. "There will be such a prevalence of the gospel on the hearts of all—rulers and people; the gospel will so modify all laws, and control all customs, and remove all abuses, and all the forms of evil; men will be so generally under the influence of that gospel, that it may be said that *He* reigns on the earth, or that the government actually administered is *his*." The view flies in the face of such passages as Psalm 146:10; Isaiah 9:6–7; Hebrews 1:8; and Revelation 11:15. The reign of Christ will involve His personal presence on earth. In sharp contrast with the view held by Barnes, Wenham comments on this passage that "Daniel's repeated references to a future 'kingdom' have obvious linguistic affinities with the New Testament references to the 'Kingdom of God.'"[42]

Hammer understands the figure as an angel guaranteeing "the promise to Israel that she will fulfill her divine destiny."[43] Israel, however, does not receive the final kingdom. That is reserved for the Lord. In view of the fact that the Lord will one day reign over the whole earth, we who know Him as our Savior should faithfully serve Him now. He is the king. We are His subjects and should live accordingly, v. 14.

Interpretation of the Vision 7:15–28 Although the remainder of the chapter interprets what Daniel has earlier seen, it is also part of his vision. He is "grieved" (*ʾetkᵉrîyat*) at what he has seen. This is the only time the verb *kᵉrâ* occurs. It is cognate to the Akkadian *kšr*, "daze, depression, or stupor." In this context, the idea of "dazed" is appropriate. Daniel is "troubled" (or "alarmed," *bᵉhal*, see 2:25)

---

[42]Barnes, II, 67; Gordon J. Wenham, "The Kingdom of God and Daniel," *ET* 98 (Feb 1987): 132.

[43]Hammer, pp. 78–79.

in his "body" (*nidneh*) at his inability to interpret the vision to this point. This is the only occurrence of *nidneh*. Its Hebrew cognate, *nᵉdanah*, also occurs only once, at 1 Chronicles 21:27, where it must mean "sheath." While this meaning does not fit here, it does suggest a receptacle of some kind. Here, the receptacle is the "body" in which Daniel's troubled spirit resides. He has seen symbols of obvious significance but does not understand them, v. 15.

Daniel approaches one of the myriads of angelic beings standing near him (cf. v. 10) to ask for an explanation of what he has seen. Goldwurm cites the view that the angels stand because they have no joints in their legs.[44] It is more likely that they are represented as standing because they are involved in active service for God. John 20:12 shows that angels can sit; Acts 12:8–9 pictures them as walking; and Genesis 28:12 as ascending and descending a ladder. These activities require jointed legs.

The angel interprets the vision for Daniel, v. 16. The four beasts represent four kings that "shall arise out of the earth," coming forth from mankind to rule. Charles considers this an "incorrect statement." He first objects that the kingdoms rise from the sea, cf. v. 3; and second, that the rise of Babylon is not future.[45] The objection involving the earth rather than the sea is trivial. Once the kingdoms have risen from the "sea" of mankind, they are earthly kingdoms. The imperfect tense verb which is translated "shall arise" simply indicates incomplete action, something still continuing. At the time of Daniel's vision, Babylon's future was not long but was still real. The angel naturally uses the imperfect tense. From the further explanation in v. 23, the four kings represent the four kingdoms that successively dominate the biblical world. These have earlier been described in 2:31–45, v. 17.

Despite the domination of the four kingdoms throughout history, the "saints" of the "most High [*ᶜelyônîn*]" God will "take" (better "receive," see *qabbel*, 5:31) the kingdom. The descriptive name *ᶜelyônîn* is plural. Since it refers to God, it is natural to understand this as a plural of majesty, "highest" or "most high." The name occurs four times, all in this chapter and all plural (vv. 18, 22, 25, 27). It is comparable to the

---

[44]Goldwurm, pp. 207–8.
[45]Charles, p. 190.

Aramaic name ʿillay (see 4:17), "most High," which occurs widely as a shortened form of ʾelahaʾ ʿillayʾa, "most high God" (see 3:26).

Lederach understands the "saints" as angels. These "receive the kingdom and possess the kingdom through the gift of God, in behalf of and with the people of the holy ones." Goldingday argues that ʿelyônîn is "epexegetical or adjectival" and that the phrase refers to "holy ones on high." He identifies these as celestial, either "angels or glorified Israelites."[46] While the word "saints" elsewhere refers to angels, 4:13, 17, 23 ("holy one[s]"), in this chapter it refers to the people of God, vv. 18, 21, 22, 25, and 27. Nowhere does the Bible teach that angels receive the kingdom. In light of eschatological teaching elsewhere, we should not limit the word to Israelites. The Bible teaches that the saints will rule with the Lord (e.g., Matt. 19:28; 1 Cor. 6:2; 2 Tim. 2:10–12; Rev. 1:6; 2:26; 3:21; 5:10; 20:6). They will possess the kingdom "for ever and ever" (cf. vv. 22, 27), v. 18.

Daniel inquires into the nature of the fourth beast. From the description in vv. 7–8 and the additional details given as Daniel asks his question, this beast is obviously more complicated to understand. It is "diverse" from the other beasts, exceedingly "dreadful" (dᵉḥal, see 4:5).[47] We find here that it had iron teeth and bronze claws, so that it "devoured" and "brake in pieces" (dᵉqaq, see 2:34), tearing apart those it trampled upon, v. 19.

Daniel also wants to know more about the ten horns, and about the eleventh horn that subdued the other three horns. The phrase "whose look was more stout [rab, see 2:10] than his fellows" is better "whose appearance was larger than his associates," i.e., the size of the horn dwarfs that of the other horns. This hints at the dominant position held by this king over the other kings, v. 20. Further, the horn makes war and prevails against the saints.[48] The horn represents Antichrist.

---

[46]Lederach, p. 164; John Goldingday, "'Holy Ones on High' in Daniel 7:18," *JBL* 107 (Sep 1988): 495–97.

[47]C. C. Caragounis, "Greek Culture and Jewish Piety: The Clash and the Fourth Beast of Daniel 7," *ETL* 65 No. 4 (1989): 282, sees the difference as "sought on the religious and cultural levels." Since Daniel goes on to develop the difference as "dreadful," it is unlikely that he thinks of religion and culture in describing the beast as "diverse." Caragounis also errs in identifying the fourth beast as Greece.

[48]Porteous, p. 96, understands vv. 21–22 as "the ill-conceived attempt of an interpolator to add something to the vision to correspond to something in the later

The Antichrist will be a real man whom Satan will control. We can see his character in the names given to him in the Bible: "man of sin" (2 Thess. 2:3); "wicked [one]" (2 Thess. 2:8); "antichrist" (1 John 2:18); and "beast" (Rev. 13:4). He will "subdue three kings" (Dan. 7:24) in his rise to power. He will be an eloquent speaker (7:8, 11, 20, 25) but also one of a "fierce countenance" who has access to hidden knowledge (8:23). He will make a covenant with Israel but break it after three and one-half years (9:27). His capital city, by this time, will be in Jerusalem (11:45). He will oppose God (8:25) and the people of God (Rev. 13:7). He will accept the worship of mankind (Rev. 13:8, 12, 15). His coalition of nations will fall apart. Egypt will attack him (Dan. 11:40a). Although he will successfully defeat this attack (Dan. 11:40b–43), the Lord will later overcome him (8:25; 11:45; Rev. 19:11–21).

As an indication of Antichrist's persecution, Zechariah 13:8–9 tells us that two-thirds of the Jews will die. Without giving the details, Revelation 13:7 describes his war against the saints, v. 21. This war will last until the "Ancient of days," the eternal God (cf. vv. 9, 13), appears. At the appointed "time" (z^eman, see 2:16), judgment is given "to the saints" (better "for the saints"), i.e., in favor of the saints, again those belonging to the "most High" ($^celyônîn$), the majestic God. They receive the kingdom, v. 22.

The angel gives the interpretation to Daniel. The fourth beast represents a fourth kingdom that dominates "the whole earth," i.e., the biblical world. Daniel 11:40–44 limits this to the Mediterranean area. His kingdom will "break [this] in pieces" (d^eqaq, see 2:34) as it crushes all resistance. The focus of prophecy is on the biblical world, the world ruled by the Romans. While this "little horn" (7:8) rules only in the Mediterranean world, he will certainly have worldwide influence (Rev. 13:7–8). His dominant role among the biblical nations will let him play a significant part in world events, v. 23.

Phillips includes all of the earth in Antichrist's rule. He understands this to embrace Canada, the United States, Russia, India, China, Japan, etc. Wiersbe also visualizes Antichrist as becoming "the ruler of the world" and "a world dictator."[49] Such a wide rule is

---

interpretation." Since no textual evidence or evidence from early translations supports his view, it should be disregarded.

[49]Phillips, pp. 109–10; Wiersbe, p. 89.

not necessary to fulfill the biblical picture of Antichrist's kingdom. In addition, it goes contrary to 11:40–44, which describes open rebellion against him coming from surrounding nations. Nothing in this context gives Antichrist dominion over the whole world. He controls the nations that have come from the old Roman Empire. These are all countries in the region surrounding the Mediterranean Sea and extending eastward toward modern-day Iraq and Iran. Nations of the world lying outside this region are generally ignored in the Bible.

Out of the fourth kingdom, ten smaller kingdoms rise. Barrett understands "the correspondence between the ten horns and the ten kings [as] simply a way of expressing the initial unity that characterized the 'iron' stage of the kingdom. It is a picture of completeness— a king for a horn." Ford understands the number "ten" as a round number representing as many as fifteen kingdoms, fragments of the Roman Empire.[50] Since the number "ten" does often occur as a round number these views are possible. The use of so many numbers in this passage—four, fourth, vv. 17, 19, 23; ten, implied eleventh, three, vv. 20, 24—argues for taking the numbers literally.

We cannot identify these kingdoms with certainty. It is enough to say that the ten kingdoms will come out of the old Roman Empire. The description portrays these kingdoms as contemporary, not sequential. An eleventh king will rise who will overcome three of the ten kingdoms. Smith understands the eleventh horn as the papacy. The three kingdoms overcome are the Heruli, the Vandals, and the Ostrogoths, all of which opposed "the teachings and claims of the papal hierarchy."[51] The view misapplies the passage to history and ignores the prophetic implications given by the agreement of the book of Revelation with Daniel.

Driver misapplies the second and third beasts as representing the Medes and the Persians. He then makes the fourth beast the Grecian Empire and its successors. The ten horns represent "the ten successors of Alexander on the throne of Antioch" and the eleventh horn is Antiochus Epiphanes. Later, he gives various ways of identifying these kings but comes to no conclusion.[52] One problem faced by

---

[50]Barrett, p. 79; Ford, p. 149.

[51]Smith, pp. 111, 123 (a note briefly discusses Smith's view at 2:41).

[52]Driver, pp. 84, 101–2.

those who adopt the view held by Driver is that there were more than ten kings of Syria between Alexander and Antiochus. The view also limits the interpretation of Daniel to the four kingdoms supposedly existing before his authorship of the book.

Lacocque suggests that the "three kings" are those subdued by Antiochus Epiphanes as he seized the throne. These included the two sons of Seleucus IV, the legitimate heirs, and his own son Antiochus, who served as co-regent 175–170 BC. Cowles identifies the three kings as Ptolemy Philometor, Antiochus the Great, and Seleucus Philopator.[53] According to the mindset of those adopting these positions, prophecy is not possible. Comparing the chapter with c. 2 and c. 11 argues for a prophetic application of the chapter rather than making it historical. In addition, 7:22 sets the fulfillment of the prophecy in the end times.

Verses 24–25 were the text for John Knox's first sermon at St. Andrews, in Scotland. He applied them to the Roman Catholic Church, v. 24.

The angel gives three characteristics of this eleventh king, who is undoubtedly to be identified as Antichrist.[54]

(1) He will speak "against [ṣad, lit. 'at the side of'] the most High [ʿillay, see 4:17]." The word ṣad occurs again only at 6:4, where it is translated "concerning." There, however, the joined preposition (miṣṣad) gives it the sense "from the side of," i.e., "touching, concerning." It is cognate to the Hebrew ṣad, which occurs more than two dozen times as "side" or "sides." Here, the word conveys the thought that Antichrist elevates himself to the same level as God (cf. 2 Thess. 2:4).

(2) He will "wear out" (or "wear away," figuratively, "harass") the saints who belong to the "most High" (ʿelyônîn). Once again, the plural ʿelyônîn denotes God's majestic nature.

---

[53]Lacocque, *The Book of Daniel*, p. 153; Cowles, pp. 361–62.

[54]Leupold, p. 323, identifies the Roman Catholic pope as "the outstanding manifestation of the Antichrist to date." While the papacy has often opposed true Christianity, it cannot be the Antichrist in view here. Rev. 17–18 describes the destruction of Rome by Antichrist. While he works with the Roman Catholic Church for a time to achieve his purposes, he eventually turns against it and destroys Rome, the seat of the church's power.

(3) He will try to "change times [z^eman, see 2:16] and laws [dat, see 2:9]," i.e., change the normal ways of life, especially with respect to morality and religion. This undoubtedly includes attacks on the worship of the Jews as he changes the normal festival times by making them point to himself.

Thomson suggests the trivial view that changing "times and laws" refers to changes by Julius Caesar in modifying the calendar. Keil and Leupold broaden both z^eman and dat by making them general. These are not limited to the Jewish festivals and laws but refer to general human institutions. Antichrist, however, will not be able to accept the worship of man without changing the worship of the true God. He does that either by letting the festival times point to him as God or by substituting other festivities that honor him. The context here is that of the Great Tribulation. Since z^eman refers to appointed times and dat refers to divine law in half of its occurrences, I prefer to let a religious sense stand here. Barrett is closer when he says, "This will involve the creation of a new calendar devoid of any Christian reference."[55] Current trends now point in this direction. We emphasize family and eating turkey at Thanksgiving without much effort to offer gratitude to God for His goodness to ourselves and the nation. We celebrate Christmas without mentioning Christ. Easter is now simply a spring break in the school's calendar. The abbreviation BC (before Christ) is now BCE (before the common era), while AD (*Anno Domini*, the year of our Lord) is now CE (common era).

The Antichrist will have power over men for "a time and times and the dividing of time." Similar expressions occur in 12:7 and Revelation 12:14. The phrase is also similar to the half-week of 9:27; cf. 12:11; Revelation 11:2–3; 12:6; 13:5. These all refer to a period of three and one-half years that takes place in the last half of the Tribulation.

Despite this clear association with other biblical passages, alternate interpretations have been put forth. Leupold denies that three and one-half years fulfills this phrase. He instead describes Antichrist as beginning to dominate the world scene for a "time," then succeeding for an indefinite period of "times" and having a "half

---

[55]Thomson, p. 219; Keil, p. 242; Leupold, 324; Barrett, p. 81.

time" of success. The overall weight of evidence from other passages that use this phrase, however, supports a period of three and one-half years.[56]

Auchincloss makes the word "time" equal seven years. With questionable logic, he makes the phrase "time, and times, and the dividing of times" equal "70 plus 490, plus 35," a total of 595 years. He begins this period at the reign of Cyrus, making it extend to AD 38. The "setting up of the kingdom" begins the next year, AD 39. This is the time when the Gentiles come into God's kingdom. The view relies on equating things that have no natural connection in the Bible.[57]

Hartman sees the fulfillment in the persecution of Israel by Antiochus Epiphanes. Since this "lasted, at the most, three years and eight days [1,103 days]," he concludes that the author "made his insertions in ch. 7 some time in 167 BC, when he could foresee the success of [Judas Maccabaeus's] military operations, but not the speed with which it would be accomplished." Hammer adopts this view except that he sees the persecution lasting "three years and ten days." These views, of course, reject the accuracy of the book.[58]

Ford understands the "little horn" as representing "religion run to seed—the system of church and state that dominated medieval times." The "time and times and the dividing of time" is 1260 years, from AD 537 to 1798. In 537 the Roman Catholic Church overcame heathen powers opposing it, but in 1798, secular opposition overcame the church. The view is highly speculative.[59]

The Bible also calls this period of time the "great tribulation" (Matt. 24:21) and the time of "Jacob's trouble" (Jer. 30:7). The last three and one-half years of the Tribulation will be a time of terrible natural disasters and increased persecution of the Jews by Antichrist. Daniel 9:27 tells us that Antichrist will break his covenant with Israel in the middle of the Tribulation "week." The Gentiles will control the temple for this time (Rev. 11:2). Antichrist will receive the worship of mankind (2 Thess. 2:4). He will persecute Israel (Dan. 12:1; Matt. 24:21). In retribution for mankind's sin, God will unleash

---

[56]Leupold, pp. 325–26.
[57]Auchincloss, pp. 100–101.
[58]Hartman, pp. 215–16; Hammer, p. 82.
[59]Ford, p. 151.

devastating calamities (Rev. 16:1–12). The period will close with the Battle of Armageddon, when God vanquishes the godless armies of the world (Zech. 14:2–3; Rev. 19:11–21).

There is a close correspondence of this passage with Revelation 13. The "dreadful and terrible" beast here (v. 7) is described there as having characteristics of a leopard, bear, and lion (Rev. 13:2). The ten horns with three subdued before an eleventh horn here (7:7–8) parallel the "seven heads and ten horns" there (Rev. 13:1). The "war with the saints" here (7:21) equals the "war with the saints" there (Rev. 13:7). The "time and times and the dividing of time" here (7:25) is the same as the "forty and two months" there (Rev. 13:5). The "mouth speaking great things" here against the "most High" (*ᶜelyônîn*, see 7:18) is identical to the "mouth speaking great things" there (Rev. 13:5). Daniel's prophecy, then, is an early prediction of Antichrist and his opposition to God, v. 25.

After that, "the judgment [or 'court'] shall sit." The expression is virtually identical with that found in 7:10 and has the same meaning. The court will be set as God prepares His judgment. The dominion of Antichrist will be ended, v. 26. The kingdom "under the whole heaven," over all the earth, will be given to the saints. This will be an "everlasting kingdom." The implied thought is that wickedness will never again prevail. All will serve the "most High" (*ᶜelyônîn*), the majestic God to whom the kingdom belongs (cf. v. 14), v. 27. The interpretation ends at this point. Although Daniel is "much [*śaggîʾ*, see 2:6] troubled [or 'alarmed,' *bᵉhal*, see 2:25]" and his "countenance" (*zîw*, see 2:31) shows his emotions, he keeps his thought to himself, v. 28.

RAM AND GOAT 8:1–27

From this point on in the book, Daniel writes in Hebrew rather than Aramaic.[1] From 2:4 to 7:28, Daniel has written in Aramaic, the language spoken and read in Babylon. That section of the book deals primarily with the development of the heathen world powers; hence, it is appropriate to use Aramaic. In 1:1–2:3 and 8:1–12:13, the book focuses on the nation of Israel. Where this part of the book mentions the heathen powers, it is generally in their relationship to Israel. The use of Hebrew is more appropriate here. Daniel therefore changes back to his native language as he continues his writings.

Daniel's Vision 8:1–14 The vision occurs ca. 551 BC, Belshazzar's "third year." The vision takes place "after that which appeared . . . at the first," the earlier vision of c. 7 that Daniel saw in Belshazzar's first year (553 BC). The vision also occurs before the events in c. 5, Belshazzar's final year (539 BC), v. 1. Among others, Knoch and Cowles make Belshazzar's third year his last year or nearly his last year as king.[2] Akkadian records, however, show that he served as co-regent for most of the reign of Nabonidus. This co-regency covered approximately the years 553–539 BC. The date places the prophecy before the fall of Babylon and, as with all prophecy, shows clearly God's knowledge of the future.

Daniel is in the "palace" (or "fortress," *bîrâ*) at "Shushan," the biblical name of Susa, located in the province of Elam. The noun *bîrâ* occurs widely in later Hebrew—Chronicles, Nehemiah, Esther, and Daniel. It refers to the temple at Jerusalem (1 Chron. 29:1, 19), to a fortress at the corner of the north and east walls apparently for the defense of the temple (Neh. 2:8; 7:2), and to a fortress located in Shushan (Neh. 1:1; Esther 1:2). The word has this last sense here.

---

[1] From c. 8 on, Hartman, p. 232, assumes that the Hebrew translates an Aramaic original. This makes his comments on 8:1–9:27 (and Di Lella's comments on 10:1–12:13) subjective, based on reconstructions of the Aramaic. Archer, p. 40, speculates that Daniel wrote c. 2–7 "before he saw the vision of chapters 8–12 [*sic*] and that these earlier chapters even became available for Gentile scrutiny, as well as for the captive Jews themselves, who by this time knew Aramaic." The view overlooks the date given in 8:1, Belshazzar's "third year." This is well before the conquest of the city described in c. 5.

[2] Knoch, p. 256; Cowles, p. 372.

Shushan also figures in the records of other biblical figures. Nehemiah served as the cupbearer to Artaxerxes, the Persian king at Shushan (Neh. 1:1). Esther, the queen of Ahasuerus, was in Shushan at the time of the events recorded in the book of Esther (e.g., 1:2; 4:16; 9:12). The city has archaeological importance as well. The French archaeologist Jean-Vincent Scheil discovered Hammurabi's Code there in 1901–2. This law code from the early eighteenth century BC contained 282 laws that covered generally every area of life and business. Some of the laws (nos. 13, 66–99) are missing, but the majority of them remain to illustrate the nature of the code. The eight-foot-high stele is located now in the Louvre Museum in Paris.

West and Whitcomb are two of several authors who understand Daniel's presence in Elam as part of the vision. Strauss also understands Daniel's presence in Shushan as part of his vision. He sees the significance of Shushan as being the capital of Persia, the next of the world kingdoms to follow Babylon. The emphasis of the chapter, however, is on the third kingdom, Greece. Watkinson argues that Daniel could not have been at Shushan since Babylon at this time was at war with Persia.[3] The war, however, did not start until several years later, with Babylon falling in Belshazzar's fifteenth year (539 BC). The two empires may well have had political relationships at this time. Only vv. 3, 4, and 7 refer to Persia.

These authors argue that, while remaining bodily in Babylon, Daniel sees himself in Persian territory. There is no reason, however, for Daniel to mention his location if it was only part of a vision that he received. The location has nothing to do with the vision except to give the background for Daniel's seeing it. The account reads as though Daniel was physically present (cf. vv. 16–18).

The name Shushan means "lilies" and reflects the growth of these in the neighborhood about the city. The province of Elam was southeast of Babylon. A residence of the Persian kings, Shushan was located a little more than 200 miles east of Babylon and about 140 miles north of the Persian Gulf. The city was on the Ulai River (ʾûbal), called the Eulaeus River in secular writing, possibly another name for the Kerkhes River and probably a branch of the Coaspes River. The noun "river" (ʾûbal) is from *yabal*, "to bear along." The

---

[3]West, p. 31; Whitcomb, *Daniel*, p. 108; Strauss, p. 233; Watkinson, p. 221.

word occurs only in this chapter (vv. 2, 3, 6) although related words occur elsewhere (e.g., Isa. 30:25; 44:4; Jer. 17:8). The ESV, NASB, and NIV are some of several translations that interpret *'ûbal* as "canal." Since the location of the river is not certain, "canal" is a possibility. The Eulaeus River flowed west of the Zagros Mountains.[4]

We can only speculate about Daniel's reason for being in Shushan. Verse 27 tells us that he was there on "the king's business." While Daniel had apparently retired from his active service, he may still have been involved in representing the Babylonians in some way. Retired governmental leaders often take on special responsibilities. The account in c. 5 occurs about twelve years after the vision described in this chapter. It is not unreasonable that Belshazzar should have forgotten Daniel in that time (5:10–16).

While the Babylonian kings did not control Shushan at this time, it is clear that they had contact with the region. There was likely trade between the regions. There may have been political agreements. Ezra 4:9 indicates that some Elamites had been resettled in Palestine after Babylon's victory over Judah, v. 2.

Daniel sees a ram with "*two* horns." One of the horns is higher than the other and comes up after the first horn. While the number "two" is italicized in the KJV, the dual form of the word here makes it clear that this is the meaning of the phrase. Throughout the chapter, the word "horn" (*qeren*) alternates between the dual (vv. 3 [2X], 6, 7, 20) and singular forms (vv. 5, 8, 9, 21) depending on whether it refers to the two horns of the ram or the one horn of the goat (and, in v. 9, the "little horn" that follows the first horn). The description makes it clear that these horns were unique. A ram normally has two horns. This ram initially had only a single horn, with the second horn coming up later and growing larger than the first horn. From v. 20, it is clear that the ram represents the Medo-Persian kingdom.

The first horn pictures the kingdom of the Medes. The second horn that is higher than the first stands for Persia, dominant after

___
[4]Hartman, p. 224, notes that the LXX and Vulgate translate *'ûbal* as "gate." There is also an Akkadian cognate *abullu* meaning "city gate." The argument from Akkadian goes two ways since there is also a cognate *abālu*, "to bring, carry, conduct," similar to the Hebrew root *yabal*, "to conduct, bear along." As for the LXX and Vulgate, they likely struggled with the sense of the word just as we do today. The occurrences in vv. 3, 6 shed no further light. Verse 16, however, while not using *'ûbal*, seems to refer to the river.

defeating the Medes and gaining their cooperation, v. 3. The ram "push[es]" (*nagaḥ*, "to push, thrust," in this context "to butt") to the west, north, and south in his conquests. The Medes and Persians first conquered to the west. In this direction, they controlled Asia Minor, territory extending to the Aegean Sea and including Babylon, Assyria, and Lydia. They next campaigned in the north, where they conquered Armenia, Bactria (roughly corresponding to northern Afghanistan), and regions around the Caspian Sea. To the south, they dominated Palestine, including Israel and the smaller kingdoms of that region, and Egypt. Although the alliance also campaigned in the east, the vision makes no mention of that direction since that part of the empire was comparatively minor and plays no significant part in the biblical record.

At this time, no other "beasts" can stand before the ram, and none can deliver from his "hand" (*yad*). Although *yad* is normally translated "hand," it is often used figuratively to represent "power" (e.g., 8:7; 9:15; 11:11, 16; 12:7). Using the symbolism already introduced, the other beasts represent the conquered kingdoms. The ram does "according to his will" (or "as he pleases") and becomes "great," having significant power and influence over the nations, v. 4.

As Daniel considers what he has seen, another animal appears in his vision. A "he goat" comes from the west with respect to the Medo-Persian kingdom. He moves "on the face of the whole earth." Apparently, the goat weaves back and forth contacting various countries as he comes. Verse 21 identifies this goat as "the king of Grecia," with its "first king" being Alexander the Great (discussed at 2:39*b*). That he "touched not the ground" suggests the speed with which he comes. The goat has a "notable horn" (better "a conspicuous horn") between his eyes, v. 5.

The conspicuous horn represents Alexander the Great, the king who led Greece to its position as the third of the world kingdoms mentioned in Daniel (2:39; 7:6; 11:3–4). Alexander, the son of Philip of Macedon, was born in 356 BC. After Philip's assassination, Alexander became king. After local campaigns and an expedition against Thebes, he prepared to conquer Persia. This is the campaign taken up in Daniel's vision. Although Daniel does not mention Alexander by name, 1 Maccabees 1:1, 7 refers to his conquest and twelve-year reign.

The "he goat" attacks the ram with two horns that Daniel had seen standing before the river. The attack takes place "in the fury of his power" (or "with great rage"), v. 6. "Moved with choler" (or "enraged") against the ram, the goat breaks his horns. The ram has no power to stand against the goat. The goat destroys the ram, throwing him to the ground and trampling him. No one can deliver the ram from his "hand" (*yad*), v. 7.

The he goat "waxed very great" (or "was greatly magnified"). Alexander led his army of 35,000 soldiers against the Persian army under Darius Codomannus, also called "Darius the Persian" (Neh. 12:22). The name Codomannus occurs spelled in different ways. It is thought to be the Greek form of his Akkadian name, Artashata, with the meaning "holding the good." He took the throne-name Darius at his coronation as king over the Persian Empire. He was not in the direct line to become king. After the death of Artaxerxes, he was selected to become king since he was a relative who had earlier distinguished himself in battle.

Alexander first defeated the Persian army at the Granicus River, near the Hellespont, 334 BC. Darius collected an enlarged army, estimated at up to one-half million soldiers. Alexander fought this army on the Plain of Issus, 333 BC, where the terrain did not let the Persians take advantage of their superior numbers. Alexander then turned south where he gained the submission of Phoenicia, Judea, and Egypt. In 331 BC, he brought his army into Mesopotamia where he defeated the Persian army for a third time at Gaugamela, on the northern part of the Tigris River. The assassination of Darius by one of his own followers ended the resistance of Persia.

At the height of Alexander's power, however, the "great horn," the king of the empire represented by the he goat, is broken. The picture is of Alexander's death at the age of thirty-two. Appianus, the Roman historian, aptly commented that "the empire of Alexander was splendid in its magnitude, in its armies, in the success and rapidity of his conquests, and it wanted little of being boundless and unexampled, yet in its shortness of duration it was like a brilliant flash of lightning."[5]

In place of the "great horn," four "notable" (again "conspicuous") horns, also representing kings, come up. They are directed toward "the four winds of heaven," i.e., toward the north, east, south, and

---

[5]Appianus, *Roman History*, trans. Horace White (Cambridge, Mass.: Harvard University Press, 1964), Preface 10.

west. As in 7:6, the horns represent Alexander's generals (Seleucus Nicanor, Lysimachus, Cassander, and Ptolemy). These gained power over the major parts of the empire. In the north, Lysimachus took Thrace and Bithynia. Toward the west, Cassander gained command over Macedonia and Greece. Seleucus controlled Asia, including Syria, Babylonia, and the eastern countries. In the south, Ptolemy ruled over Egypt and Arabia, v. 8.

A gap of about 150 years separates vv. 8 and 9. At this time, a "little horn" comes forth from one of the four horns. This horn represents Antiochus Epiphanes, a descendant of Seleucus Nicator, one of the kings to rule over part of Alexander's empire. Among others, Steen and Tregelles understand the "little horn" as picturing Antichrist. It is true that Antiochus is a type of Antichrist. The passage here, however, has a natural historical fulfillment in Epiphanes. The "horn" of 7:24 comes after the development of the ten kingdoms from the Roman Empire. Nothing here refers to that. Further, there is no connection between the 2,300 evening-mornings of 8:14 and Antichrist. Smith interprets the little horn as Rome.[6] This cannot be so. Rome replaces Greece in 2:39–40 and 7:6–7 and does not continue the third kingdom, 8:8–9. Further, the 2,300 days has nothing to do with Rome.

Since the Antichrist comes on the scene after the Roman Empire rather than after the Grecian rule, Antiochus Epiphanes better satisfies the description in the chapter. He is "little" (see *miṣʿar*, 7:8), coming from an insignificant background (v. 9) "out of one of" the original horns. This refers to his descent from one of the four kings that followed Alexander (v. 9). He opposed the "host" of God's people (v. 10). He magnified himself, taking the name Epiphanes ("the illustrious one") to call attention to his glory (v. 11). He stopped the sacrifices in the temple (v. 11) and opposed divine truth (v. 12). He caused the Jews' temple and a "host" of the Jews to be "trodden under foot" (v. 13).

Although this wicked king exercised great influence on the earth during his reign, in God's sight he is a "little" [or 'insignificant,' see *miṣʿar*, 7:8] horn." His "little" beginnings include being a younger brother of Seleucus IV Philopator. When Rome defeated his father,

---

[6]Steen, pp. 71–72; Tregelles, p. 81; Smith, p. 158.

Antiochus III, Antiochus IV went as a hostage to Rome. He remained a prisoner there for thirteen years. During this time, Seleucus Philopator assumed the rule after the death of Antiochus III. After several years, Seleucus exchanged his own son Demetrius for Antiochus IV, possibly to let Demetrius gain a Roman education.

Before Antiochus arrived in Syria, Seleucus IV died under mysterious circumstances. It is possible (but not clear) that his treasurer, Heliodorus, assassinated him. In any case, Heliodorus claimed the throne. Antiochus made an alliance with Eumenes, the king of Pergamum in Asia Minor, and defeated Heliodorus.

Although Eumenes had helped Rome in its victory over Antiochus III, he assisted Antiochus IV in gaining the throne of Syria. In all likelihood, this suited Rome since Antiochus IV had received his education while a hostage in Rome. Pergamum was at this time a smaller kingdom in Asia Minor. Rome awarded Eumenes II control over additional territory in return for assistance that he had given them. He commemorated his victory on a frieze on the great altar dedicated to the god Zeus at Pergamum, about 100 miles north of Ephesus. He ruled Pergamum 197–159 BC.

Epiphanes reigned 175–164 BC. The notes at 11:21–35 give additional information about him. Verse 9 tells us that he, the little horn, "waxed exceeding great," a summary of his military accomplishments. He conquered toward the south, as far as Egypt, and the east, conquering Parthia and Armenia. He dominated the "pleasant [or 'beautiful, glorious,' the same word as in 11:16, 41, 45] land," here referring to Palestine, a land with glorious spiritual significance, v. 9.[7] This "little horn," now great in his influence over the Mediterranean world, wars against the "host of heaven," here representing faithful Israelites, those called by the God of heaven. Some of the "host" and its individual "stars," both terms referring to the godly in Israel, are cast down and trampled on.

Thomson applies the phrase "host of heaven" to the angels. He states "all interpretations that make this mean either the people of God or the Levites must be thrown aside." When a nation is defeated, its

---

[7]The word "land" is supplied from 11:16 or 11:41. For this reason, Walvoord, p. 185, suggests that the reference here is to "Jerusalem in particular rather than the land in general." The view is possible; however, Antiochus Epiphanes conquered the land, not just its capital. Verse 24 refers broadly to his oppression of the land.

angel is regarded as "thrown to the earth and trodden underfoot." He argues that the phrase "host of heaven" never refers to people elsewhere. It refers either to the literal stars (e.g., Deut. 4:19; Isa. 34:4) or to angels (e.g., 1 Kings 22:19; Neh. 9:6).[8] Thomson neglects the context in stating his view. The surrounding verses support the meaning of God's people. Verses 12 through 13 are best understood to refer to people. Verse 24 refers to the persecution of the "holy people." Since the word "host" does refer to people elsewhere (e.g., 1 Sam. 11:11; Obad. 1:20), it is reasonable to understand it so here.

Heaton sees the stars as representing "the gods of the heathen." In assaulting them, Antiochus makes an "attack on all forms of religion." Again, the context opposes the view. Lederach also refers the phrase to angels: "A defeat of the Jews is also a defeat of their guardian angels."[9] It is difficult to accept this as a defeat of God's angels when the persecution of the Jews under Antiochus carried out God's will to bring judgment on His people for their wickedness, v. 10.

When Ptolemy VI died in 173 BC, Antiochus claimed Palestine. This brought about war between Syria and Egypt, a war won by Syria, and one in which Ptolemy Philometor was taken prisoner. Epiphanes proclaimed himself the new ruler of Egypt. The Egyptians, however, rebelled and chose Philometor's younger brother Euergetes as their king. Rather than fight a prolonged war, Antiochus returned to Syria. A second invasion of Egypt in 168 BC was aborted when Rome demanded that he withdraw. Returning through Palestine, Epiphanes sacked Jerusalem and robbed the temple of its treasures. Antiochus forbad the Jews to worship God; rather, they were to worship Zeus. His attempt to force this worship upon the Jews brought about the Maccabean Revolt (discussed at 11:32), a rebellion that eventually led to Israel's independence from Syria.

Antiochus magnifies himself to the level of the "prince of the host," i.e., the commander of the "host," God Himself. The phrase "by him" is better "from Him." In his arrogance, this king robs God by taking away the daily sacrifices.[10] He also defiles the

---

[8]Thomson, pp. 241–42.

[9]Heaton, p. 104; Lederach, p. 189.

[10]Watkinson, pp. 260–61, sees Herod as the fulfillment of this prophecy. Herod, however, did not take away the daily sacrifice or cast down the temple.

"sanctuary,"[11] the temple at Jerusalem, v. 11. 1 Maccabees 1:41–49 describes this:

> Then the king wrote to his whole kingdom that they should all become one people, and everyone should give up his particular practices. And all the heathen assented to the command of the king. And many from Israel agreed to his kind of worship and offered sacrifices to idols and broke the sabbath. And the king sent word by messengers to Jerusalem and the towns of Judah to follow practices foreign to the country and put a stop to whole burnt offerings and sacrifices and drink offerings at the sanctuary, and to break the sabbaths and profane the feasts and pollute sanctuary and sanctified; to build altars and sacred precincts and idol temples and sacrifice hogs and unclean cattle; and to leave their sons uncircumcised and defile themselves with every unclean and profane practice, so that they might forget the Law and change all their religious ordinances.

This interruption of the temple worship by Antiochus Epiphanes continued a little more than three years.

Verse 12 recaps vv. 9–11. This horn has power over a large "host" of people in the area of the "daily sacrifice." He receives this power as God judges Israel's "transgression" (*pešaᶜ*) of failing to follow Him. The noun *pešaᶜ* refers here to rebellion against God's authority.[12] Antiochus casts "the truth" (or simply "truth") to the ground.[13] He "practised" (or "acted"), carrying out his wishes, and prospering in this, v. 12.

---

[11]Lacocque, *The Book of Daniel*, p. 162, understands the "prince of the host" as the archangel Michael and the "sanctuary" (*miqdaš*) as the people of Israel. There is, however, no sacrifice made to Michael that could be "taken away." The phrase clearly refers to God Himself. In addition, the word *miqdaš* occurs more than 70X in the OT but never refers to people.

[12]Leupold, p. 349, understands the *pešaᶜ* as "the thing for which the regular daily offerings were given over." In other words, "the 'transgression' [of wicked sacrifices] took the place of the daily offerings." The preposition here, however, is best understood as the *bêt causa*, which gives the *pešaᶜ* a causative sense.

[13]Whitcomb, *Daniel*, p. 113, refers "the truth" to the OT books. He cites 1 Macc. 1:56–57, "Wherever they found the book of the Law, they tore them up and burned them, and if anyone was found to possess a book of the agreement or respected the Law, the king's decree condemned him to death." The view is possible. Although the definite article does not occur in the text, it may be supplied.

Daniel hears one "saint" (better "holy one") speaking. The word "saint" here refers to an angel rather than to a saint among the people. A second angel asks a question of the "certain [*palmonî*] saint" that has spoken.[14] This is the only time that *palmonî* occurs. The word is difficult since it does not clearly relate to any word in a cognate language. From the context, it likely is a variant spelling of *pᵉlonî*, "a certain one." Where *pᵉlonî* occurs elsewhere, it is coordinated with *ʾalmonî*, "some one" (Ruth 4:1, "such a one"; 1 Sam. 21:2 and 2 Kings 6:8, both "such and such"). For this reason, some understand *palmonî* as a compound of *pᵉlonî ʾalmonî*.[15] While this is possible, there is no way to verify it since the word occurs only here.[16]

The second angel asks how long it will be until the fulfillment of the vision of the daily sacrifice and the "transgression" (*pešaᶜ*) that causes desolation and lets both the sanctuary and the people be trampled. The question essentially asks, "How long will this period of persecution last?" The conversation illustrates the interest that the angels have in the affairs of men (1 Pet. 1:12), v. 13.

The second angel responds to "me." While the words are spoken to that "certain saint," Daniel hears them. The angel apparently means that he should. The time will cover 2,300 days. Then the "sanctuary," the holy place, will be "cleansed" (better "made right," i.e., restored to its intended use). This period of time has several interpretations.[17]

---

[14]From v. 16, Newell identifies the angel as Gabriel. It is unlikely, however, that Gabriel would ask a question here regarding the vision, then interpret the vision in vv. 17–26.

[15]BDB, p. 812, tentatively suggests this. *Gesenius' Hebrew and Chaldee Lexicon to the Old Testament Scriptures*, trans. Samuel Prideaux Tregelles (Grand Rapids: Baker Book House, 1979), p. 677, makes it compounded from the two words. Lacocque, p. 159, adopts this view.

[16]Bultema, pp. 248–49, tentatively identifies the speaker as Christ. While this is possible, the reference is too general to be certain of the speaker's identity.

[17]In addition to the views listed here, there are other lesser views not widely held. Auchincloss, pp. 61–62, 103, equates the "sanctuary and the host" with the "national government." He then makes 2,300 days equal "308 yrs. 6 mos. 21 days." This extends from Oct. 14th, 450 BC to May 4, 141 BC, when Simon Maccabeus cleansed the temple. He bases the view on the odd conclusion that a prophetic day "equals 49 ordinary days of 24 hours each." Goldwurm, p. 229, makes this the time until "Jewry's sin will have been atoned for [making them . . . righteous]," so that

(1) William Miller (1782–1849) was a farmer and a Baptist preacher in upstate New York. His study of Daniel led him to interpret the 2,300 days as 2,300 years that began in 457 BC. At the end of this time, in 1843, Christ would return. When this failed to happen, a recalculation moved the predicted coming to October 22, 1844.[18] Many of Miller's followers had sold their possessions to await the day. When Christ did not appear, the Millerites broke up. Out of the group, Mrs. Ellen G. White joined other Millerites. She taught that Christ had come in 1844 to cleanse the heavenly sanctuary. At that time, He had begun His investigative work of judging the righteousness of the living and the dead. Her beliefs led to the formation of the group known as the Seventh-day Adventists. Although Miller himself had begun the process which led to formation of this group, he never became a member.

(2) Some take the number symbolically, representing something less than a full seven-year period of judgment; cf. v. 26, which refers to the same period.[19]

Two additional major views are more commonly held:

(3) The word "days" is ʿereb boqer, "evening-morning." Some take this as 1,150 days, 3+ years, probably alluding to the

---

their suffering will end. Israel's atonement comes from the sacrifice of Christ. Only when they accept His sacrifice will their suffering end.

[18]William H. Shea, "Supplementary Evidence in Support of 457 B.C. as the Starting Date for the 2300 Day-Years of Daniel 8:14," *JATS* 12:1 (Spring 2001): 97–105, understands the 2,300 days as 2,300 years, beginning at the same time as the 490 years of 9:24–27. He argues that *dabar* (9:25) normally means "word" and does not necessarily refer to a king's decree. He refers it to Ezra's word to rebuild Jerusalem. This took place after he had dealt with the marriage problem of foreign wives, early in 457 BC. The period extends to 1844, when the heavenly sanctuary began to be cleansed. Saying, however, that *dabar* does not necessarily refer to a king's decree is not the same as saying that it cannot refer to the king's decree. The word occurs often of the king's speech, e.g., 1 Kings 2:38; 12:7; 2 Kings 18:27–28. Further, the book of Ezra gives no decree by Ezra to begin building the city. That takes place in Nehemiah. More importantly, it is difficult to apply the day = year association here since the phrasing is so radically different from c. 9. The phrase "evening-morning" does not occur again. Logically, it refers to a day.

[19]So Lederach, p. 191. Tregelles, p. 105, and Phillips, p. 129, suggest that the 2,300 days is included within the 2,520-day Tribulation period. It begins with the assassination and resurrection of Antichrist, Rev. 17:8. The context, however, refers to Antiochus Epiphanes, not Antichrist.

evening and morning sacrifices offered by the Jews. This is just about the period of time that took place between the desolation of the temple at Jerusalem by Antiochus Epiphanes and the rededication of the altar. The "transgression of desolation" spoken of in v. 13 refers to an altar of Jupiter set up by Antiochus in the temple to replace the Altar of Burnt Offering (see also the additional discussion at 11:31). The rededication of the altar took place a little more than three years later (1 Macc. 4:52). The Jews celebrated this rededication by establishing the Feast of Dedication (John 10:22). While we cannot verify the exactness of the dates, the 1,150 days come close to the historical actions of Antiochus Epiphanes, v. 14.[20]

(4) Some understand "evening-morning" as an idiom that signifies a day. This period of time—a little less than six and one-half years—refers to the whole period of time that Antiochus persecuted the Jews rather than just the period in which he forbid offering the daily sacrifice.[21] This persecution began with the murder of Onias III, a former high priest, in 170 BC (2 Macc. 4:34–36). It ended with the rededication of the altar in December 164 BC (1 Macc. 4:52).

Once again, it is not possible to verify the exact period of time covered by the persecution. This final view has the advantage of understanding "evening" and "morning" as defining a "day," just as it does elsewhere (e.g., Gen. 1:5, 8, 13, 19, 23, 31; 1 Chron. 16:40; 2 Chron. 2:4; Ps. 65:8). It is also the older view, supported by the LXX, Vulgate, and older Jewish commentaries. Further, nothing in v. 14 refers to morning or evening sacrifices. The phrase is simply "evening morning two thousand three hundred." It is interpretive to refer this to sacrifices.

Gabriel's Interpretation 8:15–27 Daniel "sought for the meaning" of the vision. As the result of his prayer, an angel, later identified as Gabriel (v. 16), appears before him.[22] The pages of Daniel

---

[20]Archer, p. 103; Bultema, p. 250; and Hammer, p. 86, are among those who adopt this view.

[21]Several authors hold this position, among them, Calvin, II, 199; Gaebelein, p. 101; and Walvoord, p. 190.

[22]Miller, p. 231, identifies the "man" (*gaber*) as "God himself." He bases this on the use of *gaber*, which normally refers in some way to "might," and the fact that

forcefully illustrate his dependence on God in prayer. On five separate occasions, the book records Daniel's prayers over the various matters with which he is involved. In 2:17–18, he and his friends pray that God will reveal Nebuchadnezzar's dream to them. When the revelation comes, Daniel immediately goes to the Lord to express his thanks, 2:20–23. In 6:10–11, we find that Daniel prayed to God three times each day. It was his faithfulness in prayer that his enemies used in their attempt to have him executed in the lion's den. In 8:15, he seeks the meaning of the vision he has seen. In 9:3–19, Daniel confesses Israel's sins and asks God to end their captivity, a prayer made at the time of the evening sacrifice, 9:20–21. In 10:2–3, he spends three weeks in fasting and prayer. In 10:12, the angel refers to Daniel's prayer. The angel there begins the answer to Daniel's requests.[23] Daniel's pattern of prayer gives a practical example for Christians to follow today.

That the angel here has the "appearance of a man" is normal; cf. Genesis 18:2, 22, v. 15. A "man's voice," the voice of the Lord as heard by Daniel,[24] sounds from between "the banks of the Ulai." The MT is lit. "between the Ulai." This logically means "between the banks of the Ulai." It is also possible, however, that the voice comes from within a bend of the river or from within the angle formed by a tributary

---

Daniel prostrates himself before him, v. 17. Except for the messianic prophecy in Jer. 31:22, the word *gaber* never refers to God. That Daniel falls on his face before the man is natural. Both the context of the vision and the close approach of the angel have affected him emotionally. In addition, v. 18 indicates that the angel awakens him and brings him to an upright position rather than accepting his prostration as worship.

[23]Whitcomb, p. 122, is too strong: "It may be safely asserted that nothing of significance happens in God's program on earth apart from the persistent and believing prayers of His redeemed ones." Prayer is important, more so than most Christians realize. Significant events do take place, however, that no Christian would think of praying for. Such matters as Hitler's slaughter of the Jews reflect God's punishment of the nation for sin. God has used tidal waves, earthquakes, and volcanic eruptions to bring judgment on cities and nations. These illustrate significant events for which believers have not prayed.

[24]Goldwurm, pp. 226, 229, identifies the unnamed speaker as "Michael, Gabriel's superior in the heavenly hierarchy." The view is speculative. The Scripture does not make clear the relationships between the archangels. Michael is "one of the chief princes," 10:13.

flowing into the river.[25] The voice both identifies and commands the angel Gabriel to help Daniel understand the vision.

The Bible mentions Gabriel more frequently than any other angel except Michael. He not only explains Daniel's visions to him, 8:16; 9:21, but he also announces the birth of John the Baptist to Zacharias his father, Luke 1:19, and the birth of Jesus Christ to Mary, Luke 1:26. The apocryphal book of Enoch (20:1–8) identifies him as one of the "holy angels who watch." The Koran (Sûrah 26:192–94) states that he revealed the Koran to Mohammed.

The Talmud mentions Gabriel several times, most notably as "one of the four archangels" (*Soṭah* 10*b*), and, relating to the book of Daniel, gives him credit for saving Hananiah, Mishael, and Azariah from the fiery furnace (*Pesaḥîm* 118*a*). *Šabbat* 55*a* states that he is "God's messenger, who executes His will on earth." He was one of the angels who accompanied the Lord on His visit to Abraham in *Yoma* 37*a* and was in fact the angel responsible for overthrowing Sodom in *Baba Meziʾa* 86*b*. *Soṭah* 12*b* says that Gabriel beat the servants of Pharaoh's daughter "to the ground" when they opposed her decision to save the baby Moses from the Nile. According to *Sanhedrin* 95*b*, he was the angel who slew the 185,000 Assyrians that had besieged Jerusalem during Hezekiah's reign. *Šabbat* 56*b* and *Sanhedrin* 21*b* relate the fanciful view that he placed a reed in the sea, which gathered land about it that eventually became the location for the city of Rome. Whether or not Gabriel performed all that the Talmud credits him with, it is clear from the biblical references to Gabriel that the Lord chose him to communicate important messages to God's people.

This is the first time that the Scriptures name an angel of God. Elsewhere the Bible also names Michael (discussed at 10:13) as an angel who serves God. In the Apocrypha, Tobit 12:15 states that "the seven holy angels . . . offer up [to God] the prayers of the God's people." The book of Revelation refers to "the seven angels" used by God to send plagues on the earth, e.g., 8:2; 15:1. Some think these are the archangels.

---

[25]Thomson, p. 245, suggests that the Ulai here divides into two branches. He admits, however, that the normal grammar would use the plural for the Ulai if this were the case. Hartman, p. 227, understand the phrase to refer to two "flanking towers of the gateway."

The apocryphal book of Enoch, 20:1–8, names seven archangels: Uriel (mentioned 16X in Enoch, e.g., 9:1; 10:1; 21:5, 9, and in 2 Esd. 4:1, 36; 5:20; 10:28), Raphael (mentioned 9X in Tobit, e.g., 3:17; 12:15), Raguel, Michael, Saraqael, Gabriel, and Remiel. The book gives a brief summary of their responsibilities. Uriel is the angel placed over the world and Tartarus; Raphael is over the spirits of men; Raguel is the angel who takes vengeance on the earth and heavenly bodies; Michael is set over Israel (identified as "the best part of mankind") and over chaos; Saraqael (or Sariel) is the angel over "the spirits, who sin in the spirit," a phrase subject to differing interpretations; Gabriel is over the serpents, Paradise, and the Cherubs; and Remiel (elsewhere called Jeremiel) is the angel set over those who rise from the dead. In Enoch 40:9; 54:6; and 71:8, 9, 13, the book identifies four chief angels: Michael, Raphael, Gabriel, and Phanuel, v. 16.

Daniel is "afraid" (or "terrified") at the approach of Gabriel, a natural response when we consider that he was facing a completely unknown situation. Similar fear occurs at other times when angels appear to individuals (e.g., Judg. 6:22; Matt. 28:2–4; Luke 1:9). Gabriel begins his explanation by telling him that the vision is for "the time of the end" (^{c}et qeṣ). The phrase occurs five times in Daniel (also 11:35, 40; 12:4, 9), and nowhere else in the OT. At every occurrence, it has an eschatological meaning. While there is a historical fulfillment of the vision here, the historical figure is a type of the greater fulfillment in the Antichrist. The knowledge that Antichrist's opposition to Israel will not last (cf. v. 25) will serve to encourage Israel in the end times.

The visions of Daniel are the indisputable foundation of biblical prophecy. Even though much of the book has been fulfilled already, Daniel's prophecies of the end times are fundamental to the understanding of the Tribulation. The visions described here find their culmination in the Antichrist and his actions toward the people of God, v. 17.

As Gabriel speaks, Daniel is at first in a "deep sleep" (radam), perhaps having fainted at the appearance of the angel; cf. 10:9. The word radam occurs seven times in the OT (here and 10:9; Judg. 4:21; Ps. 76:6; Prov. 10:5; Jon. 1:5, 6), consistently referring to "deep sleep." A related noun may denote insensibility or an unconsciousness caused by God.

Gabriel awakens Daniel by lifting him to an upright position, v. 18. He tells him again that the fulfillment of the vision will be "in the last end of the indignation [za'am]." The noun za'am occurs twenty-two times. Except for Jeremiah 15:17 and Hosea 7:16, it refers to God's wrath. The word often refers to the wrath of God poured out on the earth during the Tribulation judgments (e.g., Isa. 26:20; Dan. 11:36; Zeph. 3:8).

The phrase here refers to the Tribulation that is yet to come: "At the time appointed the end *shall be*" (better "at the appointed time of the end"). The historical information that follows leads to Antiochus Epiphanes. His activities picture the work of Antichrist during the Tribulation, v. 19. Barnes, Young, Hartman, and Lacocque are typical of many authors with an amillennial or liberal view of eschatology. They refer the prophecy to Antiochus Epiphanes but do not recognize any further prophetic fulfillment.[26] The overall teaching of Daniel, however, clearly points to the Tribulation and the persecution of the Jews by Antichrist. See 7:24–27; 9:24–27; 11:36–45; 12:11.

The ram with the two horns represents the kings of the Medo-Persian alliance. The taller horn of v. 3 represents the Persian dominance of the alliance. This occurred when Cyrus (discussed at 5:30) came to power in Persia and led the Medo-Persian alliance to its greatest position of world dominance. The ram butts its way "westward, and northward, and southward" (v. 4) as it overcomes other nations.[27] As mentioned above, the minor Medo-Persian conquests to the east play no significant role in the biblical record, v. 20.

The "rough goat" (better "shaggy goat") represents the king of Greece. He comes "from the west" (v. 5), the direction of Greece with respect to the Medo-Persian kingdom. The "great horn" is its first king, Alexander. The fact that he "touched not the ground" (v. 5) suggests the speed of his conquests over the biblical world. He offered favorable terms to cities and nations that submitted to him, often reducing the tribute they were paying. This led many to reject the oppressive Persian rule and to accept Alexander's terms without a battle.

---

[26]Barnes, II, 119; Young, p. 177; Hartman, p. 235; Lacocque, p. 150.

[27]Thomson, p. 239, concludes, "A direction has dropped out." He assumes Babylon as the point of reference and notes that the Persians did rule to the east. The bulk of the Medo-Persian rule extended from Persia toward the three directions mentioned. A relatively small part of their empire lay to the east of Persia.

Alexander's conquest of Persia was particularly critical since this marked the transition of power from one world power to the next.

The Greeks under Alexander subdued the Mediterranean world in his twelve-year reign. Alexander succeeded his father Philip as king in 336 BC. Shortly afterward, in 334 BC, he crossed the Hellespont with his army. The Hellespont (now called the Dardanelles) is the strait at the southeastern border of Greece. This strait connected the Sea of Marmara with the Aegean Sea and separated Greece from Asia Minor. In the next four years, Alexander conquered Syria, Phoenicia, Cyprus, Tyre, Gaza, Canaan, Egypt, Babylonia, Persia, Media, and several smaller countries.

In his *Antiquities of the Jews* 11.5, Josephus records an interesting historical note. He states that when the Jews opened their gates to Alexander and showed him Daniel's prophecy that "one of the Greeks should destroy the empire of the Persians, he supposed that himself was the person intended." He gave the Jews the right to continue worshiping according to their law and the freedom not to pay tribute on the seventh year. Unfortunately, there is no other historical confirmation of this report, v. 21.

At the height of Alexander's power, when he was only thirty-two years old, he died. Verse 8 notes that the horn was broken "when he was strong." Following his death, his generals fought over the division of the kingdom. Eventually, four of them achieved control. These are the "four notable ['conspicuous'] ones" of v. 8. None of these, however, achieved the power of Alexander, v. 22.

The "king of fierce countenance" draws on the earlier description of the "little horn" (v. 9). There it represented Antiochus IV, who was later known as Antiochus Epiphanes. He ruled the Seleucid Empire 175–164 BC. The thought now, however, goes beyond Antiochus to the Antichrist that he symbolizes. He will be "of fierce countenance," aggressive, and will "understand . . . dark sentences [ḥîdâ]." The ḥîdâ is a riddle, an enigma, or some matter that is difficult to understand. Numbers 12:8 and Psalm 78:2 show these to be truths not readily available to all. Antichrist will understand these secret matters as he schemes and intrigues to advance his cause, v. 23.

Goldwurm gives the view that the king of vv. 23–25 is a Roman king. To accept this position, he has to include several Roman rulers, culminating in Titus, who destroyed the temple in AD 70. This goes contrary to the text, which describes a single king. Gaebelein identifies this king as an Assyrian, "the king of the north," mentioned seven times in c. 11. He supports this with several OT Scriptures, some of which are prophetic and some of which are historical. Thomson applies the verse to Antiochus Epiphanes. He suggests that the reference to "dark sentences" (ḥîdôt) refers to "tricks of strategy and chicane of policy." Keil and Driver are similar, both referring to the use of "dark sentences" by Epiphanes as "dissimulation." Lang sees the phrase as describing Antichrist's "rivalry of the Christ in His character of . . . Revealer of secret things."[28] While Antichrist will undoubtedly claim such powers, it goes beyond the statement here to find that assertion. Elsewhere, the word refers to unclear speech, riddles or parables, and hard questions, but never to chicanery.

From the description of his opposition to the "Prince of princes" (v. 25), a transition to Antichrist must occur at some point. It is reasonable to place it here. He will possess great power but "not by his own power," i.e., he will draw on the resources given him by Satan to achieve his goals (cf. Rev. 13:2). Leupold understands the phrase "not by his own power" as referring to God allowing "this man to achieve what his measure of talents would never have warranted." While this is possible, it is an unusual way to credit God with the accomplishments of this wicked man. Thomson refers the phrase to the help given to Antiochus by Eumenes and Rome in taking the throne of the kingdom. Miller sees the power as that given by Satan to advance Antiochus.[29] These views are possible only if the passage refers to Antiochus.

With this power, Antichrist will bring about extensive destruction. He will prosper and practice his will in what he does. In particular, he will oppose "the mighty and the holy people." Among his "mighty" foes are the kings he overthrows when he sets up his reign. The "holy people" undoubtedly refers to his opposition to Israel during the last part of the Tribulation. Israel is "holy" in that they have been set apart for God's purposes, v. 24.

Through his "policy" (or "cunning"), he will cause his craftiness "to prosper," i.e., the various undertakings "in his hand [yad, see v. 4]" will succeed. He will be proud. By "peace" (šalwâ) he will

---

[28]Goldwurm, p. 234; Gaebelein, pp. 107–17; Thomson, p. 247; Keil, p. 317; Driver, p. 123; Lang, p. 110.

[29]Leupold, pp. 366–67; Thomson, p. 247; Miller, p. 234.

destroy many others. While the word *šalwâ* may have the nuance of "prosperity" (cf. Ps. 122:7), its more normal sense is of being "quiet, at ease, secure." The Aramaic cognate *šᵉlewâ* means "at ease, carefree." Since Daniel was writing in an Aramaic atmosphere, the word likely has the sense "peace, security" here.

The time comes, however, when Antichrist will lift himself up against "the Prince of princes." From its use elsewhere in the book, the "princes" are the angels; cf. 10:13, 20, 21; 12:1. The "Prince of princes" is the Lord Himself; cf. 9:25. Wood aptly notes that the title "Prince of princes" is similar to such titles as "Lord of lords" and "King of kings" that refer to Christ (1 Tim. 6:15; Rev. 17:14; 19:16).[30] Antichrist's opposition to the Lord will come to nothing. He himself will be "broken" (*šabar*, often translated with the sense of "destruction," e.g., 1 Sam. 4:18; 2 Chron. 20:37; Prov. 29:1). This will take place "without hand [*yad*]," i.e., not by human power but by divine punishment. Taking into account the whole description of vv. 23–25, it seems best to place this setting as Antichrist in his final battle against the Lord (Rev. 19:19–20), v. 25.

The angel Gabriel confirms to Daniel the truth of the vision that concerns "the evening and the morning," the 2,300 evenings and mornings mentioned in v. 14. He tells him to "shut thou up the vision," i.e., to preserve it for the end times by means of the written record of what he has seen.[31] The vision is "for many days," i.e., for future generations, v. 26. The emotional experience of the vision overwhelms Daniel and causes him to be exhausted for several days. Eventually, he recovers enough to take up his responsibilities under the king. Throughout this time, the astonishment of the vision remains with him. He discusses it with others although "none understood it," v. 27.[32]

---

[30]Wood, p. 228.

[31]Goldwurm, pp. 226–27, understands Daniel to have concealed that part of the vision which dealt with the events of the end times. Knowing that the fulfillment was a long time in the future would discourage the faithful Jews. Lederach, p. 182, understands that "references to *end* refer primarily to the end of [Antiochus Epiphanes] rather than to end-time in an eschatological sense." This, of course, removes much of the teaching about Antichrist from the book.

[32]Heaton, p. 200, calls the last verse "difficult to understand." He thinks that Daniel at this time "has ceased to be . . . a real character, and has become simply a peg on which to hang a series of encouraging homilies drawn from history and Scripture." His difficulty in understanding the verse comes from his rejection of Daniel as a real person with a real physical response to his vision.

SEVENTY WEEKS 9:1–27

Prayer of Daniel 9:1–19 "The first year of Darius" is 538 BC. Darius the Mede, "the son of Ahasuerus . . . was made king over the realm of the Chaldeans [*kaśdîm*, see 1:4]" in 539 BC. His first full year followed in 538 BC. This is the same Darius introduced in 5:31 and trapped in the plot against Daniel in c. 6. He reigns under the authority of Cyrus the Great (discussed at 5:30).

Hartman considers Darius a "fictitious Median ruler" and Ahasuerus an "invented . . . father." Aside from repudiating the inspiration of Daniel, the view also ignores what we know of Median history. In rebutting this position, McLain notes that the identification of Darius (his name, descent, ethnicity, title, and subjects) is the most complete designation of any king in the book. This emphasizes the transition from the Babylonian reign to the Medo-Persian rule.[1]

The Hebrew Ahasuerus (probably meaning "mighty man") is equivalent to the Persian *Khšayâršâ*, a name that translates into Greek as Xerxes. He is not the Ahasuerus of Ezra or Esther but is variously identified as Astyages or Cyaxares, Median kings. This would make Darius related to Cyrus, although the exact relationship would depend on the women by whom the births came. In any case, Cyrus defeated the Medes to end their separate kingdom.

Daniel 1:1 tells us that Israel went into captivity "in the third year . . . of Jehoiakim," 605 BC. Daniel writes this chapter "in the first year of Darius." The nation now has been in captivity almost seventy years, v. 1. Daniel repeats the chronological information, "in the first year of [Darius's] reign," to emphasize this date. It is significant because of its closeness to the ending of Israel's seventy years of captivity.

At this time, Daniel understands "by books" (better "in the books [*seper*, see 1:4]"), including the prophecy of Jeremiah. Through his reading, Daniel gains additional knowledge of the revelation of the Lord (*yᵉhwah*). The name *yᵉhwah* occurs only seven times in Daniel, all in this chapter (vv. 2, 4, 10, 13, 14 [2X], 20). The name *yᵉhwah* stresses the interaction of the Lord with man. It is the name by which God entered into a covenant relationship with Israel (Exod. 3:14).

---

[1]Hartman, pp. 36, 240; Charles E. McLain, "Daniel's Prayer in Chapter 9," *Detroit Baptist Seminary Journal* 9 (2004): 268.

It speaks of His gracious and redemptive nature, as well as of His justice (Exod. 34:6–7). It is the appropriate name to use when Daniel thinks of God graciously ending the seventy-year period of captivity.

The chapter illustrates this gracious nature. The Lord communicates His Word to Jeremiah, v. 2. Daniel prays to the Lord, v. 4, confessing that the people have turned from the gracious guidance of the Lord, v. 10, and have failed to pray to Him, v. 13. He has graciously punished the nation (with the intent of bringing them back to Himself), v. 14a, righteously conforming the punishment to His Word, v. 14b. God answers Daniel while he is praying and confessing to the Lord, v. 20.

Daniel's reading includes Jeremiah 25:11–12. Jeremiah 29:10 also mentions the seventy-year period, but only 25:11–12 refers to the punishment of the Jews. The word "desolation" ($horbâ$) occurs in 25:11 (singular) and here (plural) but not in 29:10. The plural here emphasizes the severity of Judah's punishments, repeated on several occasions as God punished their sins. Further evidence that Daniel read in Jeremiah comes from v. 15. The reference there to the deliverance from Egypt agrees closely with Jeremiah 32:21. What Daniel reads shows him that the seventy-year captivity is nearing its end.

Driver relies on this prophecy to reinterpret Jeremiah. The seventy years there are now understood to be seventy weeks of years, 490 years. He mentions Leviticus 26:18, 21, 24, 28, where God promises to punish His people "seven times" for their sins. The seventy years of Jeremiah are thus repeated seven times, 490 years. As with other liberal views, Driver finds the fulfillment in the period between the fall of Jerusalem and the persecution of Israel by Antiochus Epiphanes. Gowan concludes that Daniel speaks of "an approximate time period . . . never intended for calculation." He ignores the history, which tells us that the seventy years are exact (605–536 BC). Gurney suggests that the seventy years refers to "Babylon's period of power."[2] Logically, Daniel was more concerned with Israel's captivity than with Babylon's power. His prayer focuses on Israel rather than Babylon, v. 2.

---

[2]Driver, p. 135; Gowan, p. 128; R. J. M. Gurney, "The Seventy Weeks of Daniel 9:24–27," *The Evangelical Quarterly* (Jan–Mar 1981): 30.

Daniel begins to seek God through prayer, asking that He will bring about His previously stated will.[3] The phrase "I set my face unto the Lord [*ᵃdonay*, see 1:2] God [*ᵉlohîm*, see 1:2]" suggests a conscious turning toward God.[4] There may as well have been a literal turning toward Jerusalem as he had done before (cf. 6:10). Genuine prayer begins when the Holy Spirit places a burden on your heart (cf. Rom. 8:26–27). As you turn to the Lord in prayer, you show your agreement with God that His will should be done.

From the description, it is clear that this is a special prayer, not part of Daniel's normal daily prayers. He accompanies his prayer with "fasting, and sackcloth, and ashes." The Jews practiced fasting when the burden of prayer was so great that the individual did not want to take time to eat. The Bible often joins fasting together with prayer (Neh. 1:4; Ps. 35:13; Matt. 17:21 [cf. Mark 9:29]; Luke 2:37; 5:33; Acts 10:30; 13:3; 14:23; 1 Cor. 7:5). The idea behind fasting is that there is some spiritual burden so great that the person needs to go to the Lord in prayer. This leads to the person spending extra time in prayer without taking time for ordinary matters such as eating. The OT law required only the fast on the Day of Atonement (Lev. 23:27–29). Christians today no longer keep this fast or the other fasts added by the Jews. These included a fast in the fourth month, remembering the capture of Jerusalem (Jer. 39:2); one in the fifth month, remembering the burning of the temple (Jer. 52:12–13); one in the seventh month, remembering the death of Gedaliah (Jer. 41:1–3); one in the tenth month, remembering the beginning of the attack on Jerusalem (Jer. 52:4); and the fast of Esther 4:16. While believers no longer keep these fasts of the Jewish ritual, voluntary fasting is still appropriate.

---

[3]Wood, p. 233, suggests that Daniel did not know the starting point of the seventy-year captivity. It could have been 605 BC, the date of his own capture (2 Kings 24:1–3); 597 BC, the date of the second transportation of Israel's people to Babylon (2 Kings 24:11–16); or the third deportation of the Jews (2 Kings 25:11). Daniel prays that God will be gracious "and consider the *terminus a quo* as 605 B.C." In my judgment, it is unthinkable that Daniel would not consider his own captivity the primary one and the completion of seventy years from that point as the end of the prophesied time in Babylon.

[4]The word *ᵃdonay* refers to the Lord in Daniel eleven times in c. 9 (vv. 3, 4, 7, 8, 9, 15, 16, 17, 19 [3X]) and only at 1:2 elsewhere, where it is discussed.

Daniel also dons sackcloth and sprinkles ashes over himself. Sackcloth was a coarsely woven dark cloth made from goat's hair. This served to the Jews as an outward symbol of an inward grief (cf. Gen. 37:34; Esther 4:1–4). Ashes were likewise a symbol of grief and mourning (cf. 2 Sam. 13:19; Jer. 6:26). They were scattered over a person as an outward sign of that person's feelings.

While there is no mention of other Jews with Daniel during his prayer, it is likely that some were present. Since the focus of the chapter is on Daniel and the additional revelation given him, there is no need to refer to the others. He uses plural pronouns forty-seven times, in every verse of the prayer. In addition, he refers to "all the people" or "all Israel" three times, vv. 6, 7, 11. The sackcloth and ashes symbolically showed Daniel's burden to the other people as well as to the Lord, v. 3.

Note the praise and confession of sin in Daniel's prayer to the "Lord" (*yᵉhwah*). He begins by praising the "Lord" (*ᵃdonay*, see 1:2), acknowledging Him as "great and dreadful" (better "great and awesome"). Further, God is faithful, keeping His covenant with Israel and showing "mercy" (*ḥesed*) to those who love and obey Him. This is the only time in Daniel that the word *ḥesed* refers to the Lord. Throughout the OT, *ḥesed* refers to lovingkindness, mercy, or goodness. It often has a sense of loyalty to God's covenant with His people. The translation "loyalty" or "steadfast love" is appropriate.

Daniel's statements here show his familiarity with other Scripture. The phrase "great and dreadful" describes God in Deuteronomy 7:21 ("mighty . . . terrible") and 10:17, 21 (both "great . . . terrible"); in Psalm 99:3 ("great . . . terrible"); and in Joel 2:11, 31 (both "great . . . terrible"). Daniel parallels Nehemiah 1:5 with his thoughts that God is "great and dreadful" and keeps His covenant, and that He blesses those that love Him and keep His commands. While the book of Nehemiah is postexilic, Daniel and Nehemiah may well have drawn on teaching received by the Jews in their captivity. The OT frequently refers to God keeping His covenant (e.g., Deut. 7:9, 12; 1 Kings 8:23; 2 Chron. 6:14; Neh. 1:5; 9:32; Ps. 89:28). The ideas of loving God and keeping His commands often occur as well (e.g., Exod. 20:6; Deut. 5:10; 7:9; 30:16).

Charles considers the prayer in vv. 4–19 "as an addition made to the text," taken "from existing liturgical forms" by a Jew living in Judea. He offers no support of the conclusion other than his subjective view. Redditt likewise concludes that "the author . . . incorporated a previously existing prayer (vv. 4–19) into the narrative." Redditt relies on the "consensus" of "critical scholars."[5] These views fail to recognize that the "seventy years" of v. 2 lead naturally to Daniel's prayer, vv. 4–19. This prepares Daniel to receive the new revelation of the "seventy weeks" developed in vv. 24–27. There is unity in the chapter. The attempt to disregard this unity rests on a critical view of the book that accepts a late date and rejects the existence of the historical Daniel, v. 4.

Daniel now begins to confess Israel's sin to the Lord. Although the major focus of the prayer is on Israel's sin, by using the plural "we," Daniel includes his own sin as well as the sin of others (cf. v. 20). His confession sets a pattern that is still true for Christians. There is a need for a right relationship with the Lord before He can give His blessing (cf. Ps. 66:18; Prov. 15:29; 28:9). Daniel does not gloss over Israel's wickedness. The word "sin" (*ḥaṭaʾ*) has the idea of missing a mark (con. Judg. 20:16, *loʾ yaḥᵃṭiʾ*, "not miss"). In its use as "sin," it refers to the failure to satisfy God's standards in life. Israel has missed the mark of God's perfection.

They have committed "iniquity" (*ʿawâ*), a word that refers to distortion or twisting, as in turning aside from God's will.[6] They have "done wickedly" (*rašaʿ*), becoming involved with evil actions and therefore violating God's standards of righteousness. They have "rebelled" (*marad*) by turning against the ways of God and godliness. The verb *marad* occurs in the book only here and in v. 9. Elsewhere, the word appears about two dozen times. It may refer to rebellion either against God (e.g., Josh. 22:29; Ezek. 2:3) or against man (e.g., Gen. 14:4; Neh. 2:19).

This multiplication of synonyms emphasizes the greatness of Israel's sin. All of this has come as the people have departed from God's "precepts" (better "commandments") and "judgments" (or "ordinances"), v. 5. The people have also failed to follow God's servants, the prophets, men such as Isaiah and Jeremiah, who told

---

[5]Charles, p. 222; Paul L. Redditt, "Daniel 9: Its Structure and Meaning," *CBQ* 62 (Apr 2000): 8–9.

[6]Goldwurm, p. 246, links *ḥaṭaʾ* to "inadvertent sin" and *ʿawâ* to "intentional sin." These words occur in parallel, however, where this cannot be the distinction (e.g., 2 Sam. 24:17; 1 Kings 8:47; 2 Chron. 6:37).

them of God's will. This failure included the leaders of the nation ("kings . . . princes") and its inhabitants ("fathers [i.e., ancestors] . . . people"), vv. 5–6.

Daniel acknowledges that the "Lord" (*ʾᵃdonay*) is righteous. Israel deserves the "confusion [better 'shame'] of face" that has come to them when God dispersed them into other nations. This punishment included both "the men of Judah," in captivity in Babylon, and "all Israel," the ten tribes that had earlier gone into captivity and were now "near" and "far off" in the various countries to which they had been taken. This punishment has come because of their "trespass" (*maʿal*). The noun *maʿal* carries with it the nuance of acting unfaithfully. Israel has been unfaithful to God in that they have spurned His Word and, in fact, spurned God by turning to idols, v. 7. Once more, as Daniel speaks to the "Lord" (*yᵉhwah*), he includes the leaders and people in this indictment; cf. v. 6. They deserve "confusion [again 'shame'] of face" because they have "sinned" (*ḥaṭaʾ*) against God, v. 8.

Despite Israel's rebellion (*marad*), the "Lord" (*ʾᵃdonay*) has extended "mercies [or 'compassions,' *raḥam*] and forgivenesses [*sᵉlîḥâ*]." The word *raḥam* occurs in Daniel only here and in v. 18. When used of God elsewhere in the OT, *raḥam* refers to His deep-seated emotional feeling toward man (e.g., Neh. 9:31; Ps. 51:1). The noun *sᵉlîḥâ* occurs only three times in the OT (also Neh. 9:17; Ps. 130:4), although the verb occurs more often. In every case, the word refers to the forgiveness given by God. This is appropriate. Because sin is fundamentally against God, only God can grant forgiveness for sin. The plural of both words shows God's boundless grace toward His people, v. 9.

Daniel continues to confess the nation's sin. The people have disobeyed "the voice of the Lord [*yᵉhwah*]" to live according to His "laws" (*torâ*). God's *torâ* not only refers to His Law but also includes teaching given to guide the people. The noun *torâ* occurs in the book only in this chapter (vv. 10, 11 [2X], and 13). This guidance came from God's "servants the prophets," as in v. 6 the familiar prophetic voices raised up by God, v. 10. The people have "transgressed" (*ʿabar*) by "departing" (*sôr*) from God's "law" (*torâ*). In Daniel, *ʿabar* does not occur again with the sense of "transgression." The word occurs more than 550 times in the OT, normally with a sense related to the thought of "passing over." The sense of transgression comes from passing over the standards of God and thus going away from the practices of righteousness. The verb *sôr* occurs more than 290 times in the OT. Although it may simply refer to motion, it also has the sense of departing from God and His Word. With this, it often indicates apostasy (e.g., Exod. 32:8; Deut. 9:12; 11:16).

The curse that has come on the people is that found in the writings of Moses, the servant of "God" (*ʾelohîm*, see 1:2). These spoke of the judgment that would fall on the nation when they "sinned" (*ḥaṭaʾ*, see v. 5) against their God. God had sworn there an "oath" that turning away from the "law" (*torâ*) would cause judgment to fall on them (e.g., Lev. 26:14–20; Deut. 28:15–68), v. 11. God has "confirmed" (*qûm*) His words by bringing upon the people and their leaders the judgments that He had promised. The verb *qûm* normally means "to stand," most often referring to a physical position, e.g., Daniel 8:27 ("rose up"). Here the verb has a causative sense ("causing His word to stand") and thus refers to confirming or carrying out His word.

This "evil" (or "disaster") is greater than any other nation has suffered. Daniel does not speak merely of the difficulties that have come on Israel. Other nations have suffered similar difficulties, some even being annihilated as nations. But the difference lay in that with Israel, the difficulties were a divine judgment. God had told Israel that He would judge their sin (e.g., Lev. 26:14–39; Deut. 28:15, 48–50, 58–67). No other nation had such foreknowledge when divine judgment fell on them as punishment for their sin. Barnes limits the statement by making it true "at that time." Lacocque restricts the scope of the statement to the destruction or the profaning of the temple.[7] The emphasis here, however, relates the judgment to God confirming "his words, which he spake against us" (v. 12), and to that which is "written in the law of Moses," (v. 13), v. 12.

The Mosaic "law" (*torâ*) had predicted all that has happened.[8] Despite this, Israel has not entreated the "Lord" (*yᵉhwah*) in prayer. The people have not repented of their "iniquities" (*ʿaôn*) by turning

---

[7]Barnes, II, 132; Lacocque, p. 184.

[8]Hartman, p. 242, mistakenly makes the phrase "Torah of Moses" the "earliest occurrence of the phrase introducing a citation from Scripture." The phrase occurs 6X in earlier books, appearing as early as Josh. 8:31–32, introducing Scripture written by Moses.

from them. The word ʿaôn comes from the root ʿawâ (see v. 5), which means "to bend, distort." This leads to the thought of crooked behavior or perversion. The word occurs again in Daniel only in vv. 16 and 24. In addition, the people have not sought to understand the truths that God wanted them to practice, v. 13.

The "Lord" (yᵉhwah) has justly punished the nation because of their disobedience. In doing this, the "Lord" (yᵉhwah), Israel's God, is righteous since He had conformed His actions to His Word. Just as God punished Israel for her sins, so He punishes His children today (cf. Gal. 6:7–8). This punishment does not come from the hand of a cruel, vindictive God Who delights in tormenting others. No, it rather shows us the loving care of the righteous God Who wants the best for His followers. He sends His punishments to draw believers back into the way of blessing (cf. Heb. 12:11; Rev. 3:19), v. 14.

Daniel now begins the first petition of the prayer. Earlier verses have dealt with God's greatness, Israel's sin, and God's justice in punishing the nation. Daniel begins the petition by recalling Israel's past deliverance from Egypt. God had brought them out "with a mighty hand [yad, see 8:4]," i.e., with great power. There is likely the implied thought that what God has done once, He can do again by releasing the nation from its bondage. Despite this past favor shown to Israel by God, they have "sinned" (ḥaṭaʾ) and "done wickedly" (rašaʿ, see v. 5), v. 15.

The Lord elsewhere relates the seventy-year captivity to Israel's failure to keep the Sabbath-year rest. Leviticus 25:1–7 commanded that the land should be left fallow every seven years. The people had failed to keep this command. Their desire to work and to gain personal wealth brought them into God's judgment. Leviticus 26:32–45 and 2 Chronicles 36:20–21 prophesy judgment on the nation if they fail to rest during the Sabbath-year. This period of judgment would be one in which Palestine experienced the Sabbath-rest that Israel had withheld from it.

Daniel now asks the "Lord" (ʾᵃdonay) to turn away His anger for Israel's sin. He bases his plea upon God's "righteousness," the characteristic of His nature that allows God to pardon those who are penitent. Daniel mentions Jerusalem, a "holy mountain" in that it was dedicated to God. Leupold and Keil refer the phrase "holy mountain" in vv. 16 and 20 to Mt. Zion as the location of the temple, a possible view.[9] The phrase, however, refers elsewhere either to the temple (e.g., Isa. 56:7; 65:11) or to the city (e.g., Ezek. 20:40; Joel 3:17). In its only other occurrence in Daniel, 11:45, it refers to the city. The parallelism here between "thy city Jerusalem" and "thy holy mountain" favors identifying the mountain as the city's location. In addition, Daniel's prayer in v. 20 is likely for the city since the sanctuary had been destroyed. The phrase must be taken in v. 20 as it is understood here.

The city is on Daniel's mind because he realizes that the seventy-year captivity is about to end. He naturally thinks of the possibility that the people could return to their land. Their "sins" ($hata^{\circ}$) and "iniquities" ($^{c}a\hat{o}n$) have brought their captivity. This caused others to think of them as a people worthy of "reproach," v. 16. Daniel asks God to hear his prayer. He pleads that God will "cause [His] face to shine" upon the desolate sanctuary of the Lord in Jerusalem. Causing the "face to shine" is equivalent to extending favor and blessing (cf. Ps. 31:16; 80:3, 7, 19), v. 17.

Once more, Daniel beseeches God to hear his prayer on behalf of the nation.[10] He asks God to see how desolate the nation has become. He pleads with Him to look upon "the city which is called by thy name," i.e., Jerusalem, elsewhere called the "city of God" (Pss. 46:4; 87:3) but now no longer populated by God's people. Daniel does not pray because of his personal righteousness or because of any merit of the people. He simply relies on the "mercies" (or "compassions," *raham*) of God, v. 18. He asks the "Lord" ($^{2a}donay$, repeated three times) to hear his prayer, to forgive the sin of the people, and not to delay the answer to his prayer.[11] God's work would be for His "own sake" because "thy city and thy people are called by thy name." With

---

[9]Leupold, pp. 391, 400; Keil, pp. 333–34.

[10]Goldwurm, p. 254, refers the plural pronoun "we" to "the whole Jewish community," including "the prophets Chaggai, Zechariah, and Malachi, as well as Ezra and Nehemiah and other great men [who] were alive in this period." Since the text does not mention any of these men, it is more likely that Daniel simply speaks on behalf of the captive nation. Neither Haggai nor Zechariah had begun their prophetic ministry at this time, and Malachi had not yet been born.

[11]Bultema, p. 274, understands the repeated "Lord" as an allusion to the Trinity. This topic appears nowhere else in the book and is not likely in Daniel's mind here. The threefold mention of the "Lord" seems rather to be an emotional cry from Daniel's heart as he commits Israel's plight to the Lord.

this statement, Daniel recognizes the reproach to God when His possession lies waste and His people remain in captivity, v. 19.

Revelation from Gabriel 9:20–27 Daniel confesses his own "sin" (*ḥaṭṭaʾt*, cf. v. 5) and the sin of his people as he prays to the "Lord" (*yᵉhwah*) on behalf of Jerusalem, "the holy mountain of . . . God," i.e., that God might restore it as the home of His people, v. 20. As Daniel is praying and confessing his and the nation's sins, the angel Gabriel (discussed at 8:16) comes to him. He is called "the man" because he is man-like in appearance; cf. 8:15–16. This is the same Gabriel "whom I had seen in the vision at the beginning," in the previous vision of 8:15–26.

The phrase "caused to fly swiftly [*muᶜap bîᶜap*], touched me" is better "reached me in [my] extreme weariness." Among others, Calvin and Wood derive the verb from *ᶜûp*, "to fly." This verb, however, does not occur elsewhere in the *hopᶜal*. It is better to see the verb as the *hopᶜal* of *yᶜp* and to translate as above. The root *yᶜp*, which occurs here, always occurs elsewhere with the sense of "faint" or "weary" (e.g., Isa. 40:28, 31; 44:12). Young is better, "to fly in weariness." It is doubtful, however, that Gabriel would be too wearied from a flight to communicate with Daniel. Cowles translates "being wearied with a great weariness" but applies this to Gabriel.[12] Again, it is unlikely that Gabriel would be wearied from carrying out his mission. The doubled root *yᶜp*, "to grow weary," gives emphasis to the phrase, i.e., "extreme weariness." The phrase refers to Daniel's physical condition in the earlier vision, when he was faint for a period of time, 8:27. Giving the participle a sense of time, the phrase reads, "whom I saw in the vision at the beginning when I was extremely weary."

Gabriel appears at "the time of the evening oblation [or 'sacrifice']," about 3 p.m. Numbers 28:3–8 describes the evening sacrifice in great detail. Because the Jews were in captivity, they would not have been able to make such a sacrifice. This time, however, was a natural time for prayer (1 Kings 18:36; Ezra 9:5; Ps. 141:2), v. 21.[13]

---

[12]Calvin, II, 187; Wood, p. 245; Young, p. 190; Cowles, p. 400.

[13]Redditt, pp. 242–43, recognizes that the prayer, vv. 4–19, must come from 586–516 BC since "vv. 8, 12, and 16 presuppose extreme calamity in Jerusalem, from which it had not recovered, and v. 17 speaks of the 'desolated sanctuary.' " He then arbitrarily dates the other parts of the chapter to the second century BC. Again, his conclusion rests on the critical view, which denies the authorship to the historical Daniel; see v. 4.

Gabriel's purpose is to give Daniel "skill [better 'insight'] and understanding" of Israel's future, v. 22. God had given Gabriel the "commandment" (better "word"). This refers to the revelation given in vv. 24–27. This had come in response to Daniel's prayer and because he was "greatly beloved" (or "highly esteemed," $h^a m\hat{u}d\hat{o}t$). The word $h^a m\hat{u}d\hat{o}t$ is from the root hmd, "to delight, desire, take pleasure in." The abstract noun is plural here, expressing a quality, and thus "greatly desired, highly esteemed."[14] Although written with a $qibb\hat{u}s$ rather than a $\check{s}\hat{u}req$, the plural noun occurs again in 10:3, 11, 19; 11:38, 43. Daniel should understand the "matter" (or "word") and the "vision." Both of these terms refer to the prophetic material about to be given him by Gabriel, v. 23.[15]

The earlier verses of the chapter serve to introduce the final four verses, one of the most significant prophecies of the Bible. Keil describes the verses as "the most important revelations regarding the future development of the kingdom of God." Walvoord calls the passage "one of the most important prophecies of the Old Testament." Neal describes it as "the key to the understanding of all Old Testament prophecy." Leupold calls this "one of the grandest revelations made in the prophetic word."[16] These verses set forth God's plan for Israel from Daniel's time to the establishment of God's rule over the world.

Daniel's prayer had focused on Judah's "seventy years" (v. 2) of captivity. God's messenger says nothing about this but, instead, concentrates on the nation's future. It is as though the seventy years in Daniel's prayer serve as a springboard leading into the seventy-times-seven years of Israel's future. Daniel's concern is with the present. God's concern is with the future.

Hammer sets forth the typical liberal view of the prophecy. The first seven weeks cover the period from 586 to 538 BC, the fall of

---

[14]So Waltke and O'Connor, 7.4.2a.

[15]Bultema, p. 278, understands "the matter" and "the vision" to refer to two separate areas "to which [Daniel] must pay heed." The following verses are "the matter," and "the vision" relates to that given in c. 8. Bultema does not clearly develop this distinction in his following explanation. It is simpler, and equally valid, to let "the matter" refer to the following verses and "the vision" refer to Gabriel's appearance as he delivers the message to Daniel.

[16]Keil, p. 336; Walvoord, p. 216; Marshall Neal, "The Seventy Weeks," *BV* 8:2 (Nov. 1974): 132; Leupold, p. 405.

Judah to the end of the exile. The second period of sixty-two weeks lasts from 538 to 171 BC, the end of the exile to the murder of Onias, the Jewish High Priest, by his brother who bought the office from Antiochus Epiphanes. This period is only 367 years. Hammer excuses the difference with the comment that "the precise length of the Persian period was not known to later Jewish writers." The final period of seven years falls between 171 and 164 BC. This is the period of persecution by Antiochus Epiphanes, divided by his desecration of the temple in 168 BC.[17] The interpretation relies on a late date for the book. It denies inspiration and, rather than prophecy, treats the book as history.

God has "determined" (or "decreed," *ḥatak*) a period of "seventy weeks" for accomplishing His will for the nation and Jerusalem, its capital city. This is the only place that *ḥatak* occurs in the OT. The LXX translates ἐκρίθησαν, "determine, decree." The Latin Vulgate translates *abbreviatae*, "to cut off," and the Aramaic cognate is *ḥᵃtak*, also "cut off." That sense is appropriate here. From the idea of "cutting off," i.e., eliminating other decisions, we derive the meaning "to decree."

The "seventy weeks" (*šabuᶜîm šibᶜîm*), lit. "seventy sevens," most naturally represents 490 years. The noun *šabûaᶜ* appears twenty times in the OT, six of them in this chapter (9:24, 25 [2X], 26, 27 [2X]). The word always refers to the number "seven," with the context indicating either an ordinal or the seven days of a week. The context here leads us to think of years.[18] Earlier in the chapter, 9:2, Daniel has been thinking in terms of years. Further, the nature of the prophecy requires years rather than days. Since the prophecy refers to the rebuilding of Jerusalem, the coming of the Messiah, and His being "cut off," "seventy sevens" of days are nonsensical. Nothing of

---

[17]Hammer, p. 98.

[18]Leupold, pp. 407–10, argues against taking the phrase as "seventy-sevens of years." He notes that the number "seven" does not elsewhere refer to weeks of years but to weeks of days. Leupold translates the phrase as "seventy heptads" and gives it a symbolic sense, the period when God brings His work to perfection. This ignores the evidence from other passages of Scripture; cf. Gen. 29:27–28, where the word unquestionably refers to years. West, pp. 70–71, adds the Jubilee year after each forty-nine year group of years. This brings the total to 500 years. Nothing here suggests, however, that the Jubilee year should be treated separately from other years. "Seventy-sevens" most logically is 490 years, not 500 years.

this sort happened in a 490-day period. Further, the prophecy speaks of a period of persecution that begins in the middle of the last week. A 3½-day persecution does not agree with the prophecy in 7:24–25 ("a time and times and the dividing of time"). Revelation 12:13–14 quotes this phrase after earlier defining the period as 1260 days, 12:6. Daniel had prayed about the period of Israel's physical bondage. God graciously gives him a vision of the "seventy-sevens" of years necessary to free Israel from its spiritual bondage.

The remainder of v. 24 contains six statements. In my opinion, they occur in three groups of two statements each. Among others, Keil and Wiersbe group the six statements into two groups of three each. The first three deal with the removal of sin, while the last three treat the restoration of righteousness. Ignoring the fact that the third statement is positive rather than negative, this also is a possible grouping of the phrases. Keil refers the second statement to unbelievers and the third to believers. It is more natural to let all six phrases refer to the same group.[19]

Understanding the phrase in three groups of two each, (1) the first group deals with the *restraining of Satan's work*. God will "finish" (*kalleʾ*) Israel's "transgression" (*pešaʿ*, see 8:12). The *piʿel* infinitive *kalleʾ* intensifies the action. It indicates "restraining completely" (cf. Gen. 8:2, stopping the rain after the Flood; Ps. 119:101, avoiding sin completely; Jer. 32:2–3, restricting Jeremiah's movement by imprisoning him). The *piʿel* of *kalaʾ* does not occur elsewhere. For this reason, there is dispute over this word. Some authors derive it as here, from the root *klʾ*. Others derive it from *klh*, with the word borrowing the form of a *lamed-ʾalep* root; cf. GKC 76 *nn–rr*.[20] Since the root *klh* occurs five times elsewhere in Daniel written normally

---

[19]Keil, pp. 341, 343; Wiersbe, p. 114. Jacques Doukhan, "The Seventy Weeks of Dan 9: An Exegetical Study," *AUSS* 17 (Spring 1979): 10–11, also views the statements as two groups with three prophecies each. He relates the first three statements to the phrase "thy people" and the final three statements to the phrase "thy holy city." He then makes statements four, five, and six complete, in order, statements one, two, and three. While this organization is possible, a poetic structure of $a{:}b{:}a^1{:}a^2{:}a^3{:}b^1{:}b^2{:}b^3$ is unique.

[20]The majority derive the word as above, from the root *klʾ*, e.g., Stuart, p. 269; Wood, p. 248; and Young, p. 198. Archer, p. 119; Lacocque, p. 193; and Walvoord, p. 221, are among those who derive it from *klh*.

(9:27; 11:26, 36; 12:7 [2X]), it is unlikely that we should derive the word from *klh* here.

In parallel with this thought, God will also "make an end of" (*ḥtm*) their "sin" (*ḥaṭṭaᵓt*, cf. v. 5), no longer letting them sin with impunity. There is also dispute over the root *ḥtm*. The *kᵉtîb* is *ḥᵉtom*, the *qal* infinitive construct from *ḥatam*, "to seal up." The *qᵉrê* is *hatem*, the *hipᶜîl* infinitive construct from *tamam*, "to finish, come to an end."[21] There is little difference in the meaning, and no strong argument exists for accepting the *qᵉrê*. The verb itself has a variety of nuances, depending on the context. A seal may refer to stopping something (Lev. 15:3; Job 9:7). It may identify and authenticate something (1 Kings 21:8; Esther 3:12). It may indicate something that is stored away, preserved for some future time (Deut. 32:34; Job 14:17). Something may be sealed in that it is hidden (Isa. 29:11; Dan. 9:24*b*). In 9:24*a*, the parallelism with *kalleᵓ* virtually demands the first of these meanings. God intervenes in Israel's history to stop them from their wickedness.

(2) The second group describes *the initiation of Messiah's work.* God will "make reconciliation" (*kapper*, "to cover, atone") for their "iniquity" (*ᶜaôn*). The *piᶜel* infinitive *kapper* regularly occurs in passages discussing the sacrifices offered for sin (e.g., Lev. 1:4; 4:20). These assume offenses in which there was sincere repentance and for which sacrifice could be made. God will also "bring in everlasting righteousness," made possible by the sacrifice of the Lord on the cross (cf. Rom. 8:3–4; 2 Cor. 5:21). While the sacrifice of Christ at Calvary is sufficient for all mankind, the emphasis here most naturally falls on Israel. The Jews will accept this sacrifice and be converted (cf. Zech. 12:10; 13:1–2). With the culmination of God's work on earth, He will bring the everlasting ages to pass, a period marked by righteousness (Rev. 21:27).

(3) The third group involves *the establishment of kingdom worship.* God will "seal up [*ḥatam*] the vision and prophecy." Since the establishment of the kingdom brings their purpose to completion, no further need exists for vision and prophecy. Finally, the Lord will "anoint the most holy [*qodeš qadašîm*]." The doubling of *qdš* in the phrase *qodeš qadašîm* emphasizes the thought. The KJV translation

---

[21]Barnes, II, 142–43, and Stuart, p. 279, adopt the *kᵉtîb*. Goldwurm, p. 260, and Miller, p. 260, accept the *qᵉrê*.

"most holy" is appropriate. The Hebrew phrase occurs more than twenty times in the OT, always referring to inanimate things used in the temple or dedicated to the Lord (e.g. Exod, 30:10, 29, 36; Lev. 2:3, 10; Ezek. 48:12). The thought in Daniel is of the temple in the kingdom, anointed for use in worship.

Young refers the phrase to the anointing of Messiah, but this is contrary to its general use of things and places but not people. The phrase *qodeš qadašîm* never elsewhere refers to a person. Leupold understands the phrase as speaking of "Christ among His own" in eternity. He justifies this by citing 1 Chronicles 23:13.[22] The phrase there, however, more accurately refers to "most holy things" rather than to people. The NASB and NLT supply a word and translate "most holy place," referring the phrase to the Holy of Holies. This is also a possible view.

It is important to note that these six parts of the prophecy have not yet been fulfilled. Satan's work among the Jews has not been completed. The Lord's redeeming work has not been accepted by Israel. The kingdom worship has not yet begun. This suggests that the prophecy spans the gap in time from Daniel to the initiation of the millennial kingdom, v. 24.

Horne makes the 490 years a continuous period, including the last "week" of years. He applies v. 27 to the work of Christ. He confirms the "covenant of grace" with the nation. His death causes sacrifices to lose their meaning. The rejection of Christ by the Jews brings wrath "poured upon the desolate." Newton also ends the 490 years with the death of Christ. He refers the final half-week to the conquest of the Jews by Rome. This begins with an invasion by Vespasian in the spring of AD 67 and ends with the ravages of Titus in AD 70.[23] The problem with these views is that desolation did not come on the nation until AD 70, long after the "week" was concluded. It is more natural to apply the final week to the time of Antichrist.

The starting point is the giving of the "commandment" (*dabar*). From there, the 490 years divides into three periods of time: seven sevens of years (forty-nine years), sixty-two sevens of years (434 years), and one seven of years (seven years). The first period of forty-nine years refers to the rebuilding of Jerusalem that took place

---

[22]Young, p. 201; Leupold, p. 416.
[23]Horne, pp. 78, 89–94; Newton, pp. 226–230.

under Nehemiah and the following leaders of the nation. The statement that "the street shall be built again, and the wall, even in troublous times" supports the rebuilding of the city.

There are three decrees that relate to the return of Jews to Palestine. The *first* of these allowing a return of the Jews from Babylon occurred at about the same time as this chapter. Cyrus issued this decree ca. 536 BC. A large group of Jews under the leadership of Zerubbabel took advantage of this to return, Ezra 1:1–11. Cyrus was followed by his son Cambyses. In turn, Cambyses was followed by the usurper Pseudo-Smerdis (Gaumata). After his death, Darius the Mede took the kingdom. His son Xerxes ascended to the throne after his father's death.

After the death of Xerxes in 465 BC, Artaxerxes Longimanus murdered two of his brothers in his zeal to gain the throne. He received the name Longimanus because his right hand was longer than his left hand.[24] We know of two rebellions put down by Artaxerxes. His brother Hystaspes led the first in Bactria, about one thousand miles east of Mesopotamia. A man named Inaros led the other in Egypt. In the seventh year of his rule, Artaxerxes issued the *second* decree. This let a group of Jews return to Jerusalem under the leadership of Ezra, 457 BC. They could begin there to worship in the temple. Ezra 7:11–26 describes the decree. Thirteen years later, 445 BC, he authorized Nehemiah to lead a *third* return of the Jews from their Captivity, Nehemiah 2:1, 7–8. Artaxerxes died of natural causes in 424 BC.

The only decree in Scripture relating to the rebuilding of Jerusalem is that found in Nehemiah 2:8, the decree of Artaxerxes Longimanus, ca. 445 BC. The second decree of this king (and the third return of the Jews to Palestine) marks the beginning of the periods of time mentioned in the verse.

Leupold places the start at the decree of Cyrus that let Israel return, which he dates at 538 BC. Cyrus's decree (2 Chron. 36:22–23; Ezra 1:2–4), however, did not mention rebuilding the city but focused on the nation's worship. Leupold feels that while Cyrus "mentions the temple and implies the city," Daniel "mentions the city and implies the eternal temple." The Anointed One is Christ, who comes

---

[24]So *Plutarch's Lives*, trans. Bernadotte Perrin (Cambridge, Mass.: Harvard University Press, 1975), 11.1.

after "seven heptads." Leupold ignores the literal meaning of "seven" and "sixty-two" by making them a relatively short time followed by a longer period. He does not explain why such a peculiar number as "sixty-two" is chosen for this. The reference to rebuilding refers to the growth of the church, a view that spiritualizes the passage.[25]

Smith begins Daniel's seventy weeks with the decree of Artaxerxes in 457 BC, commissioning Ezra's return to Jerusalem. Adding 483 years to this brings the time to AD 27, the time of the Lord's baptism. He is "cut off" after this "in the midst of" the final week of seven years, i.e., three and one-half years later in AD 31. The week ends three and one-half years later, in AD 34, with the martyrdom of Stephen. Gurney adopts the same view.[26] The view involves manipulation of numbers to bring them to known dates. The decree of Artaxerxes in 457 BC did not mention the rebuilding of the city. The phrase "in the midst of" comes from v. 27, where it refers to Antichrist, not the Messiah. Stephen's martyrdom has nothing to do with this prophecy.

Thomson also places the date in the seventh year of Artaxerxes, which he dates at 458 BC, when he authorized Ezra to re-establish the worship of Israel, Ezra 7:11–26. Thomson feels that this implies the rebuilding of the city. Aside from the problem of reconciling this date with the total of 483 years, the decree said nothing about building the city and is therefore suspect as a starting point. Archer also begins at the decree in Ezra 7. He argues for taking the years as normal years, and notes that 483 years from a starting point of 446 BC, his date for the decree, would end at AD 38 or 39, too late for the death of the Lord. Starting at Ezra's decree in 457 BC, 483 years ends at AD 27 (adding a year for the transition from 1 BC to AD 1). This is the date at which the Lord began His ministry. "After" that, He is "cut off." The view is possible but suffers from the lack of any mention of rebuilding Jerusalem in the decree.[27]

---

[25]Leupold, pp. 418–23.

[26]Smith, p. 215; Gurney, pp. 32–34.

[27]Thomson, p. 268. Archer, p. 114. Archer is also inconsistent. He rejects the first decree since it does not mention rebuilding the city. He accepts the second decree, however, since Ezra would have understood that "the commission . . . included permission to rebuild the wall."

Nehemiah 2:1 gives the date as "the month of Nisan [March–April], in the twentieth year of Artaxerxes," 445 BC. From this time to the end of the Lord's earthly ministry (April AD 30) is a total of 475 years. Daniel, however, gives it in two groups, forty-nine years and 434 years, a total of 483 years. Months in the OT may involve thirty-day periods of time. The time relating to the Noahic Flood includes a 150-day period, which Genesis 7:11 and 8:3–4 show as equaling five 30-day months. When we compare the times given in 7:25; 12:7; Revelation 11:2–3; 12:6, 14; and 13:5, it seems that the times in Daniel also involve thirty-day months.

A 360-day year makes the 483 years equal 173,880 days, about the same as the 173,859 days in 476 years of 365¼ days each. When you consider that we do not know the exact beginning or ending dates, this is essentially equal to the 475 years that span the time between the decree of Artaxerxes ca. 445 BC and the death of the Lord ca. AD 30. Messiah will be "cut off" at some point following the sixty-two week period. The second period, then, 434 years, includes the time between completing the building of Jerusalem and the Messiah.

King closes the period with the entrance of the Lord into Jerusalem the week before His crucifixion. The phrase "shall Messiah be cut off" argues against this. Price argues that the "time" refers to the baptism of Christ, Mark 1:15. Again, the phrase "be cut off" argues against this. Price refers it to the Crucifixion, which occurs "after" Christ's baptism and ministry. This doesn't seem to be the intent of the sixty-two weeks. Paisley attributes Simeon's knowledge that he would live until the coming of the Messiah to this prophecy, Luke 2:25–35.[28] The view is possible, although his knowledge may also have come from direct revelation by the Holy Spirit rather than the knowledge of this prediction.

Some have concluded that the initial decree to rebuild Jerusalem happened on March 14, 445 BC, and that the Lord entered Jerusalem on April 6, AD 32. The interval is exactly 173,880 days. Sir Robert Anderson first set forth this view. Others have also adopted the position. While the view is interesting, it rests upon several assumptions since we do not know the exact dates involved. The prophecy

---

[28]Sir Robert Anderson, *The Coming Prince*, 10th ed. (Grand Rapids: Kregel Classics, rpt. 1957), pp. 127–28; King, pp. 178, 241–42; Paisley, p. 14.

does not need to be fulfilled to the exact day to be accurate. Other references to time are often approximate, e.g., genealogies (Gen. 9:28; 11:11), historical notes (2 Sam. 5:4–5; Jer. 52:1), prophecy (Isa. 23:15; 61:2). Where the record states time more precisely, it often specifies the month or the month and day (e.g., Jer. 52:31; Ezek. 1:1).

The word "Messiah" (*mašîaḥ*) refers to an "anointed one," normally the high priest or king. The word also refers to the Messiah (Ps. 2:2; cf. Acts 13:32–33; Heb. 1:5; 5:5). The Greek word χριστός, translated "Christ," is the Greek equivalent of *mašîaḥ*. The title "Messiah" here refers to "the anointed One," a reference to the Lord's priestly office.[29] The title "Prince" refers to His kingly office. The full title "Messiah the Prince" sets forth both the kingly and priestly role of Jesus Christ.[30]

The final phrase continues the first part of the verse. The "street [*reḥôb*] . . . and wall [*ḥarûṣ*]" of the city will be built during troubled times. The words *reḥôb* and *ḥarûṣ* naturally suggest a contrast, "broad places and streets." Leupold translates as "extensively, yet within fixed limits." Keil is similar: "wide space, and yet also limited." These indicate that the city includes wide places but is not unlimited in width. While these translations draw a contrast, they are too free with the Hebrew. Hartman understands *ḥarûṣ* as "cut," a trench cut into rock outside the walls to increase their height. Hammer translates as "conduits." Wood gives "moat."[31] While these views are possible, they do not contrast with *reḥôb* as well as "wall."

---

[29]Charles, pp. 244–45, identifies the "anointed one" as "Jeshua the son of Jozadak," Ezra 3:2. This leads to the closing of the first seven "weeks" at 538 BC. Since Charles applies the final week to Antiochus Epiphanes, 171–164 BC, he faces the difficulty of explaining how the sixty-two week period (434 years) can be fulfilled in the 367 years between Jeshua and Antiochus. He concludes that the "author followed a wrong computation." The view requires that we abandon the inspiration and inerrancy of Scripture.

[30]Heaton, pp. 213–17, identifies Joshua the High Priest at the return in 538 BC as the "Messiah." He then adds 434 years to 538 to arrive at 171 BC, a date that is off by several years but is convenient since it is the year in which Onias, a former high priest, is murdered. Heaton understands this as the "cut[ting] off" of Messiah. After this, Antiochus Epiphanes successfully gains support among "hellenizing and apostate Jews." He later proscribes worship in the temple. The author of Daniel speaks with faith in predicting the restoration of the temple worship and the death of Antiochus. Heaton's view is a typical liberal view that ignores the details of the prophecy in order to support a non-messianic view.

[31]Leupold, p. 417; Keil, p. 359; Hartman, p. 244; Hammer, p. 99; Wood, p. 251.

Just as trenches or conduits, streets also require the digging suggested by *ḥarûṣ*. This building of the city occurred after the return of the Jews led by Nehemiah, v. 25.

After the 483 years, Messiah is "cut off" (*karat*) at the Crucifixion.[32] The *nip'al karat* suggests a complete "cutting off," often with violence. This word occurs more than one hundred seventy times in the OT. It refers to a variety of matters, e.g., cutting off all flesh at the Flood (Gen. 9:11); judgment on those who violated the Law by eating flesh with blood (Lev. 17:10, 14); judgment of the wicked (Ps. 37:9; Prov. 2:22; Jer. 44:7, 8, 11). In Daniel, the word occurs only here.

The Messiah is "cut off" but "not for himself" (or "he shall have nothing," *ʾên lô*). The phrase *ʾên lô* is difficult. The negative *ʾên* refers to the complete non-existence of something. This normally has an object, "there shall be no blood" (Exod. 22:2) or "he hath no son" (Num. 27:4). There is, however, no object here, a construction found elsewhere only at Exodus 22:3, "if he have nothing."

Phillips understands the phrase to mean that there was "no successor to carry on His name." Calvin states that the phrase refers to His death as being "without any attractiveness or loveliness." Neither of these views is appropriate. He needs no successor since He will one day receive His kingdom, and death in any form is not attractive.[33]

Keil understands the phrase to refer to Messiah's position; the place that He should have had among His people is lost. Henry combines two thoughts. Messiah is cut off but not for His own sins, nor for His benefit. The phrase, however, does not have a dual meaning. Leupold focuses on the outcome. Messiah is cut off and therefore loses "all influence and prestige that He ever had before men."[34]

---

[32]Auchincloss, pp. 69–70, changes the order into "1 week plus 7 weeks plus 62 weeks." Accepting the view that a week is seven years, and beginning with the return from Babylonian Captivity in 458 BC, the 8 (1 + 7) weeks goes to 402 BC, the time when Persia lost its power to Alexander (discussed at 3:29*b*). The additional 62 "weeks" ends in AD 33 when Messiah is crucified. He then brings the one "week" back, with the first half referring to the Lord's ministry, and the last half to the persecution of the church under Rome. Auchincloss does not explain how the first week can have two applications.

[33]Phillips, p. 152; Calvin, II, 227.

[34]Keil, p. 361; Henry, IV, 1044; Leupold, p. 427.

While these views are possible, I would suggest that since He is cut off, the Messiah receives no immediate benefit. The people do not recognize His death as sacrificial, and thus they reject Him as the means of salvation. Although He is the One Who will one day reign over this world, He does not receive a kingdom at the time of His crucifixion.

It is also possible that the phrase refers to His death as being alone, with the priests denying Him (Mark 15:31; John 19:15), rejected by His nation (Matt. 27:20–22), and abandoned by God the Father, the One with Whom He had enjoyed perfect fellowship throughout His life (Ps. 22:1, quoted in Matt. 27:46 and Mark 15:34).[35] I have chosen the above view since there were a faithful few who did remain with the Lord at His crucifixion (Mark 15:40–41; Luke 23:48–49; John 19:25–27).

Following this rejection, "the people of the prince that shall come," the Romans, will "destroy the city and the sanctuary." Verse 27 supports identifying the "prince that shall come" as the Antichrist. Hulst, Lederach, and Porteous adopt a standard liberal position. They identify the "Messiah" (or "anointed one") as Onias III, the high priest who was martyred during the reign of Antiochus Epiphanes (2 Macc. 4:23–34). Antiochus himself is the "prince that shall come" who sends his armies as "a flood." The timing of the verse—"threescore and two weeks" (434 years)—does not agree with the time of Antiochus's rule.[36]

The "people" of Antichrist are the Romans in that he will come out of the Roman Empire; cf. 2:40–43; 7:23–25. The destruction took place in AD 70, when the Roman armies under Titus sacked Jerusalem. Its description as being like "a flood" pictures the multitude of soldiers who overran the city. Continuing "desolations" will mark the city until "the end of the war," i.e., until Armageddon. The Battle of Armageddon receives its name from the location at *har m^egiddô*, "the mountain of Megiddo." This lies in the south of the Plain of Esdraelon. This was the location for several of the major OT battles: Israel's victory over the Canaanites (Judg. 4:14–16); Israel's defeat by the Philistines, including the death of King Saul (1 Sam. 31:1–6); and Josiah's defeat by the Egyptians (2 Kings 23:29–30; 2 Chron.

---

[35]This view is held by Bloomfield, p. 65, and Wood, p. 255, among others.
[36]Hulst, p. 228; Lederach, p. 217; Porteous, p. 142.

35:22–24). The Battle of Armageddon will take place at the end of the Tribulation when the Lord returns to fight against the armies of Antichrist.

It is important to note that this passage anticipates the sacrifice of Jesus Christ for those who place their faith in Him as their Savior. When the Messiah is "cut off," He is the infinitely righteous provision that satisfies the wrath of a holy God against those who have sinned. Jesus Christ bears the sins and the punishment of those who trust Him for their salvation.

Daniel closes v. 26 with the sixty-ninth week and begins v. 27 by referring to the seventieth week. The sixty-ninth week ends with the crucifixion of the Messiah, followed by the destruction of Jerusalem. In the seventieth week, the Antichrist makes a covenant with Israel. Between these verses is a gap of unspecified time. This gap is the church age, a period of time not discussed in the OT.

In Luke 4:18–19, 21, the Lord applied Isaiah 61:1–2 to Himself. His statement in Luke is significant in that He quoted all of Isaiah's passage except the final two phrases, "the day of vengeance of our God" and "to comfort all that mourn." These refer to the judgments of the Tribulation and to the millennial kingdom when God's people receive comfort. The Lord's failure to mention the Tribulation and Millennium implies the church age, the undefined period of time between His crucifixion and the final end-time events.

The church is a "mystery," concealed in the OT (Rom. 16:25; Eph. 3:1–6) and unknowable to man by his reasoning ability alone. The truth that God would bring both Jews and Gentiles into a single body is revealed only in the NT (Rom. 16:26–27; Eph. 3:7–11; Col. 1:25–27). Nowhere, however, is the length of this age discussed. While we can look at contemporary events and feel that the rapture of the saints is near, we cannot set a date. This is deliberate, intended by God for the purpose that Christians should live as though it could take place at any time (1 Tim. 6:11–14; Titus 2:11–13; 1 John 2:28; 3:2–3), v. 26.

Gabriel now introduces the final "week." At this time, "he shall confirm the covenant." The "he" looks forward to the Antichrist who makes a covenant with "many," i.e., with Israel, in the end times. The word "many" has an article attached, indicating "the many." Archer considers this "a technical term referring to the true believers among the people of God." References elsewhere, however, indicate that all

Israel will be included in the time of tribulation that follows Antichrist's breaking of the covenant (e.g., Jer. 30:7, "Jacob's trouble;" Rev. 11:2, treading underfoot "the holy city"; Matt. 24:15–16, the flight of those in the "holy city").[37]

Antichrist "shall confirm [or 'strengthen']" the covenant in that he imposes this covenant on Israel. Ford sees no gap between the 69th and 70th weeks. In the middle of the 70th week—after 3½ years of ministry—the Lord is cut off. The destruction spoken of in v. 27 relates to Rome's destruction of Jerusalem in AD 70. The remaining 3½ years brings us to AD 34, when the Jews "sealed their rejection of the Christian gospel by stoning Stephen to death." Then, after emphatically finding a messianic fulfillment in the seventieth week, he states "that the inspiring Spirit intends us to make some connection here between the work of the typical antichrist and the true Christ." The explanation is confusing and contrived. Ouro is better but still incorrect. He finds the antecedent of "he" in "Messiah" in v. 26a. He rejects the closer possibility, "the prince that shall come" in v. 26b, because it "is subordinated to the subject of the clause 'the people.'" He then applies the passage to the doing away of the Mosaic law at Christ's death "in the middle of the week."[38] He does not explain what happens in the rest of the week. Ouro's conclusions stand or fall with his identification of "he" as the Messiah. But Christ, the Messiah, made no "covenant with many for one week." Further, identifying the pronoun with Antichrist agrees with the teaching elsewhere (see the notes at 7:25). Finally, relating the pronoun to the "prince," i.e., Antichrist, does away with the awkwardness of explaining the last half of the week.

The covenant made by Antichrist with Israel will be an enforced covenant that culminates in the restrictions on temple worship in the last half of the "week," the time of "Jacob's trouble" (Jer. 30:7).[39]

---

[37]Archer, p. 117.

[38]Ford, pp. 201, 233–35; Roberto Ouro, "Daniel 9:27a: A Key for Understanding the Law's End in the New Testament," *JATS* 12 (Autumn 2001): 183–98.

[39]Thomson, pp. 275–76, understands "the midst of the week" to refer to the end of the Lord's ministry of about 3½ years. He thus makes this refer to the crucifixion of the Lord. The overall prophetic nature of Daniel's visions in c. 2, 7, 8, 10, and 11 argues against this. Thomson tentatively makes the end of the "week" refer to "the end of time." He does not explain the gap between the first and last halves of the week.

At that time, Antichrist will "cause the sacrifice and the oblation to cease" as he changes the temple worship of the Lord (2 Thess. 2:4). He will have the assistance of the False Prophet as he introduces idolatry (cf. Rev. 13:15). The idol is an image of himself that the nations are to worship. It is likely that other images of Antichrist are also placed throughout his kingdom for the people to worship.

This worship is the "overspreading of abominations," better phrased as "upon the wing of abominations." Young interprets the phrase "wing [*kanap*] of abominations [*šiqqûṣ*]" as the "wing of the temple." The temple is "a house of abominations" since "the true worship of Jehovah had ceased." Neither *kanap* (109X) nor *šiqqûṣ* (28X) is rare, and nowhere else do they refer to the temple. There is therefore no justification for taking them in that sense here. Hengstenberg understands "wing" as "a figurative designation of the summit." The temple is "so desecrated by abomination, as no longer to deserve the name of the *temple of the Lord* but that of the *temple of idols.*" The Lord therefore brings ruin on the temple.[40] While the view is possible, it is also subjective, with nothing in the text to suggest it. The view expressed above sees the destruction as that of Antichrist rather than merely the temple.

It is better to see Antichrist as a mighty bird, swooping across the land and establishing the abomination of idolatry as he goes. He uses idolatry as he establishes himself at the center of his religious emphasis. He will set an idol in the Jewish temple itself (cf. 11:31; 12:11). These impious actions will continue until the "consummation" (or "complete destruction"), predetermined by God, is poured out upon the "desolate" (or "one who makes desolate"), i.e., upon the Antichrist himself, v. 27.

---

[40]Young, p. 218; E. W. Hengstenberg, *Christology of the Old Testament,* abridged, Thomas Kerchever Arnold (1847; Grand Rapids: Kregel Publications, rpt. 1970), p. 425.

GOD'S GLORY 10:1–11:1

The last three chapters of the book form a unit, giving the background and interpretation of a single vision. This is the last of the prophetic visions given to Daniel. Chapter 10 serves as the introduction to this prophecy. Chapter 11 provides an extremely detailed body of information—more than one hundred separate prophecies—as it sets forth the interpretation of the vision. Chapter 12 concludes the vision and gives the final instructions to Daniel.

Vision of Daniel 10:1–9 The "third year of Cyrus" was ca. 536 BC. Daniel 1:21 says that "Daniel continued even unto the first year of king Cyrus." This refers to Daniel's service in government. Due to his age, it is likely that he has stepped back from active service for the king. He is now about ninety years old. While many of the captive Israelites have returned to Israel (Ezra 1:1–2:70), Daniel's age and possible responsibilities under Cyrus have precluded the possibility of his leaving. He still lives with enough mental clarity that God chooses this time to reveal the future to him. Since his captivity began ca. 605 BC, he has been in Babylon approximately seventy years.

In addition to his own name of Daniel, he gives his Babylonian name of Belteshazzar (see the naming of the Israelites in 1:7) to clearly identify himself to all who read the account of this final vision. He has received a revelation so startling he feels compelled to add the statement "the thing [better 'word'] was true." In the vision, "the time appointed was long" (*ṣabaʾ gadôl*, better "the war was great"), i.e., the vision concerned great conflict.

Henry follows the KJV in understanding *ṣabaʾ gadôl* as "the time appointed was long." The word *ṣabaʾ*, however, relates to "war" or "battle" better than "time." Similarly, the adjective *gadôl* means "great, high, mighty," but not "long." It is translated "great" in vv. 4, 7, and 8 of this chapter. The phrase has also been taken in other directions. Montgomery understands *ṣabaʾ* as "trouble" and refers this to the task assigned to Daniel. Leupold understands it as "warfare" but concludes that since war involves suffering, "suffering . . . is the best rendering." Keil is similar, calling it figurative for "difficulty." Lacocque refers it to the "great slavery" of Jerusalem, a meaning not found elsewhere for *ṣabaʾ*. Thomson refers *ṣabaʾ* to the angelic hosts, a great number of them understanding the vision.[1] This introduces an unnecessary third party at this point and ignores the *waw* that sets off the phrase "and he understood," which refers naturally to Daniel rather than angels. Since c. 11 deals with many wars and conflicts between kings and nations, I prefer to relate the sense to the conflict about to be revealed to Daniel. From the development of the interpretation in c. 11, this description does not overstate the nature of what Daniel saw. He had full understanding of the "thing" (again "word," here best taken as "message") and of the "vision," v. 1.

Daniel has fasted for "three full weeks." Goldwurm follows an older Jewish view that understands "three weeks of years," i.e., twenty-one years. The Hebrew phrase translated "full weeks," however, is lit. "weeks of days." In a book where weeks may equal years (9:24–27), Daniel clarifies the length of time spent fasting (see the discussion of fasting at 9:3). This clearly limits the time.

Barnes suggests that the fast was at the time when the people faced difficulties in organizing their return to Israel from Babylon. Driver states that Daniel mourned over the nation's sin. Newell offers the view that he grieved over the willingness of the people to remain in Babylon, "away from true worship of Jehovah." Walvoord thinks that "his concern for the pilgrims who had returned to Jerusalem two years before" occasioned the fast. These views are possible; however, vv. 12 and 14 seem rather to refer to Daniel's burden to understand some previous revelation from God concerning the nation. West relates the fast to Daniel's grief over Cyrus's decree stopping the rebuilding of the temple (Ezra 4:5).[2] Cyrus, however, did not make such a decree. That came from Pseudo-Smerdis during his brief time as king. The chapter does not give a clear reason for the fast other than that suggested by vv. 12 and 14, that Daniel spent his time praying for understanding of Israel's future, v. 2.

The Jewish law did not command such a fast, so this must have been due to some spiritual burden carried by Daniel. The events of the chapter interrupt his fast on the twenty-fourth of Nisan (v. 4). The interruption follows the Passover meal on the evening of the fourteenth

---

[1]Henry, IV, 1096; Montgomery, p. 405; Leupold, p. 443; Keil, p. 497; Lacocque, *The Book of Daniel*, p. 204; Thomson, p. 368.

[2]Goldwurm, pp. 269–70; Barnes, II, 192; Driver, pp. 152–53; Newell, p. 139; Walvoord, p. 240; West, pp. 99–100.

of Nisan (Lev. 23:5) and the Feast of Unleavened Bread from the fifteenth to the twenty-first of Nisan (Lev. 23:6–8). While the Jews could not carry out the biblical commands for temple sacrifices at this time, this would have been a natural time to devote to the Lord.

During his fast, Daniel abstains from "pleasant [$ḥ^amûdôt$, see 9:23] bread," the richer foods available at the king's court, and from "flesh" and "wine." Driver suggests that Daniel's fast was partial in that he abstained only from "pleasant bread" and from "flesh and wine," normally available at festivities or special occasions. Price also considers this a partial fast. He contrasts "pleasant bread" with "bread of affliction," e.g., Deut. 16:3, "a form of unleavened cakes."[3] Since the chapter mentions only briefly this period of mourning, we cannot be certain of its nature. The very mention of it, however, indicates that this was unusual for Daniel. In addition, he does not anoint himself with oil, commonly practiced in hot and dry climates to soften the skin (cf. Ruth 3:3; 2 Chron. 28:15). The OT elsewhere connects the lack of anointing with mourning (2 Sam. 14:2; Mic. 6:13–16).

From v. 12, Daniel's purpose was "to understand" the vision he had earlier received (9:20–27), v. 3. On the twenty-fourth day of the "first month," Daniel and some other men (cf. v. 7) are at the river "Hiddekel," i.e., "rapid," the name coming from its swift current. The word is another name for the Tigris River. This name comes from the Old Persian word *tigrâ*, meaning "arrow," and is semi-descriptive of the river's generally straight and rapid flow of water.

Charles and Heaton identify the river as the Euphrates, not as the Tigris. There is no reason, however, to reject the common identification (cf. Gen. 2:14). The LXX translates as Τίγρης, "Tigris." Watkinson interprets Hiddekel as a spiritual river that denotes Daniel's reasoning ability. He thus understands the vision because his reasoning is clear.[4] As is so often true with Watkinson's interpretation of the book, his views rest on his own understanding and do not let the book speak for itself.

Boutflower and Calvin think that Daniel sees the river only in his vision, and that he was located away from the river's bank.[5]

---

[3]Driver, p. 153; Price, p. 265.

[4]Charles, p. 256; Heaton, pp. 220–21; Watkinson, p. 227.

[5]Boutflower, p. 213; Calvin, II, 239–40.

Although it is possible that Daniel is at the river only in his vision, it is more reasonable to place him physically there. The river does not figure in the vision. There is no reason to mention it unless Daniel was there. The description in v. 7 of other men being with Daniel and fleeing in fear is a detail that supports Daniel's actual presence at the river.

It is possible that the Lord sends the vision to Daniel in this location because of the connection between the Seleucids, who are the subject of much of the prophecy in c. 11, and the river that ran through their homeland. The city of Seleucia, named for the dynasty, lay on the Tigris about twenty-five miles away from Babylon at the point at which the Tigris River curves close to the Euphrates.

The month Nisan, also called Abib, is the first month of the Jewish religious calendar. This goes back to the first celebration of the Passover ritual at the time when God delivered Israel from their bondage in Egypt (cf. Exod. 12:2). Nisan is the equivalent of the period from mid-March to mid-April in our modern calendar, v. 4.

A "certain man," later identified as an angel (vv. 11–13), suddenly appears to Daniel. Later, 12:5, two other angels appear. At this time, however, Daniel sees only the first of the angels. From the description, it seems that there was a certain amount of glory associated with the angel. Daniel refers to him as a "man," i.e., manlike in appearance; cf. 9:21; 12:6, 7. It is clear, however, that this is an angel. From the role assigned to him in the passage, he is undoubtedly a powerful angel on a par with Gabriel and Michael.

Because of the similar description of Revelation 1:13–15, some identify the man as Jesus Christ. Miller, Van Impe, West, and Young are among those who identify the person as the Lord.[6] For this to be so, an additional angel, accompanying the Lord, must be introduced to explain vv. 9–21. Nothing in the text, however, signals that a new character appears. Whitcomb also sees the Lord appearing here. He explains the need for help by pointing to the NT when "in His nonglorified incarnate state, following His temptation by Satan, 'angels came and began to minister to Him' (Matt. 4:11)." In the NT, the Lord is incarnate in human flesh. The being here, however, appears in a glorified state.[7]

---

[6]Miller, p. 281; Van Impe, p. 177–78; West, p. 99; Young, pp. 225, 258.
[7]Whitcomb, *Daniel*, p. 141.

The description in Revelation 1:13–15 differs from the description here. While the descriptions are similar, they are not identical. This one's garment girds his loins with gold. That one has a golden "girdle" (or "sash") about his chest. The body of this one is like "beryl" (or "chrysolite"), likely yellowish in color. That one has a white head and hair. Angels also wear linen (Ezek. 9:2, 3, 11; Rev. 15:6). The narrative later rules out the identification of this "man" as the Lord. This one is sent, v. 11; requires help, v. 13; and is an equal with Michael, 10:21, 12:1. His statement that he "remained . . . with the kings of Persia," v. 13, is puzzling if this is the Lord. He swears an oath by "him that liveth for ever," 12:7, an improbable oath for the eternal Son of God. Angels interpret the other visions given to Daniel (7:16; 8:16–17; 9:21–23), and it is reasonable that an angel explains this vision received by Daniel here.

The angel is not Gabriel, mentioned in both c. 8 and c. 9, since Daniel does not recognize him. King, Lederach, and Phillips identify the angel as Gabriel. They do not, however, explain Daniel's failure to recognize him after having seen him twice before, 8:16; 9:21. Leupold correctly identifies him as "one of the mighty angels of God, neither Gabriel nor the Angel of the Lord but one who is on a par with other mighty angels like Michael."[8] He wears a linen robe and a belt decorated with gold from the region of "Uphaz," an unknown location. Charles suggests that "the linen garment may represent the angelic body as composed of light."[9] It seems rather that the linen garment is an actual garment. Otherwise, there is no purpose for the belt of fine gold that gathers it in.

The name Uphaz occurs again only in Jeremiah 10:9. The noun *ʾûpaz*, "Uphaz," is commonly thought to be a variant spelling of *ʾôpîr*, "Ophir," from the association of both names with gold (e.g., Job 28:16; Ps. 45:9; Isa. 13:12), v. 5.[10] Ophir is variously located in Eritrea, on the northeastern coast of Africa; across the Red Sea, on the southwest coast of Arabia; or somewhere in India. No other locations are postulated for Uphaz.

[8]King, p. 205; Lederach, p. 231; Phillips, p. 160; Leupold, p. 448.
[9]Charles, p. 258.
[10]So Julius Fuerst, *A Hebrew & Chaldee Lexicon to the Old Testament*, trans. Samuel Davidson (London: Williams & Norgate, 1885), p. 40.

The skin of the angel is the color of "beryl" (*taršîš*). From the name *taršîš*, transliterated as Tarshish, the stone seems to be one found in southern Spain near Gibraltar. While this may be the source of *taršîš*, it does not let us identify it with certainty. Henry does not identify *taršîš* but makes it "a sky-color." Barnes gives topaz. Leupold tentatively makes the stone "a crystal of cinnabar" from the mines in Spain. This would account for the name *taršîš*. Heaton offers a "pale green emerald." BDB suggests "perhaps yellow jasper." Calvin gives it "a golden hue." Miller offers "chrysolite" and gives it a golden color although this mineral generally has a greenish tint.[11] Clearly, we cannot be dogmatic. While we do not know the exact color, it is clear that his skin coloring was distinct. His face shines with the brightness of lightning, his eyes burn with a bright light, and his feet and arms shine as polished brass. His voice is loud, compared with that of a large crowd, v. 6.

Although others accompany Daniel, only he sees the vision. This is similar to the vision given to Paul in Acts 9:3–7. The men that are with Daniel sense that something unusual is happening even though they cannot see it. The Talmud, *Megillah 3a*, identifies the men as Haggai, Zechariah, and Malachi. Aside from the speculation, the dates of the ministries of these men lie after that of Daniel. Haggai prophesied in 520 BC, Zechariah in 520 BC and following, and Malachi in the mid-fifth century BC or later. Although Daniel could possibly have known Haggai and Zechariah as youths, his ministry had ended by the time their ministries were beginning.

Trembling with fear, the men flee to hide themselves, v. 7. Daniel remains by himself as he sees the vision. He is utterly overwhelmed. His "comeliness [*hôd*] was turned . . . into corruption [*mašḥît*]," i.e., he reacts in some way to what he saw and understood. The phrase must be interpreted in some way. The word *hôd* often refers to glory, honor, or majesty, particularly when referring to God. When referring to man, it may refer to honor due to position or success (Ps. 21:5) or to dignity (Prov. 5:9). It also refers to appearance (of a horse, Zech. 10:3, or tree, Hos. 14:6). I have referred *hôd* here to Daniel's appearance. This turns into *mašḥît*. This word elsewhere consistently refers to "destruction, corruption." The thought here is

---

[11]Henry, IV, 1097; Barnes, II, 194; Leupold, p. 449; Heaton, p. 221; BDB, p. 1096*b*; Calvin, II, 242; Miller, p. 281.

that Daniel's ruddy complexion turns pale from the fright he experiences, v. 8. After hearing the angel's voice, he falls into a "deep sleep" (*radam*, see 8:18), apparently fainting and falling prostrate on the ground (as at 8:18) when he becomes conscious of the angel's words, v. 9.

Interpretation of the Vision 10:10–11:1 The angel strengthens Daniel, first setting him (*nûaᶜ*) on his hands and knees. The *hipᶜîl* verb *nûaᶜ* means "to shake, cause to totter." It describes here the unsteady condition of Daniel. He first rises with trembling to his hands and knees, then staggers to a standing position, v. 10. The angel calls Daniel "a man greatly beloved" (or "highly esteemed," *ḥᵃmûdôt*, see 9:23), the plural emphasizing God's pleasure in him (cf. 9:23; 10:19). He urges Daniel to stand and, with trembling legs, Daniel complies, v. 11.

The angel encourages Daniel to "fear not." He tells him that his prayers have been heard "from the first day" he made them when he purposed "to understand" and, to this end, "to chasten himself" by fasting. The angel has come to him in response to his prayer, v. 12. He has, however, been delayed by "the prince of the kingdom of Persia." This must be an evil angel since no human could withstand the power of an angel (cf. 2 Kings 19:35).

Henry understands the princes here and in v. 20 as the kings of earthly nations in the warfare against God's people. He understands the phrase "one [*ᵓeḥad*] of the chief princes" as "the first of the chief princes." He identifies him as "Christ, the church's prince."[12] The number *ᵓeḥad*, however, occurs as an ordinal in connection with day, month, or year. The ordinal "first" with ordinary nouns is *riᵓšôn*, not found here. When *ᵓeḥad* occurs as *ᵓaḥad*, as it does here, it has a construct relationship, "one of the chief princes."

Price likewise understands the king of Persia resisting an angelic influence of some kind. Michael comes to relieve the angel so that he can come "to enlighten Daniel." Price adopts the view since he denies any "conflict behind the scenes between . . . antagonistic spirit beings." Such references as Zechariah 3:1; Jude 9; and Revelation 12:7 refer to conflict between good and evil angels. Meadowcroft asserts that the princes are "human figures subject to the attention

---

[12]Henry, IV, 1101.

of Michael and his angelic colleagues." He argues unconvincingly from the context of the book. While the word "prince" may refer elsewhere to humans, e.g., 1:7–11, 18, the immediate context argues strongly that this is a heavenly being. The "man" of 10:5–6 is clearly an angelic being, as is Michael "one of the chief princes." It is unthinkable that a human prince could require the combined efforts of two angelic creatures to overcome him.[13]

Apparently, every nation has evil angels that influence them. After twenty-one days, Michael, "one of the chief princes," had come to help. Michael is the only angel clearly distinguished in the Bible as an archangel (see Dan. 10:13, 21; 12:1; Jude 9). Price considers "Michael" as a name "which is applied to the pre-existent Son of God, who in His career of condescension took the place of one of the angels before He became human." The view cannot be reconciled with the overall teaching of Scripture. Angels are created beings (Ps. 148:2–5; Col. 1:16). Michael hesitated to rebuke Satan but said, "The Lord rebuke thee" (Jude 9). The final conflict will involve Michael and his angels warring against Satan and his angels. Will Christ become Michael again? Theologically, there is no purpose served by making Christ assume an intermediate position as an angel. Watkinson asserts that "Michael does not designate an individual spirit, but a grand man, society, or power of angels combined."[14] This novel idea cannot stand in view of the description of Michael. He is called "one of the chief princes" (10:13), a "prince" (10:21; 12:1), and an "archangel" (Jude 9) and has angels serving under him (Rev. 12:7). These terms describe a single being, not some vague power of a combination of angels.

From the phrase "one of the chief princes," there are other archangels, but the Bible names only Michael. Toward the middle of the Tribulation, Michael and his angels will fight with Satan and his hosts and will cast them out of heaven (Rev. 12:7–9). Michael is probably the archangel who sounds the trumpet to signal the resurrection (1 Thess. 4:16). From Daniel 10:21, "your prince," and 12:1, "standeth for the children of thy people," it is clear that Michael has

---

[13]Price, p. 267; Tim Meadowcroft, "Who are the Princes of Persia and Greece (Daniel 10)? Pointers Towards the Danielic Vision of Earth and Heaven," *JSOT* 29:1 (Sep 2004): 103.

[14]Price, p. 268; Watkinson, p. 232.

special responsibilities toward Israel. In the Talmud, *Ḥagigah* 12*b* identifies Michael as "Israel's Guardian Angel."

With Michael's help, the evil angel is driven away and the good angel remains to help the "kings of Persia." Miller notes that the phrase "kings of Persia" is plural. He sees the idea that the angel remains to help the Persian kings as "untenable." For this reason, he makes the phrase refer to "spiritual rulers who attempted to control Persia."[15] While this is possible, it seems unnecessary. If the wicked angel has been vanquished, why would godly angels need assistance? If these were ungodly angels, why is only the one wicked angel driven away? It is more likely that the plural word "kings" refers to royalty—the king and princes—at all levels of government.

From this narrative, we see that unseen evil forces oppose the work of God. For this reason, it should not be surprising when there is opposition to your efforts to serve the Lord. It is worth remembering, however, that "greater is he that is in you, than he that is in the world" (1 John 4:4), v. 13.

As part of his help, the angel reveals to Daniel what will happen to Israel in the "latter days." The phrase encompasses Israel's future up to the days that end with the coming of the Messiah. The vision that Daniel receives is for "many days" (or "the last days," *be'aḥarît hayyamîm*), i.e., will be fulfilled in the end times. Although this is the only time the phrase *be'aḥarît hayyamîm* occurs in Daniel, it occurs twelve other times in the OT. It normally has an eschatological sense (e.g., Isa. 2:2; Hos 3:5; Mic. 4:1). From the development in c. 11, the phrase here refers specifically to the Tribulation era, v. 14. At this speech by the angel, Daniel is overcome. He turns his face to the ground, not falling down but simply looking down. He is not able to speak, v. 15.

The angel touches Daniel to give him strength. The only identification of the angel is that he is "one like the similitude of the sons of men." Since the narrative mentions no other angel, it is likely that this is the same angel as in the previous verses. In Daniel's emotional state, he may not have recognized him. The touch on Daniel's lips lets him speak to the angel. He refers to his "sorrows" (*ṣîr*). The noun *ṣîr* refers to severe pain such as that experienced by a woman

---

[15]Miller, p. 284.

in childbirth (1 Sam. 4:19; Isa. 13:8; 21:3). It best indicates here the weakness coming from Daniel's extreme emotional reaction, v. 16. He asks how the angel can continue to speak with him in his present condition. From the description here, he refers to his emotional state, one of tremendous upset. He is weak, without the normal "strength" and "breath" of life. With these words, Daniel conveys to the angel his physical and emotional weakness. He is not able to deal with such startling truth as has been revealed, v. 17.

The angel again strengthens Daniel by touching him, v. 18. He reminds Daniel that he is "greatly beloved" ("highly esteemed," the same grammatical structure as in v. 11). He then gives Daniel a threefold challenge: (1) "fear not" the nature of the revelation; (2) "peace be unto thee" since there is no need to fear what he has received; and (3) "be strong," probably more directed to Daniel's emotional strength than his physical wellbeing. After this Daniel gains strength and urges the angel to continue speaking with him, v. 19.

The angel now supplements the information given in vv. 12–14. He asks if Daniel understands why he has come. In view of Daniel's emotional state, this is a logical question to ask. Although the evil angel that is the "prince of Persia" has been defeated, he will not accept the defeat. The angel of this chapter must therefore return to continue the battle with him. This conflict will continue until "I am gone forth," finished with his battle on behalf of God's people in the kingdom of Persia. The "prince of Grecia" will then come at the time when Greece replaces Persia as the dominant world power. Barnes identifies the "prince of Grecia" as Alexander the Great.[16] The reference, however, is to a "prince" rather than a king or emperor. The context of the "prince of Persia" who fights with God's angels supports identifying the "prince of Grecia" as an evil angel that opposes the nation of Israel. This angel will no doubt influence the kingdom of Greece in Satan's war against God. While the angel does not give details regarding Satan's battle against the Lord, it is clear that he has organized his forces as he opposes God. It is foolish to oppose Satan without relying on the strength and guidance of the Holy Spirit, v. 20.

---

[16]Barnes, II, 204.

Despite these angelic conflicts, the angel takes the time now to show Daniel the truths recorded "in the scripture [better 'writing'] of truth." This is not the Bible but rather the divine record of what is to happen. The angel develops this account in the next chapter, and thus it is about to be added to the OT Scriptures. Of the angelic hosts, only "Michael your prince" stands with this angel to assist him. Michael is the "prince" of Israel in that he is the angel that is specially the guardian of Israel (cf. 12:1). We see his conflict against Satan in Revelation 12:7–9 when his angelic forces cast Satan and his evil angels out of heaven. The only other clear mention of Michael in Scripture is in Jude 9. Jewish tradition holds that God Himself, "accompanied by Gabriel, Michael, and Zagziel, the former teacher of Moses," came to Moses at his death.[17] Satan tried to take the body back to Israel in the hope that the Israelites would make it into an idolatrous shrine. Michael refused to usurp the place of God by himself condemning Satan. He rather said, "The Lord rebuke thee," v. 21.

In point of thought, the first verse of c. 11 belongs to c. 10. It ends the thought of the cooperation of Michael with the unnamed angel in c. 10. To show Daniel that Michael's help was not unusual, he mentions that "in the first year of Darius the Mede," two years before (cf. 10:1), he had assisted Michael in some way.[18] He gives no details of this event other than to say that he had served "to strengthen [*maᶜôz*, '*be a* stronghold to'] him." The noun *maᶜôz* occurs seven times in Daniel, all in c. 11 (vv. 1, 7, 10, 19, 31, 38, 39). It comes from the verb *ᶜôz*, "to take or seek refuge." The *mem* prefix gives it the sense "a place of refuge," often a fortress. The "him" in the angel's statement of course refers to Michael, v. 1.[19]

---

[17]J. Z. Lauterbach, "Moses," *The Jewish Encyclopedia*, ed. Isidore Singer (New York: Ktav Publishing House, Inc., n.d.), IX, 54.

[18]Thomson, p. 306 argues that *daryaweš*, "Darius," should be *kôreš*, "Cyrus." The LXX and Theodotion support this change. It is difficult to see, however, that this change would take place in Hebrew. The Vulgate supports the MT.

[19]Henry, IV, 1101, refers "him" to Darius the Mede. In some way, Gabriel had strengthened "him." Logically, however, v. 1 concludes the thought of c. 10. If it introduces a new thought, it has no relation either to the previous or following words.

PTOLEMIES AND
SELEUCIDS 11:2–45

Daniel 11 is unique among the chapters of the Bible. No other chapter contains such a concentrated group of prophecies. These verses contain more than one hundred specific and often detailed prophecies of the future history of the region. The material in vv. 1–35 develops the history of the biblical world until Antiochus Epiphanes. (Chapter 8 summarizes the reign of this wicked king.) Although this portion of the chapter is historical now, it was prophetic at the time of its writing. The remaining verses of the chapter leap past the church age and focus on Antichrist, the one who fulfills the type established by Epiphanes.

History of Persia and Greece 11:2–4 Verse 1 has been discussed with c. 10, to which it logically belongs. The speaker in v. 2 is the angel previously seen in 10:18–21. He reveals to Daniel "the truth" of things to come. Cambyses (530–522 BC), the usurper Gaumata (also called Pseudo-Smerdis, 522 BC), and Darius Hystaspes (522–486 BC) are the three kings "yet" (*ʿôd*) to appear in the Medo-Persian Empire.

Henry and Calvin identify the three kings as Cyrus, Cambyses, and Darius. The particle *ʿôd* ("yet"), however, implies additional kings. Since Daniel lived during the reign of Cyrus, this logically refers to later kings. Hammer excludes Pseudo-Smerdis and identifies the three kings as Cambyses, Darius I, and Xerxes. This creates a problem in identifying the fourth king in v. 2. He adds Cyrus to the list and makes the fourth king also Xerxes. It is unlikely that Xerxes is both the third and fourth king in the same verse. Montgomery identifies the kings as Cyrus, Xerxes, Artaxerxes, and Darius III Codomannus. He does not explain the omission of Cambyses, Gaumata, Darius the Great, or several other Persian kings before Darius III. The view also forces him to ignore the fact that Xerxes, the king fighting against Greece, is not the fourth of the kings in his own list. Lederach understands "three *notable* kings" and identifies them as Cambyses, Darius I, and Xerxes. He makes the fourth king Darius III. His list of notable kings omits Artaxerxes, king for forty years. In addition, Darius III was not "far richer than they all."[1]

---

[1]Henry, IV, 1101; Calvin, II, 270; Hammer, p. 107; Montgomery, p. 423; Lederach, p. 236.

Ezra 4:6 names Cambyses, the son of Cyrus, as Ahasuerus, a name that means "mighty man." This is the Hebrew transliteration of the Persian name *Khšayâršâ* which, in turn, represented the Greek name Xerxes. To avoid succession problems, Cyrus named Cambyses as his heir shortly after he defeated Babylon. Before Cyrus went into his final battle, he named Cambyses as regent to rule in his place while he was gone. After the death of Cyrus in battle in 530 BC, Cambyses became the king. He began his rule by putting his brother Smerdis, a potential rival, to death. He successively married his sisters, Atossa and Roxana.

The historical record of Cambyses shows his instability. Herodotus 3.27–38 records that he murdered Egyptian leaders and priests, killed his brother Smerdis, killed his sister-wife Roxana, buried twelve Persian nobles alive up to their necks, and condemned King Croesus of Lydia to death, then changed his mind and killed the servants who had spared Croesus. He opened Egyptian coffins and examined the bodies in them. He was also subject to epileptic seizures.

Beginning in 526 BC, Cambyses campaigned successfully in Egypt. He defeated Psammeticus III, an unlucky pharaoh who ruled only six months. Cambyses occupied Memphis and ruled Egypt from there. He alienated the Egyptians by degrading the worship of their gods. While Cambyses campaigned in Egypt, a priest named Gaumata pretended to be the dead Smerdis and usurped the throne. The record is not clear regarding Cambyses at this point. He may have died fortuitously, or he may have committed suicide after hearing of the actions of Gaumata.

Ezra 4:7 calls Gaumata, the one who had claimed the throne, by the name of Artaxerxes. History knows him as Pseudo-Smerdis, the false Smerdis. He pretended to be the brother of Cambyses and therefore the heir to the throne of Persia. With the support of several of the nobles and in the absence of Cambyses, Gaumata claimed the throne in 522 BC. He ruled seven months before being overthrown by Darius, the general of the Persian army who was also in the bloodline of the Persian kings.

Darius I (or Darius the Great) was called Hystaspes after his father. The Bible mentions Darius in Ezra 4:5, 24; 5:3–6:15; Haggai 1:1, 15; 2:10; and Zechariah 1:1, 7; 7:1. After the rebellion by Gaumata and the death of Cambyses, Darius led the army back to Persia and seized the throne. He describes this in the Behistun Inscription, chiseled into the rocky side of a cliff near Behistun, Persia, about 200 miles northeast of Babylon. The inscription, written in three languages—Old Persian, Elamite, and Akkadian—was discovered and translated in the mid-nineteenth century by the archaeologist Henry C. Rawlinson. This trilingual inscription was the key that unlocked the cuneiform writings of that part of the world. The inscription reads in part, "Nobody dared to say anything in regard to Gaumata, the Magian [a Persian priestly class], until I came. Then I pleaded with Ahuramazda [a Persian god]. Ahuramazda brought me help. . . . Then I killed with a few men that Gaumata, the Magian, and the men who were his chief retainers. . . . Nineteen battles did I fight. According to the will of Ahuramazda I slew them and took nine kings prisoners."[2]

After devoting his early years as king to putting down rebellions, Darius showed great administrative ability. He organized a postal system to connect parts of his empire. He divided the empire into satrapies (provinces), placing nobles over each one. In Egypt, he joined the Nile River with the Red Sea by means of a canal. Rebellions occurred in Greece and Egypt toward the end of his long rule (522–486 BC), but Darius died before he could put down either of them.

The fourth king is Xerxes (486–465 BC), the last strong king of Persia. The book of Esther calls him Ahasuerus almost thirty times. He followed his father Darius as the ruler of the Persia Empire. With this position as a base to provide income, he became extremely wealthy. Herodotus 3.89–97 relates that he divided the empire into twenty satrapies and records the tribute paid by each one. History confirms the statement in Esther 1:1 that Xerxes ruled "from India even unto Ethiopia."

He crushed a revolt in Egypt and another rebellion in Babylon. He accumulated wealth in preparation for a campaign against Greece. He failed, however, in several attempts to conquer Greece. The Greeks defeated his navy in battle at the Bay of Salamis, 480 BC. A year later, he defeated the city of Athens but lost in battle at Platea in Greece. A second naval fleet was destroyed in the battle of Mycale, off the coast of Asia Minor.

Xerxes spent the remainder of his reign in building his capital city of Persepolis, thirty-five miles northeast of modern Shiraz, in Persia.

---

[2]Translation from Siegfried J. Schwantes, *A Short History of the Ancient Near East* (Grand Rapids: Baker Book House, 1965), p. 150.

It is during this time that he became involved with Esther, toward the end of "the seventh year of his reign," ca. 479 BC (Esther 2:16). He laid a heavy burden of taxation on the people to pay for his failed military operations. He also carried out extensive building projects. In 465 BC, Artabanus, the commander of his Royal Guard, led a group of conspirators to assassinate Xerxes in his bedchamber, v. 2.

The account does not mention the other Persian kings who followed Xerxes. In general, these are minor kings with no great accomplishments. The "mighty king" is Alexander (336–323 BC), discussed at 2:39b, who does "according to his will," v. 3. When he "shall stand up," still a young man in his early thirties, he dies and his kingdom is "broken" (*šabar*, see 8:25) and "divided toward the four winds of heaven," north, east, south, and west. The phrase describes the final division of Alexander's kingdom into four lesser kingdoms: Greece, Asia Minor, Syria, and Egypt.[3]

At the death of Alexander in 323 BC, his only son was Heracles, the retarded and illegitimate son of a Persian widow. Alexander's wife, Roxane, was pregnant at the time of his death and later gave birth to a son, Alexander IV. Neither son of Alexander was old enough to rule. One of Alexander's generals, Perdiccas, became regent and *de facto* ruler of the empire. Other officers, however, began taking control of parts of the empire. Perdiccas led an army into Egypt to try to put down Ptolemy's claim to that region. When his invasion failed, his own men assassinated him.

A struggle for power began among the generals with no pretense of loyalty to either of Alexander's sons. Philip III Arrhidaeus (the guardian of Alexander's legitimate son), Alexander IV (the son himself), and his mother Roxane were all assassinated. During this period of conflict, several of Alexander's leaders—Ptolemy, Antipas (followed by his son Cassander), Lysimachus, and Antigonus—began to exercise control over the major parts of the empire. Antigonus, one of Alexander's generals, took control of Mesopotamia and began military actions to gain control over much more. His son,

---

[3]Young, p. 233, sees the phrase as "merely . . . indicat[ing] that a four-fold division of the kingdom occurred." He does not see any significance in the directions implied by the phrase. I have discussed the phrase in a note at Dan. 7:2, giving my reasons for associating it with the four primary directions of east, west, north, and south.

Demetrius, became his co-ruler. Initially, Seleucus ruled the region around Shushan under Antigonus. When he found that Antigonus was moving against him, he fled south to Egypt and served under Ptolemy.

After joining forces at various times, Ptolemy, Cassander, Lysimachus, and Seleucus eventually overcame Antigonus in 301 BC. After several years of plots and counterplots, four of Alexander's officers, "not to his posterity, nor according to his dominion which he ruled," emerged as rulers of the major part of his empire. Cassander took control of Greece; Lysimachus controlled Asia Minor; Seleucus replaced Antigonus in Syria, which, at that time, included Mesopotamia; and Ptolemy ruled Egypt.

At the death of Alexander, Antipater had been the regent in Macedonia. His son Cassander had served as general over the army of Macedonia. After the death of Antipater, Cassander became ruler over the region. He overcame several plots and also was responsible for the assassinations of Roxane and Alexander IV. By 305 BC, Cassander had consolidated his claim to kingship. In 302 BC, however, Demetrius, the son of Antigonus, invaded Greece. The renewed coalition of Cassander, Ptolemy, Seleucus, and Lysimachus successfully forced Demetrius to withdraw to his father's aid in Asia Minor. In the Battle of Ipsus in 301 BC, Antigonus was killed. The remaining years of Cassander's life were spent fighting Demetrius in the effort to control Greece. Cassander died in 298 BC.

Following Alexander's death, Lysimachus took possession of the satrapy of Thrace, the region northeast of Macedonia. He joined forces with Ptolemy in Egypt and Cassander in Greece to ward off an attack by Antigonus, who at that time controlled Asia Minor. In 302 BC, Lysimachus led his army across the Hellespont to attack cities controlled by Antigonus. At the same time, Ptolemy came into Asia Minor from Egypt and Seleucus from Babylon. Ptolemy was driven back, but Lysimachus and Seleucus joined forces in the Battle of Ipsus. Together they routed the army of Antigonus, killing him in the victory and forcing Demetrius to flee for his life.

In 288 BC, Lysimachus joined with Pyrrhus, king of the western part of Greece, to conquer and partition Macedonia. Lysimachus then turned on his ally and by 285 BC controlled all of Macedonia and Thessaly. In 281 BC, the portion of his kingdom in Asia Minor rebelled against him, supported by Seleucus of Syria and Babylon. Lysimachus lost his life in the battle for control.

Seleucus I, also called Seleucus Nicator ("the conqueror"), had been an officer in Alexander's army and fought under Perdiccas against Ptolemy in Egypt. When Perdiccas handled the invasion poorly, losing three battles, Seleucus joined in the plot to assassinate Perdiccas. As a result, he was rewarded with the rule over Syria and Babylon. With the rise in power of Antigonus in Asia Minor, Seleucus joined Ptolemy, Cassander, and Lysimachus in opposing him. Seleucus had also campaigned in the east, accomplishing little but bringing back with him a brigade of Indian war elephants. Seleucus joined Lysimachus in the battle against Antigonus at Ipsus, and the elephants played a major part in the victory. Seleucus built a new capital in Antioch. In 281 BC, he extended his rule into Asia Minor by defeating and killing his former ally Lysimachus. He effectively ruled only to the Taurus Mountains. Resistance by areas to the west of that point made it impossible to establish his control there. Seleucus died in 280 BC.

Ptolemy I, also called Ptolemy Soter ("the savior"), was one of Alexander's generals governing in Egypt. Upon the death of Alexander, Ptolemy declared himself the new Egyptian ruler. By means of his navy, Ptolemy cultivated markets throughout the Mediterranean area and increased the wealth of Egypt by trade. Through the fear of Antigonus, a former general of Alexander, Ptolemy allied himself with Cassander in Macedonia and Lysimachus in Thrace. Later, Seleucus of Babylon and Syria also assisted Ptolemy.

After the defeat and death of Antigonus, Ptolemy claimed Phoenicia and Syria. Conflicts developed with Seleucus, who also claimed these areas and eventually gained control over them. The Egyptians marched over Israel in these battles, at one time compelling 100,000 Jews to return with them to Egypt. Favorable treatment in Egypt caused many other Jews to emigrate there, creating a large minority of Jews. Among Ptolemy Soter's more peaceful accomplishments was his aid in founding the library at Alexandria. Ptolemy named Philadelphus, son of his favored wife Berenice, his successor in 285 BC. Two years later, 283 BC, Ptolemy died of natural causes. Seleucus, Ptolemy, and their descendants dominate the chapter through v. 20, v. 4.

History of Egypt and Syria 11:5–20 This part of the chapter focuses on the history of Egypt and Syria because these two nations most significantly influenced Israel.[4] The geographic location of Israel between Syria and Egypt caused the interaction between these nations to seriously affect the people of Palestine. For example, within twenty-five years of Alexander's death, the rule of Jerusalem changed seven times.

From this point on, the chapter uses the titles "king of the south" and "king of the north" to refer to the rulers of Egypt and Syria. The first "king of the south" is Ptolemy Soter ("savior"), the first of Alexander's generals to control the land over which he was to rule. He is also the first ruler of the two kingdoms to conquer Israel and subject it to tribute. Josephus *Antiquities* 12.1.1 describes Soter's conquest of Jerusalem:

> He also seized upon Jerusalem, and for that end made use
> of deceit and treachery; for as he came into the city on
> a Sabbath day, as if he would offer sacrifice, he, without
> any trouble, gained the city; while the Jews did not oppose
> him for they did not suspect him to be their enemy; and he
> gained it thus, because they were free from suspicion of him,
> and because on that day they were at rest and quietness; and
> when he had gained it, he reigned over it in a cruel manner.

Soter ruled Egypt a little more than thirty years (ca. 316–285 BC), then abdicated in favor of his son Ptolemy Philadelphus.

The phrase "one of his princes" refers to Seleucus I Nicator ("the conqueror") who fled from Antigonus, a former general under Alexander.[5] After serving with Perdiccas in his ill-fated invasion of Egypt, Seleucus became a general under Ptolemy and served with him until the defeat of Antigonus at Gaza, 312 BC. At this time, he took control over the region north of Palestine formerly ruled by Antigonus. Ultimately, he became "strong above" Ptolemy with

---

[4]Lang, pp, 154–57, sees vv. 5–33 as a prophecy of "the years immediately to precede the rule of Antichrist in days still future." Since the future is unknown, it is impossible to rule out the view. The events of the section agree so closely with history, however, that it more likely applies to the future of the third kingdom.

[5]Much of the information concerning the relationships between the Ptolemies and the Seleucids comes from the two volumes by Edwyn Robert Bevan, *The House of Seleucus* (London: Edward Arnold, 1902).

a greater "dominion" in Syria and Babylon. He as well controlled territory extending to the Indus River in India. In addition to his conquests in war, he built more than thirty cities, including Antioch, named for his father. His rule lasted more than thirty years (312–280 BC). He was murdered by Ceraunus, an older brother of Ptolemy Philadelphus and thus a claimant to the Egyptian throne, v. 5.

The son of Seleucus, Antiochus I Soter ("savior"), followed him as king over Syria and Babylon. After arranging a truce with the Egyptian Ceraunus, who then turned toward Macedonia, Antiochus ruled until 261 BC. He received the name Soter for his success in defeating the Gallic barbarians who were invading Asia Minor. After his death, his son Antiochus II Theos ("god") followed him as king, reigning 261–246 BC. His claim to being a "god" was given by the leaders of the coastal city of Miletus in ancient Lydia, who sought his favor. Antiochus later accepted the worship of his subjects.

In Egypt, Ptolemy Soter named his son Ptolemy II Philadelphus ("lover of brothers," i.e., "lover of fellow countrymen") the ruler of Egypt ca. 285 BC. Philadelphus was responsible for colonizing parts of Palestine, Egypt, and Syria. He displayed great interest in the museum and library at Alexandria that his father had founded. According to the Letter of Aristeas, a somewhat fanciful account giving the origin of the Septuagint, Ptolemy authorized the Greek translation of the Old Testament. He died ca. 248 BC.

Egypt engaged in a long struggle with Syria for control of the region. The ruler of Syria, Antiochus Theos, was at first successful in his wars against the Egyptian Ptolemy Philadelphus. In "the end of years" (*lᵉqeṣ šanîm*), however, in 250 BC, he entered into a peace treaty with the Egyptian leader. The phrase *lᵉqeṣ šanîm* occurs elsewhere only at 2 Chronicles 18:2. It is similar to the phrase *lᵉqeṣ yamîm*, the "end of days" (Neh. 13:6). In each of these cases, the sense is of the passing of time, here "after several years."

At that time, as prophesied, Egypt and Syria "join[ed] themselves together" in a political agreement. Antiochus Theos divorced his wife Laodice and married Berenice, the daughter of Ptolemy II Philadelphus, to seal the arrangement between the two rulers. With this, "the king's daughter of the south" came "to the king of the north to make an agreement [*mêšarîm*]." This indicates the political nature of the wedding. The word *mêšarîm* refers to "uprightnesses" or "right things." It indicates here the righting of the relationships between the two nations.

Although Berenice had a son by Antiochus, she was not able to maintain "the power of the arm," the strength of the Ptolemies. When Ptolemy Philadelphus died, Antiochus abandoned Berenice and took Laodice back as his wife. She did not welcome her husband back. Either fearing that Berenice's son would succeed Antiochus or in revenge for being set aside earlier, she had Antiochus, Berenice, and their son murdered. Thus neither Ptolemy nor the "arm," his power, could "stand."

The use of an "arm" ($z^e r\hat{o}a^c$) to represent power or strength is common in the OT (e.g., Exod. 6:6; 15:16; Deut. 4:34). Breaking the arm represents the loss of power (e.g., Ps. 10:15; Jer. 48:25; Ezek. 30:21). The NIV suggests in a footnote that the "arm" ($z^e r\hat{o}a^c$) refers to "offspring." While the view is possible, it is interpretive and departs from the normal use of the word. Elsewhere in this chapter, $z^e r\hat{o}a^c$ refers to "forces," vv. 15, 22, 31. The thought of "strength" is thus closer to $z^e r\hat{o}a^c$ than is "offspring." Knoch reads $zero^c aw$, "seed," for $z^e r\hat{o}a^c$, "arm." He concludes that Berenice was "given up" because she was sterile and failed to produce an heir to inherit both thrones. Aside from the lack of textual support, the view is contrary to history.[6]

Berenice was "given up" in her murder. "They that brought her," the ones involved in making the arrangement, lost their power. Ptolemy, "he that begat her," and Antiochus, "he that strengthened her," both lost their lives in Laodice's revenge, v. 6.[7] The son of Antiochus by Laodice, Seleucus II Callinicus ("gloriously triumphant"), a name more boastful than descriptive, succeeded his father as king of Syria.

The "branch" of Berenice's "roots" is Ptolemy III Euergetes ("the benefactor"), her brother. After the death of Ptolemy Philadelphus, his son Euergetes took the throne in Egypt, ruling 248–221 BC.

---

[6]Knoch, pp. 377–78.

[7]Di Lella, p. 266, understands the phrase "he that strengthened her" as referring to "her husband." Since the $hip^c\hat{\imath}l$ of $hazaq$ never refers elsewhere to a man marrying a woman, he cites Ginsberg, p. 47, to suggest that the Hebrew translator from the Aramaic original misread $w^e gabr\bar{a}h$ as $um^e gabb^e r\bar{a}h$. There is no evidence supporting his theory of an Aramaic original or of a misreading of a word. Di Lella solves a problem that does not exist unless we understand the word to refer to a "husband."

Shortly after this, he began to fight with Syria to avenge his sister Berenice's death. He led the Egyptian army north to "enter into the fortress [*ma'ôz*, see 11:1] of the king of the north," Syria. With the support of his strong naval fleet, he "prevail[ed]" against Syria with great success. His success included the execution of Laodice, who had been responsible for his sister's death.

The Syrian king, Callinicus, was occupied in Asia Minor. This let Ptolemy overrun Syria, Phoenicia, Babylon, and Persia and even plunder to the borders of India. Ptolemy gained control of the Aegean Sea once more, v. 7. The Egyptian army sacked many of the Syrian temples in their search for wealth. They also recovered the Egyptian gods that had earlier been taken by Persia in the campaign of Cambyses in Egypt. The church father Jerome (ca. 340–420) records that 40,000 talents of silver (about one hundred million dollars) and 2,400 idol statues ("their gods") were brought to Egypt from this campaign.[8] Ptolemy also brought Egypt's "princes" (better "molten images") back. This spectacular success gained the Egyptian ruler the name Euergetes, the "benefactor." The name came from the Egyptians, who gave it in gratitude for the wealth brought to their country. The remainder of his reign was uneventful. He died of natural causes in 221 BC.

The phrase "he shall continue more years than the king of the north" is better "he shall refrain *many* years from *attacking* the king of the north," v. 8.[9] After his return home, Callinicus regained control over northern Syria and Babylon. He was not, however, able to restore his rule in the Aegean or Phoenicia. To raise an army, he had to give his brother Antiochus Hierax ("the hawk") rule in Asia Minor. Later, he fought to take this area back but was defeated when his brother allied himself to the Galatian tribes of Anatolia, ca. 238 BC. When Hierax later was driven from Asia Minor by forces from

---

[8]Jerome, p. 123.

[9]Goldwurm, p. 289, refers the phrase "he shall continue" to the dynasty rather than the individual. He notes that the Seleucid rule lasted only to 150 BC but that the Ptolemies continued until 30 BC. The context, however, relates the exploits of individuals. The key word in the phrase is *'amad*, "continue." Elsewhere, the word occurs as some variation of "stand" more than 350X. The *min* preposition follows the word here, giving the sense of standing apart from something. This most logically refers to the failure of Euergetes to follow up his success with an additional attack.

Greece, he invaded Mesopotamia. Seleucus returned from warring in Persia to fight successfully against his brother, defeating him in several battles. Hierax escaped from his brother but was soon captured and put to death by a band of men from Gaul. Verse 9a should read "he shall come into the kingdom of the king of the south." Callinicus attempted an unsuccessful campaign against Egypt. He was forced to "return into his own land," v. 9b.[10]

After Callinicus fell from his horse and died in 226 BC, his "sons"[11] followed him as king in succession. Seleucus III Ceraunus ("thunderbolt") first took the throne. His name, given by his troops, suggests that he exhibited erratic emotional behavior. Ceraunus and his brother Antiochus III, later known as Antiochus Magnus ("the great"), joined in raising troops to move against Attalus, king of Pergamum, who had assumed control over land previously ruled by Syria. When Seleucus III was assassinated by two of his officers after reigning only three years (226–223 BC), his brother Antiochus III assumed the kingship. He raised "a multitude of great forces" and led the army to "overflow, and pass through" Egypt. The singular pronouns in v. 10 follow this change from joint leadership to a single leader.

The first Egyptian campaign under Antiochus stopped at the Orontes River when Egypt convinced Syria to make a truce with them. Antiochus soon discovered Egyptian deception. Being "stirred up," he "return[ed]" south to let his army attack the Egyptians, who defeated his army. After this, he retreated back to the "fortress" (ma'ôz, see 11:1) at Gaza and acknowledged his defeat to the Egyptians, v. 10. Antiochus successfully campaigned in Asia Minor to retake areas that had fallen to other leaders. His successful campaign to the east, in which he conquered Bactria and Parthia, led others to call him Magnus, "the great."

Verse 11 develops the conflict between Syria and Egypt first introduced in v. 10. Ptolemy IV Philopator ("lover of *his* father")

---

[10]Henry, IV, 1103, understands the phrase to refer to Ptolemy Euergetes. He states, "He shall be forced to come into his own kingdom and return into his own land, to keep peace there, so that he can no longer carry on the war abroad." There is no historical confirmation of the view.

[11]The k^etîb is "son." The LXX also reads the singular. Both Theodotion and the Vulgate, however, accept the q^erê, "sons." Since the following verbs are both plural, it is reasonable to read with the q^erê at this point.

had become the ruler of Egypt in 221 BC. Almost immediately, he faced the threat of a Syrian invasion led by Antiochus III. Through subterfuge, he convinced Antiochus that he had a large army. This delayed Syria's invasion by two years. Ptolemy took advantage of the time gained to raise an army of 70,000 men, 5,000 cavalry, and 73 elephants. This was larger than the Syrian army of 62,000 men, 6,000 cavalry, and 102 elephants.[12] Moved with "choler" (or "rage") against Syria, Philopator led his army into battle. The Syrians "set forth a great multitude" and at first were victorious. But when Antiochus III abandoned a cautious approach and gave in to the lure of plunder, Egypt gained the victory. The battle took place in 217 BC near Raphia, a coastal city about twenty miles below Gaza. Antiochus had 10,000 men killed in the battle and another 4,000 who were captured. So "the multitude" was given into Ptolemy's "hand" (*yad*, see 8:4), v. 11.

Ptolemy Philopator desired ease more than he did the hard conditions in the field. Rather than following up his victory, he returned to Egypt. Even though Egypt had "cast down . . . ten thousands [better "myriads," a poetical reference to many thousands],"[13] the nation was "not strengthened" by the victory, v. 12. The heavy taxes necessary to pay for the army created Egyptian dissatisfaction with Philopator. Further, he was a dissolute and weak king, and Egypt's stature declined under his rule. He died of natural causes, 204 BC. Although only a four-year-old child, his son, Ptolemy V Epiphanes ("the illustrious one"), followed him as Egypt's ruler. Ptolemy's rule lasted until 181 BC.

After the death of Philopator, Antiochus again invaded Egypt with a larger and better-equipped army and with many "riches" (*rᵉkûš*, better "supplies"). The noun *rᵉkûš* refers to "substance" or "goods." Depending on the context, this may refer to property, supplies, or wealth. The word occurs three times in c. 11. It refers here to the supplies of the army. In vv. 24 and 28, it best refers to riches, v. 13.

---

[12]Polybius *Histories* 5.79 gives these numbers for both the Egyptian and Syrian armies.

[13]The MT reads *hippîl ribboᵓôt*, lit. "he shall cause to fall myriads." While the word *ribboᵓôt* can mean "ten thousand," it occurs here by itself and thus is better understood simply as an indefinite large number. So Waltke and O'Connor, 15.2.5a.

At that time "many" came against the "king of the south," Ptolemy Epiphanes. Because Ptolemy Epiphanes was only a child at this time, his Egyptian ministers and Philopator's wife fought among themselves for control. Antiochus III entered into an agreement with Philip V of Macedonia to partition the empire of Egypt. Coordinating his plans with those of Antiochus III, Philip launched an attack against Egyptian possessions in the region of the Aegean Sea. There were also internal uprisings in Egypt. One of these involved "the robbers of thy people" (or "violent ones among your people"). These were a group of Jews who had been living in Egypt.[14] In fulfillment of Daniel's "vision," they rebelled while trying to gain independence. The rebellion was not successful ("they shall fall"), not achieving their "vision" of dominance over Egypt, v. 14.

Antiochus invaded Palestine, then under Egyptian control. One year after Scopas, the Egyptian general, had recovered the region for Egypt, Antiochus defeated his forces. Antiochus "cast up a mount," i.e., threw up dirt embankments against the walls of Sidon in his attack against this Egyptian-controlled city in Phoenicia. The Egyptians had retreated there for safety. Even though three armies came from Egypt to help the Sidonians, their "arms" (or "forces") did not "withstand." All were beaten back. Antiochus defeated "the most fenced cities" (better "a city of fortifications"), i.e., Sidon, a well-guarded city.

Keil understands the "city of fortifications" as a collective representing "the fortresses of the kingdom of the south generally." Goldwurm refers it to Gaza, in southern Palestine.[15] These views are possible. Since, however, the Egyptian general Scopas fled to Sidon, it is likely that this is the object of the Syrian conquest, v. 15.

Antiochus, the one coming against the forces of Ptolemy Epiphanes, now controlled the region. No one could "stand before him." He next came into "the glorious [or 'beautiful'] land" of Palestine. This was "consumed" (or "conquered"), completely brought under his

---

[14]*Antiquities* 12.3.143–44. Smith, pp. 243–44, refers the phrase to the Romans, now beginning to develop in strength. He does not explain how Rome, across the Mediterranean, can justly be described as "robbers of [Egypt's] people" (11:14) since, at this time, Rome was allied to Egypt. He also waffles on the phrase "they shall fall," letting it apply to the first part of the verse or to Rome's final overthrow.

[15]Keil, p. 440; Goldwurm, p. 293.

control "by his hand [*yad*, see 8:4]" as he did "according to his own will." Antiochus actually gave Israel favorable terms to reward them for assisting him in the battles against Egypt. Egypt had treated them harshly. Josephus relates that Antiochus released them from taxes for three years and from one-third of the taxes after that (*Antiquities* 12.3.143–44). Many of the Israelites welcomed his rule. Nevertheless Israel came under his control, v. 16.

Antiochus then "set his face," i.e., purposed, to destroy Egypt although he was not able to succeed at this. He moved against Egypt with "the strength of his whole kingdom" as he directed the full power of his army toward them. He first took control of Egyptian possessions in Asia Minor. Opposition from Rome prevented further conquests in that direction. Antiochus entered into an agreement with Egypt, offering them "upright ones," i.e., fair terms. At this time, he negotiated an agreement with representatives of Epiphanes in which the Egyptians renounced all claims to Palestine ca. 195 BC. He gave Epiphanes "the daughter of women," his own daughter Cleopatra (not the later and more famous queen of Egypt). This was for the purpose of "corrupting her" (or "for her to destroy," *hašḥîtah*).[16] Antiochus thought that his daughter's presence would give him influence in and, eventually, over Egypt. She, however, would not "stand on his side, neither be for him." Cleopatra was faithful to her husband, children, and her new Egyptian home. After Ptolemy V had entered into his treaty with Antiochus III and received Cleopatra as his wife, he died fourteen years later, 181 BC. Cleopatra was left with three small children. She remained faithful to Egypt, acting as regent on behalf of Ptolemy VI for eight years until her death in 173 BC, v. 17.

Antiochus next invaded the coastal areas and islands of the Aegean Sea ("shall turn his face to the isles") and was successful for a time ("shall take many"). Eventually, however, at Thermopylae in Greece in 191 BC, Rome forced Antiochus and his army to flee. One year later, Rome won control of the sea. Shortly after, Rome defeated

---

[16]Thomson, p. 312, follows the KJV, "corrupting her." The word *hašḥîtah* has a 3fs suffix, which identifies it as a subjective genitive referring to "the daughter of women." It is better translated "for her to destroy." If it is taken as an objective genitive, "corrupting her" or "destroying it," the verse becomes difficult. Why would Antiochus plan to corrupt his daughter? Where is the "kingdom" antecedent in the verse? The remainder of the verse shows that the plan failed.

Antiochus at Magnesia in Lydia, modern-day Turkey. A "prince" (or "commander"), Lucius Cornelius Scipio, led the Roman army. The victory of Scipio over Syria caused the "reproach" (or "scorn") of Antiochus toward Rome to cease. This victory was so significant that Scipio was given the title of Asiaticus to indicate his victory over the Asian king.

"Without his own reproach he shall cause it to turn upon him" is better "he shall not turn reproach against him." The idea is that Scipio did not follow the example of Antiochus by humiliating those he had conquered. After negotiations with Rome, Antiochus renounced all claims to territory west of the Taurus Mountains. The Romans also required him to pay an enormous amount to Rome, paying their expenses in the war and an annual tribute of one thousand talents for twelve years. They also required Antiochus to give twenty hostages, which were selected by Rome. These included his son Antiochus IV, later known as Antiochus Epiphanes. The navy was limited in its ships, the army gave up its elephants, and the soldiers received a variety of restrictions which limited the nature of their service, v. 18.

Antiochus III now returned to "the fort [better 'fortresses,' *ma'ôz*, see 11:1] of his own land," where he focused his attention on his rule. After his defeat by Rome, he attempted to raise money to pay his tribute to Rome and to rebuild his army. In 187 BC he attacked the temple of Bel in Elymais, a district in Persia. In the battle that followed, he was killed ("he shall stumble and fall, and not be found"), v. 19.[17]

Seleucus IV Philopator ("lover of *his* father") had earlier served as co-regent with his father. He now succeeded Antiochus III as the sole king, ruling 187–175 BC. Because of the thousand talents Syria was required to pay Rome each year, Seleucus Philopator was "a raiser of taxes" (or "an oppressor").[18] As one aspect of this, he sent

---

[17]Price, pp. 288–89, refers the prophecy to the assassination of Caesar. This begins a chain of references to Rome lasting through v. 35. At v. 36, he begins applying the passage to Roman Catholicism and the Pope. His view forces him to see great lapses of time between the prophecies and to make applications that strain for credibility.

[18]Watkinson, pp. 291–302, applies the prediction at this point to Rome's conquest of Palestine. He relates the phrase "a raiser of taxes" to the decree from Caesar Augustus "that all the world should be taxed," Luke 2:1. This throws his interpretation

tax collectors throughout the empire to raise money. The minister charged with collecting this wealth was Heliodorus. He went into Palestine, "the glory of the kingdom," where he made an unsuccessful attempt to confiscate the treasure of the temple. 2 Maccabees 3:1–40 records the account. That passage tells of a sobering vision God gave Heliodorus to warn him against taking the treasure.

Within a "few days," Philopator will "be destroyed" (*šabar*, see 8:25). Compared to the lengthy reign of his father, Philopator's approximately twelve-year rule was but a "few days." Driver, Price, and Thomson adopt the conceivable view that the "few days" should be measured from the mission of Heliodorus to plunder the temple at Jerusalem (or from the inception of the plan). Keil understands the phrase as "an ideal description of the war" between Syria and Egypt.[19] This is also a possible view.

Philopator's life ends "neither in anger, nor in battle." The circumstances of his death are mysterious, but it was not due to an armed rebellion or a war against another nation. One early tradition says that Heliodorus, the treasurer, poisoned him so that he could take the throne himself. Among others, Bultema, Lederach, and John Hutchinson ("Seleucus," *ISBE*) adopt this view.[20] Appian, *Roman History, The Syrian Wars* 8.45, refers to a plot by Heliodorus but does not specifically mention poison. While possible, the view is speculative with no clear evidence demanding it. It may also be that Heliodorus planned to serve as the guardian of Demetrius, the young son of Seleucus. We have no clear indication of what brought about the death of Seleucus, v. 20.

History of Antiochus Epiphanes 11:21–35 The major historical character of the chapter is Antiochus Epiphanes ("the illustrious one"), the "little horn" of 8:9–14.[21] There is a twofold reason for his prominence in the chapter. In the first place, Antiochus Epiphanes

---

of the rest of the chapter off, including the portion relating to Antiochus Epiphanes, vv. 21–35, which he refers to the Herodians. For the rest of the chapter, he inconsistently applies the text, some to Herod and some to Rome.

[19]Driver, p. 177; Walter K. Price, *In the Final Days* (Chicago: Moody Press, 1977), p. 51; Thomson, p. 314; Keil, pp. 449–50.

[20]Bultema, p. 325; Lederach, p. 241; John Hutchinson, "Seleucus," *ISBE*, IV, 2715.

[21]Knoch, p. 388, identifies the person in vv. 21–35 as Antichrist. Antiochus Epiphanes is a type of the Antichrist, but the passage does not refer directly to

was a major persecutor of the Jews. As such, Daniel's prophetic picture of Israel's history naturally emphasizes Epiphanes. Second, he introduces the most complete OT picture of Antichrist. The final section of the chapter, vv. 36–45, takes up this antitype of Antiochus Epiphanes.

Shortly before Seleucus Philopator's death, his son Demetrius had replaced Antiochus IV as a hostage at Rome. This was possibly at Rome's order to give them assurance that Seleucus would remain loyal to the agreement made after the defeat of Antiochus by Rome. This exchange gave Antiochus Epiphanes freedom to assume the throne after the death of Philopator. Antiochus Epiphanes is "a vile [or 'contemptible, despicable'] person," probably referring to the underhanded way in which he usurped the throne.[22] He was not given "the honour of the kingdom," yet he took it with the help of Eumenes II, the king of Pergamum (197–159 BC). Although Eumenes had assisted Rome in its victory over Antiochus III, he helped Antiochus IV control the throne of Syria. In all likelihood, this suited the wishes of Rome since Antiochus IV had received his education while a hostage in Rome.

Pergamum was a small kingdom in Asia Minor that rose after the breakup of Alexander's empire. Eumenes was awarded control over additional territory as a reward from Rome for his help in overcoming Antiochus III. He commemorated the victory on a frieze on the great altar dedicated to the god Zeus at Pergamum.

"In his estate," i.e., in the place of Philopator, comes "a vile person," an apt description of Antiochus Epiphanes. He came in "peaceably" (or "in a time of peace," šalwâ, see 8:25), when the nation did not suspect his purpose. Further, he attained the kingdom by "flatteries" (or "smoothnesses"), i.e., by intrigues, v. 21.

As the king, Epiphanes sometimes engaged in dissolute behavior, leaving his palace and carousing with foreigners or strangers. Polybius, the second-century-BC Greek historian, recounts some of his peculiar behavior:

Antichrist. There are numerous historical points of contrast in this paragraph that are best understood as describing Antiochus Epiphanes.

[22]Miller, p. 298, refers the description to Epiphanes' persecution of the Jews: "From the Jewish vantage point he was a monster." This is also a possible view although the character of Epiphanes has not been introduced at this point.

He . . . used to drink in the company of the meanest foreign visitors to Antioch. Whenever he heard that any of the young men were at an entertainment, he would come in quite unceremoniously with a fife and a procession of musicians. . . . He would frequently put off his royal robes, and, assuming a white toga, go round the market-place like a candidate, and, taking some by the hand and embracing others, would beg them to give him their vote. . . . To some people he used to give gazelles' knucklebones, to others dates, and to others money. Occasionally he used to address people he had never seen before when he met them, and make them the most unexpected presents. . . . He also used to bathe in the public baths, when they were full of common people, having jars of the most precious ointments brought in for him. . . . On one occasion . . . [he] had a huge jar of most precious ointment . . . poured over [another bather's] head, so that all the bathers jumped up and rolled themselves in it, and by slipping in it created great amusement, as did the king himself.[23]

Because of this peculiar public behavior, Polybius gave him the name of Epimanes ("the madman") rather than that of Epiphanes ("the illustrious one") that he had taken for himself.

The phrase "with the arms of a flood" is better "the forces of the flood," a phrase that describes the army of Heliodorus who attempted to maintain power after Seleucus. Young identifies the "arms of a flood" as the army of Egypt, also overcome by Epiphanes. He does not, however, identify the "prince of the covenant."[24] The view faces the problem of having Egypt's army led by an unknown "prince."

The army under Heliodorus was "overflown" (better "swept away") by the army of Antiochus. Even the "prince [nagîd] of the covenant" is "broken" (šabar, see 8:25). The word nagîd normally refers to a political or military leader (e.g., Dan. 9:25–26). This leader of a "covenant" is Heliodorus, broken before Antiochus. Leupold asserts that the word "covenant" refers "only to the holy

---

[23]Polybius, *The Histories*, trans. W. R. Paton (Cambridge, Mass.: Harvard University Press, 1968), 26.1a.

[24]Young, pp. 241–42.

covenant of God's people."[25] This, however, is not always the case, e.g., Genesis 9:9–16; 1 Kings 15:19 ("league"); 20:34; Job 31:1.

Henry refers the title "prince" to Demetrius, the nephew of Antiochus and the rightful heir. This is possible although Demetrius is not clearly introduced previously. Goldwurm identifies "the prince" as Ptolemy Philometor. At this time Philometor was still a child. His mother Cleopatra (sister of Antiochus IV) served as regent, ruling Egypt in his place. For this reason, it is not appropriate to see Philometor at this point. Driver and Walvoord identify the "prince" as Onias, the High Priest of the Jews, but the word *nagîd* more often refers to a political or military leader. We would also expect the "covenant" to be definite if it referred to the covenant between God and Israel. West sees the Lord as the One described by the phrase "prince of the covenant."[26] This view ignores the context, which focuses on the leaders of Syria and Egypt, v. 22.

After inducing Egypt to make a "league" with him, Antiochus Epiphanes worked "deceitfully" in regard to Palestine. He first recognized Egypt's claim to Palestine. Later, he appropriated Palestine for himself, establishing his claim with a "small people," i.e., a small army, v. 23. Thomson relates the league to the association of Antiochus and Eumenes. Leupold understands that the "league" refers to supporting the claim of Ptolemy Philometor over against that of his younger brother, Ptolemy Euergetes.[27] Since Antiochus regularly used deceit in his associations with others, these are possible views.

He enters "peaceably (or "a time of peace," *šalwâ*). The "fattest places of the province" are the wealthy parts of the empire. As was usual, Antiochus plundered the provinces. What was unusual, "that which his fathers [had] not done, nor his fathers' fathers," was that he used the spoil to buy the allegiance of others. In addition, he "forecast his devices [lit. 'reckoned his thoughts'] against the strong holds," i.e., devised plans against the enemy strongholds. Antiochus continually plotted ways of extending his rule. This, however, gave him an advantage only "for a time," v. 24.

---

[25]Leupold, p. 495.

[26]Henry, IV, 1106; Goldwurm, p. 298; Driver, p. 181; Walvoord, p. 265; West, pp. 108–9.

[27]Thomson, p. 315; Leupold, p. 426.

Ptolemy VI Philometor ("lover of *his* mother") had followed his father as Egypt's pharaoh in 181 BC. His mother, a Syrian, acted as regent for the first eight years. Upon her death, the Egyptian ministers took control and began to plot against Syrian control of northern Palestine and Phoenicia. At this time, Rome was at war with Macedonia. Antiochus took advantage of this to launch an expedition against "the king of the south," Philometor, ruler of Egypt, a Roman ally. Syria, led by Antiochus IV, invaded Egypt "with a great army" and defeated them in 169 BC. Ptolemy responded by gathering "a very great and mighty army." The Egyptian army invaded Palestine and regained the territory formerly held. The pharaoh, however, did "not stand." Antiochus was eventually successful because he "forecast devices against" Ptolemy as he plotted successfully against him, v. 25.

Philometor's own counselors, those who were fed from "the portion of his meat," had led him astray by urging him to invade Syria. This caused him to be "destroy[ed]" (*šabar*, see 8:25) and his army to be defeated, v. 26. When Philometor attempted to escape the Syrians by ship, he was taken captive. 1 Maccabees 1:16–19 describes the war as a great victory for Antiochus.

> When his rule appeared to Antiochus to be established, he conceived the idea of becoming king of the land of Egypt, so that he might reign over the two kingdoms. So he entered Egypt with a strong force, with chariots and elephants and cavalry and a great fleet. And he made war on Ptolemy, king of Egypt, and Ptolemy turned and fled before him, and many fell wounded. And they captured the walled cities in the land of Egypt, and he plundered the land of Egypt.

Antiochus proclaimed himself pharaoh, but the Egyptians recognized Philometor's brother Euergetes II ("benefactor") as their king. Euergetes was also called Physcon ("big paunch"). Antiochus withdrew to Syria, leaving Philometor behind at Memphis as the nominal head of Egypt. Euergetes continued his reign from Alexandria. After the withdrawal of Antiochus, Philometor and Physcon came together and jointly ruled the land, occasionally working together and occasionally opposing one another. Eventually, Philometor assumed control of Egypt and Physcon led Cyrenaica, west of Egypt in North Africa.

In the continuation of Epiphanes's reign, he and Philometor bargained deceitfully with one another. The deception, however, did "not prosper" because God had determined an "end" at the "time appointed." This refers to Rome's eventual domination over Syria. Keil understands "the end" as "the time determined by God for the consummation of His kingdom." Leupold is similar, referring to "the actual 'end' of all that man builds up."[28] While much of Daniel is prophetic of the end times, the section here is primarily prophetic of future history. For that reason, I have related the phrase to the end of Syria as an independent kingdom, v. 27.

As Antiochus Epiphanes returned from Egypt with the spoil gathered there, he set himself "against the holy covenant" by plundering the temple at Jerusalem. 1 Maccabees 1:20b–23 describes this:

> Antiochus . . . turned back and came up against Israel and entered Jerusalem with a strong force. And in his arrogance he went into the sanctuary and took the gold altar and the lampstand for the light, and all its furniture and the table for the Presentation Bread and the cups and the bowls and the gold censers and the curtain and the crowns and the gold ornamentation on the front of the temple, for he stripped it all off. And he took the silver and the gold, and the choice dishes, and he took the secret treasures, which he found; he took them all and went back to his own country. He massacred people and spoke with great arrogance.

This was done with the excuse of putting down a rebellion, but his ruthlessness went far beyond correcting a minor rebellion. The phrase "he shall do exploits" is better "he will act," the thought referring to his plundering of the temple, v. 28.

About a year later, "at the time appointed" by God, ca. 168 BC, Antiochus returned "toward the south" in another expedition into Egypt. This time, Philometor and Physcon cooperated in opposing him. Antiochus's invasion was "not . . . as the former, or as the latter," i.e., not as successful as his previous invasions of Egypt, v. 29. Egypt sought the aid of Rome, and Rome sent "ships from Chittim" to assist her. Originally, Chittim referred to the Mediterranean island of Cyprus. Later, Josephus (*Antiquities* 1.6.1) tells us that the term referred to the islands and coastal regions of the Mediterranean. By association, it represents areas controlled by Rome.

---

[28]Keil, p. 454; Leupold, p. 498.

At the time the ships arrived, Antiochus was beginning a siege of Alexandria. Caius Popilius Laenas, head of the Roman embassy, met Antiochus to deliver Rome's message to him. Epiphanes had invaded Palestine with the intention of occupying territory previously controlled by Egypt. Rome supported Egypt since Egypt supplied much of its needs for provisions. Upon finding Antiochus near Alexandria, Laenas gave him a letter from the Roman Senate demanding that he withdraw. Antiochus attempted to gain time to think about his answer. With a stick cut from a vine, the Roman envoy drew a circle around him in the dirt and told him to make his decision before leaving the circle. Not daring to face the power of Rome, Antiochus yielded his claim to Palestine, v. 30*a*.[29]

On the way back to Syria, Antiochus again showed his "indignation against the holy covenant." The phrase "so shall he do" refers to his oppression of the Jews. In this, he has "intelligence" (or "regard") for those who "forsake the holy covenant," Jews who had been Hellenized, adopting Greek customs, v. 30*b*.

The phrase "arms shall stand on his part" is better "forces from him shall arise." According to 2 Maccabees 5:14, "In no more than three days eighty thousand people were destroyed" by the forces under Antiochus. The Syrian king sold as many more into slavery. He polluted "the sanctuary of strength [*maʿôz*, see 11:1]," the sanctuary that served as a spiritual fortress to Israel. Syrians used the temple for immoral purposes and offered "abominable offerings" on the altar (2 Macc. 6:4–5). Antiochus also forbade the offering of "the daily sacrifice" (cf. 1 Macc. 1:44–45). The crowning desecration of the temple came when he placed "the abomination that maketh desolate." According to 1 Maccabees 1:54*b*–57,

> He erected a dreadful desecration upon the altar, and in the towns of Judah round about they built altars, and at the doors of their houses and in the squares they burned incense, and wherever they found the Book of the Law, they tore them up and burned them, and if anyone was found to possess a book

---

[29]Polybius *Histories* 29.27. The same anecdote is repeated in Appian, *Roman History, The Syrian Wars* 11.66, and in *Livy*, trans. Arthur C. Schlesinger (Cambridge, Mass.: Harvard University Press, 1968), 55.12.

of the agreement or respected the Law, the king's decree condemned him to death.

This "abomination of desolation" was an idol of Zeus, called Jupiter by the Romans, the chief god of the Greek pantheon. The "dreadful desecration upon the altar" was the sacrifice of a swine, unclean by Jewish law (Lev. 11:7). The New Testament refers to this abomination (Matt. 24:15; Mark 13:14) as it prophesies a similar defiling of the temple by Antichrist.[30] This evil work of Antiochus Epiphanes thus typifies the actions of Antichrist, v. 31.

Antiochus will corrupt those who "do wickedly" (rašaᶜ, see 9:5) by promises and bribery. However, "the people that do know their God shall be strong, and do exploits." This was fulfilled in the intertestamental revolt of the Jews led by members of the family of Mattathias the Jewish priest. This Jewish revolt against Epiphanes (also prophesied in Zech. 9:13–15) eventually led to Israel's freedom.

Mattathias was a priest who lived at Modin in Judah, about fifteen miles northwest of Jerusalem. After Antiochus Epiphanes forbade the Jews to worship their God, he tried to institute the worship of Zeus. Apelles, a messenger of Antiochus, came to Modin to conduct a worship ceremony. Being the leading citizen of the town, Mattathias was asked to offer the sacrifice. 1 Maccabees 2:19b–22 recounts his reply:

> If all the heathen in the king's dominions listen to him and
> forsake each of them the religion of his forefathers, and
> choose to follow his commands instead, yet I and my sons
> and my brothers will live in accordance with the agreement
> of our forefathers. God forbid that we should abandon the
> Law and the ordinances. We will not listen to the message of
> the king, or depart from our religion to the right hand or to
> the left.

When Apelles found another Jew who was willing to make the sacrifice, Mattathias slew both the Jew and Apelles. He and his five

---

[30]Newton, p. 264, refers the "abomination that maketh desolate" to the actions of the Romans, ca. AD 132, when they replaced the temple with one devoted to the god Jupiter. The view forces Newton to make the rest of the chapter refer to Rome. He picks and chooses Roman rulers to find parallels with phrases in the chapter but does not have a consistent chronological interpretation.

sons fled to the mountains where they organized a rebellion against Epiphanes. Mattathias led the rebellion for two years before dying of natural causes in 166 BC. He was buried at Modin, but his sons continued the fight, v. 32.

Those "that understand" (*śakal*) among the godly rebels against Antiochus will "instruct [or 'impart understanding to'] many" as they show others the spiritual issues at stake. Leupold argues that the *hipʿîl* of *śakal* here and in v. 35 has a causative sense and refers to teachers.[31] While the *hipʿîl* of *śakal* may indeed refer to teachers, it does not always have this meaning. The word occurs nine times in Daniel (also 1:4, 17; 9:13, 22, 25; 12:3, 10), always in the *hipʿîl*, and consistently referring to skill, wisdom, or understanding and never meaning "teacher." Since no teachers have been previously introduced, I refer *śakal* to godly men with spiritual insight. Despite this spiritual orientation, many of them will fall in the battle. This stand against false worship was the first step in what became a full-fledged rebellion against Antiochus Epiphanes, v. 33.

Though some of the rebels will fall, God will send them "a little help" through the slow but steady successes of the Maccabean rebellion. Many came "with flatteries," not sincerely concerned over the opposition to godly worship of the Syrians but more interested in their own advancement, v. 34. As in any war, many were killed in battles with the Syrian forces. The rebellion began with a defeat in the wilderness near Jerusalem. The Syrians attacked the Jews on the Sabbath. Because they refused to fight, about a thousand Jews died. This defeat caused Mattathias to resolve to fight, no matter what day of the week was involved.

After the death of Mattathias, his son Judas took his place and led the loyal Jews for five years, dying in battle in 161 BC. Judas Maccabaeus (a nickname meaning "the hammer") was the third son of Mattathias. He proved very successful in guerilla warfare, defeating several Syrian generals in battles. In 163 BC, he gained control over Jerusalem. In 161 BC, he defeated the Syrian army in a major battle in which Nicanor, the Syrian general, was slain.

A group known later as the Hasideans (from a word meaning "the pious") developed during this period. They acknowledged the

---

[31]Leupold, p. 505.

leadership of Judas. Later, however, when Judas tried to negotiate an alliance with Rome, many of the Hasideans were alienated and defected from him. This weakened the army so that they were defeated in battle at Elasa, 161 BC. Judas died in the battle. 1 Maccabees 3:1–9:22 gives the account of his leadership. In later biblical history, the Pharisees largely developed from the Hasideans.

Jonathan, called Apphus (questionable meaning, possibly denoting "the wary one"), next assumed leadership. He was the youngest son of Mattathias. Following the death of Judas in 161 BC, Jonathan became the leader of the Jewish rebellion against Syria. Due to pressures from other enemies of Syria, Demetrius, Syria's king at this time, made a treaty with the Jews. Balas, Syria's enemy and leader of troops from Pergamum and Egypt, recognized Jonathan as Israel's high priest in order to gain his support. After defeating Demetrius, Balas proved to be an unsuccessful ruler. Demetrius led a revolt against Balas. Jonathan again supported Balas. Egypt, however, supported Demetrius, and Balas was deposed. Jonathan was able to win recognition as Israel's leader from Demetrius. A new rebellion in Syria, led by Tryphon, deposed Demetrius. Jonathan had assisted Tryphon in the rebellion. Fearing Jonathan's power, Tryphon deceived him, and he had him captured and executed in 142 BC. The record of Jonathan's leadership occurs in 1 Maccabees 9:28–12:52.

Simon, called Thassi (uncertain meaning, possibly "gentle"), the final son, continued the leadership. 1 Maccabees 13:1–15:16 tells of his leadership. He was the third of Mattathias's sons to lead the Jews. After the death of Jonathan, Simon arranged an alliance with Demetrius II, the leader of Syria. In return, Simon was granted complete freedom from Syrian control. In 140 BC, the elders of the Jews proclaimed Simon the new high priest with broad civil and religious powers. After the overthrow of the Syrian king by the Parthian ruler Mithridates I, Antiochus VII Sidetes (from Sida, a town in Pamphylia, north-northwest of Cyprus on the coast of Asia) took control of Syria. He invaded Judah in an effort to bring it under Syrian rule again. Simon successfully resisted the invasion, but his son-in-law Ptolemy assassinated him in 134 BC in an attempt to rule Israel himself.

John Gaddi (doubtful meaning, possibly "fortunate"), the oldest son of Mattathias, had been killed early in the rebellion by marauders. After his brother Jonathan had risen to lead the rebellion against Syria, John was sent to take some possessions to the Nabateans,

south of the Dead Sea. A group of marauders, from Medeba in
Moab, attacked the convoy, killing John in the battle. 1 Maccabees
9:35–36 tells of his death.

The other son of Mattathias, Eleazar, called Avaran (unclear
meaning, possibly "white," referring either to his complexion or his
dress), fought alongside his brothers in the rebellion against Antiochus Epiphanes. In 161 BC, the Jews faced elephants for the first
time in battle. Seeing one of the elephants covered with royal armor,
Eleazar thought that it carried the Syrian king. He fought his way to
the animal, went under it, and stabbed it through the stomach. When
the animal fell, Eleazar was crushed under it. 1 Maccabees 6:42–46
gives the account.

These reverses to the Jews do not last forever. These trials have
the purpose of testing the Jews, purging those who lacked trust in the
Lord. They will "make them white," i.e., purify them (cf. 12:10; Ps.
51:7; Isa. 1:18). The "time of the end" (ᶜet qeṣ, see 8:17) is "for a time
appointed," not in the times just discussed but to a future when God
brings this age to a close. Such trials as Daniel has discussed here
always have as one of their purposes the causing of God's people
to rely on Him (Heb. 12:9–11). During the Tribulation, when the
age closes, this reliance will be all the more necessary. This phrase
makes the transition to the next section of the chapter where Daniel
discusses the activities of Antichrist during the Tribulation. This
logically concludes in c. 12 with a summary of the Great Tribulation
(v. 1) and with the mention of the resurrection (vv. 2–3), v. 35.[32]

History of Antichrist 11:36–45 This verse makes a transition to
Antichrist. Antiochus worshiped the god Zeus, and thus the "king"
of v. 36 must be different. Among others, Cowles, Lacocque, and
Montgomery refer the verse to Antiochus Epiphanes. Not only did
Antiochus worship Zeus, he came from ancestors who also warred
against others. The statement in v. 38 is contrary to this. It states
there that this king serves a god of forces not known by his fathers.
Barnes also understands the verse as describing Antiochus. His

---

[32]Watkinson, pp. 302–4, applies v. 35 "to the Arian heresy of the fourth century." In discussing the verse, however, he ignores the words and phrases of v. 35.
His misapplication of vv. 21–35 leads him to give a late date for the fulfillment of
vv. 36–45. In pp. 304–15, he relates this to the subsequent history of Rome from
the 4th to 7th centuries, picking and choosing events that seem to relate to the text.

view requires him to apply c. 12 to Antiochus, an interpretation that requires contorted reasoning. Lederach sees the fulfillment in Antiochus but recognizes that the details of vv. 40–45 cannot be related to him. He offers four explanations, all of which deny the historicity of the passage. Goldwurm identifies this king as Constantine, who "endeavor[ed] to further the Christian religion and to establish it as the state religion." While it is understandable that a Jewish commentator would consider the actions of Constantine objectionable, the Roman emperor cannot be the one who speaks "against the God of gods," v. 35. Goldwurm explains the reference to "fathers" in v. 37 as Abraham, Isaac, and Jacob. But Constantine did not descend from this line. Further, he did not "magnify himself above all" (v. 37). Calvin applies the passage to Rome, the fourth kingdom. The view leads to awkward interpretations of vv. 40–45. Horne sees the fulfillment of vv. 36ff. in the "Pope-king," the line of papal rulers leading the Roman Catholic Church and directing its influence against Judaism. The conflict between the king of the north and the king of the south, vv. 40ff., refers to the Crusades.[33] While the view is innovative, there are too many details that do not fit into the interpretation.

The self-will and pride of this king are clear. He will speak "marvellous things," i.e., unbelievable blasphemies, against "the God of gods." Paul's comment in 2 Thessalonians 2:4a comes from this verse (see also Rev. 13:5–6). This king will "prosper till the indignation [za‘am, see 8:19] be accomplished," the end of the Tribulation. These things that have been "determined" will indeed come to pass, v. 36.

He will not "regard the God [or 'gods,' ʾelohê, see 1:2] of his fathers" as he puts aside his loyalty to his ancestral religion. Many authors (among them Van Ryn, Whitcomb, and Strauss) conclude that Antichrist will be an apostate Jew who rejects the God of his fathers, the patriarchs. The view goes against Daniel's practice of attaching the definite article to ʾelohîm when the true God is in view. (See the discussion at 1:2.) Daniel does not use the article here. In addition, it is highly unlikely that Antiochus Epiphanes, a Syrian pagan, typifies a Jewish Antichrist. For this reason, it is better to understand ʾelohê

---

[33]Cowles, p. 432; Lacocque, *The Book of Daniel*, pp. 231–33; Montgomery, p. 460; Barnes, II, 240; Lederach, pp. 251–52; Goldwurm, p. 311; Calvin, II, 338ff.; Horne, pp. 120–22.

as a plural referring to the "gods" of Antichrist's heathen ancestors. Wood argues against the position that the "God of his fathers" is the God of the Jews by noting that the singular *ᵉloah* occurs later in this same verse, in v. 38 (2X), and in v. 39. Daniel thus makes it clear when he refers to the singular rather than the plural.[34] Both the NASB and NIV translate the word as plural, supporting the view that these are heathen gods.

Further, Antichrist will not regard "the desire of women." Different suggestions have been made to explain the lack of regard toward women. Archer understands the phrase as simply pointing to the cruelty of Antiochus "toward all women he was sexually involved with." Henry suggests that the reference is to either the "barbarous cruelty" toward women or "his unnatural lusts," or "his contempt of every thing which men of honour have a concern for." Keil refers the phrase to the "affection of human love . . . for which even the most selfish . . . of men feel some sensibility." Leupold does not see a god here at all but rather loyalty to womankind—his wife, sister, and mother.[35] These views go against the context, which brackets the phrase with two phrases clearly referring to Antichrist's rejection of other gods. He does not regard his ancestral gods, and he does not regard any other god.

After acknowledging "it is almost imperative that it be an object of worship that is here referred to," Thomson suggests Adonis or Tammuz. Auchincloss suggests Astarte. Phillips supports the view that this is a nature goddess, worshiped under various names throughout human history.[36] In view of this rejection of other "gods" and the attempt to promote his own deity, it is reasonable to say that Antichrist will not regard any god, including the false "gods" of his fathers or the Son of God. In this context, the phrase "desire of women" refers to the hope of Jewish women to become the mother of the Messiah. Antichrist will reject any Messianic hope because he will not regard "any god." He exalts his own deity above all gods worshiped by this world, v. 37.

"In his estate" (or "in his place," i.e., "instead"), the god of Antichrist will be that of "forces" (*maᶜôz*, "fortresses," see 11:1), i.e.,

---

[34]Van Ryn, pp. 89, 141; Whitcomb, p. 154; Strauss, pp. 342–43; Wood, p. 306.

[35]Archer, p. 144; Henry, IV, 1109; Keil, p. 465; Leupold, p. 515.

[36]Thomson, p. 320; Phillips, pp. 190–91.

he will devote himself to taking the strongholds of other nations.[37] He comes from ancestors who had no such designs. He will use his "gold and silver" to accomplish his goals, v. 38. He will move against "the most strong holds [ma⁽ôz]" (or "strongest of fortresses"). The "strange [or 'foreign'] god" assisting him is the god of force. This god is foreign to his ancestors, possibly implying the possession of weaponry not previously held by those who have ruled before him. The phrase "whom he shall acknowledge and increase with glory" is better "he will give great honor to those who acknowledge him." He will reward others who assist him with wealth and positions of responsibility under him, v. 39.

In the "time of the end" (⁽et qeṣ, see 8:17), the time that precedes the return of Christ to establish His rule over the earth, Antichrist's coalition of nations will fall apart. The "king of the south," Egypt, will attack "him." The "king of the north," Antichrist, will come against the king of Egypt. Among others, Gaebelein, M. R. DeHaan, and Walter K. Price see three kings here rather than two. The "king of the north" and the "king of the south" join in opposing the Antichrist. Keil gives three arguments supporting the view that the passage mentions only two kings: (1) the nearest antecedent of the second pronoun "him" is the "king of the south"; (2) vv. 40–43 describe an invasion from the north against the south; and (3) the passage does not mention an attack against both the "king of the north" *and* "the king of the south." Tanner dismisses these arguments as not conclusive. He argues that the Antichrist cannot be the northern king because Antichrist has a connection with the Roman Empire, not the Seleucid Empire.[38] The Roman Empire, however, included Syria, with parts of Mesopotamia subject to it. For this reason, it is likely that Antichrist will come from this region. If the Syrian Antiochus Epiphanes is the type of Antichrist, it logically suggests that the antitype will also be from this same region.

---

[37]Thomson, p. 321, understands the "God of forces" as Jehovah. The defeats suffered by Antiochus brought honor to the Lord. The view is contrived and does not fit the context that focuses on the continuing warfare of this "king," Antichrist.

[38]Gaebelein, pp. 192–93; M. R. DeHaan, *Daniel . . . the Prophet* (Grand Rapids: Zondervan Publishing House, 1948), p. 300; Walter K. Price, *In the Final Days* (Chicago: Moody Press, 1977), p. 172; Keil, p. 470; J. Paul Tanner, "Daniel's 'King of the North': Do We Owe Russia an Apology?" *JETS* 35 (Sep 1992): 321–22.

Henry, still clinging to his view that this section refers to Antiochus, explains this as a fourth expedition against Egypt. There is no support in history, however, for a fourth campaign by Syria against Egypt. It is doubtful that Antiochus would have invaded Egypt after Rome had already stated clearly that it did not want him to do so. Thomson also applies the section to Antiochus. Realizing, however, that a fourth invasion of Antiochus into Egypt is not possible, he makes the paragraph repeat what has previously been discussed. He admits, however, that "against this is the chronological statement at the beginning." Gowan also recognizes that Antiochus did not lead another campaign into Egypt. He makes vv. 40–45 a genuine prediction by the author, who was wrong in his attempt to guess the future. Paul Niskanen describes vv. 40–45 as a "fictional account . . . of the death of Antiochus." He develops parallels with the death of Cambyses and concludes that the author constructs this account to show that "a sacrilegious king met with a fitting end." Tatford understands the "king of the north" as heading the "Scythian, Cimmerian, Armenian and Arabic peoples" in opposing Antichrist. Harton identifies the "king of the north" as Russia. She joins with "the king of the south," a confederation of Arab nations headed by Egypt, in an attack of Israel. Up to this point, however, the "king of the north" has referred to the Syrian king (vv. 6, 7, 8, 11, 13, 15). It is more consistent to apply the phrase to Antichrist, the leader of a coalition that includes Syria at that time, as he invades Egypt. Leupold refers the phrase "glorious land" to "the church of God."[39] This spiritualizes the text and disregards the meaning of sensible terms.

There may be a confederation of nations under the leadership of the king of the south. Antichrist will move "like a whirlwind" as he sweeps through the "countries" of these that have opposed him.[40]

---

[39]Henry, IV, 1110; Thomson, pp. 322–23; Gowan, p. 151; Paul Niskanen, "Daniel's Portrait of Antiochus IV: Echoes of a Persian King," *CBQ* 66 (July 2004): 380–81, 86; Tatford, p. 220; George M. Harton, "An Interpretation of Daniel 11:36–45," *Grace Theological Journal* (Fall 1983): 214–15, 225–26; Leupold, p. 521.

[40]Since the Antichrist comes from the Roman Empire (9:26–27), Archer, p. 147, tentatively suggests that he will be an Italian. The "king of the north" is everywhere else the Syrian king. As noted before, the Roman Empire included Syria. It is more logical that the Antichrist will also be from this region of the world.

He comes with "chariots, and with horsemen, and with many ships," obvious representations of more modern weaponry, v. 40.

Antichrist will also enter "the glorious [or 'beautiful'] land," Israel, a beautiful land because of its special relationship to the Lord. From there, he directs his attack against the surrounding nations. He will overcome "many *countries* [or '*people*']." The regions occupied by Edom, Moab, and the "chief of the children of Ammon," referring to the more heavily inhabited part of Ammon near the Jordan River, will be delivered from his "hand" (*yad*, see 8:4). It is possible that Antichrist spares those countries on the East Bank of the Jordan River because he is occupied with the rebellions coming from Egypt and, later (v. 44), from the north and east. In addition, these areas are predominantly Arab and will support Antichrist as he acts against Israel and its worship. The discussion in Revelation 12:5–6, 13–16 shows that God will supernaturally protect those who have fled to these areas for safety, v. 41.

Antichrist will extend his "hand" (i.e., "power," *yad*) over many "countries," including Egypt, v. 42. He will take a great spoil of "treasures" (*mikman*) from Egypt. This is the only occurrence of *mikman* in the OT. It comes from an unused root *kmn*, "to hide." Aramaic and Arabic cognates support the meaning of "hidden things," treasures placed in storehouses away from public view. Libya, to the west of Egypt, and to Ethiopia, south of Egypt, will be "at his steps," i.e., in submission to him, v. 43.

"Tidings" (or "news") from the east and north will cause alarm.[41] Antichrist will send his army out to destroy his enemies. This may refer to the invasion of the "kings of the east" (Rev. 9:13–21; 16:12) and the coalition of nations from the north (Ezek. 38–39). Antichrist will send out his army "to destroy and utterly to make away [or 'exterminate']" his foes, v. 44. He will establish the seat of his government

---

[41]Those who apply this section to Antiochus Epiphanes resort to speculation to support their view. Thomson, p. 324, suggests "a Parthian war" to the east although "there is . . . no record of such a Parthian war." He relates tidings from the north to "the arrival of the Roman envoys, headed by Popilius Laenas" even though Antiochus did not war against Rome. Lacocque, p. 233, and Di Lella, pp. 304–5, both refer to Antiochus campaigning against the Parthians and the Armenians in his final days. There is only weak evidence to support such campaigns. Even if such warfare is accepted, there are too many details in the chapter that do not fit Antiochus Epiphanes. See discussion at v. 36.

in Jerusalem, between the Dead Sea and the Mediterranean Sea, in the "glorious [or 'beautiful'] holy mountain," Mount Moriah, the location of the temple. Despite this location, he will be defeated (2 Thess. 2:8; Rev. 19:19–21) in the final battle of this age, the Battle of Armageddon (Zech. 12:4–9; 14:1–3; Rev. 16:13–16), v. 45.

END TIMES 12:1–13

Blessings of the Righteous 12:1–4 These verses logically finish the thought of c. 11. "At that time" refers to the time of the end mentioned in 11:40 when Antichrist will rule his kingdom from Israel and direct his battles against the nations. Michael (discussed at 10:13), the "great prince," referring to his position as an archangel (cf. 10:13, 21; Jude 9; Rev. 12:7), then will watch over "thy people," the nation of Israel to which Daniel belonged. Henry identifies the "great prince" as Jesus Christ since He is "prince [ἄρχων] of the kings of the earth" (Rev. 1:5). Calvin also adopts this view.[1] The word ἄρχων, however, could just as well be translated "ruler" in the NT passage. The context here does not support introducing the Messiah.

This will be such a time of "trouble" (ṣarâ) for Israel as has not previously come on any nation. Leupold refers this time of trouble to the worldwide calamities that will take place during the Tribulation. He notes that "the world, which has times without number seen distress of the most acute sort, will never have seen anything like this last distress."[2] While this is true, the context here relates more to Israel than to the world. The archangel Michael is uniquely the angel who guards Israel (10:21, "your prince"). There is no reason to mention him unless this is a trouble that involves Israel.

The word ṣarâ may also be translated "anguish" or "distress" and thus includes emotional turmoil. The promise of trouble "such as never was since there was a nation" is broad but justified by the remainder of the verse. The statement draws attention to the difficulties faced by Israel (cf. Jer. 30:7, "Jacob's trouble"). Matthew 24:21 and Revelation 7:14 also refer to this period of tribulation. As in 9:12, we can justify the superlative nature of the statement by looking at this trouble as a divine judgment. God has not warned any other nation of such judgment because of their sin.

Thomson continues to see Antiochus Epiphanes in the verse. Michael delivers the nation from his persecution. Only in v. 2, where the reference to the resurrection leaves him no option, does Thomson

---

[1]Henry, IV, 1111; John Calvin, II, 369.
[2]Leupold, p. 528.

look to the time of the end. Auchincloss refers the "time of trouble" to the conquest of Jerusalem by Rome when, according to Josephus, 1.1 million people perished. Watkinson makes each day equal a year. The phrase "time, times, and an half" (v. 7), three and one-half days, equals 1260 years. He makes this end in AD 513. Watkinson also sees a second period of 1260 years that follows the first period. He concludes that during this period "Michael and his angels fought against the dragon and his angels."[3] The view rests on the faulty assumption that "days" in Daniel always equal years.

Through the work of Michael, those whose names are "written in the book," the Book of Life, cf. 7:10, will be spared. The Book of Life (Exod. 32:32; Ps. 69:28; Phil. 4:3; Rev. 13:8; 17:8; 20:12, 15; 21:27; 22:19) is that book in which the Lord keeps the listing of all that belong to Him by faith in His sacrifice at Calvary for salvation. The names of all the living are recorded in the book. Those who fail to receive Christ as their Savior have their names "blotted out" at the moment of death (Rev. 3:5). While the Book of Life contains the names of all Christians, the stress here is on the deliverance of Israel. Calvin and Young refer this to all believers.[4] The repetition of "thy people" most naturally limits the application. While NT believers will also receive deliverance, the Bible does not develop that thought until the NT. The emphasis here is on the nation of Israel as it turns to the Lord during the Tribulation (Zech 12:10; 13:1) and the Lord delivers them from Antichrist's persecution. Although many will die from this persecution, their eternal future will be with the Lord. Daniel repeats the phrase "thy people" to draw attention to this emphasis, v. 1.

The word "many" (*rabbîm*) emphasizes the great number involved in the resurrection. Leupold and Barnes rely on the NT to conclude that "many" may mean "all."[5] The word *rab*, however, here translated "many," never has the sense of "all" in the OT.

Those that "sleep," a common picture of death (e.g., Deut. 31:16; 2 Sam. 7:12; Job 7:21), will awake. Knoch thinks it is a "problem to account for the interval between the death of Daniel and other saints of his class, and the deliverance of the Kingdom." He solves this

---

[3]Thomson, p. 334; Auchincloss, p. 85; Watkinson, pp. 316–17.

[4]Calvin, II, 372; Young, p. 255.

[5]Leupold, p. 530; Barnes, II, 259.

by letting dead believers "sleep" and thus be "unconscious of the millennia of misery which intervene."[6] Sleep, however, is simply a picture of death. The Bible does not teach that the souls of departed saints sleep until the resurrection. The dying thief was assured of being with the Lord "to day" (Luke 23:43). Lazarus died and joined Abraham in paradise (Luke 16:22). Many "come from the east and the west, and . . . sit down with Abraham, and Isaac, and Jacob" in heaven (Matt. 8:11).

The just will wake to "everlasting life [$hayy\hat{e}$]," and the unjust to "shame [$h^arap\hat{o}t$] and everlasting contempt." Although the word $\check{s}^e\hat{o}l$ does not occur in Daniel, Driver refers to this as he expresses the common liberal view that the Jews viewed the dead as in Sheol, with "a shadowy, half-conscious, joyless existence, not worthy of the name of 'life,' where communion with God was at an end, and where God's mercies could be neither apprehended nor acknowledged."[7] This is not the teaching of the OT. The Hebrew word $\check{s}^e\hat{o}l$ may refer either to the grave or to the abode of the righteous (Pss. 16:10; 30:3) and wicked (Pss. 9:17; 31:17). The dead have a conscious existence and a personal identity (Isa. 14:9, 15). The Lord will bring the righteous out of Sheol (Pss. 49:15; 86:13). The noun $hayy\hat{e}$ here is plural, indicating the fullness of the life enjoyed by the saints in heaven.

The abstract noun $h^arap\hat{o}t$ is plural, conveying the quality of shame.[8] This is appropriate in view of the "everlasting contempt [or 'abhorrence']" connected with their punishment. Heaton denies the accuracy of the prophecy, insisting on the universal blessing of mankind in eternity. He states, "To our finite minds, the status of man as a moral and spiritual being endowed with freedom of choice may demand the possibility of hell; but the revelation of God's sovereign love in the NT, which is greater far than our minds can conceive, demands with greater insistence that there will be no need for this hypothesis when God is all in all."[9] Heaton ignores the teaching elsewhere of God's judgment on the wicked (e.g., Isa. 66:24; Matt. 25:46; Rev. 20:12–15).

---

[6]Knoch, pp. 423–24.
[7]Driver, p. xc.
[8]So Waltke and O'Connor, 7.4.2*a*.
[9]Heaton, p. 247.

Price presents a novel view of the resurrection. He suggests that many of the wicked experience a preliminary resurrection so as to act as witnesses to the second coming of Christ. He justifies this from Revelation 1:7, "every eye [of them living at that time] shall see Him." Smith is similar in his understanding of the resurrection. The view goes contrary to the NT teaching of an interval of time between the two resurrections. Pentecost argues that vv. 1–2 are chronological and that Israel is not raised until the glorious appearing of Christ at the end of the Tribulation.[10] The NT passages that deal with the resurrection (e.g., 1 Cor. 15:51–54; 1 Thess. 4:13–18) make no distinction between Jews and Gentiles in the resurrection. When Paul uses the word "we," he obviously includes himself.

Such passages as John 5:28–29 (quoted from this verse) and Revelation 20:4–6, 11–15 show that an interval of time separates the two resurrections. Together, this includes all of the dead. Leupold rejects "the idea of two resurrections." He states that "a dual resurrection is taught nowhere in the Scriptures." He explains this verse by making "many" refer to "all." In view of the teaching in Revelation 20:4–6, his argument is weak. Gaebelein and Ironside deny that the passage refers to a physical resurrection. They see the resurrection here as a "figure of the national revival of Israel" in the end time. They are buried throughout the nations of the world, and the Lord will bring them back to Palestine. The faithful will enter into the kingdom, while the wicked will be judged.[11] The view requires a great deal of imagination to see the resurrection as a figure here. If everything else in the chapter is understood literally, this should also be so understood. It is an early prediction of the resurrection, with the NT supplying additional details later. The connection between vv. 1 and 2 lies in the fact that the deliverance spoken of in v. 1 extends even to those who are martyred for their faith, v. 2.[12]

---

[10]Price, pp. 328–29; Smith, pp. 305–8; Dwight Pentecost, *Things to Come* (Grand Rapids: Zondervan Publishing House, 1958), pp. 209, 255, 395, 411.

[11]Leupold, p. 530; Gaebelein, pp. 200–201; Ironside, pp. 231–32.

[12]Watkinson, pp. 317–18, spiritualizes the passage. Those that "sleep in the dust of the earth" are the unsaved "whose spirits are death to the light of life." They will awake "to the glory of the star whose beams are shedding the light" of salvation. The star is John Wycliffe, with the "stars" of v. 3 including "other Reformers." The view is subjective. It makes Watkinson the authority rather than the Bible. The discussion above mentions the NT application of the passage.

Those who are "wise" (or "have insight," i.e., spiritual discernment; *śakal*, see 11:33) in these troubled times will "shine" (*zahar*) like "the brightness [*zohar*] of the firmament [or 'expanse,' i.e., the sky]," the noonday sun. Barnes understands "the brightness of the firmament" as "that of the sky at night, thick set with bright and beautiful stars." While this parallels the second half of the verse, it is contrary to the quote by the Lord in Matthew 13:43. Wolters argues that the noun *zohar* refers "to a specific celestial luminary." He concludes that this is Halley's Comet, "which made one of its periodic returns at precisely the time to which this verse refers."[13] While I agree that *zohar* refers to a specific luminary, Halley's Comet cannot possibly be that luminary. In the first place, Matthew 13:43, which mentions the sun, alludes to this verse. In the second place, Wolters dates the book at 164 BC to relate the passage to the comet. The conservative date places the book about 536 BC. At this date, Halley's Comet was more than twenty years past its perihelion and not visible from earth.

The verb *zahar* means "warn" almost everywhere else it occurs. That translation comes from the sense of being enlightened to some danger. Here, the comparison phrase "brightness of the firmament" makes the translation "shine" appropriate. Those who have helped others come to righteousness will shine brightly as the stars of heaven. The Talmud, *Baba Bathra* 8*b*, adopts a trivial view of the verse. "They that be wise" are judges who give "true verdict[s] on true evidence." "They that turn many to righteousness" are the "collectors for charity." Nothing here or in the NT limits the verse in such a manner. God delights in righteousness. We see here His evaluation of those who are righteous themselves and who help others to become righteous. Matthew 13:43 adapts the verse.

It is refreshing to see this teaching that God will reward the faithfulness of believers. Daniel does not limit faithfulness. It may include spiritual growth through reading, memorizing, and meditating on the Bible; it may include evangelism, seeking to win others to Christ; it may include giving tithes and offerings to support the work of the Lord; it may include a host of other things. Even though

---

[13]Barnes, II, 261; Al Wolters, "Zōhar hārāqîaʿ (Daniel 12:3) and Halley's Comet," *JSOT* 61 (1994): 111–20.

faithful service to God may seem difficult at times, it is still the right way to follow. In His time, God will right the wrongs of this life as He rewards those who have put Him and His will first in this life, v. 3.

The angel now commands Daniel to "seal" (*hatam*, cf. 9:24) his writings, i.e., to preserve them, until "the time of the end" (*ʿet qeṣ*, see 8:17). Keil relates the sealing of the book to guarding it, keeping it "securely from disfigurement." While *hatam* may have the sense of guarding, its earlier use in 9:24 (2X) supports the thought here of stopping (i.e., hiding) its meaning until a future time. In addition, v. 9, where the angel repeats the thought of sealing, supports this idea. Bultema understands the seal as a mark of authenticity.[14] This is also a possible view; however, the continuing of the book until its inclusion in the Bible seems to speak more of preservation.

Driver and Hammer consider the book historical, not prophetic. The reference to sealing is necessary since the book claims a sixth-century-BC origin. They understand the unsealing of the book as the meaning becoming clear in the time of Antiochus Epiphanes, the actual time of its writing.[15] The discussion of the date of the book in the Introduction rules out the possibility of this late date for its writing.

Daniel's writings conclude with the record of this vision, but it will be some time until believers know its application. Because of the nature of its prophecies, many specific to a future king and others relating to eschatology, this final vision (11:2–12:3) would remain a mystery for many years. Since this vision amplifies earlier visions given to Daniel, the reference to a "book" here must include all of Daniel's prophecies. Leupold limits the "book" to the final vision.[16] It is hard to see how this vision can be separated from Daniel 2, where Daniel sketches the broad outline of the future for Nebuchadnezzar; Daniel 7, where the "little horn" is first introduced; Daniel 8, where Daniel elaborates on the activities of the "little horn"; Daniel 9, which introduces the time and nature of Antichrist's activities; and Daniel 11, which gives a fuller account of Antichrist's work.

---

[14]Keil, p. 485; Bultema, p. 348.

[15]Driver, p. 202; Hammer, p. 117. Ford, p. 281, sees the unsealing of the book beginning in 1844. The notes at 8:14 discuss this view, held now by Seventh-day Adventists.

[16]Leupold, p. 534.

The "time of the end" is the church age, the period before the return of Christ. We should not expect to find the fully developed church in the OT since it is founded upon the death and resurrection of Jesus Christ. It is the baptism of the Holy Spirit, received at salvation, that brings a person into the church, the body of Christ (1 Cor. 12:13). With this as background, we say that the church age began at Pentecost and continues today. It will end with the coming of Jesus Christ for believers at the rapture of the church. Since the return of the Lord can take place at any time, the Bible considers this whole period as the end times. In Matthew 24:15, the Lord Himself commissioned the "understanding" of Daniel's prophecies. The preservation of the book makes it possible for the church to now understand and heed it.

Many "shall run to and fro" (*šûṭ*). The verb *šûṭ* occurs in different contexts with a sense of going back and forth, e.g., gathering manna (Num. 11:8) or rowing (Ezek. 27:26). It also occurs several times with a sense of going back and forth while searching (e.g., 2 Chron. 16:9; Zech. 4:10). The word has this sense here. In light of the context of Daniel's "book" (*seper*, see 1:4), the word here refers to study, the diligent search for the knowledge of the vision in the effort of understanding it. Knoch understands the going "to and fro" as the actions of unbelievers who "swerve" from God's Word because they do not know it. The view ignores the context of increased knowledge. Knoch justifies his view by emending *daʿat*, "knowledge," to *raʿôt*, "evil," a change with little to commend it. DeHaan and Smith refer the going to and fro to the increase of air travel and automobiles in our age.[17] This ignores the thought of increased knowledge that results from going "to and fro." The sense of study is appropriate here as mankind explores Daniel's writings with the result of increased "knowledge," v. 4.

Questions from Daniel 12:5–13 Daniel sees two other angels standing on the banks of the "river." While Daniel does not name the river, it is probable that it is the Tigris River, the same river mentioned in 10:4. These angels are "other" in that they differ from the angel of 10:5 who communicates the vision to Daniel, v. 5. One of the two angels speaks to the angel "clothed in linen" who has been with

---

[17]Knoch, p. 428; M. R. DeHaan, *Daniel . . . the Prophet* (Grand Rapids: Zondervan Publishing House, 1957), p. 309; Smith, pp. 313–14.

Daniel. Daniel describes both this angel and the angel in 10:5 as being "clothed in linen." This angel has knowledge of the vision given to Daniel. It is likely, then, that he is the same as the angel in 10:5.

The angel now stands "upon [better 'above'] the waters of the river." Since waters elsewhere are a symbol of people, Bultema and Henry spiritualize the angel's appearance here with Christ's standing upon the waters referring to His dominion over mankind.[18] I have argued at 10:5 that this angel is not the Lord. In addition, while waters *may* signify people, they normally do not represent anything but water. Nothing here suggests that we spiritualize the word.

The angel asks the other angel, "How long shall it be to the end of these wonders?" The question refers to the events embraced in the vision of c. 11:2–12:3. As in 8:13, the question illustrates 1 Peter 1:12, the interest of angels in the events of mankind, v. 6.

In answering the question, the second angel raises both hands to heaven in a gesture to accompany his oath. In taking an oath, it was normal to raise one hand (e.g., Gen. 14:22; Deut. 32:40). Where an action involves both hands, the picture often conveys emphasis (e.g., Prov. 3:16, the complete blessing of wisdom; Isa. 9:20, the full judgment upon the people; Ezek. 39:3, the totality of judgment on Gog). The action here serves as a visual signal that the oath was made in the presence of the all-seeing God. The raising of both hands emphasizes the truth of what the angel is about to say.

The angel swears by the eternal God that the persecution of Israel will last for "a time, times, and an half." The notes at 7:25 give the reasons for interpreting this as three and one-half years. At that time, Antichrist will "scatter" (better "shatter") the "power [*yad*, see 8:4] of the holy people" as he overcomes Israel (cf. 9:27). Then "all these things," the events of the vision culminating in the deliverance of Israel by Michael, the resurrection of the dead, and the judgment of the wicked and the righteous (12:1–3), will "be finished." Calvin makes the phrase "time, times, and an half" an "indefinite period." He refers this to the cleansing of the temple in the time of Antiochus Epiphanes.[19] Taking together the several uses of the phrase and similar periods of time (7:25; 12:11–12; Rev. 11:2–3; 12:6, 14; 13:5), an eschatological application of the phrase is more likely, v. 7.

---

[18]Bultema, pp. 350–51; Henry, IV, 1114.
[19]Calvin, II, 383–84.

Since Daniel does not understand this answer, he repeats the thought of the angel's question (v. 6) about the "end" (or "outcome," *ʾaḥᵃrît*) of the vision. In directing the question to "my Lord," he follows customary usage with no hint that this is the Lord God (e.g., Gen. 23:6, 11, 15; 2 Sam. 14:22; Dan. 4:19). Keil understands *ʾaḥᵃrît* as "last," referring to the last event before the end. This is kept hidden so that men will not know the end of all things with certainty.[20] Elsewhere, though, the OT makes clear that the future will climax with the Tribulation (9:27; Isa. 24:1–22), the kingdom (2:44; Isa. 25:1–8), and the eternal ages (Isa. 65:17–20), v. 8.

The angel directs Daniel not to inquire further since the words are "closed up and sealed" until the end times. As earlier in v. 4, so again the angel emphasizes that the truths revealed in the visions will not be understood until "the time of the end" (*ᶜet qeṣ*, see 8:17), i.e., the church age, v. 9. As the angel thinks of the end times, he describes the character of the righteous and the wicked in that period. The oppressed righteous will be "made white," purified, and "tried" (or "refined"). Through this persecution, they will be brought to "understand" spiritual truth.[21] Such understanding will come from the indwelling presence of the Holy Spirit in them (cf. 1 Cor. 2:14). The wicked, not having the Spirit, will continue to "do wickedly" (*rašaᶜ*, see 9:5) and will lack an understanding of spiritual truth, v. 10.

The angel now gives a time frame for the last part of the Tribulation. In some unknown way, Antichrist will duplicate the desecration of the temple by Antiochus Epiphanes (who is discussed in the notes at 8:23 and 11:21–35; the notes at 11:31 refer to his desecration of the altar in the temple at Jerusalem). He will stop the offering of the "daily sacrifice" and will set up "the abomination that maketh desolate." From the Lord's reference to this (Matt. 24:15), it is clear that this is future, not something that occurred during the reign of Antiochus Epiphanes.

---

[20]Keil, pp. 494–95.

[21]In v. 10, Auchincloss refers to the conversion of 3,000 people. In v. 11, he returns to the desecration of the temple under Antiochus Epiphanes. This movement from AD 70 to Pentecost (ca. AD 30) to Antiochus (ca. 141 BC) is in the wrong direction. Auchincloss relates phrases in Daniel to convenient parallels in history but in doing so ignores the sequential nature of the prophecy.

From that time until the end will be 1,290 days, a little more
than 3½ years. King suggests that the extra thirty days are to give
the Jews a month to repent and to recognize their Messiah. Such
passages as Jeremiah 30:7 and Zechariah 13:1, however, indicate
that the Jews will repent and turn to Christ during the Tribulation,
not after its close. Cowles considers the "time, times, and an half"
of v. 7 an approximate time and 1,290 "the more exact." He does
not explain the difference from the 1,260 days of Revelation 11:3
and 12:6. Cowles applies the passage to Epiphanes. He makes the
additional forty-five days bring us to the death of Antiochus after
the victory of the Jews and the rededication of the sanctuary. Since
the earlier part of the chapter is eschatological, and v. 13 speaks
of Daniel's resurrection, there is no warrant for wrenching these
verses out of context and applying them historically to Antiochus.
Susan Fournier Matthews sees the numbers as "rounded approxi-
mations of Pythagorean plane numbers" having symbolic meanings.[22] Her argument amounts simply to playing with numbers and
cannot be taken seriously, v. 11.

In addition to the 1,290 days, the angel informs Daniel that
there also will be an additional forty-five days until full blessing
comes. Some attempt to explain the additional seventy-five days as
symbolic. Keil, followed by Young, concludes that both numbers
in this section—1,290 and 1,335 days—are symbolic, not historical, and are meant as comfort that "the severest time of oppression
shall not endure much longer than half the time of the whole period
of oppression." They refer this to the time of Antiochus Epiphanes. Since the "time, times, and an half" of v. 7 is literal (cf. Rev.
11:2, 3; 12:6, 14; and 13:5), it is doubtful that these numbers are
symbolic. Wallace ignores the definite numbers to draw a spiritual
lesson. Blessing will come to those who wait, "even if two hundred
and ninety are lengthened to three hundred and thirty-five past
the thousand, and even more." It is unlikely, however, that specific numbers would be given unless they have some significance.
Leupold also understands the numbers as symbolic. Since the 1260
days refers to a time of tribulation, those who live to the longer

---

[22]King, p. 246; Cowles, pp. 451–52; Susan Fournier Matthews, "The Numbers
in Daniel 12:11–12: Rounded Pythagorean Plane Numbers?" *CBQ* 63 (Oct 2001):
634–46.

period are blessed since they have survived the evil and come into a good period.[23] Again, it is doubtful that the numbers should be understood symbolically, since the verses cited above from the NT book of the Revelation of Jesus Christ deal with the same span of time. It is more likely that the extra seventy-five days in these verses have a specific purpose.

Price holds the contrived view that the 1,260 days are years, culminating in the union of church and state. This begins in AD 538, when the bishop of Rome was decreed the head of the Roman Catholic Church. It ends in 1798, when Napoleon took the Pope prisoner. He begins the 1,290 years 30 years earlier, in AD 508 when Clovis became the first civil power to accept the church of Rome. The additional 45 days (years) thus ends in 1843, when the followers of William Miller (later Seventh-day Adventists) began to look for the Lord. While they were disappointed, this period proved to be one of great blessing to those who anticipated the Lord's return.[24]

Walvoord offers the view that this time lets the judgment of Matthew 25:31–46 and the gathering of Israel from the nations around the world take place. The return of Israel to Palestine takes place during the kingdom, not before it. Knoch suggests that the thirty days give time to organize the priesthood so that true worship of God may begin. The additional forty-five days allow the resurrection and reward of the "saints of former eras." His view of the resurrection is faulty. Goldwurm gives a view based on the phrase "time and times and the dividing of time" (7:25). He relates the "time" to the 480 years from the Exodus to the first temple. The "times" are a second period referring to the 410 years that the first temple stood. The total of these two periods is 890 years. Half of that is 445 years, a third period. Adding the three periods together gives 1,335 years. "This corresponds exactly to the years until the End in 12:12." This view simply manipulates numbers. There is nothing to commend it.[25]

DeHaan states that the additional thirty days are days of grace given by the Lord to the nations between the end of the Tribulation

---

[23]Keil, pp. 502–505; Young, p. 263; Wallace, p. 196; Leupold, pp. 547–58.

[24]Price, pp. 131, 338–39.

[25]Walvoord, p. 295; Knoch, p. 435; Goldwurm, p. 213.

and His appearing to judge the nations. The following forty-five days are the time required for the Battle of Armageddon. Nothing in Scripture supports either of these views. Tregelles suggests that the blessing of Israel "is not an instantaneous result." The Lord works on the consciences of the people; they mourn and turn to the Lord. The Lord gathers them to Israel and then gives "united blessing." Tregelles concludes: "It is not improbable that these two periods may relate to the stages of the Lord's actings, the one thousand three hundred and thirty-five days bringing in the united blessing."[26] Israel will turn to the Lord during the Tribulation (Zech. 12:10; 13:1). They will not, however, be gathered to Palestine until the kingdom.

These two periods are likely necessary for the full establishment of the kingdom. Some time is necessary for the judgment of the sheep and goats (Matt. 25:31–46), determining those of the people left after the Tribulation who will enter the millennial kingdom of Christ. Following this, an additional period of time allows the setting up of the government. The saints will reign as the representatives of the Lord at this time (Isa. 32:1; Rev. 5:10; 20:6).

There are a wide variety of other suggestions to explain this time. Van Impe adopts the above view but reverses the preparation time and the time for bringing the Jews back to Palestine. Harry Ironside suggests that the extra thirty days is devoted to purging out offensive and evil things from the kingdom. The extra forty-five days "points us on to the full establishment of the kingdom in power and glory."[27] These are possible views that may well be included in the above view.

Talbot refers the thirty days to judging the nations, cleansing the sanctuary, and purifying the earth. He is vague regarding the additional forty-five days.[28] The variety of opinions shows the difficulty of a clear understanding of the prophecy. We may speculate but should not be dogmatic.

---

[26]DeHaan, pp. 334–35; Tregelles, pp. 161–62.

[27]Van Impe, p. 222; Harry Ironside, *Lectures on Daniel the Prophet* (Neptune, N.J.: Loizeaux Brothers, 1973), p. 236.

[28]Louis T. Talbot, *The Prophecies of Daniel* (Wheaton, Ill.: Van Kampen Press, 1940), pp. 221–22.

Thomson suggests several ways of understanding the period but concludes that "no solution is possible."[29] He is right in this conclusion. The wide variety of attempts to interpret these numbers shows the difficulty in making a dogmatic interpretation. We cannot be certain because the passage does not state the purpose of this time, v. 12. Daniel is to "go [his] way" until the end of his life. He will "rest," referring to his death. "At the end of the days," however, the end times, however, he will "stand," a statement of his resurrection, in his "lot" as he receives his reward for faithfulness, v. 13.

---

[29]Thomson, p. 341.

SELECTED BIBLIOGRAPHY

Commentaries and Other Books on Daniel

Anderson, Sir Robert. *The Coming Prince*. 10th ed. Grand Rapids: Kregel Classics, rpt. 1957.

Archer, Gleason L., Jr. *Daniel*. In *The Expositor's Bible Commentary*, ed. Frank E. Gaebelein. Grand Rapids: Zondervan Publishing House, 1985.

Auchincloss, W. S. *The Book of Daniel Unlocked*. New York: D. Van Nostrand Company, 1905.

Barnes, Albert. *Daniel*. 2 vols. In *Notes on the Old Testament: Explanatory and Practical*. Edited by Robert Frew. Grand Rapids: Baker Book House, 1950.

Barrett, Michael P. V. *God's Unfailing Purpose: The Message of Daniel*. Greenville, S.C.: Ambassador-Emerald International, 2003.

Bevan, Anthony Ashley. *A Short Commentary on the Book of Daniel*. Cambridge: University Press, 1892.

Bultema, Harry. *Commentary on Daniel*. Grand Rapids: Kregel Publications, 1988.

Calvin, John. *Commentaries on the Book of the Prophet Daniel*. 2 vols. Translated by Thomas Myers. Grand Rapids: Wm. B. Eerdmans Publishing Co., 1948.

Charles, R. H. *A Critical Commentary on the Book of Daniel*. Oxford: Clarendon Press, 1929.

Cowles, Henry. *Ezekiel and Daniel: With Notes, Critical, Explanatory, and Practical*. New York: D. Appleton & Company, 1868.

DeHaan, M. R. *Daniel . . . the Prophet*. Grand Rapids: Zondervan Publishing House, 1948.

Driver, S. R. *The Book of Daniel*. In *The Cambridge Bible for Schools and Colleges*. London: Cambridge University Press, 1936.

Ford, Desmond. דניאל. Nashville: Southern Publishing Association, 1978.

Gaebelein, A. C. *The Prophet Daniel*. Grand Rapids: Kregel Publications, 1955.

Gangel, Kenneth O. *Daniel*. In *Holman Old Testament Commentary*. Edited by Max Anders. Nashville: Broadman & Holman Publishers, 2001.

Ginsberg, H. Louis. *Studies in Daniel*. New York: The Jewish Theological Seminary of America, 1948.

Goldwurm, Hersh. *Daniel*. Brooklyn, N.Y.: Mesorah Publications, 1980.

Gowan, Donald E. *Daniel*. In *Abingdon Old Testament Commentaries*. Edited by Theodore Hiebert, Carol A. Newsom, Kathleen O'Connor, and Choon-Leong Seow. Nashville: Abingdon Press, 2001.

Hammer, Raymond. *The Book of Daniel*. In *The Cambridge Bible Commentary*. Edited by P. R. Ackroyd, A. R. C. Leaney, and J. W. Packer. London: Cambridge University Press, 1976.

Hartman, Louis F., and Alexander A. Di Lella. *The Book of Daniel*. Vol. 23 in *The Anchor Bible*. Edited by William Foxwell Albright and David Noel Freedman. Garden City, N.Y.: Doubleday & Company, Inc., 1978.

Heaton, E. W. *The Book of Daniel*. In *Torch Bible Commentaries*. Edited by John Marsh, Alan Richardson, and R. Gregor Smith. London: SCM Press, Ltd., 1956.

Henry, Matthew. *Commentary on the Whole Bible*, vol. IV. 1910. Reprint, New York: Fleming H. Revell Company, 1935.

Horne, E. H. *The Meaning of Daniel's Visions*. London: Marshall, Morgan & Scott, n.d.

Horner, Joseph. *Daniel, Darius the Median, and Cyrus*. Pittsburgh, Pa.: Joseph Horner, 1901.

Ironside, H. A. *Notes on the Minor Prophets*. Neptune, N.J.: Loizeaux Brothers, 1909.

Jerome. *Commentary on Daniel*. Translated by Gleason L. Archer Jr. Grand Rapids: Baker Book House, 1958.

Keil, C. F. *Daniel*. In *Commentary on the Old Testament*. Translated by M. G. Easton. Reprint, Grand Rapids: Wm. B. Eerdmans Publishing Co., 1978.

King, Geoffrey R. *Daniel: A Detailed Explanation of the Book*. Grand Rapids: Wm. B. Eerdmans Publishing Co., 1966.

Knoch, A. E. *Concordant Studies in the Book of Daniel*. Saugus, Calif.: Concordant Publishing Concern, 1968.

Lacocque, André. *The Book of Daniel*. Translated by David Pellauer. The Society for Promoting Christian Knowledge. Atlanta: John Knox Press, 1979.

———. *Daniel and His Time*. Translated by Lydia Cochrane. Columbia, S.C.: University of South Carolina Press, 1983.

Lang, G. H. *The Histories and Prophecies of Daniel*. London: The Paternoster Press, 1950.

Lederach, Paul M. *Daniel*. Scottsdale, Pa.: Herald Press, 1994.

Leupold, H. C. *Exposition of Daniel*. Reprint, Grand Rapids: Baker Book House, 1969.

Miller, Stephen R. *Daniel*. In *The New American Commentary*. Edited by E. Ray Clendenen and Kenneth A. Matthews. Nashville: Broadman & Holman Publishers, 1994.

Mitchell, T. C., and Ray Joyce. *Notes on Some Problems in the Book of Daniel*. London: The Tyndale Press, 1965.

Montgomery, James A. *A Critical and Exegetical Commentary on the Book of Daniel*. Edinburgh: T. & T. Clark, 1927. Rpt. 1972.

Newell, Philip R. *Daniel: The Man Greatly Beloved and His Prophecies*. Chicago: Moody Press, 1951.

Newton, Isaac. *Sir Isaac Newton's Daniel and the Apocalypse*. Edited by William Whitla and translated by W. H. Semple. London: John Murray, 1922.

Phillips, John, and Jerry Vines, *Exploring the Book of Daniel*. Neptune, N.J.: Loizeaux Brothers, 1991.

Porteous, Norman W. *Daniel: A Commentary*. Philadelphia: The Westminster Press, 1965.

Price, George McCready. *The Greatest of the Prophets: A New Commentary on the Book of Daniel*. Mountain View, Calif.: Pacific Press Publishing Association, 1955.

Pusey, Edward Bouverie. *Daniel the Prophet*. New York: Funk & Wagnalls, 1885.

Rowley, H. H. *Darius the Mede and the Four World Empires in the Book of Daniel*. Cardiff, Wales: University of Wales Press Board, 1964.

Smith, R. Payne. *Daniel*. Cincinnati, Ohio: Cranston & Curtis, n.d.

Smith, Uriah. *The Prophecies of Daniel and the Revelation*. Mountain View, Calif.: Pacific Press Publishing Association, 1944.

Steen, J. Charleton. *God's Prophetic Programme*. London: Pickering & Inglis, n.d.

Strauss, Lehman. *The Prophecies of Daniel*. Neptune, N.J.: Loizeaux Brothers, 1969.

Stuart, Moses. *Commentary on the Book of Daniel*. Boston: Crocker & Brewster, 1850.

Tatford, Frederick A. *The Climax of the Ages: Studies in the Prophecy of Daniel*. London: Marshall, Morgan & Scott, 1953.

Thomson, J. E. H. *Daniel*. In *The Pulpit Commentary*. Edited by H. D. M. Spence and Joseph S. Exell. New York: Funk & Wagnalls, n.d.

Tregelles, S. P. *Remarks on the Prophetic Visions in the Book of Daniel*. 1863. Reprint, London: The Sovereign Grace Advent Testimony, 1965.

Van Impe, Jack. *Final Mysteries Unsealed: Opening the Door to Your Destiny*. Nashville: Word Publishing, 1998.

Van Ryn, August. *Daniel: The Man and The Message*. Kansas City, Kans.: Walterick Publishers, 1969.

Wallace, Ronald S. *The Lord Is King: The Message of Daniel*. Downers Grove, Ill.: InterVarsity Press, 1979.

Walvoord, John F. *Daniel: The Key to Prophetic Revelation*. Chicago: Moody Press, 1971.

Watkinson, Redford A. *The End, as Foretold in Daniel*. New York: C. S. Westcott & Co., 1865.

West, George W. *Daniel: The Greatly Beloved*. London: Marshall, Morgan & Scott, Ltd., n.d.

Whitcomb, John C. *Darius the Mede: A Study in Historical Identification*. Grand Rapids: Wm. B. Eerdmans Publishing Co., 1959.

———. *Daniel*. Chicago: Moody Press, 1985.

Wiersbe, Warren W. *Be Resolute*. Colorado Springs, Colo.: Victor, 2000.

Wood, Leon. *A Commentary on Daniel*. Grand Rapids: Zondervan Publishing House, 1973.

Young, Edward J. *The Prophecy of Daniel: A Commentary*. Grand Rapids: Wm. B. Eerdmans Publishing Co., 1949.

General Works

Ammianus Marcellinus. Translated by John C. Rolfe. Cambridge, Mass.: Harvard University Press, 1972.

Appianus. *Roman History, The Syrian Wars*. Translated by Horace White. Cambridge, Mass.: Harvard University Press, 1972.

Athenaeus. *The Deiphnosophist*. Translated by Charles Burton Gulick. Cambridge, Mass.: Harvard University Press, 1967.

Bevan, Edwyn Robert. *The House of Seleucus*. 2 vols. London: Edward Arnold, 1902.

Cartledge, Paul. *Alexander the Great*. New York: The Overlook Press, 2004.

Diodorus of Sicily. Translated by C. Bradford Welles. Cambridge, Mass.: Harvard University Press, 1963.

Dougherty, Raymond Philip. *Nabonidus and Belshazzar: A Study of the Closing Events of the Neo-Babylonian Empire*. New Haven, Conn.: Yale University Press, 1929.

Herodotus. *Histories*. Translated by A. D. Godley. Cambridge, Mass.: Harvard University Press, 1960.

Hospers, J. H., T. Jansma, and G. F. Pijper, eds. *Aramaic Texts from Qumran*. In *Semitic Study Series*. Translated and annotated by B. Jongeling, C. J. Labuschagne, and A. S. Van Der Woude. Leiden: E. J. Brill, 1976.

Jastrow, Morris. *The Religion of Babylonia and Assyria*. Boston: Ginn & Company, 1898.

Josephus. *The Works of Josephus: New Updated Edition*. Translated by William Whiston. Peabody, Mass.: Hendrickson Publishers, Inc., 2000.

Livy. Translated by Arthur C. Schlesinger. Cambridge, Mass.: Harvard University Press, 1968.

Oates, Joan. *Babylon*. London: Thames & Hudson, Ltd., 1979.

Plato. *Alcibiades*. Translated by W. R. M. Lamb. Cambridge, Mass.: Harvard University Press, 1964.

Pliny. *Natural History*. Translated by H. Rackham. Cambridge, Mass.: Harvard University Press, 1968.

Plutarch's Lives. Translated by Bernadotte Perrin. Cambridge, Mass.: Harvard University Press, 1975.

Polybius. *The Histories*. Translated by W. R. Paton. Cambridge, Mass.: Harvard University Press, 1968.

Pritchard, James B., ed. *Ancient Near Eastern Texts*. Princeton, N.J.: Princeton University Press, 1955.

Singer, Isidore, ed. *The Jewish Encyclopedia*. New York: Ktav Publishing House, Inc., n.d.

Statius. Translated by J. H. Mozley. Cambridge, Mass.: Harvard University Press, 1961.

Strabo. *The Geography of Strabo*. Translated by Horace Leonard Jones. Cambridge, Mass.: Harvard University Press, 1966.

Thomas, D. Winton., ed. *Documents from Old Testament Times*. New York: Harper & Row, Publishers, 1958.

Thucydides. *History of the Peloponnesian War*. Translated by Charles Forster Smith. Cambridge, Mass.: Harvard University Press, 1962.

Wigoder, Geoffrey, ed. *The New Encyclopedia of Judaism*. Washington Square, N.Y.: New York University Press, 2002.

Wisdom, Thurman. *A Royal Destiny: The Reign of Man in God's Kingdom*. Greenville, S.C.: Bob Jones University Press, 2006.

Wiseman, D. J. *Nebuchadrezzar and Babylon*. New York: Oxford University Press, 1985.

Xenophon. *Anabasis*. Translated by Carleton L. Brownson. Cambridge, Mass.: Harvard University Press, 1968.

———. *Cyropaedia*. Translated by Walter Miller. Cambridge, Mass.: Harvard University Press, 1968.

———. *Memorabilia and Oeconomicus*. Translated by E. C. Marchant. Cambridge, Mass.: Harvard University Press, 1988.

Linguistic Aids

Brown, Francis, S. R. Driver, and Charles A. Briggs, eds. *Hebrew and English Lexicon of the Old Testament*. Reprint, Oxford: Clarendon Press, 1974.

Fuerst, Julius. *A Hebrew & Chaldee Lexicon to the Old Testament*. Translated by Samuel Davidson. London: Williams & Norgate, 1885.

Harris, R. Laird, ed. *Theological Wordbook of the Old Testament*. 2 vols. Chicago: Moody Press, 1980.

Holladay, William L. *A Concise Hebrew and Aramaic Lexicon of the Old Testament*. Grand Rapids: Wm. B. Eerdmans Publishing Co., 1971.

Hulst, A. R. *Old Testament Translation Problems*. Leiden: E. J. Brill, 1960.

Köhler, Ludwig, and Walter Baumgartner. *The Hebrew and Aramaic Lexicon of the Old Testament*. Revised by Walter Baumgartner and Johann Jakob Stamm. Translated and edited by M. E. J. Richardson. New York: E. J. Brill, 1995.

Tregelles, Samuel Prideaux, trans. *Gesenius' Hebrew and Chaldee Lexicon to the Old Testament Scriptures*. Grand Rapids: Baker Book House, 1979.

Waltke, Bruce K. and M. O'Connor. *An Introduction to Biblical Hebrew Syntax*. Winona Lake, Ind.: Eisenbrauns, 1990.

Periodicals

Alt, Albrecht. "Zur Menetekel-Inschrift." *VT* 4 (1954): 303–5.

Archer, Gleason L., Jr. "Modern Rationalism and the Book of Daniel." *BibSac* 136 (April–June 1979): 129–47.

Avalos, Hector. "The Comedic Function of the Enumeration of Officials and Instruments in Daniel 3." *CBQ* 53 (October 1991): 580–88.

Beckwith, Roger. "Early Traces of the Book of Daniel." *TB* 53:1 (2002): 75–82.

Bell, Robert D. "The Theology of Daniel." *BV* 8:2 (November 1974): 142–44.

Caragounis, C. C. "The Ten Horns of Daniel 7." *ETL* 63:1 (1987): 106–13.

———. "Greek Culture and Jewish Piety: The Clash and the Fourth Beast of Daniel 7." *ETL* 65:4 (1989): 280–308.

Colless, Brian E. "Cyrus the Persian as Darius the Mede in the Book of Daniel." *JSOT* 56 (1992): 113–26.

Coppens, Joseph. "Dan. VII, 1–18—Note Additionnelle." *ETL* 55:4 (1979): 384.

Doukhan, Jacques. "The Seventy Weeks of Dan 9: An Exegetical Study." *AUSS* 17 (Spring 1979): 1–22.

Dyer, Charles H. "The Musical Instruments in Daniel 3." *BibSac* 147 (October–December 1990): 426–36.

Frank, Richard M. "The Description of the 'Bear' in Dn 7,5." *CBQ* 21 (1959): 505–7.

Gardner, Anne. "The Great Sea of Dan. VII 2." *VT* 49 (July 1999): 412–15.

Goldingday, John. "'Holy Ones on High' in Daniel 7:18." *JBL* 107 (September 1988): 495–97.

Gooding, David W. "The Literary Structure of the Book of Daniel and Its Implications." *TB* 32 (1981): 43–79.

Gosling, F. A. "Is it Wise to Believe Daniel?" *Scandinavian Journal of the Old Testament* 13:1 (1999): 142–53.

Grabbe, Lester L. "The Belshazzar of Daniel and the Belshazzar of History." *AUSS* 26:1 (Spring 1988): 59–66.

————. "Another Look at the Gestalt of 'Darius the Mede.'" *CBQ* 50 (1988): 198–213.

Gurney, R. J. M. "The Seventy Weeks of Daniel 9:24–27." *The Evangelical Quarterly* (January–March 1981): 29–37.

Hanhart, Karel. "The Four Beasts of Daniel's Vision in the Night in the Light of Rev. 13. 2." *New Testament Studies* 27 (1981): 576–81.

Harton, George M. "An Interpretation of Daniel 11:36–45." *Grace Theological Journal* (Fall 1983): 205–31.

Hasel, Gerhard F. "The Book of Daniel: Evidences Relating to Persons and Chronology." *AUSS* 19:1 (Spring 1981): 33–49.

Hilton, Michael. "Babel Reverses—Daniel Chapter 5." *JSOT* 66 (1995): 99–112.

Instone-Brewer, David. "*Mene Mene Teqel Uparsin*: Daniel 5:25 in Cuneiform." *TB* 42 (November 1991): 310–16.

Kraeling, Emil G. "The Handwriting on the Wall." *JBL* 63 (1944): 11–18.

Lenglet, A. "Las structure littéraire de Daniel 2–7." *Biblica* 55:2 (1972): 169–90.

Lucas, Ernest. "The Source of Daniel's Animal Imagery." *TB* 41 (November 1990): 161–86.

Matthews, Susan Fournier. "The Numbers in Daniel 12:11–12: Rounded Pythagorean Plane Numbers?" *CBQ* 63 (Oct 2001): 634–46.

McLain, Charles E. "Daniel's Prayer in Chapter 9." *Detroit Baptist Seminary Journal* 9 (2004): 265–301.

Meadowcroft, Tim. "Who are the Princes of Persia and Greece (Daniel 10)? Pointers Towards the Danielic Vision of Earth and Heaven." *JSOT* 29:1 (September 2004): 99–113.

Mercer, Mark K. "Daniel 1:1 and Jehoiakim's Three Years of Servitude." *AUSS* 27 (Autumn 1989): 179–92.

Millard, Alan. "Daniel and Belshazzar in History." *BAR* 11 (May–June 1985): 72–78.

Mitchell, Terence C. "And the Band Played On . . . But What Did They Play On?" *Bible Review* 15:6 (December 1999): 32–39.

Neal, Marshall. "The Seventy Weeks." *BV* 8:2 (November 1974): 132–38.

Niskanen, Paul. "Daniel's Portrait of Antiochus IV: Echoes of a Persian King." *CBQ* 66 (July 2004): 378–86.

Nutz, Earl. "Nebuchadnezzar: The Tree Cut Down." *BV* 8:2 (November 1974): 119–25.

Ouro, Roberto. "Daniel 9:27a: A Key for Understanding the Law's End in the New Testament." *JATS* 12 (Autumn 2001): 180–98.

Panosian, Edward M. "No Half Measures." *BV* 8:2 (November 1974): 100–103.

Paul, Shalom M. "Daniel 3:29—A Case Study of 'Neglected' Blasphemy." *Journal of Near Eastern Studies* 42 (October 1983): 291–94.

Pfandl, Gerhard. "Interpretations of the Kingdom of God in Daniel 2:44." *AUSS* 34:2 (Autumn 1996): 249–69.

Pinches, Theophilus G. "Fresh Light on the Book of Daniel." *ET* 26 (April 1915): 297–99.

Polaski, Donald C. "*Mene, Mene, Tekel, Parsin:* Writing and Resistance in Daniel 5 and 6." *JBL* 123 (Winter 2004): 649–69.

Redditt, Paul L. "Daniel 9: Its Structure and Meaning." *CBQ* 62 (April 2000): 236–49.

Royer, Wilfred Sophrony. "The Ancient of Days: Patristic and Modern Views of Daniel 7:9–14." *St. Vladimir's Theological Quarterly* 45:2 (2001): 137–62.

Shea, William H. "Daniel 3: Extra-Biblical Texts and the Convocation on the Plain of Dura." *AUSS* 20:1 (Spring 1982): 29–52.

———. "Nabonidus, Belshazzar, and the Book of Daniel: An Update." *AUSS* 20:2 (Summer 1982): 133–49.

———. "Darius the Mede." *AUSS* 20:3 (Autumn 1982): 229–47.

———. "A Further Note on Daniel 6: Daniel as 'Governor.'" *AUSS* 21:2 (Summer 1983): 169–71.

———. "Darius the Mede in His Persian-Babylonian Setting." *AUSS* 29:3 (Fall 1991): 235–57.

———. "Supplementary Evidence in Support of 457 B.C. as the Starting Date for the 2300 Day-Years of Daniel 8:14." *JATS* 12:1 (Spring 2001): 89–96.

Tanner, J. Paul. "The Literary Structure of the Book of Daniel." *BibSac* 60 (July–September 2003): 277–82.

———. "Daniel's 'King of the North': Do We Owe Russia an Apology?" *JETS* 35 (September 1992): 315–28.

Taylor, Richard A. "The Life God Blesses." *BV* 8:2 (November 1974): 104–11.

Van der Woude, A. S. "Zu Daniel 6,11." *ZAW* 106 (1994): 123–24.

Wenham, Gordon J. "The Kingdom of God and Daniel." *ET* 98 (February 1987): 132–34.

Wittstruck, Thorne. "The Influence of Treaty Curse Imagery on the Beast Imagery of Daniel 7." *JBL* 97 (March 1978): 101–2.

Wolters, Al. "Untying the King's Knots: Physiology and Wordplay in Daniel 5." *JBL* 110 (Spring 1991): 117–22.

———. "Zōhar hārāqîaʿ (Daniel 12.3) and Halley's Comet." *JSOT* 61 (1994): 111–20.

Woodard, Branson L., Jr. "Literary Strategies and Authorship in the Book of Daniel." *JETS* 37 (March 1994): 39–53.

Yamauchi, Edwin M. "Daniel and Contacts Between the Aegean and the Near East Before Alexander." *The Evangelical Quarterly* 53 (January–March 1981): 37–47.

———. "The Archaeological Background of Daniel." *BibSac* 137 (January–March 1980): 3–16.

HEBREW AND ARAMAIC WORDS

s

sabbᵉkaʾ 3:5
sᵉgan 2:48
sᵉleq 6:23
sûmponᵉyâ 3:5
sarbal 3:21

c

ᶜiddan 2:8
ᶜillay 4:17
ᶜillî 6:10
ᶜelyônîn 7:18
ᶜilᶜîn 7:5
ᶜaqar 7:8
ᶜiśbaʾ 4:25

p

paḥᵃwataʾ 3:2
paṭṭᵉyšêhôn 3:21
pas 5:5

pᵉsanterîn 3:5

ṣ

ṣᵉdaʾ 3:14
ṣᵉlaḥ 3:30

q

qabbel 5:31
qᵒbel 5:1
qᵉṭar 3:8
qaytᵉrôš 3:5
qarnaʾ 3:5

r

reʾš 7:1
rab 2:10
rᵉgaš 6:6
raḥᵃmîn 2:18
raᶜᵃnan 4:4

ś

śaggîʾ 2:6
śeṭar 7:5

š

šegᵉlateh 5:2
šᵉḥat 6:4
šêzib 6:16
šalû 3:29
šaᶜâ 3:6
šᵉraʾ 5:12

t

taltaʾ 5:16
taltî 5:7
tᵉmah 4:2
tiptayeʾ 3:2
tᵉraᶜ 3:26